Blind Allegiance
to
Sarah Palin

Blind Allegiance
to
Sarah Palin

A Memoir of Our Tumultuous Years

FRANK BAILEY
with Ken Morris and Jeanne Devon

HOWARD BOOKS
A DIVISION OF SIMON & SCHUSTER, INC.

New York Nashville London Toronto Sydney

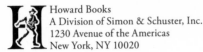

Howard Books
A Division of Simon & Schuster, Inc.
1230 Avenue of the Americas
New York, NY 10020

Copyright © 2011 by Frank Bailey, Ken Morris, and Jeanne Devon

All rights reserved, including the right to reproduce this book or portions thereof in any form whatsoever. For information address Howard Books Subsidiary Rights Department, 1230 Avenue of the Americas, New York, NY 10020

First Howard Books hardcover edition May 2011

HOWARD and colophon are trademarks of Simon & Schuster, Inc.

For information about special discounts for bulk purchases, please contact Simon & Schuster Special Sales at 1-866-506-1949 or business@simonandschuster.com.

The Simon & Schuster Speakers Bureau can bring authors to your live event. For more information or to book an event, contact the Simon & Schuster Speakers Bureau at 1-866-248-3049 or visit our website at www.simonspeakers.com.

Manufactured in the United States of America

Library of Congress Cataloging-in-Publication Data

Bailey, Frank (Frank Thomas), 1970–
    Blind allegiance to Sarah Palin : a memoir of our tumultuous years / Frank Bailey ; with Ken Morris and Jeanne Devon.
      p. cm.
    1. Palin, Sarah, 1964–   2. Alaska—Politics and government—1959–   3. Bailey, Frank (Frank Thomas), 1970–   4. Governors—Alaska—Biography.   5. Women governors—Alaska—Biography.   6. Vice-Presidential candidates—United States—Biography.   7. Presidents—United States—Election—2008.   8. Palin, Sarah, 1964—Friends and associates.   I. Morris, Ken (Kenneth Jacob), 1952–   II. Devon, Jeanne.   III. Title.
    F910.7.P35B35 2011
    979.8'052092—dc22
    [B]   2011012643

10 9 8 7 6 5 4 3 2 1

ISBN 978-1-4516-5440-0
ISBN 978-1-4516-5441-7 (ebook)

The emails and many quotes are printed here as they were originally written or spoken. Most were of a casual nature; thus, any errors were part of the original quoted material.

This book contains expletive language. Howard Books is sensitive to language issues and we know our readers are too. As with any Howard book, we do not want to offend readers with coarse material; however, we felt to fully demonstrate the context and validity of the emails and working relationships detailed in *Blind Allegiance to Sarah Palin*, we decided to keep the language as is, with no alterations or substitutions.

Scripture quotations marked NKJV are taken from the New King James Version. Copyright © 1982 by Thomas Nelson, Inc. Used by permission. All rights reserved. Scripture quotations marked NIV are taken from the Holy Bible, New International Version®, NIV®. Copyright © 1973, 1978, 1984 by Biblica, Inc.™ Used by permission of Zondervan. All rights reserved worldwide. www.zondervan.com.

Scripture quotations marked NLT are taken from the Holy Bible, New Living Translation, copyright 1996, 2004, 2007 by Tyndale House Foundation. Used by permission of Tyndale House Publishers, Inc., Carol Stream, Illinois 60188. All rights reserved. Scripture quotations marked KJV are from The King James Version of the Bible. Public domain. Scripture quotations marked ASV are from the American Standard Version, Thomas Nelson and Sons, 1901. Public domain in the United States.

To Momma
Your life inspired me to work passionately, dream, and
value those the world had discarded.
Even two days before you left us,
you were fighting for what you believed in.
It's a few months too late for you to share this with us,
but, Momma, the "fiddle fartin'" is done.
I miss you deeply.

CONTENTS

PART FOUR: *Death Spiral*

PART FIVE: *End Times*

I thought today—what would this campaign have turned into without [Frank Bailey]? We'd have fizzled. I'm so thankful things evolved the way they did and he took over so many, many important tasks. Pretty much everything is what he handles!

—SARAH PALIN, EMAIL, TUESDAY, JUNE 20, 2006

Since the 2006 campaign, no one person has been closer to the epicenter of the Palin campaign and administration than Frank Bailey.

—ANDREW HALCRO, ALASKA GUBERNATORIAL CANDIDATE,
IN HIS BLOG, NOVEMBER 6, 2009

FOREWORD

Tricks and treachery are the practice of fools
that don't have brains enough to be honest.
—BENJAMIN FRANKLIN

Frank Bailey's memoir began when, through third parties, he and I got in touch via email. After extensive dialogue, we decided to begin a collaboration. Because Frank's association with Sarah Palin's campaign and administration involved one of the most controversial political figures in recent memory, we elected to tread lightly and work in anonymity. Two months into the project, it became evident that extensive knowledge of Alaskan politics and personalities demanded the addition of another brilliant mind. To that end, we invited Jeanne Devon, creator and editor of website The Mudflats (www.themudflats .net), to join our team. Amazingly, from that day forward, the three of us worked for over a year without a leak to the public. In late February 2011, we found an agent and finished the initial draft of the manuscript. All was well.

Then, as most of the world now knows, only days after submitting our rough draft manuscript to publishers for consideration, the unthinkable happened. Over Presidents' Day weekend, we woke to find our working manuscript being quoted on websites, television shows, and in newspapers. How did this unpublished manuscript become so famous so fast?

In brief, the copyrighted words and work were distributed by a competitor. Not in America, we told ourselves. And certainly not initiated by an award-winning bestselling author—with his own Palin tell-all due to publish soon. Yet that is exactly what happened.

Joe McGinniss received an unauthorized copy of our manuscript and then took our property—the product of thousands of man-hours—and electronically distributed it en masse.

McGinniss undoubtedly knew this was, at a minimum, an ethical breech. In an effort to deflect blame, McGinniss's attorney admitted in a letter to us (also released to the media) that while McGinniss did send *Blind Allegiance* "to a few people and media outlets in Alaska," he'd advised them "that they should not reproduce any of the manuscript before contacting the authors for permission." If it is true that McGinniss did attach such a warning—and we have at least one source who suggests that is not the case—why then did he not follow his own warning?

McGinniss contacted none of us prior to distributing our copyrighted work.

The simplest of Sunday school lessons would require recipients to report the violation to the appropriate people, starting with us, the authors, or at least ignore what was sent. In several cases, we did receive a heads-up. In many other instances, though, newspapers and television shows read and commented on excerpts, by and large agreeing that the revelations were significant, insightful, and entertaining.

Likely, the offenders may say of stealing our intellectual property, "It's not really stealing." They are as wrong as Sarah Palin was when she issued similar rationalizations for inexcusable behavior. In a line from one chapter, Frank noted, "Only later did I realize that everywhere we traveled in our campaign to make Alaska a better state, ethical challenges were so thick we no longer had the ability to see them, except, that is, in others."

However, the unethically distributed manuscript was an early draft of the book you now hold. In addition to our adding new material to the original manuscript, as is customary in any editing process, our plight inspired a source to come forward and confirm in its entirety one of the most controversial of our many spectacular revelations in the book. Having painstakingly reconstructed the story of the coordination between the Palin campaign for governor and the Republican Governors Association in violation of election law (chapter 14, "The Republican Governors Association and Our Limbo Dance with Truth"), we had no question about the information Frank Bailey supplied. However, supporters of Sarah Palin who read the leaked text took exception by suggesting that there was only circumstantial evidence and "no smoking gun." We now provide additional and incontrovertible evidence of this inappropriate coordination. And in that unsolicited confirmation is added credibility to the analysis and mountains of evidence provided in these pages. As such, it is impossible for me to deny that there is great truth in the cliché that the Lord works in mysterious ways.

On behalf of my cowriters, we thank Howard Books for recognizing that within the pages of this book there is an inspirational personal story of faith and redemption that accompanies the important look at how dangerous it is to elevate individuals to our highest offices based on image alone. We also wish to thank those brave people who came to us after witnessing the treachery of others to lend a hand and tell their stories. All of you helped salvaged our many months of work.

—Ken Morris

PROLOGUE

I Quit

But if any harm follows, then you shall give life for life,
eye for eye, tooth for tooth, hand for hand, foot for foot,
burn for burn, wound for wound, stripe for stripe.
—BOOK OF EXODUS 21:23–25, NEW KING JAMES VERSION

You have heard that it was said,
"An eye for an eye, and a tooth for a tooth."
But I tell you, do not resist an evil person.
If someone strikes you on the right cheek,
turn to him the other also.
—JESUS OF NAZARETH, BOOK OF MATTHEW 5:38–42,
NEW INTERNATIONAL VERSION

A year before her July 3, 2009, resignation, Sarah said to me when discussing her husband, "Frank, we're not like other couples; we don't talk." In some matters, like resigning from the governorship, that appeared true enough when Sarah said in her speech, "And I'm thankful that Todd flew in last night from commercial fishing grounds in Bristol Bay." Hours earlier, Todd was rushed from his commercial fishing venture in Dillingham, a 360-mile journey from Wasilla made possible only by plane to be present for the shocking main event. About forty-five minutes before the press conference, he phoned me, sounding agitated when I said I'd known about the announcement for a few days; I guessed that he was perturbed at being the last to know. He tried to explain his wife's reasoning for quitting but couldn't recall the term "lame duck," so I prompted him and he then said, "Yeah, she'll be a lame duck." It sounded as if he were rehearsing unfamiliar lines he'd just learned, using me as a test audience.

On resignation day—at the Palin home with family, a single-

engine plane, with shimmering Lake Lucille in the background—
Todd stood in stoic silence and assumed the role of obedient prop,
listening maybe for the first time to his wife's puzzling explanations.
He struck me as uncomfortable, if not a little dumbfounded.

I'd seen Sarah freeze out family and former friends many times
before and had heard her say, "Watch out what you say to Todd; he
can't be trusted," so my feeling that she excluded her husband from
this monumental decision shouldn't have come as a surprise. Nevertheless, it did.

Much later, when I heard from others that Todd had received a cell
phone call from Sarah with the shocking news only the day before
while waiting for the brief but lucrative "opener"—when the Alaska
Department of Fish and Game determines that enough salmon have
returned upstream to allow fishing to begin—I tended to believe the
report to be true. Sometimes, despite all the pain he'd caused me, it
was hard not to feel sorry for the man.

In her opening statement, Sarah said, "People who know me know
that besides faith and family, nothing's more important to me than
our beloved Alaska. Serving her people is the greatest honor I could
imagine." For those of us by her side from the beginning until the end,
we understood the words as another instance of Sarah parceling truth.
Most decidedly, she did *not* enjoy serving the people of Alaska and she
did imagine greater honors on a regular basis.

In reality, the seeds of this head-scratching development were
planted long ago.

Sarah Palin may best be described as "serially dissatisfied." It is well
known that she enrolled and left *four* colleges before finally graduating
after nearly six years from the University of Idaho in 1987. During her
earliest political days, aspects of being the mayor of Wasilla enraged
her—including dealing with an aborted recall; firing Police Chief
Irl Stambaugh, for what he claimed was supporting her opponent in
the election; and dismissing the city's librarian, until being forced to
rehire her. When Alaska's newly elected governor, Frank Murkowski,
appointed her to a highly paid job on the Alaska Oil and Gas Conser-

vation Commission (AOGCC) in 2002, she openly complained about having to work with men whose loyalty was to big business. Palin quit that job about a year after accusing a powerful co-commissioner of unethical behavior. She first threatened to abandon her own run for governor in early 2006 before she'd even won the GOP nomination—and repeated that threat numerous times thereafter. Then, at what should have been her finest hour, during the 2008 presidential race, she rebelled against playing second fiddle on a ticket with John McCain, a man she didn't support in the primary, thought "weird," and whose wishy-washy politics she disliked.

On April 16, 2009, *Conservatives4Palin*, a blog dedicated to raising money for and furthering Sarah's career, wrote as part of a longer piece:

> It is irrelevant to us whether Sarah Palin runs for governor again, runs for president, or runs for any other elected office. If she were to say, "I've had enough. I'm going to retire and ride snowmachines in the winter and fish in the summer," we would still support her.

By intimating that there was a wellspring of support that would flow no matter what she did—including quitting—the article greatly buoyed Sarah's spirits. On April 28, 2009, a full nine weeks before walking away from her commitment to the state, Sarah wrote a simple but frequently repeated message: *"I hate this damn job."* She sent the words to me, Frank Bailey, her director of boards and commissions, and to former administrative aide Ivy Frye, and then added, *"I'll quit in a heartbeat if we have the right message for Alaskans to be able to understand that I can affect change outside the system better than inside this flippin' kangaroo court joke of a job."* Two days later, she wrote of blowing this *"popsicle stand"* in favor of *"effectiveness outside this Juneau zoo."* Agreeing with a written assessment by Ivy, Sarah needed to *"travel the country talking to people unfiltered every day [because] Rs/Independents will love it . . . the dems won't know what to do with themselves."*

Several of us, including me, contributed to the dream of breaking the shackles of government scrutiny. Not that Sarah needed encouragement. In June I'd written to her—without consciously thinking that it would come to pass—*"Again, can you affect more change from the outside? You certainly would lose the ties that hold you down."*

The Friday morning that Sarah resigned—symbolically timed to coincide with the nation's own Independence Day—I was out of state, driving from Olympia, Washington, to Sedro-Woolley, Washington. Sarah had instructed key advisor and aide Kris Perry to alert me on the previous Tuesday of her plans, so when the time came, I was dialed into the press conference.

In a word, Sarah's speech was confounding. Rambling and nearly incoherent, she attacked critics, spoke of dead fish going with the flow, and said, "You can choose to engage in things that tear down or build up. I choose to work very hard on a path for fruitfulness and productivity." Those words made me choke. To say her path had been one of "fruitfulness" or "productivity"—at least as she intended those listening to believe—was ludicrous. Governing in any sense of the word had barely been on the to-do list.

Since she had no intention of running again for the *"damn"* governor's job, she added something about not wanting to be a lame duck; there was, however, no mention of the multimillion-dollar deal for an autobiography that her inner circle had spent dozens of hours helping construct. Nor did she discuss the marketing and speaking arrangements that would net millions more dollars.

In her mind, Sarah had suffered enough and was entitled to riches, just like biblical Jabez (a frequently used Palin password), whose prayers for wealth were similarly answered by God. All those promises to deliver a better Alaska to our children and use her job "to usher change" were uttered before she understood how un-fun and unglamorous being governor would become—a realization more apparent after biting the apple of national acclaim as *the* future of the Republican Party.

On April 21, 2009, five months after she and McCain were defeated by the Obama-Biden ticket, in an email she wrote of the embarrassing fallout from her actions along the campaign trail:

> **Ridiculous . . . paying for the damn McCain campaign's attorneys to vet me!!! Unflippinbelievable. The campaign was so disingenuous, who in the heck has to pay for themselves to be vetted when**

they didn't ask for it??? I didn't hire any attorney—they did! They ran up a bill and left me with it—just like they did with the damn clothes issue. Paying out of my family's pocket . . . for the privilege of campaigning with a bunch of rich, connected people who have no burden after the campaign ends. . . . They have $ left over in different campaign accounts, but we're stuck with their bill and a lot of embarrassment. This is an unbelievable chapter in a book.

(Note: the McCain campaign later revealed that this was not a vetting expense, but a legal bill associated with defending Sarah Palin against ethics charges in her dismissal of Public Safety Commissioner Walt Monegan in a scandal that became known as "Troopergate.")

While Sarah Palin's charisma energized followers, her fragile emotional makeup was unnerving. To stay in her good graces, counterattacking anyone who opposed her became top priority. We went after opponents in coordinated attacks, utilizing what we called "Fox News surrogates": friendly blogs, ghostwritten op-eds, media opinion polls (that we often rigged), letters to editors, and carefully edited speeches. Nobody needed to be told what to do; we understood Sarah's silent mandate to do something *now*. I personally participated in character assassinations, effectively casting undue ethical shadows on her opponents—something I deeply regret.

Minor slights, many of which would have withered under their inconsequentiality, became magnified obsessions that made governing the state of Alaska a lesser priority. An opponent uttering a statement Sarah regarded as an attack demanded retribution and, if possible, the destruction of that person's reputation.

Love thy neighbor? Turn the other cheek? Forgiveness? These New Testament concepts were not part of Sarah's Old Testament temperament. *Both* eyes for an eye was the rule, and vanquishing enemies became a goal. Nothing was more important, to any of us working alongside Sarah, than preserving her image or achieving retribution. Not our families, not our friends, not our financial well-being, not the state's business. Nothing.

I have no doubt Sarah's belief in God is real and passionate. Hers just isn't the same God that I knew growing up, the One who preached the importance of love, honor, and charity. That I turned my back on these teachings and offered her blind allegiance is a cross I will bear forever. As for Sarah, her values—in and of themselves—have little to do with my writing this book. From my insider's perch from November 2005 well into 2009, I write because I am convinced that her priorities and personality are not only ill suited to head a political party or occupy national office, but would lead to a disaster of, well, biblical proportions.

———

How we arrived at this day, where the once most popular governor in America would suddenly leave her fellow Alaskans high and dry, is an incredible story. In our tumultuous journey together, there is much to be learned about human nature, politics, and the dangers of investing blind allegiance in any one person.

Having reviewed with my coauthors over fifty thousand emails (my nongovernment Yahoo! account emails, either to or from me) during the campaign and administration, my intention is to let recollections and Sarah's own words tell the tale. You'll find that the emails quoted in this book provide important insights—not only into the workings of Sarah's inner circle and how her campaigns were run; but more important, they give us a picture of the mind and motives of Sarah Palin. All emails are reproduced as written—without correcting grammar, spelling, etc. Great care has been taken to quote these emails accurately and fairly, so let me tell you how we've identified them in text. Longer emails are set off from the regular text in a bold font; emails that are reproduced within a paragraph are identified with quotation marks and italic type. And one more detail: many of the email quotes are not the entire email, but just portions of it. When you see ellipses marks within an email, part of the email has been left out at that place. And following publishing style form, if the quoted portion of the email begins somewhere other than the beginning or ends somewhere other than the end, no ellipses are used at the beginning or end.

I remain a staunch Fox News conservative, so let me say—to borrow a phrase—my observations throughout these pages are heavily documented in an effort to remain "fair and balanced."

PART ONE

Only in Alaska

1

Alaska: Right Time and Right Place

There is a place. Like no place on Earth.
A land full of wonder, mystery, and danger!
Some say to survive it: You need to be as mad as a hatter.
—THE MAD HATTER, FROM DISNEY'S
ALICE IN WONDERLAND, 2010

Within weeks of Sarah declaring her candidacy for governor of Alaska in November 2005, I joined her crusade for change. Once in office, I continued as a troubleshooting jack-of-all-trades while holding the title director of boards and commissions. Working up to eighty hours a week, I maintained that position during her selection as Senator John McCain's vice presidential running mate and continued after their defeat.

Over our three years and nine months together, my perceptions of Sarah evolved radically, but whatever I thought, Sarah Louise Palin was becoming an amazing political and social phenomenon. Without experience, pedigree, or worldliness, individuals like her don't often achieve statewide, much less worldwide, acclaim. Her story is a patchwork quilt of equal cuts beauty queen, lottery winner, political populist, Paris Hilton celebrity, and barnstorming evangelist. There is myth and reality to nearly every one of her story lines, whether it is God's chosen one, devoted wife, mother, and political maverick— or unhinged diva, thin-skinned attack dog, and self-absorbed zealot. Sarah slipped into and out of these roles and personalities, unpredictably mixing and matching one to another. The complexity of the

Palin psyche kept those around her alert, if not eternally anxious. That Sarah achieved eventual political rock stardom amid such interpersonal turmoil is an only-in-Alaska story.

Despite being a geographically massive state, Alaska's population is less than that of Austin, Texas. Of our roughly 700,000 residents, about 40 percent live in and around the city of Anchorage. Juneau, the state capital, has no direct roads leading in and is accessible only by boat or plane. While Alaska could literally reach from the Atlantic Coast to the Pacific Coast in the lower forty-eight, locals refer to the state as the "biggest small town" in America. Outside of Anchorage (population 280,000), Fairbanks (metropolitan area population of about 90,000), and Juneau (31,000), we Alaskans hail from towns too small to be dots on most maps.

———

When I was two, my father moved our family from central California to Kodiak Island where he taught instrumental music and third grade. While the second largest island in the United States, Kodiak's population was less than 10,000 back in 1972, with our hometown of Kodiak City home to about 1,100 of these residents. The island boasts rainforests and heavy timber harvesting in the northeast, black shale cliffs in the south overlooking both the Gulf of Alaska and the Shelikof Straits, and sandy, rural, windswept vistas in the southwest, down near Alitak Bay and Olga Bay.

Like much of Alaska, Kodiak was a throwback to an earlier time, with bars outnumbering churches and schools several times over. Our first stoplight—a blinking affair at a three-way intersection—was installed around 1980. For my parents, the adjustment from sunny California couldn't have been easy. In the worst of the December nights, I gathered branches or snapped apart pallets for firewood, but there was still little heat. In fact, it was not uncommon to find ice in the toilets come morning. We were poor even by local standards. If it wasn't for the charity of our church, the Kodiak Bible Chapel, and the abundance of salmon, halibut, and crab, we'd have likely starved. As it was, our family of six (two brothers and a sister) often went to bed hungry. Paper routes, frying burgers at a Dairy Queen, and eventually working aboard sometimes dangerous commercial fishing boats became my way of contributing to the family income at an early age. These long hours instilled in me a willingness to work slavishly and an appreciation for people who struggle to keep their heads above water financially.

And while a person never becomes accustomed to hardship, we on Kodiak Island accept our relative isolation, fickle weather, and the ever-present potential for natural disaster as the price we paid for a lifestyle of freedom and self-determination. For instance, we have a volcano just across Shelikof Strait, Mount Katmai, whose sixty-hour eruption in 1912 represented the largest of the twentieth century. The resulting blanket of soot washed down and covered Kodiak homes with ash that is still evident today when one digs down only a few inches. It was nearly seven years before the acid-choked waters of Kodiak could support a salmon industry again, but most of the island's early-century population of five hundred elected to remain and rebuild their lives.

On March 27, 1964, a second massive devastation struck the island. Centered less than one hundred miles away, the largest earthquake ever recorded in North America—magnitude 9.2 on the Richter scale—struck on Good Friday. Chimneys fell, windows shattered, and roofs caved. Devastating waves from an ensuing tsunami splintered homes and moorings. Like before, the citizens picked up, rebuilt, and started over. This far north, we know that it won't be *if* we face a next challenge, but *when*.

With these extremes, neighbor depends on neighbor when life hangs in the balance. Once we give our loyalty and word of honor, we do so with conviction and faith.

In Alaskan politics, it is no less true.

———

As Sarah Palin rose to prominence as a visible and sometimes controversial mayor from 1996 until 2002, she spoke from the heart about what we had in common as Alaskans, including a desire for freedom, a return to ethical governance, and the protection of our most prized and state-owned resources, especially oil. A tough-talking woman with a reputation for backing her words with action appealed to a broad cross section of our population. Head down, children in tow, and confrontational when necessary, she represented our unique spirit.

She was photogenic, she was charming, and she spoke to our concerns. Sarah Palin seemed worthy of our faith and trust. She arrived on the political scene at the right time, at the right place; she was accessible, willing to boldly state her case, say "hello," or simply smile and shake a neighbor's hand.

As for her experience, starting out as mayor of a tiny town like Wasilla from 1996 to 2002 wouldn't inspire executive credibility in most of the civilized world. Yet with only six thousand residents, Wasilla was growing rapidly; it is now Alaska's fourth-largest city with a population of eleven thousand. With a citizenry that prides itself on being independent thinkers—over 57 percent of registered Alaskan voters are not affiliated with either major political party—the burden of inexperience is not a major priority for most voters. That she engineered the construction of an indoor sports complex in tiny Wasilla was, by our standards, a big deal. (As we discovered years later, it also displayed her ability to downplay critics who complained she raised costs dramatically by failing to secure the land prior to construction, left the city $22 million in debt, and raised taxes to help with financing.)

Natural resources and the state's legacy of political corruption are by far the two most critical issues on voters' minds. Not surprisingly, oil industry money was the primary engine in producing the massive ethical lapses in what eventually became known as the Corrupt Bastards Club: a group of eleven lawmakers who received large campaign contributions from executives of the state's oilfield service companies in return for political favors; the ensuing investigation resulted in five fraud-related indictments. Emphasizing her record for combating and attacking those whom she called evildoers, Sarah practiced the art of sticking to talking points that resonated with voters: business as usual, bad; oil companies, bad; all establishment politicians and bureaucrats, very, very bad. In a close but unsuccessful bid for lieutenant governor in 2002, she put herself in a bright statewide spotlight.

Friend and foe began predicting that this "no more business as usual" candidate was a force to be reckoned with. Stories of the house-wife-ex-mayor who was toting kids door to door in a red wagon to solicit votes brought to mind that all-important pioneer spirit and mother-bear tenaciousness. Later that image would transition with her famous campaign question, "What is the difference between a hockey mom and a pit bull?"

By this time, I was married, with a toddler and an infant, and I had spent several years in Anchorage working in the airline industry, first as a baggage handler and then in middle management. These responsibilities did not, however, lessen my financial struggles or grueling hours. With economic and personal struggles unabated, I became aware of the nasty state of Alaska's political elite, people who sold out to special interests in what was a reverse Robin Hood. Our bountiful state wealth was being handed over to oil and gas company executives, to the detriment of Alaskan citizens. My own Republican Party, including Frank Murkowski, had sold us out for political gain.

When then senator Frank Murkowski (a man we came to call "Murky") ran for and won election as the state's tenth governor in 2002, he couldn't wait to pounce onto a pile of political scat. The seventy-year-old lifetime politician had, as governor, the privilege of appointing his own successor in the U.S. Senate. After interviewing several candidates for show (including Sarah), he appointed his daughter Lisa to the powerful position. In a backroom deal, the senate seat went from father to daughter as if it were a family-owned asset. The governor's subsequent self-serving actions galled Sarah and thousands like me.

Much later, in reference to Governor Murkowski's shocking appointment, Sarah wrote to me, *"I despise dynastic succession."* As far as Sarah and many of us on the sidelines were concerned, differences with the Alaska GOP political machine were irreconcilable. Somebody needed to address this egregiousness. I for one knew in my heart that this upstart beauty was the only person willing and able to take on that challenge. While Murky had the GOP machine and big donors, I believed that Sarah Palin had God's blessing and people's love and faith. Check and mate.

As a distant observer, I perceived a principled, clean-house Republican, unafraid of the entrenched good ol' boys. Possessing Ronald

Reagan's conservatism and principles, she was David to Murkowski's Goliath. And many of us suspected this was only the beginning. Sarah held similarly larger ambitions. During her 1996 run for mayor of Wasilla, her campaign manager, Laura Chase, once said to her, "You know, Sarah, within ten years you could be governor."

"Governor?" Sarah answered. "I want to be president."

As if hand delivered by fate, Sarah found a way to establish her anti-corruption chops. Shortly after the outrage over dynastic succession—and maybe in an attempt to placate a potential foe—Governor Murkowski appointed the increasingly vocal Sarah Palin to a prestigious and well-paid post on the Alaska Oil and Gas Conservation Commission (AOGCC), an agency that helps determine how best to safely bring Alaska's North Slope oil and gas to market. Within the first year of a six-year term, Sarah called out a fellow commissioner for ethical lapses and later resigned when told she was under a gag order and could not publicize her complaints. The commissioner in question happened to be the Republican Party chair, Randy Ruedrich. He eventually paid a hefty fine for passing along confidential committee documents to oil interests. Equally troubling to many was that as GOP Party chair, Ruedrich's job was to solicit oil money from the industry's top executives for political candidates. That he was simultaneously on the AOGCC was another example of grimy politics. What's more, Sarah also exposed him for running Republican Party business from his AOGCC office, a violation of using state resources for political activity.

When later running for the GOP nomination for governor, Team Palin summarized this saga in an email written to counteract an editorial in the conservative *Anchorage Times* suggesting that she was a political lightweight:

> **Ruedrich was fined the largest ethics violation amount in state history. . . . I was the chairman of AOGCC, and was Ruedrich's ethics supervisor. I was not going to let the integrity of this quasi-judicial agency go down the toilet by allowing the many questionable actions of a political appointment (who also happened to be the GOP boss) go unchecked. . . .**
>
> **As Ruedrich was investigated by the Dept. of Law, Murkowski**

promised to set the record straight . . . so the integrity of AOGCC, which regulates 20% of the U.S. domestic supply of energy, would be restored. Murkowski broke that promise . . .

I'm the only Republican candidate who stood up to Ruedrich and Murkowski . . . I did so at personal cost, including leaving a $124,000-year top-level state job.

While Sarah exaggerated the importance of the AOGCC (Alaska supplies not 20 percent but only about 2.4 percent of the U.S. domestic supply of energy), she displayed an early hyperbolic willingness to attack and defend.

In 2004 Richard Mauer reported in the *Anchorage Daily News* on the lengths to which Sarah went to uncover Ruedrich's violation:

The next week, when Palin went back to work at the AOGCC, she noticed that Ruedrich had removed his pictures from the walls and the personal effects from his desk. But as she and an AOGCC technician worked their way around his computer password at the behest of an assistant attorney general in Fairbanks, they found his cleanup had not extended to his electronic files . . .

Palin found dozens of e-mail messages and documents stacked up in trash folders, many showing work Ruedrich had been doing for the Republican Party and others showing how closely he worked with at least one company he was supposed to be regulating.

With this widely reported and praised resignation for principle and antiestablishment rhetoric, Sarah branded herself the people's champion. Sacrificing the arrogant party stalwarts to gain favor with true conservatives, she traded up.

––––––

Upon learning Sarah might take a run at unseating Frank Murkowski as governor in the 2006 election, I felt drawn to volunteer. I looked up the name Palin in the phone book. The Wasilla phone number was listed right there in the White Pages. (Don't forget, this is Alaska.)

"Hi, is this Sarah?"

I explained about wanting her to run for governor and how the state, the party, and the people needed her. I said that I'd do whatever I could to help her win.

My wife, Janeen (Neen), thought I was nuts. "You just picked up the phone and called her like that, right out of the blue? Isn't that kind of weird?" I hadn't really thought about the implausibility, but, yeah, there was a certain amount of serendipity in what I'd done. Certainly Frank Murkowski wasn't listed in the phone book, and I doubt he'd be interested in having Mr. Nobody do much more than write him a check.

Apparently my immediate follow-up email expressing disgust with Governor Murkowski struck a chord.

From: frank bailey
To: spalin
Sent: Wednesday, June 29, 2005 8:23 PM
Subject: Campaign Volunteer

Hi Sarah,
Once again . . . sorry about the odd phone call this afternoon. If you want a resume to see my skill set just let me know. I just decided that I wanted to get behind anything that could possibly make a positive change. I do know this . . . I will likely vote for a Democrat before I would vote for Murkowski again. His arrogance and his "slow to act" style of addressing ethics issues have disappointed me. We are a better state then we have become.
    Let me know if there is anything I can do to help.
Frank Bailey

Sarah responded, indicating that she'd be in touch if she decided to run. More than three months later, in October, she officially announced her candidacy. I sent another email:

From: frank bailey
To: sarah palin

Sent: Tuesday, October 18, 2005 8:16 PM
Subject: Re: Campaign Volunteer

Hi Sarah,
I caught you on Channel 2 tonight. You were AWESOME on TV.
You spoke to the heart of most Alaskans . . . ethics, small govern-
ment, practical experience vs a comfortable career politician.

Let me know if/how I can help in your campaign. My experience is fairly broad, but I'm willing to clean toilets if that's what it
is needed. I can send a resume so you can see my skill sets, but my
involvement has been mostly management in the airline industry
for the past 12 yrs . . . I . . . have done quite a bit with budgets (not
huge budgets . . . 1mil/yr). Let me be clear though, I am not looking for anything in return. What I know of you and what I've seen
of you in the media makes me excited about the future of kids. Let
me know what I can do to help!
Frank Bailey

The next day, Sarah emailed back:

From: Sarah
To: frank bailey
Created: 10/19/2005 11:56:52 PM
Subject: Re: Campaign Volunteer

Thank you so much Frank! And it's great to hear from you. I'm glad
you're happy to hear the decision. This all happened pretty quickly
and we didn't have the luxury of having any time between filing a
Letter of Intent and then formally announcing the run for Gov. So,
we're hustling!

Thanks again Frank. I sincerely appreciate your support.
God bless,
Sarah

While I don't wear Christianity on my sleeve, I know in my core that God's teachings are best for this world, me, my family, and all of our relationships. Having attended Capernwray Bible College in England for a time and been an active member of the evangelical ChangePoint church in Anchorage, Sarah's "God bless" sign-off didn't seem strange to me at all. As for Sarah, the connection between her faith and politics seemed profound; in my mind, God had chosen her, and this was His will.

Even after this second email, I heard nothing back. It wasn't until I approached Sarah at her first official fund-raising event at the Reagan Building in Wasilla in November 2005 that matters moved forward.

Present that day were several individuals I would grow close to in the coming years, including prominent longtime local attorney Wayne Anthony Ross, better known as WAR; Sarah's husband, Todd; Don Benson, a volunteer from nearby Palmer; and Kris and Clark Perry, friends of Sarah's from Wasilla.

At that fund-raiser, in front of notables and nobodies, Sarah inspired us, talking about how, "Man was created to work." With the Murkowski administration, she said, this wasn't happening. I took her words about being created to work personally and applied it to a verse that my mother instilled in me as a preteen that says, "Work heartily as unto the Lord."

At this time, the depressed price of oil was damaging Alaska's economy, and people were scraping to get by. Pouncing on that theme, Sarah pointed out that Murkowski's Petroleum Profits Tax amounted to an oil company giveaway. The people who actually owned the resource in the ground—by state constitution, Alaskan citizens—were being shafted. Rather than receiving potential increased revenue from the resource itself, they received a piddling tax while business enjoyed the windfall. Her words convinced me anew that our current governor was taking the state in the wrong direction. All the heads in the room nodded like bobbleheads. When she uttered the phrase "time for change," the room broke out in spontaneous applause. For the first time in all the years I'd observed politicians, someone was uttering unvarnished truth.

In the midst of the excitement, I made my way in her direction to meet face-to-face. What, I wondered, could a simple man, a political novice, a kid raised in a small town on a remote island, possibly do to aid a future governor? All I knew was that I had driven almost an hour because I wanted to make a difference. Maybe I could offer ten words of encouragement. Maybe I'd hand off a check for fifty dollars. Whatever she'd accept from me was on the table.

"Sarah. Hi. I'm Frank Bailey. We exchanged emails . . ." In a voice that surely betrayed my nerves, I explained I hadn't heard back from anyone about volunteering.

"Frank, I am sorry nobody contacted you." She sounded annoyed with her current unpaid staff.

"I can paint. Clean floors and toilets. Wash windows." What I really wanted to say was that I'd help flush and scrub away Alaska's massive political corruption.

While I did not know then the level at which I'd be working for the campaign, my naively sincere offer struck the right chord. With little more than this brief introduction, Sarah invited me inside the campaign. As I've learned since, only in Alaska is it possible to be invisible one day and in the middle of a political movement the next. After all, I'm just an amateur musician and former airline manager of average height, balding, with a hefty build. I have a wife, whom I love deeply, and two wonderful children, along with a German shepherd named Shiloh and a cat named Kalsin (named after a picturesque bay in Kodiak). I have a hankering for burgers, fries, shakes, and most anything sweet and salty. We live modestly in middle-class South Anchorage, about twenty-five minutes from downtown. If Sarah were an unlikely political icon, my future intimate role—in her election, governance, and resignation—was even more so. As I made plans to turn my life inside out at the age of thirty-five and devote massive amounts of time in pursuit of landing Sarah Palin in the governor's office, I felt light-headed. What an adventure lay ahead. I walked away convinced that if my future boss applied her potential to running the state, better days lay ahead. This woman from Wasilla had a down-home charisma, a laudable work ethic, and she would *never* lose her ideals.

In hindsight, I guess I forgot the adage "Never say never."

2

Rag Tags: On Your Marks, Get Set, Go

Part of my message is to let swing voters know I recognize
the Governor's job is to serve all Alaskans, all parties,
not just members of the party in which I'm registered.
—SARAH PALIN, EMAIL TO VOLUNTEERS,
THURSDAY, DECEMBER 22, 2005

In November 2005, driving my weary blue 1997 Isuzu Trooper
SUV, I barreled along the Seward Highway under a white canopy
of a sky that blended in with the snowcaps of Sleeping Lady Mountain
and distant dormant volcanoes. I was armed with a five-gallon bucket
of tools, including a paintbrush, toilet bowl cleaner, and a hammer,
and there was never a man more ready to roll up plaid sleeves, get
down on denim-covered knees, and do "work unto the Lord" than
me. Window washer, painter, gofer deluxe, whatever it took was more
than okay.

I was on my way to Palin campaign central in Anchorage. After
passing an Avis car-rental dealer and an adult bookstore, I pulled up to
the curb in front of the ground-floor office. White butcher paper covered the windows as if to hide whatever went on inside, casting back
my reflection. Short of breath, I felt goofy and reminded myself, *Don't
forget to smile, be confident; let Sarah know how grateful you are.*

A pessimist might suggest that the building's grimy exterior,
cracked cement and brick, and rusted railings foreshadowed a future
with crumbling dreams, but as an incurable optimist, I saw the reverse. To me, the disrepair of the headquarters, which was the former

home of the Alaska Aces minor league hockey team administration, symbolized the current sorry state of Alaskan politics. In a moment, I'd enter and meet a team of people who had the heart and soul to fix 'er up into a shining jewel. As I surveyed the chosen building for launching a governor, I decided that—modest digs aside—this location had merit. On the corner of busy West Fifth Avenue and B Street, the eventual campaign banners would attract plenty of eye contact from pedestrians and drivers. The offices were set within a building that housed the well-worn 5th Avenue Mall parking garage, the far end of which had a sky bridge leading to the trendy shopping area anchored by the Nordstrom department store. Traffic noise and busy streets were perfect for campaigns operating on a shoestring.

As I'd soon discover, we were a half lace short at that.

I yanked open the metal door, which stuck against the base plate before yielding. Water-stained overhead tiles and spotted blue carpet led to an elongated lobby with a built-in countertop for a nonexistent receptionist. Cartoons, a pinup-girl calendar, and sheets of tacked-on paper littered the walls, floors, and windows. Were it not for the optimism filling my heart, the word *dump* might have crossed my mind.

With a bathroom that self-locked and required a credit card to pick open, a large storage closet, two mini-offices, and a third office for candidate Palin, command central was a diamond in the rough. Sarah's ex-brother in law, Jack McCann, had contributed some decent desks and chairs, so we had at least a small sense of office potential.

I'd arrived at around ten o'clock and met a small group of volunteers who came and went over the next hours. I would soon learn that with the exception of me and an ex-correctional officer named Kelly Sharrow, this was a family affair.

Sarah arrived shortly after me, dressed for work in jeans and with her hair pinned back. She set down paint supplies next to her omnipresent oversized red shoulder bag.

"Frank, thank you," she said, shaking my hand. A radiant smile, framed by chocolate colored eyes that would later charm hardened members of the media like Bill Kristol and Sean Hannity, lit up the room. Sarah asked me repeatedly about my wife, kids, and extended family. When I explained that my father had passed away two years earlier—and was unable to mask the pain of that loss—her condolences were sincere. She asked questions and got me talking about myself. Her interest in a person she'd known for all of an hour was flattering, endearing, refreshing, and energizing all at once.

For me, it took only a minute to see beyond her physical charm to a warming heart. Though not yet a powerful political voice, Sarah was more than a former beauty queen (Miss Wasilla, 1984), she was a concerned Alaskan woman on a mission. As we spoke, there was none of that "You betcha!" folksy manner that provided so much material for political satirists, standup comics, and impressionists during the 2008 presidential campaign. It was straight-up, neighbor-to-neighbor or parishioner-to-parishioner, from-the-heart conversation. Later on, in March 2006, as I was recruiting a woman to join us as a fund-raiser, I summed up my impressions this way:

> Sarah is an absolutely wonderful woman . . .
>
> She's a mother of 4, her husband works on the slope. They are commercial fishermen in the summers out in Bristol Bay. Just regular folks, but she was a 2 term Mayor out in Wasilla and really pulled that city out of its regulatory doldrums to turn it into one of the fastest growing cities in the U.S. . . .
>
> Her last run for political office was for Lieutenant Governor. She went up against Loren Lehman, who outspent her 5 to 1, and he only beat her by 1400 votes or 2% . . .
>
> I have had people write to us at the campaign and tell us that while they don't agree with a stance Sarah has taken, they support her run for Gov, because they respect her being open on the issues . . . She is not fake, but a real everyday person.
>
> She is EXTREMELY fiscally conservative.

It took no more than a minute for me to appreciate her honesty and integrity; a theme she emphasized throughout the campaign. In one early bout of pique about a gift she'd received after speaking to the local Bartlett Democratic Club, she answered a question about a gift disclosure this way: *"That was just a $4.00 cup they gave me . . . I'm so dam honest I even disclosed that gift!"*

While I was surprised at how few of us there were on that first day—maybe ten or twelve people in and out—we accomplished a great deal. Over seven hours, we completed most of the painting (the best touch being the gold stars of the Big Dipper on the Alaska state flag splashed across the entryway ceiling), shampooed carpets, vacuumed floors, and cleared trash.

Sarah had brought along her younger daughters, four-year-old daughter Piper and eleven-year-old Willow. During the morning, the girls quietly shuffled in and out, more interested in organizing a shopping trip across the avenue with their cousins than getting down on hands and knees to scrape gum off splintered floorboards. Sally Heath, Sarah's mother, was there as well. She spoke with a slight tremor and possessed a sweet, caring nature. Sally is not one to speak up against stronger personalities in the family, especially Sarah or her husband, Chuck Heath, but she is the spiritual rock of the family. She joined me in applying coat after coat of paint to bury the grime and muck left behind by hockey execs who apparently enjoyed the ambiance of a frat house after rush week. All the while, Sally lathered me with endearments such as "Oh, you are so wonderful to help us, Frank," and "It's so good of you to take away time from your family to help Sarah."

Lesson learned on that November day: Sarah Palin clearly had the gift for motivating people through emotional osmosis. I don't recall her directing anyone to task. We directed ourselves. Galvanizing people to work tirelessly on her behalf are strengths; prioritizing tasks, delegating minutiae, and big-picture focus less so. We'd confront the need for that second skill set later, when attempting to run a campaign and eventually the state. For now, all of us assumed that Sarah had more than enough fortitude to reshape Alaska.

Late that afternoon, with my brand-new Levi's 501s speckled with paint, we wound down. While they were ruined, I never did toss those jeans; they remain a reminder of the best of our days together, the beginning of what Sarah would come to fondly call her "Rag Tag Team"—especially when she grew disappointed with the performance of her so-called political professionals, as was often the case. The name, an immediate source of pride, stuck.

I'd return to this office and a second midtown office we opened in August 2006 regularly for the duration of the campaign, watching it fill with campaign detritus such as posters, bumper stickers, and Palin-Gov buttons, along with a growing army of volunteers and supporters. My initial job was to coordinate many of the early personalities through the upcoming campaign—when not responding to daily requests from Sarah for computer tutoring (*"Frank. i'm totally numb to the real world of computer technology. glad you and Stevie know the language!"*) or dishing out the positive reinforcement she needed to sustain focus (*"Sarah. You are real and that's why everyone loves you"*). Within a few weeks, the sound of voices pitching ideas for an all-Alaska gas pipeline, spending cuts, and the elimination of waste, fraud, and "same ol', same ol' " filled the rooms seven days a week. Nurturing emotions, soothing egos, and assigning wildly divergent personalities to daily tasks consumed my life as the campaign and Sarah's prospects grew from that first day forward.

By the time we closed the office in November 2006—just after our successful gubernatorial election—it had become as unrecognizable as the woman whose career it launched as well as those of us who marched in lock step alongside her.

Definitely different, but would it be better?

3

An Honestly Cheap Campaign

I brought you a track-ball, because I gave away all of the extra
computer mice I used to have. Try it out. If it's still frustrating
we'll get you a mouse. I put in a request for a free one so
maybe in a day or two we'll get one without having to pay for it.
—FRANK BAILEY, EMAIL TO FELLOW VOLUNTEER,
MONDAY, JANUARY 30, 2006

Only a few weeks after my volunteer debut, the campaign for the
Palin GOP nomination was under way, and I was right in the
thick of it.

"Frank, can you answer this guy's question about picking up campaign signs?" I'd answer that question, and the next one would be,
"How do we send out this campaign message to everyone who's submitted an email address?"

Before addressing that issue, Sarah might say, "This is flippin' confusing. I just wrote a letter in Word, and now it's disappeared. Frank,
where'd it go?"

For all the chaos, this was more nonfamily fun than I'd ever had.

While our message to the voters was simple and did not yet include major policy directives, Sarah's business-*unusual* tone, Reagan
populism, and unwavering ethics resonated. Sarah didn't need to understand how to cut and paste in Word or how to save a document.
When she spoke of God, home, family, "real Alaskans," change, less
government, and more accountability and transparency, she believed
what she said, and so did we. Hope and ideology guided and motivated us—so much that I threw myself into this with every molecule

of my being. Nothing seemed half as important as the outcome of the next election.

By this time, I was commuting to the Anchorage headquarters on a full-time basis and assumed the duties of an office manager, a job that included setting up phone systems (initially cordless, then refurbished cell phones), a groaning first-generation fax machine (a loaner we called Smoky Joe because it literally did just that, smoke), second-hand computers, and discount laptops while also coordinating a growing legion of volunteers.

At both ends of the day, extending my hours to as many as twelve, I also fielded emails. As such, I soon discovered that for Sarah, not all advice was welcome. One concerned supporter wrote: *"Sarah, I am a Teamster, a family man, a Christian and I am angry. . . . Your name is not out there. If I were wealthy I would give you what you needed, but alas I am not. Fifty dollars is my commitment. I think you WILL bring honesty back to Alaska."* Sarah snapped, *"Man, I get annoyed with messages like this one."* Any criticism, in this case tiny and wrapped in support, did not sit well with her.

More than anything, issue number one in getting Sarah elected was money—or more precisely, the lack thereof, especially when compared to our GOP rivals: former state senator John Binkley and Governor Murkowski. In Binkley's July 24 filing with the Alaska Public Offices Commission (APOC)—the state agency charged with enforcing all campaign finance laws—he reported spending $794,000, with many of his 1,100 donors coming from his hometown of Fairbanks. He also tossed in $379,000 of his own money over a six-month period. Murkowski's 438 donors contributed $260,000, of which $50,000 was his own. Not surprisingly, most state department commissioners—many of them appointed by Murkowski—contributed the maximum $1,000, as did oil industry executives from VECO Corporation and Udelhoven Oilfield System Services. In contrast, Sarah's 1,200 contributors managed to raise $194,000, of which only $1,500 came from Palin bank accounts. The vast majority of our contributors gave less than $250, with many below $50. By typical election standards, we were scrapping for funds, and so I became preoccupied with making a loaf of bread and a fish or two feed the hungry masses of a gubernatorial campaign. A financial number that might look small to the rest of the political world represented a fortune to us.

One of the first strategic goals was to create a sea of yard and building signs with Palin for Governor in white letters set against a blood-red background. In Alaska, these low-tech anachronisms mean something to voters in the same way they did in 1952, when the slogan I Like Ike appeared across the nation and helped elect Dwight D. Eisenhower president. And just as General Ike's name meant something important to his generation, to us the name Sarah Palin symbolized fearlessness in the face of huge corporate interests.

During each Alaskan election cycle, armies of volunteers with hammers pound signs into the ground—or on trees, if the ground is frozen. Each camp battles for prime location. The visuals along well-traveled roads, on lawns, and in the parking lots of local businesses, serve as indicators of public sentiment. Local businesses often display a favorite's sign. I even had a barge owner ask if we had a sign seventy feet long: he wanted to hang the biggest banner in Alaskan history from his vessel anchored off the Port of Anchorage in Cook Inlet. I laughed and told him we did not. He pledged to make one out of tarps and canvas. We needed these kinds of believers to offer up a window or a rooftop (or a boat) and join sides with our underdog upstart.

We knew the importance of primacy and wanted to be first in the race to generate and distribute pins, buttons, bumper stickers, wristbands, logoed Frisbees, and those glorious signs. Sarah felt this urgency acutely and wanted to get her signs out before the opposition got its out.

Her goal was to see *"a sweet splash of red all over the areas. . . . Rural AK needs them sooner rather than later."* Somehow we'd figure a way to impress upon the state's seven hundred thousand residents this message: *A vote for Palin is a vote for change.* Conservatives, ironically, later compared our hero to Barack Obama: they both sailed the winds of change, just tacking in different directions.

The first batch of Palin signs arrived just prior to Christmas 2005, and that delivery of fifty small yard signs and four four-by-eight-foot signs confirmed for us that, wow, this was really official now! The freshly minted signs had a just-off-the-press smell that I associated with our growing confidence, and a few were so new that the damp ink smudged (providing an excuse to haggle for additional signs at a reduced price). These early posters were plain with few variations. Later we added a photo of Sarah and the motto Take a Stand. The one thing that never varied was that signature shade of red—the same color that Sarah's high school girls' basketball team wore in 1982, the year that its star point guard, nicknamed Sarah Barracuda, led the Wasilla Warriors to a state championship. Eventually we constructed over 6,800 yard signs, a huge number by Alaskan standards. It made our rivals' signs look like random weeds in a countryside of red flowers.

As for the cost of distributing our handiwork, especially to remote rural communities, we had a plan for that too, as I shared with Sarah in an email: *"Love the idea of having people carry signs out when they go. Kerm is working on lightweight-sturdy packing to accommodate that."*

Sarah endorsed the human mule concept wholeheartedly: *"In fact people can transport them for free as carry ons or luggage when they travel to their communities."*

Strategic sign placement, we learned, was as important as volume. We targeted the properties along the most traveled roads. Each prime spot we found became a cause for celebration. In one instance, when we secured a spot on the Palmer Flats—a wide-open area that is the only north-south route between Anchorage and the scenic Mat-Su Valley, which includes Sarah's Wasilla—we took that as a coup. Since billboards are outlawed in Alaska, there was nothing to obstruct the view for the thousands of weekday commuters who zipped along Glenn Highway. Palin supporter and valley resident Don Benson, who owned a parcel of land on the inlet side of the highway, built a large riser and mounted one of our impressive four-by-eights surrounded by American flags and ribbons. Sarah, unable to contain her enthusiasm, wrote, *"Whoo Hoo!!! This is awesome!!! I saw it tonight on my way into town. It's the sweetest spot in the entire state of Alaska."*

Later, when future radio host Eddie Burke secured a building owner willing to hang a large sign, Sarah had a similar outburst: *"Oh baby—yeah!!! We'll owe Eddie for this one."* If Sarah's *Whoo-hoo's* and *Oh baby's* made it sound as if we were easy to please, we were.

The larger signs cost $40 each, while the yard signs ran us around

$8. In the volume we desired—thousands—this represented a staggering sum. Saving money to buy these visuals meant soliciting donations of desks and chairs and shopping in thrift shops. We researched at length matters that were budgetary trifles for our opponents, such as calling around town to price out a four-drawer locking file cabinet that could be bolted to the floor. Of course, I'd do the bolting myself for free. In the meantime, Sarah noted, *"I'm looking around for a table or whatever . . . we can't purchase any furniture so we have to scrounge around for desk, table etc."* We became great fans of Craigslist and the giveaway cyber-community known as the Freecycle Network. Since I lived much of my life on tight budgets, Sarah learned that if she wanted to run a campaign on the cheap, I was her guy.

For example, I devised a double-up scheme to cut down on parking costs in the Fifth Avenue Mall garage: *"For the garage behind us we can get a $54/mo rate per vehicle . . . if 2 people coordinated, one person could park, then exit, THEN somehow drop the card back in the office for the next person to use later that day."*

Sarah added this partial solution: *"And remember I have quarters for you now in the office—for those stinkin' parking meters."*

Not to belabor the point, but when I say we were not above collecting coins from sofa cushions, I am not exaggerating. I sent the following e-blast to our volunteers:

> Hi folks,
> If anyone has a good quality 10-key calculator that we could borrow for the next 5 months that would be great.
>   ALSO . . . we're in constant need of washers & wood screws for our signs (as well as scrap lumber to build stakes out of). If you have some lying around in your garage that you'd like to donate, bring 'em on down! We have some extremely resourceful minds working on this project, but it takes the resources of all, not just a few, to make stuff happen.
> Thank you so much!

Volunteers extraordinaire Cathy Fredericks and husband Dave made thousands of campaign buttons in their living room, printing out sheets of round designs on an ancient inkjet printer; our cost of 19 cents per button compared to $1.20 for those of lieutenant governor candidate Sean Parnell (later our running mate). The buttons bore simple logos like Sarah Gov or simply Sarah, but they got our name out the door and pinned onto coats and shirts. When we could afford to, we purchased a $350 machine and had volunteers stamp out more sophisticated buttons by the thousands. Truly, we were learning that necessity is the mother of invention—or in our case, the mother of low-cost innovation.

In most of the political world, media-buy decisions revolve around whether there is more bang for a million-dollar commercial on CNBC or on Fox News. Or the campaign controller might have to decide between taking out a half-page black-and-white ad in the *New York Times* at a cost of $35,000, and splurging on a full-page color ad for $100,000. But for the Rag Tag Team, when it came to advertising, we agonized over a $362 ad in a local newspaper announcing a campaign event. One insider fired off an email advising, *"That is an expensive ad and perhaps not the best use of our dollars."* Literally, we were a campaign for which a $100 outlay might require the attention of Sarah, me, and as many as three or four others.

In the midst of all this financial caution, Sarah was keenly aware that her legitimacy as a candidate was, in some measure, dependent on showing the media (and by extension her rivals) that she had the ability to raise money. The amounts we're talking about seem trivial in an era where a Meg Whitman can spend more than $144 million of her own money in California's 2010 gubernatorial election. Our goal? On December 19, Sarah put her request in an email to staff:

> **We need to raise another $15,000 before Dec. 31st. That's when APOC closes this year's recordings, the press does a story on how much has been raised by the candidates, and our credibility is measured in part by the amount we've raised. . . . Thanks!!**

We made that $15,000 with a few thousand to spare. Nonetheless, Binkley, the GOP hierarchy's favorite son, swamped us. Money, when you're not in the party's good graces, is as hard to find as the end of a rainbow.

However, our seat-of-the-pants operation suited us. I believed that the way we operated was how government should run and *would* be run under Sarah Palin: cutting waste and chopping expenses to the bone; fiscal conservatism at its finest. Sell assets, reduce government, and simply do more with less. I didn't know much about government, but I did know that politicians spent a lot more of our hard-earned money than necessary. Sarah and I spoke the same language: Waste not, want not.

4

Thrilling Chaos

Does the flap of a butterfly's wings in
Brazil set off a tornado in Texas?
—EDWARD LORENZ, A MATHEMATICIAN SPECIALIZING
IN CHAOS THEORY, DECEMBER 29, 1979

As crucial as funding was, the need for volunteers was equally important. Having people man phones, distribute flyers, and hold
banners across a freeway overpass can make or break a candidate in
our state.

When a new volunteer came on board, Sarah often personalized
a note that might sound corny in most circles, but it played perfectly
at this time, in this place. In one such note to Red Secoy, a Mat-Su
Valley acquaintance of Sarah's who enthusiastically committed to the
cause, she gushed, *"Right on Red! I'm excited about you being on board.
You're a hoot . . . and a good worker & good man. Thanks so much!"*

All of us cherished each willing body, and with Sarah's charisma,
the body count grew rapidly.

Over time, our Rag Tag Team included Sarah's immediate family
(especially husband Todd) as well as early arrivals like ever-loyal Ivy
Frye (attacked mercilessly by her critics); father figure and decades-long
Palin family friend Kerm Ketchum; tech guru Stephen (Stevie) Bailey,
my baby brother; gas-line brainiac Bruce Anders, brilliant attorney Jeff
Lowenfels, whom Sarah tried to recruit as running mate; my "sister
from a different mister" and untitled campaign manager for the general
election, Kris Perry; and early campaign spokesperson Curtis Smith.

Others joined our group after Sarah won the governorship, including sometimes problematic and controversial spokesperson Meg Stapleton (with her pejorative nickname, Stapletongue), attorney Thomas Van Flein (ultimately private council to the Palins), eventual state attorney general Talis Colberg, radio host Eddie Burke (if we needed a story reported, Eddie was our local guy), and conservative radio shock jock Dan Fagan.

One person in particular epitomized what this wave of volunteerism was all about. Marvin Morrisett, a highly decorated veteran, was eighty-six years old during the '06 campaign. Marvin lived with his wife in a beautifully stained wood house in Chugiak, a bedroom community between Anchorage and the Mat-Su Valley. Shortly after he joined us, we noticed a sudden shortage of yard signs. When I caught Marvin on his third trip in and out of the office, loaded up with Palin-Gov posters, I realized he was hauling placards and hardware to his house, assembling the signs, and then walking house to house up and down Eagle River, Chugiak, and nearby Peter's Creek. This octogenarian single-handedly planted over two hundred signs. After that, whenever he showed up with his enthusiastic smile, we did our best to treat him like royalty. Standing eye to eye with me at about five foot seven, he would say, "Don't want to take up your precious time, Frank. I know you are so busy. I just need more signs." Marvin was always humble and polite, as if I were doing him a service instead of the other way around.

People started calling in, saying, "Eagle River's all red, Frank! You guys are doing an amazing job there!" It was all Marvin. On top of that, when kids stole signs from an entire street, Marvin discovered them in a ditch, cleaned them up, and hammered 'em right back into the ground. His motivation for all this effort? "Sarah's so refreshing, Frank," he used to say to me. "She's exactly what this state needs."

While Sarah would gush her thanks in personal emails, when I repeatedly asked her to please pay a quick visit to Marvin, she never did. I didn't understand her unwillingness. My wife and I had the honor of visiting Marvin in his beautiful home filled with pictures of grandchildren and extended family. Sarah missed out on something special.

Sarah was sometimes dismissive of others as well. Bill Arnold, working alongside two elderly volunteers from the Kenai Peninsula, spent ten hours a day pounding signs, lobbying voters, and doing communications work. In private, the candidate referred to them as the "crazy old men's club" on the peninsula. While that might sound endearing, Sarah's tone was belittling. After election night, Bill Arnold presented Sarah with his lucky fedora, festooned with campaign buttons, and told her to keep it through her reelection in 2010. Rather than being touched by the gesture, Sarah quickly tossed the beloved hat in the trash, explaining to me that it was "icky." She seemed to have a callous streak and a way of trivializing others' efforts on her behalf. I began to wonder if Sarah didn't view relationships based primarily on what folks could do for her.

However, at the time, I convinced myself that I was merely misreading her intentions. Maybe in Marvin's case, Sarah didn't feel that visiting a single volunteer was the most productive use of her time. If so, she had a lot to learn about time management, as she spent countless hours on details that likely deserved delegation. If a request for bumper stickers came in, Sarah would typically handle it personally.

In yet another time gobbler, Sarah read and responded to hundreds of individual emails. For example, when a woman expressed concern that Sarah was in favor of a ban on bear baiting—luring bears with food, then shooting them as a means of predator control—Sarah replied personally:

> Hi Nahtalie.
> I've never changed my position on predator control or bear baiting. I don't support the ban on bear baiting, and I also support scientifically sound practices of predator control, too, so human consumption of our game resources can continue in a strong manner.
> Thanks for asking . . . Please contact me anytime.

Was this efficient? We didn't initially think in those terms. In her first campaign for Wasilla mayor, in 1996, she'd won by just 211 votes: 651 to 440. In even closer races, Mark Begich (now a US senator) won the mayorship of Anchorage by 14 votes in 2003, while the following year, Mike Kelly of Fairbanks won election to the US House of Representatives by 4 votes. Wasn't this just a bigger Wasilla or Fairbanks campaign, with the results possibly hinging on a handful of votes? If there was a disgruntled voter, like Nahtalie, Sarah either responded directly or had staff do so ASAP on her behalf. Win that voter over, no matter how long it took or how inefficient that strategy would become. Unfortunately for our earliest efforts, this wasn't the Wasilla mayor's race and our candidate needed to woo an entire state, not just a handful of local voters.

———

By the end of February 2006, the volumes of email and paperwork began to swamp our primitive and inefficient systems. In classic understatement, I wrote to Kris Perry: *"Don't really like the idea of Sarah taking credit card stuff home, as I think she'll make lots of stops and would hate for that to get stolen out of her car."* My suggestion that we hold contributions and records under lock and key instead of having them pile up in Sarah's backseat seems obvious, yet we went months without a solution.

As for controlling email traffic, Sarah felt overwhelmed. Five months into the campaign, I literally had to teach her how to cut and paste a Word Document, a technique she did not master easily (frequently having a patch-quilt email containing multiple font types and sizes as a result). Accessing email remotely was itself a new skill for Sarah. In February 2006 she asked me how to log on to the campaign email system to read her emails:

> In case I run into anyone at the store who asks if I've received their message, I won't have a blank look on my face like I did the other day when a lady asked if I thought about what she'd written. I had no idea what she was talking about. . . . Also, when we do a blanket email . . . can I be copied . . . so I can see what we've sent out and/or communicated to a particular area?

In late April '06, Sarah was still typing individual addresses onto emails when sending out policy pieces. In frustration, she wrote me, *"It would be great to have the email addresses so i could cut a paste 'em on my op-ed submittals to news sources around the state."* Only then did we get around to building an address book for media contacts so that she did not have to type individual names and addresses on each email.

Our lack of sophistication went well beyond computer efficiency. When a disgruntled voter asked if we had received a contribution from the union group AFSCME, Sarah wrote, *"Does anyone know what union group this guy is talking about in his attached message?"* I certainly didn't, nor did anyone else. In a minipanic—fearing that this might be an organization whose affiliation would tarnish our reputation—we researched and discovered that the American Federation of State, County, and Municipal Employees was not only the largest employee union in Alaska, representing approximately 8,500 state and munici-pal employees, but also the largest in the United States. And we *had* received a contribution.

How could we not have been aware of this union? Sarah, along with the rest of us, was completely unaware that many of her future employees were members of AFSCME and that they were currently supporting us. There were many things we didn't know, but we'd learn, sometimes the hard way.

In one instance, we hit a financial landmine planted by a public re-lations firm that Sarah had hired. Given our monetary woes, it was the last thing we needed.

From: Sarah
To: frank bailey
Created: 12/15/2005 7:35:33 AM

i just got another bill from the original web guy . . . it was the most ridiculously expensive and inefficient thing we've done so far—asking a PR firm to get that thing up and running. i'm em-barrassed to admit they've charged us around $7,000 for the web-site (which took forever to get up and running, then had mistakes throughout). . . .

HUGE lessons learned with that!!! we found out after the fact that we were charged for every visit and phone call . . . i made to the firm. we weren't told up front what all they expected, and i guess i didn't ask the right questions because we got snookered and we're still paying for it.

anyway—onward and upward.

Despite the occasional financial hiccup, we believed that there was nothing wrong with inexperience and learning on the job. In June I sent Sarah talking points for her to use if questioned about inexperience:

They attack me for lack of experience. If experience means tainted by large corporations, then it is true: I do not share that kind of experience.

Does "experience" mean more of the same? Alaskans are telling me every day that they are ready for a change from what you call "experience."

In sum, we believed that Sarah's common sense trumped factual knowledge and good-ol'-boy experience every dang time.

———

Despite the chaos of these initial months, we felt a thrill similar to the early days of a marriage, when pennies are pinched amid the promise of everlasting love. I once heard an older, wealthier, and not particularly happy couple say of their earlier life together, "Those were the best times, when we had nothing more than love and great expectations. Passion was enough back then." That's where we were, in a place where passion seemed enough. Despite everything, Sarah *was* flying high. Her earlier confrontation with Republican Party chairman Ruedrich and her stance against Governor Murkowski and his daughter were paying dividends. Big money didn't flow in, but small bites did, as did poll numbers. According to an early 2006 Ivan Moore Research survey, Sarah held a formidable 15-point lead in the three-way Republican primary, with 42 percent of polled voters preferring her over Murkowski (27 percent) and Binkley (16 percent).

We had a simple formula: work hard, trust in God, and stay true to our principles. And while I'd have appreciated Sarah reprioritizing—especially when it came to the lack of attention she paid to volunteers—it was her feeling overwhelmed that ensured many of us an important role in the campaign. In some ways, her imperfections were perfectly fine with me.

5

Dark Clouds

[I was] warned how pressurized things get in politics,
I naively assumed I'd be immune from it all, but this "half
way point" has been pretty significant in terms of some
pressure manifesting itself. Just need God's guiding hand!
—SARAH PALIN, EMAIL TO FRANK BAILEY, MARCH 21, 2006

Eventually, those of us who doted on Sarah became known
throughout the blogosphere as "Palin-bots," and with some
truth, I was the first of these. A second term of "respect" for her army
of avid fans was "Palin Gremlins," of whom it was said, "The more
she's beat up, the stronger her gremlins come back, and they come
back in ever larger numbers." Nobody in his right mind ever suggested that our prior two governors had corps of "Murkowski-bots" or
"Knowles-bots." The terms applied uniquely to Palin devotees, those
seeking her approval even as they were strapped to her personal and
professional roller coaster.

And as we Palin-bots built our campaign, we simply overlooked,
ignored, or rationalized signs that suggested things weren't as sanguine
as we envisioned. Worse for me, behaviors I had previously considered
myself incapable of condoning would become acceptable and com-
monplace. I slipped from passive observer to participant.

While I might suggest this unfortunate morphing began subtly,
almost innocently, that's a weak excuse. I should have seen the creep-
ing insanity.

Definitely should have seen, but blindly did not.

One of the things I noticed early on was that Sarah was unable or unwilling to separate her personal life from her political life.

At times, the Palins shared with me and staff moments of humor and love. In one instance, Sarah described oldest son and hockey star Track Palin's concerns over a "goofy" picture of Sarah playing hockey with him on the official Palin for Governor website:

> He says it's the worst picture he's ever seen because I'm not even holding the stick correctly.
>
> He just called from his school library where he was visiting the website. I promised him I wouldn't embarrass him and I'd remove the dumb thing . . .
>
> So . . . take that one off & replace it with anything else? Or just delete it and replace it with nothing.
>
> Thanks so much! Track can then come back out from hiding.

Her subsequent thank-you for taking care of the matter was equally charming: *"Thanks so much for the quick work on deleting the hockey picture! My son says, 'Sweet . . . thanks.'"*

At other times, the family sacrifices tore me apart. I often felt the kids, in particular, paid a stiff price for Sarah's political single-mindedness. With Todd traveling up to the North Slope for his union job with British Petroleum and Sarah focused intensely on her campaign, the four children were left on their own for large stretches of time. We heard that their school grades suffered. Sarah's concern did not, however—as near as I could tell—translate into hands-on action. She blamed coaches for not alerting her or school administrators for not providing enough resources or not contacting her often enough, but there was never a mention of taking a night off to help with homework or schedule additional parent-teacher conferences.

I recall one day when Bristol phoned from school crying while Sarah sat in my office. Sarah rolled her eyes and held the phone out, as if to say, "You wanna listen to this?" She responded to Bristol in clipped one-word answers meant to quickly wrap up the call. I felt pained for Bristol; whatever was going on, she was obviously upset, and Sarah's indifference made me uncomfortable. Her reaction felt callous—a new facet of her personality that I hadn't noticed before. Later, in June 2006, as a throw-in line to a light-hearted string of emails, Sarah wrote something that struck me as similarly insensitive: *"Bristol's mad at me. Says this isn't fun. Too bad."*

I sought to rationalize my concerns over the children's welfare by assuming that the older kids were sufficiently mature to manage their days and occasional nights alone, and that Sarah and Todd surely had family members supervising them. The children had, after all, a mother whose moral compass I believed ran true at all times. And Sarah had abilities to juggle priorities in ways I could not possibly fathom. I simply wasn't seeing the whole picture. The Palins knew their children and I didn't. Maybe the way Sarah handled her daughter's earlier call was a tough love moment?

In contrast to these moments, there were times when she felt the mounting toll the campaign was taking on family, as when she wrote an email asking, *"Please pray for the Lord's guidance . . . I know you already are praying. Yikes, the attacks on family are not much fun."* I understood that any criticism of family hurt, and I did pray: "God, please protect our future governor, take care of her family, and provide Your peace to her endeavors. As imperfect as I am, God, please hear my prayer for Sarah and the future of Alaska." In moments like this, I came to feel sorry for all of us. I too was sacrificing time with family. That this vibrant woman was willing to dedicate so much for others simply meant that we all needed to do more and try to make up for lost time later, after we won the governor's race.

A month or so into the campaign, Sarah sent an email addressing a family matter that sent my jaw dropping:

From: Sarah
To: Scott Heyworth Cc: Todd Palin
Sent: Friday, January 06, 2006 10:19 AM
Subject: Todd's son

Scott:
Todd just told me you had spoken with him awhile back and reported that some law enforcement friends of yours claimed some

dumbass lie about Track not being Todd's son? This really, really disgusts me and ticks me off.

I want to know right now who said it, who would ever lie about such a thing . . . this is the type of bullshit lie about family that WILL keep me from running for Governor. . . .

I want to know NOW what this latest b.s. is all about because I want to get to the bottom of this garbage rumor mill . . . AND IF UGLY LIES LIKE THIS ARE BELIEVED BY ANYONE AND ADVERSELY AFFECT MY HUSBAND AND KIDS

. . . I WILL PULL OUT OF THE RACE BECAUSE IT'S NOT WORTH IT—AT ALL—TO LET MY FAMILY BE VICTIMS OF DARK, UGLY POLITICS LIKE THIS.

When Sarah forwarded this message to a tight group of her inner circle, she added a final note: *"this is total crap that a candidate (me) and their family would have to put up with this garbage."* Scott Heyworth, to whom Sarah addressed her first email, was a reliable volunteer with substantial political experience. Whenever asked to, he offered seasoned advice and organizational skill but was not considered part of the inner circle and didn't receive many emails from Sarah. As one of the few, this was a doozy.

My initial response to the message was shock. Maybe 10 percent of me wondered if the assertion was true, but I didn't care. I felt as if I was back in the fifth grade, watching a bully pick on a helpless little girl. This was the very, very first moment where I felt that I needed to protect Sarah. With a knot in my stomach, I said something to her like, "That's junk. Let *us*"—as in, not you—"deal with stuff like that." Naturally I had no inkling how to possibly deal with this "stuff," as my repertoire did not yet include retributive strategic thinking.

Despite what most saw as justified anger, if we'd looked more closely and read between the lines, we would have seen Sarah's penchant for inflaming issues that, if left alone, might have disappeared. I knew nothing about this rumor nor did I care anything about it—until she brought me into the discussion, that is. When Sarah demanded to know *"NOW"* who'd said these things, I'd eventually learn that her desire for names wasn't just idle curiosity—she wanted to know where to set her sights and counterattack.

Another aspect of this extraordinary exchange is that Sarah believed this to be *"DARK, UGLY POLITICS."* When I spoke later with Heyworth, he observed, "Politics is tough. Sarah needs to be able to hear this crap because you know Binkley and Ruedrich will be coming at her with everything they've got." I silently agreed with Heyworth. Sarah often spoke of Ronald Reagan's "steely spine," and, as Heyworth implied, she'd need to find hers, or this would be a hard row to hoe. And did this actually constitute *"DARK, UGLY POLITICS?"* Disgusting, yes, but it seemed more like barroom gossip by ignorant individuals with eighty-proof mouths. Are idiots really worth the hassle? That's hard for me to say, as it wasn't my family, but for Sarah Palin, no slight, whether real or imagined, ever went unpunished.

At that time, what troubled me most was her threat to pull out of the race. Surely, I thought, this was merely a gut reaction without intent. Too much was at stake for her to scuttle the campaign over a mere insult. In that moment, Sarah's Rag Tags likely joined Sarah's Prayer Warriors (a self-named group that actually existed) in asking God to grant her peace. No less than the fate of our great state depended on that.

As for Sarah, she never did completely forget, and she certainly did not forgive. During the campaign, an accusation arose that as mayor she'd inappropriately used her office to conduct campaigning for her unsuccessful run at lieutenant governor in 2002. She likened the criticism to the attacks on her family. To a large list of supporters, she repeated the Track Palin parentage rumor and gave life to several others—some that eventually became well known on the national stump.

This reminds me of the allegation that was "anonymously" leaked to the media that falsely accused me of having a felony on my record by attaching a false court document to the lie that was sent to the press. It's also reminiscent of the false allegations that my children aren't really mine and my husband's. Oh, and of course, the ol' "I saw her on a train headed to Seward with a guy she's having an affair with" lie that also got back to me. Oh please. This aspect of politics stink, this is why good folks sometimes don't offer themselves up to serve in public office. . . .

It's almost funny that this is all they've got. Let me help them out a bit and make their search for "dirt" a little easier. I got a "D" in a micro-econ course once in college, 20 years ago, Todd and I eloped—we didn't have a real wedding. . . . I make mistakes everyday. Heck, today I hollered at the wrong child when I accused one of not taking out the trash on their day to do so. I was wrong. I apologize. That's about it. All the skeletons are out of the closet.

Defensive emails like this did more to breathe life into speculation than end it. That Sarah raised sordid issues to a previously unaware audience generated new questions. Personally, I never made the connection, nor did I read the blogs that did, nor did I follow up and wonder who Track's father was if not Todd? Or what guy on what train? But thousands (eventually millions) of others did.

Not surprisingly, few people—certainly not me—had the guts to tell Sarah to put to rest the offending commentary by simply taking the high road, ignoring critics, and thereby allowing matters to wither and die. Why not simply focus on issues instead of chatter? In July 2006, I sent her a message hinting at this advice:

Sarah,
If you're able to show your strength, and your passion, but stay above the fray and gracefully smile off the personal attacks as just that (and label them as that!), that the voters of Alaska will come to your aid. . . . There's a certain grace that you can show in there that shows that you're dismissing so much of this as mean spirited, personal, juvenile, and not affecting you (even though is sucks bigtime). But I tell ya . . . THAT is the person that people will stand up out of their bleacher chairs for!

In her response, Sarah intellectually understood and wrote, *"I agree. A woman can't get pissed without sounding pissy. And we don't like pissy women. No one does."* But in most instances, a suggestion from staff or a voter would send her into a mini-tirade. In response to a constituent's email asking for the campaign to differentiate Sarah's positions from independent gubernatorial candidate Andrew Halcro's, Sarah emailed:

> ok—i have to clone myself or something . . . or i'm going to have a nervous breakdown. . . . i just returned home (to pick up kids and cook dinner) and I see a dozen more email questions i have to add to my list of 81 other emails needing answers. we have to have a different system . . . or i must concentrate on only this task and forget many other things that are piling up. it will take me long than "soon" to respond to all these.

Within months of my joining the campaign, these rants were becoming frequent. In April 2006, my concerns over Sarah's mental discomfort became so acute that I contacted an executive coach, writing, *"I see this as a crucial pivotal point for Sarah. I'd like to see her energized and not bogged down by the challenges we've had. I have a feeling that this . . . will be an emotional draw on her, and that concerns me. Her #1 worry is letting down her supporters."* When I courageously floated the idea past her, she said bluntly, "That's something I do not need, Frank." Her tone made it clear that a suggestion of personal weakness was unwelcome.

In a battle between Sarah's mind and emotions, the latter nearly always prevailed. As much as she might understand the wisdom of forgive and forget, I would soon discover it wasn't gonna happen. Not with her, and ultimately not with anyone else who survived in her campaign and administration. Eventually we repressed pacifism altogether.

6

Stuck in the Middle

It takes two to get one in trouble.
—MAE WEST

Todd Palin was himself an unpredictable factor in the life of the campaign. His interest and input ebbed and flowed. At times, he might be involved via emails in something as simple as organizing signs as in this message: *"We'll be ordering knew signs soon, so this is a good time to re-group and be ready for sign displacement when the knew signs arrive. I will work with the sign team to answer any further questions regarding signs."* And on a much larger scale, Todd might direct staff, including me, to investigate commissioners, as he did on August 24, 2007: *"The FAA representative expressed to Jack great concern about Deputy Commissioner DOT/Aviation John Torgersons commitment to aviation safety. . . . If you would please give Jack Barber a call to get a better understanding of the situation and how this may affect the states relationship with FAA."*

When the state-owned Matanuska Maid Dairy was nearing bankruptcy and became a political liability for the administration in June 2007, Todd instructed me to do opposition research on Mat Maid executives Joseph Van Treeck and Terry Clark. In these instances, operating counterattack from the sidelines became one of Todd's special interests.

When Todd did appear in the campaign, between stints on the North Slope, his intercessions—often intent on managing Sarah's quixotic personality—weren't necessarily constructive.

My first encounter with a Todd crisis came only weeks into my joining the effort. As background, Todd and I were both aware that Sarah had a desire to control all information and micromanage the tiniest of details—including being copied on every email in and out of the campaign. Expense management down to pen reorders and yard sign purchases and placement were on that nothing-is-too-small-for-me list. Todd's directives, however, conflicted with Sarah's. He'd say to me, "Sarah doesn't need to know what's going on; she needs to be shaking hands."

No argument that what Todd said made sense. However, Sarah had—and we knew in no uncertain terms—different ideas. Her oft-repeated line was "I've run five campaigns," blah, blah, "and I know what I'm doing and know what I need to know." Which was a need to know *everything*.

I'd relay this to Todd, and he'd order us, in his my-way-or-the-highway voice, "No more emails to Sarah. Quit bothering her; she's getting distracted and frustrated."

I learned to ignore many of Todd's commands the hard way. In April 2006 he phoned and asked, "How are we doing?"

"Well," I said, "signs are flying out the door, and we're almost out." We'd printed and delivered hundreds already and had only a handful remaining.

"So order more."

"They take a couple or three days to make—"

"Frank. How tough is this decision to make? Just order more frigging signs. Buy 'em."

Laughing nervously, I suggested, "Yeah, okay. I'll clear it with Sarah tomorrow, when she's in the office—"

"No!" he insisted. "Just buy 'em. She doesn't need to know; she shouldn't be bothered. Worrying about signs, thank-you notes, whatever, end it. What the hell, Frank. Sarah's heading toward a mental breakdown at this rate."

It wasn't that Todd was wrong about the stress of overburdening Sarah. He was dead right. He knew his wife; I was still a new kid on the team, so why not? After all, Sarah had sent us countless messages about getting that "sweet sea of red" washing across Alaska as soon as possible. I uttered two words to Todd that I came to regret: "Sure thing."

I phoned our sign guy, Ross, ordered $2,000 worth of new signs, after having proudly negotiated down their price, and assumed I'd live happily ever after.

All was well. Until four days later when Sarah entered the office and saw the signs. Her face went from bronze to a shade of red, matching the background of our newly minted Palin for Governor posters. In front of at least two other volunteers—dedicated Cathy Fredericks and high-energy Clark Perry—she asked, lacing each word with dry ice, "Where did those come from?" At that moment, with my back pressed against a door and body withering, I spoke:

"I ordered them. We had only six or seven left—"

"Why the heck did you do that?" If it didn't look silly, I'd add about five exclamation points to adequately relay the fire-breathing emotion behind her question. "I, not you, Frank, am running this campaign."

As a man who tends to lurk in the shadows of his wife's ambition, Todd isn't one to step forward and say, "I told Frank to do that." When the Sarah thermostat revved high, nobody expected the husband to supply supportive ice to cool things down. As for me, I had no desire to implicate Mr. Palin in anything controversial, realizing that such a move would become a lose-lose proposition for me. Nodding yes to my boss and hero (as a glass-is-half-full guy, all I had to do was convince myself that a fiery temper can be an asset in politics), I said, "Okay." Feeling sucker punched, I swore to avoid falling into this trap again, naively believing that possible.

The entire sign exchange took only a minute or two and ended with Sarah storming out of the building. My fellow volunteers had retreated out of the office but heard the exchange (or at least Sarah's side of it). As was his nature, an animated Clark reentered once the future governor left. With a shake of his head and through a nervous laugh, he said, "Duuuude, you're in the shithouse now, aren't you? But you know how Sarah can get," he added. "And, Frank, I'm off signs for good."

Clark had known Sarah for years. Me? I had no idea until that moment "how Sarah can get."

That tooth-rattling pothole on the Sarah Highway was never discussed again, thankfully. Days later, I came to believe that Sarah regretted the outburst. Seldom one to offer apologies or acknowledge blame, she did purchase for me a desperately needed $500 smartphone—an enormous expense for our acorn-sized campaign. I took the gift as a peace offering meant to say, "Frank, you're here to stay, so don't sweat it." Honestly, until that moment, I wondered if this Todd-induced initiative on signs was game-set-match for me. Maybe I'm reading too much into her gesture, but with Sarah, almost nothing is done sans hidden meaning, including smartphoning me.

7

Conflicting Message

Beauty without grace is the hook without the bait.
—RALPH WALDO EMERSON

Around May 2006, Kerm Ketchum called me. Kerm, nearing seventy at the time and working long hours for the campaign despite his wife's terminal illness, is a kind man possessing significant intelligence and patience. Just seeing him you would agree, but we affectionately termed him our "campaign Einstein." He would willingly drop everything and undertake any task Sarah needed done, from emailing event announcements to delivering signs. To me, he became an advisor and sounding board. A good, good man.

With his voice quivering through the phone, I knew immediately that he had a shocking message. Kerm said he had been monitoring the email coming into the campaign account. Embarrassed, he explained that a pornographic picture of Sarah had popped up on one of the emails. The thought of such a thing sickened me; I can only imagine how Kerm, who'd known Sarah since she was in grade school, felt. Kerm forwarded the offending email, and I called Todd immediately to give him a heads-up. To my everlasting surprise, Todd's response was "Is it real?" He sounded amused.

Stunned, I said, "How the heck should I know, man?"

"Well, she walks around the house with her robe open and with all those windows we have, well, you know," Todd said, seeming not to care much either way.

If it were my wife, fake X-rated photo or not, I'd be horrified.

When I assured Todd that it had probably been Photoshopped, I felt as if I'd wasted words. Naked photos: not such a big deal.

When the photo later appeared on Craigslist, the rest of us were less amused. A campaign staffer wrote, *"To Whom It May Concern: We have just been emailed a picture of a nude woman with the face of Sarah Palin on it. This is an altered picture and is not!!!! Sarah Palin. We want it removed immediately or there wil be repercussions."*

However, at the other end of the concern scale, if a radio host suggested that Sarah had misrepresented a fact in a speech, Todd's blood boiled. In particular, he came to loathe—as we all did—the Anchorage-based conservative radio host Dan Fagan. Fagan became in fact a top-lister on what eventually grew into an extensive enemies list. At first professing love—literally—for Sarah, he soon turned on her over issues that I believed became more personal than political and ultimately backed her opponent John Binkley in the primary. What this little man said about Sarah consumed us enough that we regularly wasted three hours in the afternoon listening to the radio for his barbs, slights, or criticism. When something was said that she didn't like, Sarah's mood would darken, or she might demand that we solicit friends and family to phone in and blast "evildoer Dan Fagan." Finally, an infuriated Todd shot off an email to Sarah demanding that *she* take the upper hand in the battle with Dan and put him in his place. His tirade included suggesting that we make it known that Fagan was an *"unhealthy looking male that's not married . . . And his life is all about the next free steak and cigar. . . . He looks sick . . . no wonder he can't get a date."* Words from a clownish radio commentator were declarations of war, but the prospect of nude photos of his wife? *Whatever.*

It didn't take long for me to realize the Palins' family and marriage were complicated. What went on in the privacy of their home sometimes leaked out, as when Levi Johnston—former fiancé of Bristol Palin and father of her son, Tripp—described chaotic scenes of family and marital turmoil in his many interviews after becoming a Palin pariah. Granted, Levi is hardly an unimpeachable source. But once in

2007, when Governor Palin was weighing a month-long reality show to be filmed in their home, Bristol said, in my presence, "They'd see some shit, that's for sure." Sarah not only seemed not to react to the use of a four-letter word, she giggled in agreement.

Outside the home, there was further evidence of tension. At times, each spouse would separately instruct campaign workers to avoid informing the other of certain things, creating conflicting demands and a tough balancing act. Not only did Todd direct volunteers *not* to burden Sarah about everyday expenses and sign reorders, but he also demanded that we protect Sarah from certain types of emails as well.

For example, when a concerned parole officer wrote Sarah a lengthy list of recommendations on ways that he believed the division could improve its operation, Todd instructed us to take action that we all knew never would have met with Sarah's blessing:

> We need to stop, shield and intercept any e-mails from supporter's who have fallen through the cracks and are mad, from getting to Sarah. When she receives these e-mail she feels obligated to respond, taking valuable time away from her preparation for the next day's events.

Not only did I find this message demeaning, since we always sought to make Sarah's life easier by working seventy-hour weeks, but if Sarah discovered anyone shielding her from information—even if, as Todd suggested, it was for her own good—her reaction to my sign-ordering fiasco would have looked like a high-society double-cheeked kiss.

Similarly, Sarah phoned on at least three occasions and said, "Todd talks to lots of people. Be careful to tell him only what he needs to know." Once, in the presence of Todd, Kris Perry, and me, and without an ounce of sarcasm, she spoke wearily of trust. "Yep, our circle of trust is just that much smaller. There are only two people in this room I can trust." She then pointed to Todd and finished by saying, "And it's not him." Kris, a senior staffer who'd known the Palins far longer than I had, privately worried that anyone stroking Todd's ego might pull his talking string. And when Todd spoke, he sometimes volunteered information that was embarrassing.

––––––––

At one point, Todd actually put the campaign at risk. Jerry Mackie, a lobbyist and part-owner of the Alaska Aces, slipped Todd several sets of free hockey tickets during the campaign. If Todd failed to report these, this would be a campaign violation. When I pointed out to Todd that if unreported, these were inappropriate gifts, he tried to explain them away by suggesting what a "coup" it was, being able attend a game at the packed Sullivan Arena where he and Sarah could hand out Sarah buttons and conduct free campaigning in front of 6,600 people.

Similarly, when the Alaska State Snowmobile Association (ASSA) sent the campaign a questionnaire with intentions of publishing our responses in an issue of its official publication, the *Alaska SnowRiders*, as well as on the association's website, Todd took a personal interest in assigning this task to me and John Bitney, then the issue coordinator and opposition researcher. He copied others as well, to make certain that this was a high priority. As with the receipt of unreported gifts, Todd had little compunction about marshaling resources toward Palin family interests.

> There are groups out there that want to lock up Alaska's lands from motorized recreational use. We have a cabin in Petersville on Safari Lake. Our property taxes increase every year, while we continue to have limited parking all up and down Petersville road. . . . Can someone complete this questionnaire please.

From this message, it was clear how Todd wished us to answer the survey: let's get more parking near Safari Lake and open up the entire state, please, to motorized recreational vehicles. Dropping everything else on my lengthy to-do list, I lit a fire under sluggish John Bitney, and we got the survey completed as per Mr. Palin's urgent request.

In distrust for rules, Sarah mirrored Todd. For Sarah, less government extended to liquor, gun, helmet, cigarette, and even seat belt laws (telling me, "Heck, I don't even agree with Click-it or Ticket seat belt laws, and I filmed the damn commercial for 'em"). Because they were kindred spirits, the issue surrounding Todd was not his opinions but his lack of discretion in mouth management. His dearth of interview face time was an intelligently managed tactic.

Anxiety over Todd's ability to remain discreet, however, did not preclude Sarah from protecting his back, particularly when criticism reflected poorly on her image. For example, when a letter to the editor on the website AlaskaReport stated that "her husband is in charge of production at a field on the North Slope" and suggested that he resign to avoid a conflict of interest, she circulated the following:

> oh please! what is that guy yakking about?
> Todd is a production hand on the slope, he began his job in Prudhoe Bay 18 years ago, he's not in management (he actually works!) and doesn't call any shots for BP, he just does his job separating oil, gas and water in one of the Slope facilities. He's blue collar, grease-under-the-fingernails, pays his mandatory dues to United Steel Workers along with all his co-workers,
> he's a working-his-ass-off-for-his-family type of guy. We should be proud he's one of the few born-and-raised Alaskans up North who has the skills and work ethic that our state needs in the oil patch. What do they want me to do while I'm campaigning, as he can't quit his job, do they want me to divorce him? ;)

When Sarah saw a news story referencing a DUI of Todd's, in his defense she wrote of the hypocritical double standard: *"I saw another publicized slam of Todd's old 1980-something DUI again and wondered why does Obama get a pass for his drug use at the same time Todd got busted for drinking beer/driving in the ol' metropolis of Dillingham."*

For public consumption, she painted their relationship as perfect. When a voter wondered why her email went to Todd when addressed only to Sarah, the reply was typical Sarah: *"My husband is so wonderful, he helps go through emails so we don't miss any. We sure don't want to let any of the emails slide and not respond! Todd helps me keep them straight. He's the best helpmate a candidate could ever have, considering the amount of emails we receive!"*

Sarah's conflicting message to those of us on her staff was: don't always tell Todd what we're doing, but don't criticize him, either. These public proclamations of marital bliss, however, became what I referred to as pasting on a whole lotta frosting atop that cupcake to make it sweeter than it really is. I'm not suggesting that rumors of divorce had merit—I don't think they did—but this union for sure had its rocky side. Todd once wrote Sarah an email that he shared with me, saying she was *"once about taking a stand and shit,"* but that after being elected *"she wasn't any better than those she ran against."* Todd's email went on to express his growing dissatisfaction with Sarah. This message so unnerved my wife that she wrote me, *"It almost sounds as if he is filing for divorce if she doesn't answer his email the way he wants her to."*

For all the frictions their relationship created, however, Todd returned to home base and demonstrated as much devotion to the cause as anyone. It was hard to tell if the Palins were a loving couple, or like many couples, if they drifted in and out of affection. But whatever they shared, it was built around furthering Sarah's career, with Todd willingly assuming a supportive position.

———

As the months wore on and Sarah's personality grew increasingly unpredictable, we felt a need to understand which Sarah would show up on a given day. In particular, Kris Perry (our campaign organizer for the general election) and I would phone each other on our commute into the office and discuss early morning communications with Sarah. "What kind of mood do you think she's in?" became the overriding question. This is where Todd came to provide a valuable service. Fully on board with our need to know, he would regularly relay his wife's demeanor as she left the house for headquarters. If something distressing was going on, he'd phone me with his concerns. Some time later, Todd even took to stealing Sarah's BlackBerry in order to read her emails for emotional clues. So thick were we in this plot to monitor mood, Todd went so far as to access one of her main email accounts while working on the North Slope.

When she traveled to the state capital in Juneau, Todd became particularly alarmed as he described the "Juneau trance" she fell into: "It's where she believes everything the Juneau-ites tell her." The Juneau-ites, as Todd called them, were the bureaucrats she swore (and failed) to get rid of before being elected. Naming those he felt most offensive, Todd would say, using one of his favorite expressions, "They are just humping her leg, and she gets all mixed up, she buys it. It's disgusting." At one point, before Sarah traveled to Juneau, Todd provided me with frantic and detailed instructions.

> She will get down there and [they] will hit her with a number of the sky is falling issues to get her off track and to keep her off balance. Frank you need to be by her side for support, if she pushes you away we're in trouble. I know her well, I've seen similar situations from the past and the outcome was ugly, she ends up getting stabbed in the back. . . . She cannot have any dissuasion. . . . Please let me know if you guys think I'm overreacting to this situation. . . .
>
> Please give me a call before you send an e-mail making sure no one else is monitoring this address/computer. . . . I'm erasing all content of this e-mail after I send it. please call

I found it particularly interesting that even as her husband, Todd lumped himself in the "we're in trouble" category. If she listened to Juneau voices, she'd come home believing Todd's advice suddenly wrongheaded. Finding myself thrust into a bizarre situation, on this trip I became her full-time Juneau babysitter and Todd Palin's double agent.

Especially after Sarah took office, Todd's regular intelligence reports helped us plan ahead. Was this to be a day when Sarah was emotionally up, and we could look forward to being productive? Or was this a day when she was "in a mood"? In the latter case, we'd be looking backward at someone to blame for the state of our daily affairs.

From those early months in 2006 on, we had already learned—no matter her state of mind—to back off and avoid confrontation. In her own words, she'd say, "Man, I hate it when I'm wrong!" More than that, Sarah disliked anyone pointing out when she was wrong.

While I am certainly no psychologist, I believe this aspect of her ego prevented her from admitting mistakes. One time I suggested to her that it is important for people to see her as real and human, not some superwoman whom they'll try to shoot out of the sky. In typical Sarah fashion, when she heard something she didn't want to hear, she changed the subject.

8

A Higher Standard

I feel like we're the last of the innocents.
—SARAH PALIN, EMAIL TO FRANK BAILEY,
TUESDAY, APRIL 4, 2006

Paul Riley, Sarah's eighty-plus-year-old Pentecostal minister in Wasilla, once offered his spiritual advice by suggesting that she reread the story of Queen Esther in the Bible. As the story goes, King Ahasuerus of Persia wished to find a fair young virgin to replace his deposed queen. A beautiful girl named Esther, brought before him, "pleaseth the king" most, and he "set the royal crown upon her head and made her his queen." From that perch, Esther concealed her Jewish heritage, for Jews were Persian enemies. But when her people were threatened with annihilation, she revealed her identity and convinced the king to spare the Jews while permitting them to fight against their other enemies. This event is celebrated annually in the Feast of Purim. Assuming personal risk, Esther is famously quoted as saying, "If I die, I die."

Identifying with this perceived role model, on at least two occasions Sarah invoked identical language. The first of these instances was in June 2009 when introducing right-wing radio host Michael Reagan (and President Ronald Reagan's adoptive son) at a political gathering: "So I join you in speaking up and asking the questions and taking action, and here at home in my beloved Alaska, I just say, politically speaking, if I die, I die." The following month, when asked on *Good Morning America* why she resigned as governor sixteen months early, she replied, "I said before I stood in front of the mike the other day, you know, politically speaking, *if I die, I die.* So be it."

Many of Sarah's followers believed these biblical parallels to be 100 percent true: God had summoned Sarah Palin to lead an Esther-like mission to save fellow Alaskans from self-interested cronyism and bring down their foes.

Demonstrating her own belief in a divine calling, in June 2006, Sarah wrote about an "awesome" service at Wasilla Bible Church that spoke to her:

> **You know when you're called for something. . . . Our pastor . . . talked about Solomon having to build the temple when he was young & inexperienced & there were political tensions and struggles all over the place . . . my mom looked at me and said: do you think he's talking to you?!**

On another occasion, while Sarah drove us from Kenai to Homer in her black Volkswagen Jetta, she said, "Frank, isn't it weird that God called me to the two most corrupt professions? Media and politics."

Embedded within a list of prayer items, Sarah apparently endorsed another part of Esther's mission as well:

> **frank—is C*** still heading up a prayer list effort for us? seems like we need it—i know we need it. For strength, for joy, for wisdom in all this. For the plans of the enemy to be stopped, for God's will to be done, for favor in this race.**

In contrast to some who wear their religion in public, I never saw Sarah read or carry a Bible on any of our frequent travels together. Nor did she cite verses. We didn't hold prayers before meals or prior to meetings. Only once did we pray together, and that was during a moment of deep distress. For reasons I cannot recall, Sarah felt in early 2006 that everything was going wrong. She came into my office and spoke of problems and uncertainties, then abruptly said, "Y'know, we should pray."

Sarah and I bowed heads, folded hands, and sat in silence for a few awkward moments until I realized that she expected me to lead. I finally said, "God, I know You can see what we're going through; we need Your wisdom, God, for what we can see, and what we can't." The prayer continued, but more remarkable to me than what we said was Sarah's emotional invocation of "Lord Jesus" over and over. The desperate and heartfelt moment convinced me that despite Sarah's lacking elements of forgiveness and charity, her faith had deep roots. Confirming this sincerity, she often echoed a firm belief in the literal teachings of the Bible, explaining her creationist, pro-life, anti-gay-marriage fundamentalism.

These theocratic underpinnings influenced the campaign on matters large and small. Due to other campaign obligations and unable to attend an October 2006 gubernatorial debate organized by the *Anchorage Daily News* and British Petroleum, Sarah took a public relations hit. In summing up her frustration, she explained to a long list of supporters: *"BP put an empty 'no show' chair anyway to make a fool out of me. And Larry Persilly, the moderator, was loving it."* Her reaction was to rally her circle of Prayer Warriors: *"Hi Prayer Warriors: We are in 'damage control' mode again today because of this unfair treatment. And we need your prayers to turn this around."*

In another instance, my wife, who has always walked a firm, straight line with God, had the following exchange with Sarah:

> Sarah,
> I am asking Jesus to place a hedge of protection around you and that he will provide you clear wisdom. God is sovereign and I am thankful that He, ultimately, is in control and HIS will will be done! Thanks for serving Alaska.

> thank you Neen!
>   you guys are awesome. no way would we be doing what we're doing without you . . . and Jesus!

George W. Bush once famously said, "I listen to a higher Father" when discussing whether he took advice from his own dad, former president George H. W. Bush. Similarly, when Sarah wrestled with the possibility of forming a joint ticket with one of the candidates for lieutenant governor—being unhappy at the time with candidate Jerry Ward and eventual winner Sean Parnell—she wrote me, *"I am still praying for a running mate. I don't care if I've been told I shouldn't try and hook up with someone."* She didn't need advice from pundits or advisors. Like President Bush, she had access to a higher authority.

Though rarely seen praying in public, Sarah would send prayerful notices to her mailing list, as she did in October 2006, when the final push for the governorship was overwhelming us:

> **Reach within yourself to tap into an inner strength that can carry the day when we feel this is humanly impossible. I ask for that strength to come from God everyday, that He fills us up with more wisdom, peace, strength, etc.**

Many of us inside the campaign shared a commitment to Christ; those who did not knew enough to either be silent or feign one. Three things definitely helped in getting close to Sarah, and everybody knew what they were: have her believe that you were a devoutly conservative Christian, share a history with her (especially back to her Wasilla days), and exhibit loyalty to her above all others. We couldn't do much about past association, but whether real or faked, faith and loyalty were traits best worn on our sleeves.

———

As far as the campaign for governor went, Sarah announced proudly that her Christian principles would be a guiding light. After all, Sarah established her popularity by exposing the corrupt practices and behaviors of entrenched politicos such as GOP head Randy Ruedrich and Governor Frank "Murky" Murkowski. The message became: we're better than our rivals because we have a moral foundation that is not built on shifting sands. Nothing, certainly not the desire to win an election, would cause her to abandon that cherished principle: *If we die, we die.*

Sarah, in June 2006, wrote to us that yet another set of lies out of the mouth of radio nemesis Dan Fagan would just *"invigorate us to keep working hard and keep telling the truth."* In that same email, she continued, *"We'll be held to a different, higher standard through this guys."*

In gung-ho, bring-it-on fashion, we welcomed being held to God's higher standard. We not only had nothing to hide, we never would.

9

Nobody Noticed

If you are willing to lie about silly matters, then what
are you going to do on the big matters of the state?
—JANEEN BAILEY, EMAIL TO HUSBAND FRANK,
REFERRING TO JOHN BINKLEY'S CAMPAIGN,
TUESDAY, AUGUST 15, 2006

For major parts of our campaign, we did a darn good job of honoring our pledge to run an honest campaign. In plastering the
6,800 signs across the state, pinning buttons, and smacking stickers
to bumpers, we upheld our theocratically based principles. But even in
Alaska's relatively unsophisticated political landscape, there was more
to be done.

Just as signage and visuals built name recognition and signaled momentum, we understood that accessing and playing to what Sarah
would later label the "lame-stream media" was vital. In her own frenzied way, she surreptitiously came up with a brilliant—though not
ethically superior—way of landing free access to newspaper space. As
with many actions, this was born of her frustration with and anger at
our rivals.

Sarah grew agitated over her perception that John Binkley was
copying our campaign website and stealing her best lines. In this
email to Curtis Smith, owner of the public relations firm we used for
web design, Sarah went ballistic:

Curtis -
I mean, REALLY!!!
I'm not one to cuss, but this really ticks me off. He stole YOUR

colors, font, logo, website, bumperstickers . . . and he's stealing my message in his itty bitty speeches now!

. . . He's even slamming Frank [Murkowski] now . . . remember he'd said he couldn't think of anything he disagreed with Murky on back before he declared? I think he said that on the Fagan show.

Mackie should pay YOU for doing all the work for Bink. Those boys didn't have to do any work on this . . . they took our stuff that we've had up since October and they're running with it with a big Binky grin.

Shhhhhheeeeeeezzzzzzzzz.

Three days and much discussion later, copycat foes were still a hot-button topic, but this time Sarah was upset over our ideas being ripped by Troy Maulden, the Alaskan Independence Party candidate for lieutenant governor. It began when Sarah emailed me, *"Now Troy's doing the 'take a stand' thing, is including excerpts from his GOP address, and is referencing Abe Lincoln . . . all things we've been doing!"*

As I came to understand what was expected of me, I fed into Sarah's frenzies. Taking initiative, I emailed Maulden: *"Grrr . . . Troy. First you adopted 'more of the same' and now 'take a stand'??? Make up your own stuff buddy!!!! You're an excellent researcher . . . but this is getting frustrating man."*

Unable to shake free of her frustrations with John Binkley, whose webpage imitations continued to fester, Sarah went back to that topic in an email to me:

We may have to enlist the help of folks like Dan Fagan on this one . . . we need Dan to expose Bink's copycat crap too!

$100 says Bink will do some kind of "dear supporter" letter to be leaked after HE does an unbiased poll in the coming weeks. He'll copy us.

Guess we should feel flattered.

Next day, the outrage continued to build. *"Just heard Bink's radio commercial about ethics and experience . . . gag . . . we said that first."*

Nobody cared much that nearly every campaign in history spoke of ethics and experience; they now belonged to us.

As we swore that ours was a high-road campaign, Sarah's outrage over perceived intellectual pilfering did not seem an overreaction—the color red and references to President Lincoln, as well as ethics, were ours. Stealing her words and ideas seemed abusive and wrong, like the kid sitting next to someone copying his hard-earned math answers on the final exam. Only we couldn't raise our hand and tell our teacher. To me, there seemed little or no recourse. Sarah, however, had a brainstorm. In the midst of an April '06 outrage, she wrote a draft for a letter to the editor and asked us what we thought.

From: sarah
Created: 4/20/2006 6:06:34 PM
Subject: Rough draft idea for a letter to be sent to all editors in alaska newspapers

Dear Editor:
It's been a pleasure watching our life-long Alaskan gal, Sarah Palin, campaign for Governor these past six months. I am impressed with her leadership skills, experience, ethics and energy. And I'm most impressed with how she communicates her message that is connecting with so many Alaskans.

Sarah tells it like it is and is obviously not your typical politician. She doesn't just go with the flow or test the waters with political polls before taking action. It's clear Sarah is committed to just doing the right thing, even if her Republican Party bosses try to punish her for it. I knew she'd be my candidate when she told GOP bosses Randy Ruedrich and Frank Murkowski to take a hike.

She communicates well through her website, too, so I found it particulary interesting to see her opponent in the campaign, Johne Binkley, recently post his own website that looks exactly like the website Sarah's had for the past six months. Then I noticed Binkley even copied the same campaign colors, logo, fonts, bumperstickers, and signs that Sarah has used since October. Recently even his theme mirrors Sarah's.

This may not seem like such a big deal, but not having an original idea and taking credit for someone else's work gives us a clue of how Johne works.

Sarah should be flattered that Binkley copies her ideas and message. It shows she can lead even her political opponents. But maybe Johne should donate to Sarah's campaign to help defray her costs for all her campaign efforts that he's using now.
Signed,
XXXXXX

My response? I loved it. My only suggestion was that she change "Johne," since she was the only one I knew who called him that.

On its face, the letter looked like a joke, having Sarah sing her own praises, leaving an identity trail by using Johne instead of John, and sounding as if a random supporter might actually notice and care enough about a website rip-off to make it a major attack point. A few weeks later, the *Peninsula Clarion* newspaper carried the letter to the editor. Except for a bit of needed polishing, this was identical to the original draft. Sarah had found a name to take the place of *XXXXXX* in the husband of one of our web designers, who signed and claimed authorship.

Despite knowing about the ruse, we felt proud to have Sarah's words see the light of day. Nothing struck me as wrong about attaching someone else's name to a letter written by the candidate about herself, especially since Sarah's mounting frustration was like air pressure threatening to burst a balloon. This direct attack on Binkley provided her important psychological decompression.

Largely from this successful placement, we realized that, like omnipresent red signs, letters appearing in the editorial pages of the *Anchorage Daily News*, the *Fairbanks Daily News-Miner*, the *Juneau Empire*, and a host of smaller newspapers across the state were important for message building and demonstrating grassroots support. One supporter summed up their power when she wrote me, *"When I was talking to people in line at the post office last night, almost everyone I chatted with in line made reference to the letters to the editor. Frank, I see what you mean, that is an extremely powerful venue to get the message out to the masses."*

Sarah, deciding this would become a priority, gushed, *"That's brilliant about the letters. It's free, it's powerful. . . . I know I always read the letters to the editor, sometimes I learn more there than in any other parts of media!"* In another instance, she noted, *"It is such a quick and easy way to keep your name and message in the limelight."*

The issue became: how do we take maximum advantage of this free publicity? As with campaign buttons, we'd become a factory and mass-produced them. To do so, we enlisted secret letter writers. One longtime Palin friend sent in four letters: *"OK, I'm all lettered out for now. Here's four. Do with them as you will. I know the ADN editor is pretty sharp. I don't know how you can make sure that no 2 people sign the same letter but I'm sure you have something in mind."*

As for how we might find names to claim authorship, Sarah had ideas: *"We need to find folks to sign & submit—even Trevor— and I don't think he's considered a 'campaign volunteer' is he? so they wouldn't print that as a disclaimer. So, Trevor's one. Stephanie can be two. Tara three. Dave four. (I mean their peeps . . . or their family members.)"*

By the time we had this process humming, there were letters of high praise for Sarah and harsh criticism of opponents submitted en masse to the entire print media. Coordination became tricky, so we provided specific instructions:

Directions for those submitting letters:
I have attached two letters below. Feel free to change with your own wording, etc. Please be sure to include your name at the bottom of the letter and include your phone number. They usually will not publish without a name and phone number included. The editors more than likely will call you to verify that you did submit the letter. I would copy and paste the letter portions and then go to the media list and send an e-mail to each newspaper separately. If you send a mass e-mail to all of the newspapers, they more than likely will not publish the letter. Please do not have two people send the

**same letter. Let me know if you have any questions. I am happy to
help out in any way.**

Sarah realized there was a need for discretion.

Even while we were operating a letter-manufacturing plant, Sarah,
always aware of the importance of image, cautioned: *"gotta' just make
sure it doesn't look like a manufacturing plant of letters going on . . . and
that they're not dups. thanks guys! (I know you already know that!). love
ya . . . you're all AWESOME."*

In an email string on April 4, 2006, Sarah wrote, *"I feel like we are
the last of the innocents."* In that same email she spelled out in blunt
terms what was required of our coconspirators: *"let's remember to tell
people that when they offer to help but don't know what to do. They can
loan us their names for a letter, and they have to be ready to confirm that
they authored the letter when all those various newspapers call them for
confirmation."*

If it sounds as if Sarah was asking the borrowed names to lie when
editors asked if they authored a letter, it's because we "last of the innocents" were doing exactly that. What is amazing to me is that
nobody—not me, not Sarah, nor anyone I am aware of—regarded this
as an ethical limbo dance under that higher standard to which we'd
vowed to uphold. Maybe other campaigns also did this stuff, but we'd
promised to be unlike other campaigns. Hadn't we pledged not to be
part of the same ol', same ol'?

Scott Heyworth was not part of this massive process. At one point,
however, he became concerned we might be editing some letters to the
editor. He warned, *"My only concern was if [Sarah] and the campaign
got caught proofing letters . . . Explosive. One email could kill you."*

Editing? *Ha!* We were actively writing the darn things. Unrepen-
tant, Sarah wrote, *"Scott, I wouldn't be reading their letters! It's the
thank you's I'd be keeping in touch with."* Sarah's response had the desired effect of placating Scott Heyworth.

With that blatant cover-your-ass lie to Heyworth—witnessed by
a host of us who knew better—the limbo dance of truth had just
dropped a bit lower.

Tragically, not one Rag Tag noticed.

10

Tumultuous Victory

I am looking forward to your [radio] show on
August 23, 2006, when you have to announce,
"Sarah Palin wins primary." I guess Alaskans will
prove after all that we aren't a bunch of idiots.
—JANEEN BAILEY, EMAIL TO RADIO CRITIC
DAN FAGAN, SATURDAY, JUNE 14, 2006

On May 29, 2006, about three months before the primary, our numbers appeared strong. Hoping to build enthusiasm, we immediately emailed our supporters the current Dittman Research poll findings:

38 percent, Palin
27 percent, Binkley
18 percent, Murkowski
17 percent, unsure

Against all odds, we were trouncing the entrenched Republican machine. Everywhere Alaskans traveled and whatever media they accessed, they saw the name Palin. Button, banner, yard sign, and letter manufacturing were clipping along seven days a week. Having saved our pennies, in the last few weeks, we launched radio and television ads that featured an assured, professional candidate. The message we sent out was, "You know, thankfully, I'm going to be a different kind of governor, and, thankfully, I'm also running a different kind of campaign!"

This was the political Cinderella story, and it was up to the voters to put the glass slipper on the princess from Wasilla. When playing to ever-growing crowds, Sarah had a way of making each person feel as if she knew him or her personally. She spoke of family, hard work, and making dreams come true. As a result, citizens grew increasingly enchanted.

But our success did not come without sacrifice. On the personal side, my family struggled with time away from one another and tight finances. My wife felt the burden of balancing a starving checkbook, raising two kids, and trying to get me to pay some attention to family. In a note that tore me apart, she wrote: *"Are you sure you have been reimbursed for everything? I was only able to pay $1000.00 on our credit card this month and we still have a balance of $1587.53. . . . I am really getting nervous about our spending. The last thing we need is to be in the hole a ton after this campaign . . . it keeps me up at night and I am tired and weary."*

I told Neen that I understood, suggesting I'd do my best to be more attentive to her daily struggles. As with any compulsive behavior, however, that is a pledge I failed to keep. What if we lost the election by that one vote I might have influenced? How could I live with myself? This wasn't a forever commitment, just until Sarah became governor. I had no concrete thought that my participation might drag on for several more years. For now, the sacrifice seemed steep, but finite. Besides, I wasn't alone in the massive workload. The team needed me. Sarah and the state of Alaska needed our 100 percent commitment.

Sarah also felt the pressure, her nerves and temperament racing along an ever-sharper edge, and even the positive poll numbers could not dull the blade. If a campaign volunteer stepped out of his or her assigned shoes and she didn't approve, she'd let everyone know—*except* for the person with whom she was upset. Scott Heyworth, for example, fell out of favor on a regular basis. The reason was that he became the one person who had no hesitation in letting Sarah know what he thought. Sarah forwarded this email to several of us, with the comment: *"With friends like this—who needs enemies?"*

From: Scott Heyworth
To: Sarah Palin
Cc: Todd Palin

I am not after a job in your Administration so I can say the following.

STOP TALKING!!!!!!!! Stay off the radio shows!

You are going to be your own worst enemy.

Where is the RAFT?

Where are the issues?

Where is the flyer?

Where is the beef?

You never swim back to your RAFT and talk the issues.

You just give them lip service, then you get right back into their bloody waters.

You love to stay in the water with their sharks.

You have a lead. BE QUIET!

They are taping everything you say. . . .

I could make one ad that would just kill you from all your radio comments.

He went on to warn, *"You will be seen as whiny, vindictive, haughty, smarmy, no issues candidate!"*

As a result of his opinionated missives, which we assured Sarah were not in the least bit true, Sarah did not trust him to speak or represent the campaign on any level. When Scott made contact with a nonunion Palin acquaintance, Scott Johannes, regarding a fund-raiser, Sarah immediately wrote:

frank—why is scott Heyworth meeting with my non-union friend, Scott Johannes?

Scott J. has been trying to offer to host a fundraiser for us for some time, and Scott H. didn't even want him on Hickle's fundraiser list because Scott J. is non-union. Which is good! And it's why I wanted him on the list! We needed balance on that to temper all the pro-union and Democratic names on the invite. But Scott H. didn't hear me, evidently! . . .

Don't forward this, but tell Tara that Heyworth should NOT meet with Scott J.

As with Scott Heyworth, Sarah often shared behind-the-back criticism that at times crossed into the cruel. Just as volunteer campaign workers could go from being in favor to out of favor to back in favor again on a minute-by-minute basis, Sarah's opinions of hired staff also swung from one extreme to another.

Kelly Goode was a case in point. Sarah brought Kelly into the campaign in January 2006 after having decided that we needed a professional campaign manager. When Kelly arrived, Sarah gushed, "You'll love her. She's perfect." Kelly immediately set up shop in one of the two inner offices within the Anchorage headquarters. I occupied a middle office between Sarah and Kelly, with a door to each. The inner circle had a new member who was a hard-driving, experienced professional, and we felt confident and suddenly legitimate.

Petite, at something like five foot tall and less than one hundred pounds, Kelly was nothing if not a spitfire. She burst in and wasted no time displaying a take-charge personality, immediately pegging us for what we were: a grassroots organization without much organization. She believed that we'd been successful *despite* the ragtag operational structure, not because of it. She shot out commands and sought to coordinate everyone's time in a methodical manner, replacing a campaign wall calendar with a computerized schedule that planned events for Sarah all the way through primary Election Day. The new, stricter structure and authoritative commands made us all feel like a bunch of teenagers who'd been grounded, and office morale sunk. Kerm Ketchum and I strategized about how to approach the problem. I suggested raising the issue with both Sarah and Todd.

In a phone call shortly thereafter, I outlined to Sarah my concerns. Kelly's blunt manner (which I later deemed an absolute asset), I suggested, was turning off staff and volunteers, and we ran the risk of losing enthusiasm and momentum. The fact that Sarah agreed with these sentiments suggested that she too was tiring of Kelly's take-charge personality, despite only weeks on the job.

That Kelly made staff uncomfortable was one thing, but when she continued to insist that Sarah's top priorities be position papers and fund-raising, that was a recipe for disaffection. No doubt Kelly's strategy was sound and professional and typical of well-run campaigns. However, as John McCain would discover during the 2008 presidential race, Sarah does not like to be pigeonholed or told what to do, especially since laboring on position papers and dialing for dollars were things she disliked. In addition, Kelly played devil's advocate, always analyzing the potential downside to any action Sarah wished to pursue. Sarah had great affection for cheerleaders. Critics? Not so much.

The first sign of estrangement was Sarah's copying Kelly less often on group emails, thus freezing her out of the information loop. That coincided with snide comments about Kelly to the staff. When Sarah began referring to her sarcastically as "that Kelly girl," I knew our campaign manager's days were numbered. With Sarah unwilling to take her advice or acknowledge there might be ways to improve operations, Kelly read the interpersonal tea leaves correctly. With no fanfare or formal farewell, our campaign manager officially resigned after just two months on the job. Sarah, in classic passive-aggressive fashion, fixed the problem without the need for direct confrontation. Although Kelly was gone, she wrote in an email, *"not communicating with Kelly will be a huge mistake because of her connections."* She couldn't resist adding a sarcastic *"Oh, great."*

None of this deterred us from using Kelly throughout the campaign on a freelance basis. Her support from a distance proved valuable, as she participated in the future letter-writing effort and provided seasoned, strategic advice. Kelly hung on long enough to eventually make a return engagement; in 2008 Governor Palin appointed her legislative director, but once again Kelly soon found herself in the doghouse and resigned a second time.

Tension among staff members also began to flare as close quarters, long hours, and the stress of the campaign wore us down. In one instance, after I'd been named campaign administrator (a position that paid roughly enough to cover my children's day care expenses), I had a run-in with full-time office hand Cathy Fredericks, a middle-aged woman. One day Cathy misinterpreted an innocent request I'd made for thank-you notes as a criticism of her competence. In response, she sent a blistering email to Sarah, who then forwarded it to me. Among other things, Cathy wrote:

> Sarah, In order for you to be a Governor there are a lot of unpleasant things that need to be dealt with that you may not want to deal with but need to be dealt with. You know that Frank and I don't always get along yet you want him to deal with Me. . . . My assumption is that we are no longer a team but that Frank is the Campaign manager. . . .
>
> You always said I was in charge of the office. But I obviously am not. Why don't you just say Frank is the Campaign Manager and get it over with instead of the Team Palin crap. . . . You constantly get mad at him for spending money and roll your eyes. I guess behind my back you are doing the same thing and talking about me. . . .
>
> If you are done with me say so and no offense taken. That's what Christians are suppose to do. . . .
>
> I am truly offended.

When I phoned in an attempt to soothe her hurt feelings, Cathy hung up on me.

Perceptively, Cathy's email did hit a couple of points dead-on. Sarah often *did* roll her eyes at me when it came to spending money, and she *was* talking about Cathy behind her back—something from which nobody was immune. Demonstrating her behind-the-back candor, Sarah wrote: *"Holy moly—she has NO RIGHT whatsoever to hang up on you . . . how did she manage in the real working world? or the military? can you imagine her taking actual "commands"? I'll not get brought in by her if she whines about any of this. . . . I'll remind her I've tasked you with this."*

In an unusual direct meeting soon afterward, Sarah listened to Cathy's complaints and shut her down by saying, "Frank is emailing me late at night, early in the morning, responding to what I need when I need it. So I don't want to hear any more about Frank." Expecting that we'd lose Cathy, the next day Sarah backpedaled from her staunch Frank Bailey can-do-no-wrong support:

> **Frank, I am asking you to make it work with Cathy. Period. I know you've reiterated to her what her value is. It's not a matter of groveling. It's a matter of logistics. . . . I don't think you realize how much tougher this is going to be, paperwork-wise, without her.**

It took a couple of days—and the relationship never was what I'd call a good one—but Cathy Fredericks returned after Sarah said she was "so sorry for any offense I've caused you." To further placate her, we turned a closet into a small office so she wouldn't be bothered by unnecessary human interaction, especially with me.

———

The stress built as Election Day drew closer. Ragtag friendships faltered and cliques began to emerge while our sensitivity to criticism grew increasingly acute. Like a dog that hears a siren, whenever a radio show host, blogger, or editor at the *Anchorage Daily News* made a pejorative comment, we'd follow Sarah's lead and howl at the top of our lungs. Remarkably, after all these months, our collective skins had not thickened, and radio voice Dan Fagan remained enemy number one—as he opposed her policy to tax oil companies and what he regarded as her antibusiness bias, disagreements that eventually became angry and personal. We continued to waste hours and hours listening to his inane show, then formulating plans to counterattack his messages. We might solicit irate callers or write nasty letters. Sarah, on one occasion, personally did both. After phoning into his show to set the record straight, she sent her nemesis a confusing follow-up email that included this:

> **Dan—thanks for letting me call in to your show on Friday. I bit my tongue as long as possible as folks were telling me you were really trying to crucify me this week. . . . I did hear some of it and just had to shake my head because . . . you still characterize me as being**

unreasonable, or not knowledgeable enough to govern. Remember
we agreed to disagree on that issue?

Sarah then went through pages of supportive statements that Fagan
had emailed her prior to her campaign. They were full of praise, while
expressing love—writing an email that once said, in no uncertain
terms, "I love you, Sarah"—and suggesting that it was God's will for
her to win. She would, he said, rescue Alaska from its corrupt past.
She concluded her own email by writing:

> I am the same person with the same values as I was just months ago
> when you wrote these words. . . . I don't ask you to change your
> mind, just to consider that the values I've always held close seem to
> be appreciated by you in many previous comments you've shared
> with me—and seemed to be what public officials need to help turn
> things around in society.

After reading her e-mail, I wrote Sarah my support, and she replied
back:

> thanks Frank.
> you're right. [Fagan] makes folks feel like idiots, and he belittles us
> "little people." I think I had to go through this to understand what
> it feels like for other callers who get slammed. . . . Don't you think
> he does sound sort of scitzo? . . .
> Do you think we should get tapes of his show and go point by
> point so he is confronted with his lies.

Should we get tapes of his show? Could there be any bigger waste of
time that that? It seems looking back, the obvious answer is *no*, but
as the primary drew closer, those considerations didn't matter. We reviewed tapes and discussed how unfairly we were being treated for
hours on end. And while I am not proud of my role in stoking the
flames, I did so.

Lumping the media into a group that included Republican and
Democratic leaders, Sarah warned us, *"Political folks are not loyal . . .*

*please know that. It's the nature of their game. Trust me. Just let [them]
do the talking, don't say anything."* That last part, about not saying anything in response to criticism, was great advice we studiously avoided.

With the pressure cooker of the Palin campaign on high, the poll
numbers continued to hold steady. Endorsements trickled in and built
momentum. Former governor Walter Hickel said in his endorsement,
"The Governor needs to do what is best for Alaska and the owner
state. Sarah Palin is doing exactly that." In a second major coup, we
received the sole endorsement of Alaska's Right to Life organization.
Sarah's reaction aptly reflected the importance she attached to this:

From: sarah
To: frank bailey
Subject: Re: Good News
Date: Fri, 28 Jul 2006 00:07:40 -0800

NO WAY!!!
  WAY!!!
  OH MAN!!!
  In our camp, probably only you and Neen know how much this
one means! Yeah!!!
  Are they co-endorsing? Because Bink's gonna' freak about this
one if they don't.
  Thanks for the great news!

The Alaska Correctional Officers Association represented yet another coveted endorsement. Large and small, we welcomed these, even
when we didn't understand the rationale. When, for example, we received the blessing of a marijuana advocacy group, we accepted with
the following: *"Thank you for your support and we look forward to a
brighter future for all Alaskans. Hopefully, those who read your voters
guide, will cast all 150 plus votes for Sarah Palin during the August 22
Primary."* So long as they could fill out a voter registration card, why
not have 'em vote Palin, dilated pupils and all?

As we neared the primary election date, principal opponent John Binkley's last-minute attempt to derail us came in the form of an editorial that appeared in the *Mat-Su Valley Frontiersman* more than a decade earlier. I listened to snippets from the commercial that included:

> Announcer: You think you know Sarah Palin? Think again. This is what her hometown newspaper had to say.
>
> "Welcome to Kingdom Palin, the Land of No Accountability."
>
> "Palin Fails to Have a Firm Grasp of Something Very Simple. The Truth."

In shock, I called Sarah and described the ad. My directive came loud and clear: "Do something, Frank!"

This was beyond anything we'd seen in this election cycle, and Sarah's desperate plea hit, in me, a willing mark. I phoned attack-architect Mike Tibbles, Binkley's campaign manager.

"What are you thinking?" I asked. "You know this thing was written years ago. You're making it look like it just happened, like it was something they wrote today."

"I don't have to share our campaign strategy with you, Frank."

"Then all I have to say is this, Mike. If you guys think this is gonna work, you're crazy. On Tuesday, you are going down."

Binkley's tactic unnerved me, not because I thought it might work—I did not—but more for Sarah's reaction. Did she think the voters so easily swayed, or was it natural insecurity ahead of an election? As for me calling out Tibbles for being slimy, that part felt good. When we won, I'd allow myself to wallow a bit in the sin of pride.

Stunningly, when Sarah later brought in Mike Tibbles for the final weeks of her own general election campaign, I felt he was the one enjoying a last laugh.

PART TWO

Victory

11

Some Things Never Change

I'll do all I can to serve the people of Alaska and not
disappoint my supporters . . . and to serve Alaskans I'll
operate much better in a positive environment that gives our
campaign credit for knowing just a wee bit about what we're
doing. It's by the grace of God that we've been so successful.
—SARAH PALIN, EMAIL TO DOZENS OF
VOLUNTEERS, SUNDAY, AUGUST 27, 2006

As the day of the primary approached, we felt nervous but ready.
Let the voters have their say and get rid of the clowns and
pretenders to the GOP throne. With momentum, the Prayer Warriors, and Queen Esther's legacy on our side, I felt optimistic. Strange,
though, that while I believed in Sarah's victory with all my heart, my
slightly aching stomach seemed not to fully agree. We'd done everything we could, and this was now in God's hands. I hoped that He
would reward our efforts. "Work as if we're three points behind,"
I constantly told volunteers. Now the phrase echoed, creating that tiny
ounce of uncertainty.

To view the televised results, we reserved the ballroom at the Hotel
Captain Cook, a luxury property in downtown Anchorage with views
of Cook Inlet and beyond the foothills to the Chugach Mountains. It
was owned by former Governor Hickel. Top-hatted doormen escorted
us through the main entrance on our way into the nine-thousand-
square-foot ballroom with crystal chandeliers and a British coat of
arms above the door. When I walked into the party room, Sarah was
busy opening plastic containers of cookies from Costco to set out on
tables littered with Palin-Gov buttons and cheap glitter. Everyone,

including the candidate, seemed to be wearing a red blazer. Despite sparse decorations, piped-in elevator music, and no free beverages, the room sparked with anticipation. Sarah, in contrast to the energy of her supporters, had wrinkles around her eyes, her face drawn and hanging a bit like melting wax. She reminded me of a child the day after a long overnight with little sleep and no next-day nap. At what we expected to be her finest moment, she seemed nearly overcome by anxiety.

While others mingled and chattered away, septuagenarian volunteer Kerm Ketchum sat huddled with me in a corner staring at my computer screen, compulsively clicking the Refresh button to update the latest vote tally. Polls closed at eight o'clock, and results began trickling in about half past. When a poll watcher called in from the town of Sterling to say Palin had received 60 percent of the local vote, the crowd of over two hundred erupted.

Into the night, new election numbers led to whistles and applause. In an instant, those cathartic outbursts transitioned into a seemingly endless wait for the next update. We'd hit that Refresh button every few seconds, as a subdued Sarah hunched in her chair beside Kerm and me.

Reporter Jason Moore from KTUU, Anchorage's NBC affiliate, stopped by and asked, "Sarah, any reaction to the early results showing you with a strong lead?"

"No. It's still early, yet." She didn't want to jinx the results.

A new number flashing led to renewed bedlam that sounded like an arena-size crowd's reaction to a last-second, game-winning hockey goal. The human crush drifted toward our corner the closer we came to a final tally. When the Fairbanks numbers flashed across my bargain-basement laptop shortly after nine o'clock, showing solid support in our weakest geographical area, I knew we owned this election.

I turned to Sarah and said, "Listen, there is no way Bink can recover from losses in his hometown."

Sarah tilted her head as if to say, "Are you sure?" before mumbling, "Really?"

"Yes. Mathematically, it's just not going to happen for him. Kenai, Kodiak, and even the Anchorage precincts are yours."

With each new district reporting, Scott Heyworth shouted out the results. As our vote total grew, so did the decibel level. The rafters echoed with, "Sa-*rah*! Sa-*rah*! Sa-*rah*!"

Waiting longer than I thought necessary, at around nine thirty she turned to me and, with a little shrug meant to be a question, wanted to know if it would be safe to make a statement.

I nodded. "It's time." Before approaching the stage, she gave me a strong, warm, unbelievably appreciative embrace. There are a handful of dramatic moments in life that ink themselves indelibly in one's mind. For me, this was one of those. With a smile creasing my cheeks and tears blurring vision, I watched as Sarah wove through the crowd, noticing for the first time that she appeared to have shrunk these last few weeks. I'd heard others suggest that before elections she lost significant amounts of weight (living largely off of Skinny White Chocolate Mochas).

Sarah spoke briefly and at one point said, "It's time for new energy for Alaska." Four-time Iditarod champ Martin Buser, Wally Hickel, and legendary attorney Wayne Anthony Ross all spoke as hundreds swirled around Sarah for group photo ops.

With all the votes tallied, in a landslide Sarah Louise Heath Palin became the GOP's candidate for governor:

Candidate	Votes	Percentage
Sarah Palin	51,443	50.59
John Binkley	30,349	29.84
Frank Murkowski	19,412	19.09

Her opponent on the Democratic side of the aisle was former two-term governor Tony Knowles who, despite racking up 75 percent of his party's vote, totaled only 37, 316 votes, or some 14,000 fewer than Sarah. Add to the mix independent candidate Andrew Halcro, who didn't have much of a base, and we had reason for optimism come November.

Heavily dressed in crimson sweaters, scarves, shirts, and ties, we eventually left the hotel en masse and marched the five blocks to Election Central at the William A. Egan Civic and Convention Center, where winners and losers gathered to meet with the press and play nice after a long campaign. It got dark late in Anchorage at that time of year, so we still had remnants of light even though it was past ten o'clock. In the cool but dry air, we hoisted the leftover yard signs used to inexpensively decorate the luxurious hotel ballroom, making it look like the Palin sea of red was joyously flowing down Fifth Avenue. To me, this felt like our own march down Avenue des Champs-Élysées after World War II. The GOP war was won. Our army felt invincible. For this glorious night, petty squabbles like those between me and Cathy Fredericks ceased to exist. We were a single, living, breathing organism with but one life, one love.

At one point during these raucous events, we passed by the soon-to-be deposed governor, Frank Murkowski. While far from members of the mutual admiration society, he nonetheless smiled and stopped to shake Sarah's hand. Leaning in, he said something I'll never forget: "Sarah, you have an amazing group of volunteers." Interestingly, I never did stop to think why it was that Sarah undertook this race with few (almost no) volunteers from her previous campaigns. Was it an issue of competency, loyalty, availability? Whatever the reasons, they wouldn't have mattered much to me. What Murkowski said was absolutely true. We weren't hardened political operatives like Binkley's Mike Tibbles. We didn't run this race with a well-oiled machine or even a detailed plan—or, from time to time, any plan at all. What we did was work our tails off.

We'd invested everything—our hearts, family time, financial well-being—into this first step toward landing Sarah in the Juneau governor's mansion. This night's victory became a confirmation that without the so-called pros, we had done the impossible. All of that scrambling, late-night fighting with Smokey Joe the fax machine and printing hokey two-color fliers that we'd cut into postcards and mail cheaply across the state had, miraculously, paid off. Lost weekends going door to door, asking folks on prime street locations to join us by allowing the campaign to post a Palin-Gov sign on their fence or in their yard, were not sacrifices made in vain. For me personally, I wasn't a politico, but I knew how to treat people honestly. When necessary, I had attempted to pick up the pieces of a sometimes fractured campaign, using energy and commitment to insulate volunteers from some of the sharp Palin-edges that might have disenfranchised others.

I felt on top of the world, believing that I was a piece of history that would be recognized as great. This was like becoming a father for the first time, and feeling overjoyed after counting your newborn's ten fingers and ten toes and realizing that your healthy new baby is headed toward a blessed future. The feeling of gratitude to God for the gift of life—in this case, political life—filled me and every one of the hundreds of manic supporters who'd slaved for months and who now leaked euphoria from every pore.

It wouldn't hit me until much later, but even as we cheered, laughed, and reminisced with joy, there seemed to be an emotional cloud hovering over our candidate—a hardening forming in her personality. Her happy face was fleeting, present only when in front of cameras. When left on her own, in the hallways outside the main rooms, she more paced than walked, her head heavy, her eyes without that magic sparkle. Maybe Sarah realized that we'd won the easier battle and that the next phase would be more challenging, with real mudslinging taking the place of dust balls. On her night of nights, did she regret the journey? The future? What was going through her mind? Did she really possess Reagan's steely spine, or did she harbor doubts about her political vertebrae?

Answers wouldn't take long in coming.

———

Out of the primary, we continued with message and name placement. For the general election campaign, we nearly doubled the number of yard signs to 12,500 statewide, while distributing 21,000 campaign buttons, 23,000 bumper stickers, and nearly 1,000 of the larger four-by-eight-foot signs suitable for mounting on buildings, in vacant lots, and along Alaska's much-traveled Rail Belt, which stretches nearly 500 miles from Seward in the south to Fairbanks in the north while passing through Anchorage.

We did all this while exploring additional avenues meant to address the biggest weakness—aside from money—haunting the campaign: Sarah's lack of substantial governing experience and a perception that she spoke only in what independent candidate Halcro termed "glittering generalities." At the Captain Cook on primary night, *Anchorage Daily News* reporter Tom Kizzia had told me candidly that glossing over missing or inaccurate facts would no longer work for her. I understood that there was a need for ramping up the substance of her message, but it never occurred to me that there was a problem beyond minor naiveté, which naturally went with being the "anticandidate candidate." Our state had plenty of experience with sophisticated political hacks. Sarah would read, learn, and do what she always did: laying waste to those who underestimated her.

Sarah herself recognized the risks inherent in falling into the stereotype of empty-headed beauty queen and sought to look the part of a wise, serious executive. One simple device was the ever-present Kawasaki glasses.

"I wonder why Sarah wears those glasses," said Kerm Ketchum, a man who supported, loved, and felt almost like family to Sarah. Kerm's daughter was Sarah's high school friend and college roommate, and he was a close confidant of Sarah's parents, Chuck and Sally. On this particular day in late 2007, our paths crossed at Anchorage International Airport as Sarah and I were heading to Juneau.

"Seems strange to me she'd bother with 'em," he continued.

As Sarah mingled with a small group of people about ten yards from where we stood, I focused on the candidate's face. With hair trussed up in the signature Palin beehive, the effect was to raise her petite frame, perhaps an attempt to match her skyscraping personality.

"I'm gonna ask Sarah why she still wears glasses; Sally says her eyesight was all fixed with Lasik surgery."

Kerm, armed with a revelation from Sarah's mother, padded toward Sarah, his enthusiasm reminding me of my son asking how that model boat got into such a tiny bottle. He caught up to Sarah just as she was boarding the plane. As they spoke, Sarah's face twisted and all traces of a smile disappeared. After a rapid exchange, Kerm, head bowed, stumbling as much as walking, returned to where I stood.

"What's wrong?" I asked. "She looks upset. What—"

"She don't wanna talk about that," he said. Kerm wouldn't discuss what Sarah said to him.

In another effort to address her perceived lack of gravitas, Sarah once suggested when searching for a photo to go on a campaign mailer, *"how about including the pic where i'm speaking from the podium down in juneau (it's posted on the web site) because it looks like i may actually be speaking governor-ish."* Sarah had firm ideas on how to manage her appearance, and for the most part did so successfully.

For those digging deeper, however, no cosmetic cover-up would silence their concerns. On the conservative Voice of the Times editorial page of the *Anchorage Daily News*, the editor, Paul Jenkins, blasted her by writing,

> A few weeks back, I pointed out the glaringly obvious; that Sarah Palin is the lightweight in the Republican gubernatorial field. I should have added she is a trifle paranoid and maybe not the brightest bulb in the box.
>
> Frankly, with the notable exception of John Lindauer [the 1998 Republican Party candidate for governor], who melted down like a candle when asked about his fountain of campaign money, I've never seen a politician come unhinged so quickly as Palin when asked a few straightforward questions.

The editorial grew even more pointed:

> And how would somebody with just six years' experience as Wasilla mayor—and none at the state level—be able to manage an enterprise as complicated, complex and dynamic as Alaska? Or, if she surrounds herself with qualified people to make up for her lack of experience at the state level, who really will be running the state . . . Some guy she met at a party? Who?

These attacks, while painful, also energized supporters. Jenkins tended to write his criticisms ahead of the weekends. We called these "Jenkins Fridays." On the days immediately after his editorials, our phones rang nonstop with support and an uptick in financial contributions. Other critics elicited the same reaction. After a particularly nasty Dan Fagan attack, a man waved his checkbook in Fagan's face and declared, "I'm gonna give money to that poor gal runnin' for office."

While the public mostly tolerated vague answers, media and opponents were less charitable. The chorus asking for detailed proposals grew, and Sarah longed to build her intellectual credibility. While the letters to the editor were helpful, they did not go far enough. We could write dozens of notes expressing outrage at Jenkins-like attacks (while soliciting plenty of folks who'd be happy to lend their name and claim authorship), but constant questions about her intelligence and experience demanded something substantive. So we began methodically exploring the potential of the op-ed. These short columns, another free source of advertising and name recognition, might define Sarah's policy credentials while laying to rest the label of political lightweight.

Unfortunately, this did not play to Sarah's strengths. Even while blindly supporting her, many of us understood that she was not particularly well versed in policy matters or the minutiae of governing a state. While we didn't much care about her lack of hands-on knowledge, others did. In addition, Sarah's ability to woo a crowd with plainspeak did not transfer to the written word. At times, her communications were colossally incoherent and cut-and-paste repetitive. She sent one particularly long and bitter email to a then distinguished list of allies. Her rambling thoughts in this small portion of a much larger email included statements and attacks on familiar foe Randy Ruedrich as well as calls for blessings and expressions that there were powerful forces wishing her ill will:

> Alaskans deserve better. . . . It's a bunch of b.s. going on in this state. . . . My God . . . this stuff makes my stomach turn. . . .
>
> How much more evidence do we need . . . our vice-chair's comments yesterday that our campaign will implode so we need Randy to salvage it . . . on and on and on . . . the evidence is glaring: we have to do our part to clean up the mess. Someone has to do it. Many Alaskans are putting their faith in our campaign to do it. I am willing to do it. I think I've held back too much and that's

**why some folks are chiming in, requesting that I PLEASE don't
get sucked in to the politically correctness of the day . . . ?! They're
looking for reform!**

The essay was emblematic of a style of writing and speaking that
critics later labeled "Sarah word salad" and I internally referred to
as "hodge-podge-kitchen-sink-soup." But another noteworthy thing
about this particular email is that one recipient, Mike London—a
senior vice president of Eagle Electronic—emailed back, *"Sarah, Did
you mean to send this to me?"*

While I never saw her response, Sarah did e-mail her team:
*"Ummmm . . . oh no. Somehow he was cc'd in to this very confidential
email. Does anyone know Mike?"*

This type of faux pas was not unusual. Sarah occasionally sent messages blasting a team member, unintentionally copying the victim.
Glen Biegel, a dedicated volunteer, speechwriter, and radio host, was
the target of one such blistering email. When Sarah inadvertently
copied him, he reacted with shock and hurt feelings.

Claiming to Glen that his being copied was intentional, so that
he might know what she was thinking in an up-front manner, Sarah
wrote, *"Glen, I sent this to you and others with all due respect."* But as
she immediately emailed me, *"Yikes—I didn't know I was sending it to
him! Thot that thing was just forwarded to me . . . DANGGGIIITTT."*

Clearly, prose, editing, and attention to detail weren't Sarah's
strong suits. Even with direction, she would submit paragraphs that
challenged everybody's ability to comprehend. In an oil tax position
piece, she wrote in less than inspiring prose:

Alaskans deserve an atmosphere of trust in government. But
broken promises, averted eyes from ethical lapses, booted-out
conscientious state employees, and things like the Governor's
jet are the much ballyhooed issues that illustrate the disconnect
between established politicians and the rest of us. Hopefully
though, as we consider the most important economic issues
facing Alaska in decades, may these aforementioned reminders
of things amiss share ink so we can debate additional issues that

are also of utmost importance. As obstinate as the jet purchase
is, oil taxes and long-term gasline deals are such a focus now.

Issues advisor Paul Fuhs (also an oil industry lobbyist), when reviewing another of Sarah's position pieces, wrote to me: *"Frank, I tried
to keep this within the spirit of what sarah has written but to fill in some
details that shows she knows what she is talking about"*—the implication
being that either Sarah was not proficient at supplying details or didn't
actually know what she was talking about.

The question thus became: how does the campaign produce opinions for publication and debate that instill enthusiasm without exposing our candidate's policy inexperience, weak writing skill, or
alienating a constituency? Sarah's early attempt to cobble together an
editorial from a series of talking points did not go well and illustrated
the dilemma. In submitting a 675-word op-ed to the *Anchorage Daily
News* entitled "Nonsensical Gas Agreement," Sarah demonstrated a
prodigious ability to lard the piece with hyperbole and inaccuracy
after suggesting she would put the complex issues *"in plain English,
which I'm good at."* Editor Larry Persily's reply, after reading her draft,
was blunt in its dismissal:

> Sarah,
> Thanks for the op-ed column, but it will need some changes before
> we can publish it. As I have told all the candidates, we are not going
> to let anyone (incumbents or challengers) get by with easy political
> speeches on the page, especially on oil and gas issues.
> The public deserves specifics, not just promises. So—and noth-
> ing personal in any of this—I've added my comments where ap-
> propriate to give you an idea of what would need to be added or
> explained before we could publish the piece.

Picking up with Persily's comments in an email exchange on
Sarah's fourth point, we read:

> <u>Sarah wrote:</u> Fourth, the contract doesn't ensure gas for in-
> state use.

<u>Persily commented:</u> How do you propose to ensure in-state gas? Everyone is quick to promise in-state gas, and to attack the draft contract for being deficient in this area, but I'm not going to allow anyone to get by with more of the same promises. If you're going to raise the pledge of in-state gas, you will need to explain how you plan to fulfill that pledge.

<u>Further down, Sarah wrote:</u> As Cook Inlet supplies diminish, the concept of importing natural gas while ours goes to Canada is abhorrent.
<u>Persily replied:</u> through Canada, not to Canada.

<u>Sarah:</u> Fifth, under this contract, if gas prices dropped to certain levels, we'd actually pay oil companies for the privilege of producing our gas while they reaped profits.
<u>Persily:</u> Please explain. Yes, the state would have to pay the processing costs for its share of the gas, and the cost of removing and disposing of impurities, but we're talking around 50 cents per mcf. Do you expect gas prices to drop that low? And if gas prices were that low, and we lost money, how would the companies "reap profits"?

<u>Sarah:</u> We assume more cost and risk than the oil companies do, including contributing our land and 7/8 of our gas to make the project happen. All told, our concessions could nearly equal the cost of the entire project, yet we'd only own 20% of it.
<u>Persily:</u> How is any of this true? We would take 20% of the cost risk under the contract vs. 80% for the companies. How does that translate into the state taking on more cost and risk than the companies? And we didn't "contribute" our land, we leased it to the companies for a substantial upfront payment and royalty terms. And, if the project is $20 billion, what state "concessions" would nearly equal $20 billion?

<u>Sarah:</u> Seventh, Administrators refuse to disclose details of negotiations with viable alternatives like TransCanada, MidAmerican, and the Alaska Gasline Port Authority.

<u>Persily</u>: Not entirely true. The state eventually released most of the negotiation documents from its talks with MidAmerican. And there were no negotiations under the Stranded Gas Development Act with the Alaska Gasline Port Authority, just informal talks outside the Stranded Gas Act. This could easily be fixed by changing the allegation to a statement about the state has been less than fully honest about our projects, or something like that.

<u>Sarah:</u> Eighth, the deal was the Administration was forced to propose sweeping legislation to amend the Stranded Gas Act to retroactively legalize their deal.

<u>Persily:</u> Not quite "retroactively legalize their deal," since the Legislature has not approved the deal. It would be more accurate to say "to allow the deal to proceed under the law," or "to make the law match the deal."

<u>Sarah:</u> Ironically, other viable alternatives projects were hypocritically rejected as 'illegal under the Act.'

<u>Persily:</u> What alternatives were called "illegal?" I'm not aware of any. The state did determine that the Alaska Gasline Port Authority does not qualify under the Stranded Gas Development Act, but not qualifying for a negotiated fiscal contract is not the same as "illegal."

<u>Sarah:</u> Like other Alaskans, I crave a profitable gas line agreement. But it must pass Constitutional muster and be derived through a competitive process where all viable proposals are fairly and openly considered. My preferred alternative will first provide gas for energizing Alaska's homes and businesses, employing Alaskans, and reducing rural energy costs.

<u>Persily:</u> Again, how do you propose to ensure gas for Alaskans and how do you propose to guarantee Alaska hire? Local-hire requirements are unconstitutional, so if you're going to imply you have a way around that, you need to say how. And, as for ensuring gas for Alaskans, do you propose reserving a portion of the state's royalty gas and selling it to Alaskans at below-market prices? Whatever the answer is, you need to say what you have in mind.

Sarah did not take rejection well. That her editorial didn't accurately address the issues, misstated facts, and was devoid of proposals were unimportant. The blame went to Persily and the *Anchorage Daily News*. She wrote back, *"See?! Your piddly little 675-word limit forced me to lower my own standards. OK—back to the drawing board. Thanks for the challenge Larry."*

Not to be dissuaded Sarah had her oil advisors deal with Persily's pesky complaints while she submitted the original, error-challenged piece to her smaller hometown paper, the *Mat-Su Valley Frontiersman;* apparently its editorial board had less stringent standards. But since the much larger *Anchorage Daily News* would not publish an editorial that had already appeared in another newspaper, Sarah had to frantically unscramble her mess:

[S]hoot—Kris [Perry]—can you contact the . . . local papers (juneau, frontiersman, fairbanks & kenai) and ask them to hold on to the article until after Tuesday? otherwise the ADN won't run it. thanks sorry it's more complicated than it should be!!! but Larry just gave me this news this afternoon.

Since Sarah's participation on the Alaska Oil and Gas Conservation Commission helped build her reputation as an energy expert (in 2010 she even asked President Obama to seek her counsel on the Gulf oil spill), oil and gas issues were of great concern. As such, Bruce Anders—the man who ultimately rewrote much of Sarah's original editorial and who later served as director of oil and gas leasing and was an early point person on Governor Palin's natural gas team—took on the role of tutor in addition to ghostwriter. We also relied heavily on Tom Irwin, a former commissioner of the Department of National Resources under Governor Murkowski. Anders and/or Irwin wrote the pieces, and Sarah read and added what she called some "normal-people-speak."

When the *Fairbanks Daily News-Miner* published an article in October 2006 entitled "Big Oil, Energy Commission Spar over Pipeline Provisions," Sarah wrote to Anders, *"Bruce—care to decipher this article for me? Thank you . . . for all your prep work on debate!"*

Sarah took great pains to hide the fact that her appointment to the AOGCC had nothing to do with knowledge of the industry. Nor did she serve on the commission long enough to gain much expertise (less than one year). In early 2006 a bill that became known as the "No More Sarah Palin Bill" (House Bill 300, sponsored by Vic Kohring, a Republican state representative from Wasilla-Mat-Su) was introduced as a means of insuring that in the future nobody with so little knowledge on energy issues as Sarah Palin could serve on the AOGCC again. Originally, the commission allowed that one member "need not be . . . experienced in either the field of petroleum engineering or the field of petroleum geology." On her board, Sarah was that inexperienced person. The language in the proposed House Bill (eventually watered down before passage later that summer) stated that all members "shall have training or experience that gives the person a fundamental understanding of the oil and gas industry."

The publicity behind this bill ran the risk of diluting Sarah's claim of oil energy expertise and implied that she did *not* have even a fundamental understanding. Todd and Sarah became alarmed and angry. John Norman, who took Sarah's AOGCC seat after her resignation, agreed with the bill's intent, prompting Todd to write bitterly, *"Norman testified saying it's important for the public seat individual to have extensive knowledge of the industry, he doesn't, I guess he's grandfathered in. The machine at work."* Todd's indictment was not accurate, however, as Norman had extensive knowledge of the oil and gas industry from, at least, the resource law perspective.

When Sarah wrote to me that she'd *"uncovered an erroneous comment Vic [Kohring] made in Juneau that ended up making me look bad,"* she asked me to leak the information anonymously to The Ear, the *Anchorage Daily News*'s political gossip column as a means to embarrass him.

That Sarah did not have significant expertise was not the issue for us. Loaded with all of her common sense, she didn't *need* in-depth knowledge or background. We believed, as Sarah once emailed, *"remember: amateurs built the ark. Professionals built the Titanic."* The entire No More Sarah Palin episode boiled down to unwarranted mischief by evildoers Randy Ruedrich and *the machine*. Publicly, however, of the attacks on her credibility, this was potentially the most damaging—all the more reason to get smart advisors to pump out policy pieces, especially as they related to energy, which was the biggest campaign issue in a state that has long depended on black gold for its livelihood. As a result of this urgency to upgrade Sarah's perceived command of policy, by September, she had a handful of writers at her beck and call and came to enjoy the perception that she'd authored these well-constructed editorials

Another emerging figure in the campaign was Ivy Frye, who initially became a writing coordinator. It was Ivy's job to seek experts to contribute editorial content. At one point, Sarah told me she valued Ivy because she was single, had no life, could write, and would work lots of hours. As with most of us who survived our association with Sarah, Ivy found her role constantly in flux; eventually she became Sarah's leading opposition researcher and advocate.

Sarah ultimately guided these and other Rag Tags into creating a formal editorial team. Although utilizing experts is a sound idea, a major problem was Sarah's utter detachment from the process and unwillingness to study issues herself or become familiar with what her advisors were writing on her behalf. In other words, she wanted credit without caring about even a fundamental understanding. Much later, months after returning to Alaska after the McCain campaign, opinion pieces in her name continued to be distributed on her behalf. In one instance, she gave us a curious heads-up: "Just another weird thing— an op-ed in the *Post*, by me, that I didn't write." Sarah rarely wrote the pieces, but at times she found herself losing track of where her writers were sending them as well.

So, with Sarah's blessing but limited input, the editorial team's productivity took off. When necessary, we'd use professionals to craft a piece. In a fine example of ingratiating commerce, Pat Walsh—of the public relations firm Walsh and Sheppard—acquired a chunk of goodwill with her contribution: *"Sarah, attached are two approaches for op-ed piece. I love writing for you. It gives me a chance to pour out what I really believe. I just hope it gives you something to work with. . . . I hope there is something here to build on."*

Sarah's response to the editorial gifts: *"Right on! . . . This will be so good. I say if ADN doesn't run our OpEd, we send it to all other publications and we incorporate the copy somehow in an ad. . . . Great work Pat!"*

Graciously, Sarah referred to Pat's work as "ours." When it hit the newspapers, however, it would be solely hers, even when she had little understanding of the issue being discussed. This writing process would be duplicated years later when we all cooperated with author Lynn Vincent in the production of *Going Rogue.*

Being an equal opportunity borrower of others' ideas, contributors might come from anywhere. Lyndsay Wheeles—tireless volunteer, future Mrs. Alaska, and Sarah worshipper (eventually posting on Facebook that the one job she'd like in life is to be the "personal assistant to Sarah Palin")—wrote a piece about the controversy surrounding a rumor that Sarah wished to move the state capital from Juneau. Such a change would drop Alaska's third-largest city and its surrounding towns into an economic abyss, making such rumors political dynamite. Appreciative of Lyndsay's contribution, Sarah directed that she be included on the growing team:

> pls. hook up with Lynds for the Ed. Group . . . she's great!
>
> Amen about the doggone Move the Capitol issue. You would NOT believe how many [questions] I was pressed on that this weekend. How many Ivy—a million? I finally got ticked about it, told one last group that I'm not proposing to move it, said they could either believe me or not, but I would not be commenting on the issue again. Period. Sheeeeeeesh. Remember we even paid for an OpEd piece to run in the Juneau newspaper saying I won't propose moving it? And that no one is talking about it except Juneau people?

Interestingly, in this email, Sarah let slip that the campaign had *paid* for an editorial placement in the Juneau newspaper. That paying a newspaper to publish an editorial is antithetical to the intent of an editorial never crossed our minds. We had poll numbers to buoy and an image to polish.

Having others understand and address important issues instead of the candidate was also a terrific timesaver. As Sarah wrote us on September 13, *"I'm overwhelmed with trying to organize all this. . . . My schedule is flippin' jammed."* She preferred mundane functions such as working on signs to studying issues. In a bout of frustration, in August she wrote, *"This is all such bull crap . . . i just hope a presser goes out . . . and then i can eventually go to bed so i can get up early enough to do signs during early morning commute. after i conference with glen and bruce on the stinking gasline again, for the millionth time."*

Formal writing groups—such as opposition research and media teams—freed Sarah to do what she did best: speak to crowds, smile on camera, and listen to and respond to negative radio commentators, newspaper reporters, and Alaskan bloggers. Sarah would simply say, "Make it work. Period." In fact, the word *period* was a favorite of hers. She used it often in emails and in conversation to cut short discussion. This was another way of saying, "Just get 'er done and don't bother me with the how!" We understood.

Our rationalization that other political campaigns were worse offenders allowed us to continue believing we walked on firmer moral ground. In the end, we deceived the public *and* ourselves.

––––––

Taking these communications strategies further, eventually, after her return to Alaska from the McCain campaign, Sarah became famous for Twitter messages which largely replaced slow-motion letters and op-eds. Communications Director Bill McAllister explained to us, "We have to be able to correct the record instantaneously." However, the transition was not a smooth one. Just as she was initially challenged with the cut and paste function in Word and inadvertently sent copies of emails to those she was criticizing, this new communications vehicle produced headaches. Even while she had no understanding of the technology, messages were being posted as early as late April 2009. Sarah was anxious to see what was being written in her name, so she begged staff in emails, *"How do I even access 'my' twitter? They better tell me this morning."* Another early Twitter endeavor in May 2009, mirroring the mysterious op-ed that once appeared in the *Post,* she wrote, *"Who is twittering in my name? I haven't twittered anything, yet it's reported that I have re. Swine Flu, and maybe other subjects? How is this new form of communication going to work—it still hasn't fully been explained to me, and I am not comfortable with others twittering in my name."*

Later that same day, she added, *"This is obviously a dangerous experiment in communication, so why would we have done this? . . . I can not afford more opportunities to be hoaxed or mocked. I didn't know it wasn't secure or would never have agreed to it."*

What Sarah came to quickly appreciate and embrace, however, was the monumental and instantaneous reach this new form of communication had. Why take a public relations buggy when a jet was available? Every time she or someone she authorized posted a message, the media light lit up and whatever she said made headlines. Only three weeks after nearly pulling the plug on this *"dangerous experiment,"* she was hooked, and all of us had a new set of tasks. She ordered, *"If u guys have ideas on 140-character twitters, pls share. It's a good communications tool, but is sometimes a burden on my 'to do' list when I have to think of what to post throughout the day. . . . Need more ideas on twitter, folks, so pls contribute any you may have."*

While a *"burden,"* the Twitter love affair was blossoming, but not without another setback. The same day Sarah resigned as governor, July 3, 2009, we received a frantic message from a close friend wanting to know if Sarah had sent an invitation to her thousands of followers to join her in a July Fourth party at her Wasilla home. The message said there would be free beer for all and a chance to meet her infant son, Trig. Not only that, the messages was being retyped and sent out over an ever-extensive network. Sarah immediately responded, *"It's a lie. We'll try to shoot that down."* More dramatically, the next day she let us know, *"If I were a hater, I'd be doing the same thing w messing w fake twitter sites . . . we need to put ourselves in the haters' mindset and anticipate what they're going to do to cont to screw with us and our message so we'll be prepared to counter (or avoid) this crap."*

Problems aside, Sarah and her Twitter team eventually crafted 140-bit nuggets in steady streams, thus generating sympathy, attention, and a forum for opinions that millions read and media dissected. This became, in ways, the equivalent of letter and op-ed writing but on cyber-roids.

At least as important as opinion pieces were face-to-face radio and television debates with rivals Tony Knowles and Andrew Halcro. In all, Sarah attended approximately twenty-five formal debates. By most accounts, she held her own and often did far better than that. As far as I was concerned, our candidate dominated these events. Sarah had a remarkable ability to freeze-dry complex issues into easy-to-memorize talking points. At one point, a debate moderator praised her for saying about the death penalty, "Hang 'em up." He thought this was the kind of straight talk Alaska needed. The key was to avoid specifics. In September, leading up to the general election, advisor John Bitney suggested she do exactly that regarding benefits for same-sex couples (emphasis mine) in an email:

> Sarah: I have put an extreme amount of crafting into the words regarding same-sex benefits. *You will need to have a clear understanding of what I have crafted.* . . . I recommend that you avoid getting into a trap of whether or not the Equal Protection Clause of the State Constitution . . . you will need to be ready to avoid the land mines.

If she found herself unable or unwilling to answer a question—which was often—Sarah had little hesitation in changing direction. When, in 2008, she landed in the vice presidential debate with Senator Joe Biden, moderated by Gwen Ifill, she boldly stated this policy as "I may not answer the questions that either the moderator or you want to hear." Debate opponents felt flummoxed over her nonanswers, but many viewers cared little. Sarah had the Kennedy magic over her Nixonian rivals when it came to the camera.

Typical of what viewers saw in a Palin debate was the November 2, 2006, roundtable broadcast statewide on Juneau's KTOO-TV. Sarah sat in a bright red blazer, flanked by independent candidate Andrew Halcro on her right and Democratic candidate and ex-governor Tony Knowles on the left. Both men, as well at the two moderators, wore drab, dark suits. Sarah jumped out immediately and powerfully as if she were in Technicolor and her opponents in black and white. She captivated the viewers' attention speaking in an unusually smooth, deeper voice—exactly as ex-advisor Kelly Goode had suggested.

At one point, she boldly chastised her opponents for not answering specific questions. However, with the very next question put to her regarding a specific bill that the state legislature had passed in the previous session, Sarah ignored the moderator and launched into an attack on Governor Murkowski's last four years in office. Nobody seemed to notice the apparent hypocrisy; her manner and appearance deflected substantive deficiencies. She did, in televised debates, what she did to crowds: wowed them with image.

On that metric of appearance, Sarah scored a convincing knockout.

Later, according to Andrew Halcro, Sarah once complimented him on his encyclopedic knowledge of facts and policy, but then said, "Andrew, I watch you at these debates with no notes, no papers, and yet when asked questions, you spout off facts, figures, and policies, and I'm amazed. But then I look out into the audience, and I ask myself, 'Does any of this really matter?' "

Halcro admitted the wisdom of Sarah's advice when he later told BBC News, "The one thing I found during the debates was no matter how knowledgeable her opponents were on the issues, it didn't matter." In 2009 Halcro wrote in the *Chicago Sun-Times*, "I've debated Governor Palin more than two dozen times. And she's a master, not of facts, figures, or insightful policy recommendations, but at the fine art of the nonanswer, the glittering generality."

For instance, in one October debate, she said of health care, "My attitude and my approaches toward dealing with the complexities of health care issues is a respectful and responsible approach, and it's a positive approach. I don't believe that the sky is falling here in Alaska." As a hard-to-disagree-with nugget, this was typical Sarah-speak.

The voters tended to agree with us that Alaska did not need Egg-headed Halcro; the state needed Commonsense Sarah, even if her twisted sentences were impossible to decipher. "I feel your pain" was more important than "I have a solution."

12

Sacrificing Everything

You are spending WAY too much time on the campaign, but
I don't know what else you can do differently. This is very
frustrating to me because our family suffers and tasks aren't
getting done that we HAVE to complete. I don't know what to
do, but I definitely cannot handle this pace until November.
We really need to think about childcare for the fall too.
Anyways, I know you are overwhelmed . . . me too . . .
—JANEEN BAILEY, EMAIL TO HUSBAND FRANK

As we moved into the heart of the general election season, already intense interpersonal pressures grew. Many evenings my children's goodnights arrived in the form of emails. Too often progress reports in school and feedback from teacher conferences came via rushed phone conversations. In what I suspect were similarly hollow words uttered by others in the campaign, I promised to slow down, take time off, and reprioritize. All of us, no more so than Sarah, wished to have this satisfactorily over and done with. An email of hers summed up our feelings: *"I just wish we could skip the election b.s. & get right into governing, implementing the changes that are needed. I see more and more piling on our campaign's plate, and more 'pulling' from different directions."*

However, every time our opponents attacked or a new poll showed the lead growing or shrinking, we became amnesiacs regarding family promises and considered only our November date with destiny. Our children suffered most. *Regret* is not nearly a strong enough word to describe how I came to feel.

As for Todd Palin, throughout the campaign, he would regularly vanish, largely because his job on the North Slope required him to be away for weeks at a time. My sense was that he tended to focus more on the kids when home than on the campaign. And for all his faults, and to his credit, during his time home from the job, Todd was an engaged father, picking up family slack while Sarah focused on the GOP race. Often, he struck me as both father and mother to the kids. My prayers were that Sarah, with what little time she had, was showering them with as much attention as she could.

———

Shortly after the primary victory, Sarah sought to consolidate the inner circle. My title went from coordinator of the primary to coordinator of the general election. In sum, I continued to direct volunteer efforts and organize campaign events. But equally vital for Sarah, I screened calls from reporters, tracked down staff, chauffeured VIPs, did opposition research when required, made calls, and wrote letters in defense of Sarah's reputation.

In a short August 27 email to the staff, Sarah outlined specifically the roles of several others. Longtime friend Kris Perry, who headed the Wasilla Chamber of Commerce when Sarah sat on the Wasilla City Council, would handle *"scheduling, admin. and assisting with everything I need."* Curtis Smith would be *"focusing on admin & media/message/ spokesperson & working with"* our PR firm, Walsh and Sheppard. John Bitney's job was *"focusing on administration and writing/research (working with Bruce [Anders] and Glen [Biegel] especially on this re: crafting message on gasline, et al)."* Bitney, as a former lobbyist, required permission from the Alaska Public Offices Commission to come on board and was prohibited from raising funds for the campaign.

In October Mike Tibbles—formerly our rival John Binkley's campaign manager and co-architect of the Palin smear campaign in the waning days before her primary victory—joined to work some of his tactical magic (or, as I thought of it, tactical *tragic*). Heavyweight attorney Wayne Anthony Ross, oil and gas lobbyist Paul Fuhs, Scott Heyworth, Jeff Lowenfels, and Ivy Frye remained central players as well, adding dashes of expertise, opposition research, and moral support for our emotionally up-and-down candidate.

While Sarah realized that some organization was required, there was no way she'd relinquish tactical power a second time. Recognizing her inability to take direction during the Kelly Goode experiment in January, Sarah finalized her August summation of duties by adding, *"I'm not giving anyone the Campaign Manager title because that's passé and it's not the way we'll run a team oriented campaign."* The message was clear: Sarah now had a bone-deep desire to control her comings and goings and was de facto her own campaign manager. What was "passé" was any notion that someone else might dictate priorities. If that meant inefficiency and micromanaging, so be it. If that meant little critical feedback, all the better. Unfortunately, her attempt at assigning duties did little to relieve unending hours on the job.

––––––

Our biggest political asset, aside from our all-consuming commitment to Sarah and her message of reform, remained Democratic rival Tony Knowles himself. As an ex-two-term governor (and an ex-two-term mayor of Anchorage before that), he had name recognition, but when we ran across his volunteers and asked about their candidate, we detected ho-hum enthusiasm. Indications were that most support came strictly along Democratic Party lines or from voters believing Sarah Palin too inexperienced. Not only was he an entrenched politician in a state begging for change, but the Yale University graduate and Vietnam Veteran lacked charismatic energy. Our candidate was the latest in political fashion.

Whenever the Knowles campaign criticized her, Sarah's standard response became, "It appears to be the good ol' boy network doing business as usual. They just don't get that the public is sick and tired of such tactics." Every time she uttered these lines, it reminded people that she was the *do-gooder* being bullied by *do-badders*. And at the age of sixty-three, Knowles represented a political movement that to the relatively young and changing population of Alaska seemingly began when humans were still using chipped-stone tools. Besides his own lengthy political career (beginning in 1981 as Anchorage Mayor), the *New York Times*, in October, 2006, noted that "two of the three members of the state's Congressional delegation, Senator Ted Stevens and

Representative Don Young, have been in office for a total of 71 years. The third, Senator Lisa Murkowski, has been in office since 2002 in the seat her father held for 22 years before that." For a large chunk of Alaskans, a hundred-plus years of corrupt mismanagement was at least a hundred years too many.

In addition to experience, Knowles possessed great superiority in money and ad buys. A month ahead of the November 7 general election, campaign finance-disclosure statements showed that he and his running mate, Ethan Berkowitz, had raised $401,978. Together with Knowles's war chest left over from the primary, they had $637,025 to spend as of September 1. By contrast, Palin and her eventual running mate, Sean Parnell, had only $366,613. What money couldn't buy, however, was the fact that Sarah had captured voters' imaginations, and her name was on everyone's lips. Papers sold more copies when her name made the headlines or when the front page carried her photo. And this cost us nothing.

To the extent we could afford to, we used advertisements to hammer home electorate discontent. In one television commercial, Sarah spoke into the camera and said, "Alaska's former governor says we should gamble on his experience? I say we already have. His administration put resource development on life support, making Alaska's economic growth one of the worst in the country. He tried to grow government for eight years despite billion-dollar deficits, and when we couldn't afford his new programs, he introduced an income tax. I'm Sarah Palin, and I'm ready to lead Alaska. That's no gamble, that's a promise."

A radio spot had Sarah end by saying, "Alaska wins when *new* leaders step up to govern." Nobody was fresher or newer than ever-smiling Sarah.

Despite the buzz surrounding our campaign, the relative lack of funding remained frustrating. We attracted those $50 contributors, while Knowles had fat-cat $500 and $1,000 special interest sponsors. Independent Andrew Halcro simply threw his own fortune at his futile run. For Sarah, there were clear villains responsible for the sorry state of financial affairs, namely familiar foe Randy Ruedrich and his state Republican Party machine.

Date: Sun, 3 Sep 2006 15:44:35

frank—would you . . . start asking around about the $ that's sup-
posed to be there for our Gov's campaign. It's totally impossible to
believe they don't have funds for this race—that the [Republican
Party of Alaska] hasn't raised any money in four years for the Republican nominee. How much did they provide Murkowski four
years ago—the entire allowable $200,000?

. . . others may know where to look for truth in the statement:
there's no RPA money for the campaign.

By the next day, her frustrations grew:

Created: 9/4/2006 8:46:37 AM

this whole GOP machine stuff is going to get worse before it gets
better. I know my commitment is to leave it behind while we charge
ahead . . . and to let others battle this one for me . . . but the situation is not good. The traditional fiscal support a GOP candidate
should expect to receive is not going to be there with Randy (and
others) as the head of the party.

Sarah used this perceived slight as another opportunity to reinforce
her role as victim and maverick: *"It's one thing to spin this to the press (not
hard). We say it's an extension of the anemic support we got in the primary
and that it's a shame [Ruedrich] can have so much influence on a party
that he no longer appears in touch with. But it doesn't help us with $."*

How far did Sarah's distrust of Ruedrich go, and how much did
that preoccupy us? Here's an example: the campaign was preparing
to send out a flyer regarding her participation in a solstice event and
emailed a copy to the Republican Party, requesting that it be sent out
to its mailing list. Sarah railed in an email, *"Randy Ruedrich had better
not screw us on this. He'd better send it out today or tomorrow!"* Something as minor as a campaign flyer became a potential Ruedrich controversy, and Sarah was not hesitant to explain that *"it's bull crap is
what it is. typical Randy."* The Republican Party leader existed in our

minds as a bogeyman every hour of every day. This bore similarities to our dealings with Palin family rumors, radio critic Dan Fagan, and editorial criticism in any form. Just one more time-killing distraction. There were an infinite number of more pressing priorities. Too bad we didn't have the eyes to see.

Having built her reputation partially on exposing Ruedrich's conflict of interest while on the Alaska Oil and Gas Conservation Commission, it remained the centerpiece for Sarah's counterattacks on him. When another conservative radio critic, Rick Rydell of KENI-AM, Anchorage, spoke of Ruedrich on his show, Sarah fired off an email letting him know her facts:

> The Dept. of Law investigated [Randy Ruedrich] after so many concerns were expressed by many people who were observing Randy's activities at AOGCC. Randy's issue erupted with the Evergreen Resources proposed developments when Randy was seen traveling with Evergreen's lobbyist one too many times and providing Evergreen information. . . . Employees at AOGCC, and public members and legislators observing the conflict, knew Randy's conflict would erupt. Dept. of Law evidently didn't need an ethics complaint to investigate him.

Sarah liked her response so much that she asked, *"Should this be sent to [Anchorage television station] KTUU?"* Randy Ruedrich wore that corruption albatross and Sarah was going to make certain everyone knew. *Period.*

———

When we reminded people that *Sarah runs marathons, she's a young mom, she fishes and hunts*, it was another way of contrasting her to old, old politicians who drank Chivas Regal (paid for by oil lobbyists) through high-priced dentures. The image was a vital part of who Sarah wanted Alaskans to believe she was. Only days ahead of the election, a woman who went to school in Dillingham with Todd and his brother, J.D., challenged Sarah's claim of being a rugged Alaskan. She wrote in a nasty email to Sarah, among other things, *"[W]hen is the last time you went commercial fishing in Bristol-bay?? . . . Some one like you would hardly go unnoticed!! . . . is there maybe a fishing season I'm not aware of??"*

While the accusation appeared trivial on the face of it, we sure didn't think so, not this close to the election. Sarah, upset, wrote to us, *"Can you believe ANOTHER untruthful email now? . . . The distractions in these last hours of the campaign seem overwhelming. And hurtful to our campaign. Pray through this guys."*

Lies, lies, and more lies. With so many things being said that we believed were evil attacks, all we could do was, as Sarah advised, pray. Fortunately for the campaign, this claim never did make news.

———

Money concerns and distrust of the state political machine played out on another front as well. In Alaska, during the primaries, the governor and lieutenant governor run separate campaigns. Once into the general election, they run as a ticket. From the outset, Sarah had a distaste for her running mate, Sean Parnell. Strategist John Bitney echoed these sentiments when he wrote, *"On Lt. Governor's race . . . I feel like I'm being asked to pick my favorite Menendez brother. Should I vote the one that stabbed his mother, or the one that shotgunned the father?"*

Once we were stuck with Parnell, it infuriated Sarah that he had a $20,000 debt coming into the general. Not a dime, she made clear, of our money would go toward easing his burden. Sarah also harbored a lingering animosity based on Parnell's unwillingness to endorse her during the primary. If all this wasn't bad enough, he expressed an irrational respect for Randy Ruedrich, as Sarah pointed out in a September 4 email:

> This whole "duh . . . we've always been one big happy family" odd aura of Sean [Parnell's] is too puzzling to continue to be ignored. we need to have a Come To Jesus meeting with him on . . . his seeming respect for Ruedrich and the machine, etc.

She then wrote to Parnel directly and couldn't have been more blunt:

Are you getting closer to being out of debt? Our treasurer really needs to combine our campaigns ASAP. We can't be naive and believe Ruedrich and the party machine will go out of their way to provide the traditional, expected, and deserved GOP funds that the GOP nominees should be counting on. . . .

My supporters and I want to talk to you about the reality of this situation—that Ruedrich . . . Binkley and Murkowski's campaigns were not positive . . . and they used PR folks who didn't engage in ethical campaigning, etc. They did things I would NEVER have allowed in our campaign, nor would my campaign team have encouraged me to do. . . .

It's an unconventional way of campaigning, but it's the right way. And it's the way I will govern.

Understandably, Parnell was offended. *"I don't appreciate the inferences that I somehow would engage in anything but ethical conduct,"* he replied. *"Quite the contrary, I strive to lead a life of integrity that points people to Christ, although I don't always do this perfectly."*

In a long response that backtracked from her finger pointing, Sarah began by writing, *"No inference at all in this, Sean, that you would engage in anything but ethical conduct. Maybe my email wasn't clear . . . what I and many others have observed is unethical conduct in other campaigns . . . not in yours."*

Ruffle feathers, smooth feathers, then move on in classic Palin fashion.

Stuck with him, Sarah came to accept that Parnell had some plusses to go with his list of minuses. He began his political career in 1992 at the age of thirty, when elected to the Alaska House of Representatives. He served two terms and later won a seat in the Alaska State Senate. He had experience as a member of the Energy Council and cochaired the Senate Finance Committee. His resume added legitimacy to the ticket. However, he also had a chunk of baggage that we feared might tarnish our reputation. After his stint in the state senate, Parnell joined the oil company ConocoPhillips as its director of government relations. Later, in 2005, he worked at Patton Boggs as a full-time lobbyist, focusing on the development of oil and gas projects with clients such as ExxonMobil (his new firm being involved in the ongoing litigation over the 1989 *Exxon Valdez* oil spill). One of Sarah's ongoing attacks on Ruedrich was his cozy relationship with oil lobbyists. Now she found herself straddled with a former lobbyist, his name alongside hers on a new sea of red.

To deal with the money gap and to delay having to associate her name with his, Sarah chose to downplay Parnell on the PR until he figured a way to carry his own load. In August, when sending out invitations to 1,800 people for a fund-raiser, Sarah and Ivy Frye debated whether or not to include Parnell's name. The decision? No, wrote his running mate, not *"UNTIL Sean gets rid of his [debt]."*

And so it fell to me, as with many other between-the-crack tasks, to play Parnell's debt hound. Ten days after the primary, on direct orders from Sarah, I phoned him, awaking an ill candidate for lieutenant governor at eighty thirty in the evening.

"Sean, we need to know your plan to pay off your debt so we can get in line and begin to raise money jointly for the combined campaign." Until that moment, Parnell seemed to be under the misapprehension that we'd bail him out, at first refusing to discuss the issue. "No. That's not gonna happen," I said. "Our funds are separate from yours."

Parnell pledged to turn over every money-raising stone he could find. When I reported our conversation back to Sarah, the part of the story striking her as most significant was hearing that her running mate, sniffles or not, was sleeping at half past eight, a time most of us at Camp Palin were choking down high-salt, high-calorie fast food in the office. She added "lazy" to the negative side of the Parnell ledger.

Less than a month later, Sean continued to provoke animosity from Sarah. *"Sean is not my husband, father, mentor, speechwriter nor boss,"* she complained. *"He threw some surprising comments before and after my many speaking engagements/meet & greet functions where it was confirmed that we'll have to diplomatically remind him that he is running for Lt. Gov. Period."*

By late September, the friction and problems only worsened as Sarah complained about us working our butts off while noting: *"Sean's pretty absent from the work that's needed to succeed here . . . we need to*

put him on something and see him produce. is he out of debt yet? :) are you
guys tired of hearing me ask that yet? :)"

Ultimately, the dilemma we had with Sean Parnell came full circle
and once again hit upon the omnipresent full-time evil-doer, Randy
Ruedrich. Somehow Sarah believed that the GOP head would use her
lieutenant governor to destroy her.

From: sarah
Created: 9/9/2006 8:24:44 PM
Subject: Fw: Sean Parnell

In my paranoia it's occurred to me: if there's any perceived conflict
with Sean's attorney/lobbyist work and the Dem's try to capital-
ize on it, would Ruedrich . . . gleefully watch us sink, in their dis-
tain for this GOP ticket? Would they sacrifice Sean to destroy this
ticket?

I ask because they're not above anything. And I ask because it
was reported that our oh-so-supportive GOP vice-chair said today,
"Sarah is very fragile and when her campaign implodes, she'll need
Randy to rescue it."

Fortunately for Parnell, Sarah eventually concluded that he'd make
a fine second in command. Especially as he, once the general election
put us in office, enthusiastically joined in the ever-growing quest to
counteract any critical word uttered against our leader. When it came
to, as Sarah would say, quoting George W. Bush, "you're with us or
against us," he was cloyingly with us.

Sean, if he reads this, might take comfort in the knowledge that
Sarah was a serial complainer when it came to those who toiled for
her. Even in the case of our well-respected public relations firm of
Walsh and Sheppard, she moaned that they produced subpar work
and advice, despite dramatically cutting their fees. In July Sarah commented, *"It's odd that Walsh/Sheppard doesn't even seem to have any*
advice . . . they ask us what to do about media . . . I need them to tell me
how to do this right."

Two months later, the spats between Sarah and Pat Walsh reached a boiling point. In a terse message from Kris Perry, we learned, *"Walsh & Sheppard sent a letter of resignation this evening. They wish Sarah well and continue to personally support her in her bid for Governor."*

Sarah immediately fired off, *"I want WS back."* Less than a week later, we received this, written by Pat Walsh:

> Sarah, I just want to say your phone call Friday was very healing for Jack [Sheppard] and I. We so very much appreciate your generosity in taking the time to call when time is the most precious commodity in your day. You are a great human being, and you will be a great governor.

Sarah often stepped on toes, but when she wanted to sweet-talk someone back home, she did so like no one else. From Pat's response, whatever Sarah said was effective, and Walsh-Sheppard was back, working once again at a steep discount. In private, however, Sarah still held marginal respect for the firm. When informed that WS planned to engage in not only media buys but also press and creative tasks, Sarah responded:

> From: sarah
> Created: 9/11/2006 12:02:31 AM
> Subject: don't forward . . .
>
> NO on WS reviewing pressers for obvious reasons. . . . they're too slow on production and creativity also, unless Curtis [Smith] does it and just "hands it" to their people. . . . we need to just be able to hand off to them what we're ready to have produced and placed. . . .
>   if more feelings get bent out of shape in this, then I give up.

———

Sarah's rocky dealings with Sean Parnell, Dan Fagan, Rick Rydell, Walsh and Sheppard, Cathy Fredericks, Kelly Goode, Scott Heyworth, Randy Ruedrich, and, later, John McCain and his campaign staff, aren't by themselves seismic events, and are likely similar to the in-fighting and petty complaining that goes on in other business and political environments. But in the distance of time, what became enlightening was the accumulation of Sarah's fractured relationships. With Sarah, personal infatuation often morphed into dissatisfaction for reasons that didn't always appear logical. If that led to potentially losing an asset, she often shifted gears, turned on the charm, and recouped that asset, in one form or another. Witnessing this process on a regular basis, most of us couldn't help but wonder—as Cathy Fredericks had stated directly—what Sarah was saying behind *our* backs. Given how hard I worked and how loyal as I remained, I told myself that surely none of that hidden commentary was going on about me. Oddly enough, knowing that Sarah had a highly critical side to her personality made the rare compliment all the more important. In a perverse way, what might seem a character fault motivated us to work harder and search for ways to curry favor.

Despite dealing with limited finances, crazy interpersonal dynamics, and helter-skelter organization, we continued to successfully distribute Sarah's brand throughout the state. In the polls, we were thumping Tony Knowles no matter what he (or we) did or said. An October 6 Rasmussen poll, between the two leading candidates, put Sarah at 47 percent and Knowles at 40 percent, with 13 percent undecided. According to the same poll, the electorate ignored reality and viewed Sarah in a political light that ideally suited our purposes. Fifty-one percent of the voters saw Sarah Palin as a moderate, while only 45 percent saw Knowles the same way. Also tilting our way, 44 percent labeled Knowles a liberal, while only 37 percent regarded Sarah as a conservative. With such perceptions, we were winning the battle for the important political middle. All told, the numbers and demographics bode well for our prospects.

Unfortunately, our most shameful episodes—where we went from blurring the ethical line to ignoring it altogether—likely resulted from the marriage of Sarah's intensity and insecurity. Whatever the reasons, we began to quit believing that it was better to lose a race than to win unethically.

We officially became as bad as the others. Maybe worse.

13

Our Double Agent

Don't tell anyone I'm asking you for free
advice. Or any advice for that matter.
—SARAH PALIN, EMAIL TO WILLIS LYFORD,
INDEPENDENT CANDIDATE ANDREW HALCRO'S
MEDIA ADVISOR, MONDAY, JUNE 12, 2006

For a time, we fretted that Andrew Halcro, a clever independent with an acerbic tongue and wit, might prove to be a speed bump on our ride to Juneau. A friend of the campaign warned in an email, *"Halcro could be a spoiler. He is seen as some one that republicans would vote for if he was on the R ticket and is seen as taking more votes from Sarah than Tony."*

A second political voice wrote: *"my biggest concern . . . is the impact Halcro will have on the general election ballot. Twice Knowles has won election by a fractured conservative base. Halcro must be dealt with."* This person went on to ask, as a means to eliminate the threat, *"Would [Halcro] be a good Lt. Gov??"* For Sarah, the answer to this query was a definite no. The man was incapable of being charmed or impressed by her common sense, making him unsuitably incorrigible.

At a youthful forty-two, Halcro had an affection for sweater vests and blue blazers that draped over his slim frame. When he spoke to a camera, he gazed unflinchingly through oval wire-rims framed against a thick head of JFK-like hair. His critics saw him as an image-conscious opportunist capable of going from political wonk to rumor-mongering diva in a single sound bite. He proved to be smart, often funny, unpredictable, and routinely irreverent. As a former Republican elected to the Alaska House of Representatives in 1998 and again in 2000, he had government experience but not enough to be old guard. More troubling, he had his own mavericky reputation. After criticizing Republican legislators for taking too many junkets with taxpayer money, he lost his chairmanship of the House Transportation Committee. While Sarah's run-ins with the state GOP placed her on the party's fringes, Halcro managed to become a complete outcast.

With a personal fortune from family control over the Alaskan Avis car rental franchise, he had funds to pour into a campaign that might yet influence the outcome. Halcro would never be governor, but if he stole enough votes, he might cut into our margin of victory or, in the worst possible scenario, split the vote and usher in yet another Knowles administration.

Fortunately for us, Halcro had a consultant on his payroll who didn't mind lending Sarah free advice that proved an asset in dealing with both Halcro and Knowles.

————

Willis Lyford, a longtime political strategist and media consultant who had worked on Lisa Murkowski's legislative campaigns, met Sarah Palin when she ran for lieutenant governor in 2002. In an interview with Kenneth Vogel on the Politico website in 2008, Lyford recalled their first meeting in Wasilla: "She came out from behind her desk and was wearing a navy blue turtleneck and these leather boots that were up over her knees, like thigh high, and I thought immediately to myself, *This is not a look you often see on a Republican.* She was sharp, personable, a quick study, capable, committed—the whole package. And my assessment of her right from the get-go was all she needed was visibility and exposure."

While the Palin campaign for lieutenant governor could not afford to hire Lyford, he did suggest correctly that scheduling face-to-face meetings with the electorate would play to Sarah's strengths.

With that bit of mutual history, it wasn't unusual that he should contact the Palin campaign for governor a few years later were it not for one small complication: Willis Lyford was financially married to Andrew Halcro. Press reports during the race variously described him as spokesman and media consultant to Halcro for Governor. At the time, I actually thought he was Halcro's campaign manager.

According to Alaska Public Offices Commission records on campaign expenses, on February 2, 2006, Lyford Strategies received from Andrew Halcro as "paid accrual," $14,822.50. During the coming months, various payments ranging from $10,000 to more than $59,000 ran through Lyford's hands. In all, his firm handled over $165,000 in advertising expenses for Halcro. Lyford's efforts in creating the "Think Halcro" television ads that ran during the election season went on to win a silver medal at the 2007 Pollie Awards. (The Pollies are highly prestigious accolades voted on by the nonpartisan organization the American Association of Political Consultants.)

If Willis Lyford was wed to Andrew Halcro's campaign, he began a torrid affair with ours early on. Nevertheless, for months, while handling Halcro's media, Lyford offered Sarah free counsel and occasionally a bit of intelligence on his candidate's progress. Amazingly, Sarah embraced the relationship in spite of its unseemly nature.

Once again, the most important aspect wasn't our behavior but the fact that we kept it a secret.

Her words to us mirrored those surrounding our letter- and op-ed-writing factories. This was, she wrote, *"Totally confidential: don't let anyone know Willis wrote."* As if he needed reminding, she warned Lyford, *"Don't tell anyone I'm asking you for free advice. Or any advice for that matter."* On his end, Willis explained, *"I don't tell anyone I have any communication with you . . . Andrew [only] knows I talk to you once in a blue moon."*

The only way for Lyford's words to ring true would be if by "blue moon" he meant regularly communicating with our campaign and surreptitiously visiting our downtown campaign office as warranted. On the very day that he and Sarah shared their notes on confidentiality, June 13, Lyford composed a lengthy email offering advice on the primary campaign, which Sarah passed along to me and others. Among his recommendations:

I don't know what inside polling data you have about your perceived strengths relative to Bink or Murky. . . . Bink has worst posi-

tion of all in this primary. Who does he try to knock down, you OR
Murky. He only gets votes by dragging them from one of you two.
He can't go after you both. . . .

But for sure, experience is your weak suit. Trust, integrity, honestly, those are your great strengths. I'd expect that in a few weeks,
someone will be on the air dissing you for your lack of experience.
It is just a matter of time. It will be delicate at first, but it will get
nasty.

In early July, Paul Jenkins of the *Anchorage Daily News* penned an
editorial criticizing Sarah for using her Wasilla mayor's computer to
help campaign for lieutenant governor four years earlier. Sarah solicited Lyford for his opinion on how to handle the crisis. Willis warned
that the opposition would use the accusation to launch a *"two pronged
attack; you ain't the ethics queen you pitch yourself as, and your under-
qualitied for the job. . . . Take a deep breath. I still think you need to go
on offense with paid media."*

When the lieutenant governor story was still a hot topic two weeks
later, Sarah again begged for input, especially regarding a suggestion
by attorney Wev Shea to put the matter to rest by writing the City
of Wasilla a check compensating it for use of city resources. Ever responsive, Lyford dispensed more advice, such as, *"You need to do a few
things right away. I would not do the check thing Wev suggests. Implies
guilt. Who determines how much you should pay. . . . I mean, when did
you stop beating your wife."*

Lyford offered important feedback throughout the primary campaign, even while Andrew Halcro was preparing to oppose Sarah
once the general election cycle began in late August. He weighed
in on such matters as uncovering dirt on Randy Ruedrich (*"do a
google search for 'randy ruedrich and political contributions' "*), dealing with radio critic Rydell (*"he ain't your friend. . . . Whatever you
are saying to him, he is passing on"*), how to handle the campaign's association with attorney Wayne Anthony Ross (*"the other side needs to
be confused when Ross pops up defending you in these different media
venues"*), and leaking information to the media (*"I would . . . give*

them [*an incriminating email from*] *Murky and make sure it is on the lo-down"*).

When I needed to know of Andrew Halcro's progress in gathering enough signatures to get on the ballot for the general election, Lyford wrote back, *"We'll get the signatures. It just will take some work, right now I think he is a few hundred short, but there is a week left."* In this same email exchange, Lyford offered intelligence he'd gathered on a final preprimary ad campaign against Sarah. He also suggested *"some thoughts about what SP should say Tuesday if she should win"* the GOP primary. Staggeringly, despite being knee deep in aiding Halcro in his run against Sarah Palin once the primaries were over, Lyford wrote me, *"Just ask SP if she wants me to write [her formal victory statement] up."* Willis's rationale for doing so was *"Because what/how she says it will make a big difference, I think."* After the primary, he recommended a pollster to help us in the general election. He rationalized that it was okay for us to hire this particular outfit because *"Andrew H. does not have enough $$ to use these guys, so there is no problem in me recommending them, and I'm not sure they would sign up for an independent campaign."*

No problem in recommending a topflight PR firm to Halcro's opposition? In other words, he was pointing the Palin campaign to people who might help defeat his candidate. When, in August, Lyford advised us to wrap Binkley together with Murkowski and Ruedrich in a hard-hitting ad campaign, Sarah asked again about Halcro's signatures: *"How's AH doing on the signatures?"* She followed that up with an affectionate sign-off, *"Folks are coming out to my house today to talk issues. 1:30. Wish you could be in the middle of all this Willis!"*

Ever helpful, Lyford provided us with exactly what Sarah asked: *"Andrew will be turning in around 4K signatures on Tuesday afternoon, he needs 3100 or so to qualify, so I think he is there, fyi."* Ever mindful, he added, *"Pls no discussion of this to anyone at all."* It goes without saying he did not show up for Sarah's talk.

I am left to wonder how often in the annals of political history has a consultant for one candidate provided so much information to the opposition, going so far as to volunteer to write her victory speech?

While we welcomed the help, I knew that if someone from our camp handed out inside information, Sarah's wrath would know no bounds. One time, when she suspected Tony Knowles of ripping off material penned by our own Bruce Anders, she wrote him, *"I think you have a serious leak. The timing, his use of the EXACTLY same phaseology we've used ("don't tie our hands"), is simply too coincidental."*

In another instance, Sarah became so distraught that she suggested the staff work "in a large, open room 'bullpen' with no cubicles and no closed doors anywhere" in order to "get a handle on leaks."

As governor, when information from a closed-door meeting she'd attended wound up in Andrew Halcro's blog (ironically enough), Sarah became enraged and warned us:

> **Very, very disappointing, but also seems to be par for the course: too many "disclosures"/leaks that only aim to undermine this effort. This is unacceptable . . . —pls find out everything you can on this. It's unacceptable. Please enlist whomever else you must in order to find out who leaked . . . because it must, and will, stop. . . .**
>
> **Who attended the meetings?**

Despite her own moral outrage at leaks from within and a desire to uncover and punish offenders, all of us—none more so than Sarah—embraced Willis Lyford's efforts on our behalf. On several occasions, Sarah referred to him as "my friend," as did I.

Weeks later, in October, as we went head to head with Andrew Halcro in a bitter rivalry, we continued to hear from Lyford regarding his specialty: advertising expenditures. He reported that on our behalf, the Republican Governors Association (RGA) *"[d]umped a massive amount on money into tv late friday for SP. On KTUU alone for one week, it is nearly $52,000 for 8 days. Much more than they were doing previously. . . . Just thought you might want to know. I'd expect Tony to try to make even more hay with this than before."*

Willis Lyford was right that Tony Knowles did make hay out of our association with the RGA and what was a negative campaign strategy—something we swore we'd never condone—but so did Andrew Halcro.

At the time, none of us viewed our collaboration as inappropriate. I suppose we felt that the Golden Rule didn't apply to politics. Only later did I realize that everywhere we traveled in our campaign to make Alaska a better state, ethical challenges were so thick that we no longer had the ability to see them, except, as Willis Lyford suggested, in others.

14

The Republican Governors Association and our Limbo Dance with Truth

Our campaign can have NO participation
in any 3rd party campaign efforts.
—SARAH PALIN, EMAIL TO FRANK BAILEY,
WEDNESDAY, AUGUST 23, 2006

J ust prior to the August gubernatorial primary and while fighting fatigue on a long drive back from a pair of debates in Kenai, I received a phone call from Republican state representative Bill Stoltze. The forty-five-year-old former legislative staffer, who eventually won office and now sat on the state finance committee, said, "You're doing great with this campaign, Frank. But we're getting to the time when you need to start thinking beyond the primary and into the general election season."

While my own natural instinct was never to assume victory prematurely, Stoltze spoke confidently of our chances in November. "And I want you to know," he continued, "that I've got people who will help." While he didn't elaborate, I welcomed the sentiment, believing that we'd need all the people we could muster in a general election against Tony Knowles.

With one hand steering the pickup and the other hand pressing my cell phone to my ear, I said, "I really appreciate all your help, Bill. I'm sure I speak for Sarah when I say we're grateful. God willing, we'll win this thing." After we hung up, the drive seemed less tedious. That a man as savvy as Representative Stoltze had our primary race in the win column seemed a good omen.

True to his word, after our stunning primary victory, Stoltze visited me at campaign headquarters. Stoltze is a jovial Drew Carey look-alike on the outside but a cagey Karl Rovian political animal within. When he walked into my office and banged shut the door, I raised an eyebrow. Though it wasn't unusual for him to drop by, his manner was different. He had a wrinkled brow and a pinched forehead, the normal grin absent. Uncharacteristically, I shut off my BlackBerry so that we wouldn't be interrupted and leaned forward. Stoltze grabbed a chair, slid it forward, and began a one-sided conversation.

"Frank, remember those people I mentioned? Those friends that can help?" Bill wasn't talking about a handful of volunteers as I expected. No, what he had in mind was something that went beyond my limited imagination. We were, he explained, about to go national. His *friends*, as he put it, were running the Republican Governors Association (RGA).

There were thirty-six gubernatorial contests to be decided in November 2006, and in a media market as inexpensive as Alaska, the RGA, chaired at the time by Governor Mitt Romney of Massachusetts, felt that it could influence the race for governor.

"I'm talking some serious numbers," he said. Meanwhile, I was practically wondering if we were on some show with a hidden camera. Stoltze mentioned a dollar amount that went into the hundreds of thousands. For a campaign that once had a four-way debate about whether or not to splurge on a $360 newspaper ad, we were suddenly staring at what seemed like an absurd amount of money.

"Frank, the RGA has a keen interest in seeing Republican governors gain power, and they want Sarah to win this thing." Stoltze, an early supporter of Sarah before it was politically expedient, knew that he had her appreciation. As such, he stood to gain power if she won. More than once, he mentioned a desire to head up the reapportionment board—which controlled redistricting of the state house and senate districts—thereby giving him power to make or break political careers by redrawing political geography.

He leaned over my desk and reminded me that Knowles would

likely be doing a blitz of negative ads during the last weeks of the campaign. "The RGA wants to help counter that. I've got their contact info for you to reach out to them."

"Sure, Bill, we'd like the help. And no question money is always an issue. But . . ." I hesitated, because what he said sounded good and the thought of national backing was flattering. "Look, it sounds great, but what about the rules?" I explained that I wasn't overly familiar with election law, but I believed that our campaign was not permitted to coordinate with any outside groups.

Stoltze seemed barely concerned and insisted that this was a game-changing opportunity. Without committing, I said only that I'd pass along the information to Sarah. "She's had experience running campaigns and should know more than me."

Hoping that it *was* legal for us to initiate contact with the RGA, on August 23 I wrote Sarah: *"RGA wants to give $250k for starters than up to $750k. . . . Want to set up 3rd party? 601c4 . . . can only fundraise and advertise for 60 days . . . wants to get started right away."*

Sarah replied in no uncertain terms: *"Our campaign can have NO participation in any 3rd party campaign efforts."*

I'd had a feeling my first instincts were right. I wrote back: *"ya know . . . i knew that was the case for 527's, but he mentioned some other third party (601)."*

Suddenly the closed door and hushed conversation with Stoltze made more sense. Contact with the RGA in this context was prohibited. I felt disappointed in Stoltze and wasn't sure why an experienced sitting lawmaker didn't realize this type of coordination was forbidden.

To my dismay, several days later, Stoltze phoned. "My people at the RGA haven't heard from you, or Sarah, or anyone at the campaign. To be honest, they're getting frustrated and wondering if we really even want their help." His voice had that "What the hell is wrong with you hayseeds?!?" tone.

Equally annoyed, I thought to myself, *You think* they're *frustrated? How about me having to deal with* you? "I don't know what to tell you, Bill," I said, as politely as I could. "We can't do that, and I'm getting really uncomfortable with this." Stoltze said something about not knowing what the hell I was talking about before I cut him short. Afterward, despite the conversational heat, I felt relieved knowing that I'd ended this particular debate. Windfall money was nice, but not at the expense of sabotaging the campaign. Not for us, in any event.

Unbelievably, only days later, Stoltze stopped by the office yet again. "Frank, have you made that call?" It didn't sound like a question. My discomfort had now reached the saturation point.

"Bill, I can't be doing that," I told him firmly. "My understanding is that it is positively illegal!" This time I didn't hide my frustration.

Against a red face, and with a dot of spit forming in the corner of his mouth, the man's eyes flashed. "Don't you lecture me on what's f**** illegal! I'm a lawmaker! I know the rules!"

Wasn't I right about the ethics of this matter? There was no question in my mind that Sarah was on my side, totally committed to running a fair, legal campaign. Finally, after what seemed an eternity, Stoltze lifted his beefy five-foot-ten-inch frame and awkwardly spun around. Without so much as an *adios*, he stormed out, pushing shut my office door with the back of his hand. I had a feeling this time I would not be hearing back from him.

Unfortunately, that's not to say the matter was put to rest.

Two days later, a message came from Palin warrior and fellow campaign worker Ivy Frye: *"I talked to Kris [Perry]—we have Sarah meeting with Gov Romney and Gov [Roy] Blunt [of Missouri] on Tuesday."*

Reporter Kyle Hopkins of the *Anchorage Daily News* had gotten wind of this meeting, and on August 29 he provided readers an explanation of the potential relevance:

> [Palin spokesman Curtis Smith] said it's unclear why the governors want to talk with Palin, but here's why it's worth a second look: Romney is chairman of the Republican Governors Association, which exists primarily to get Republicans elected and keep them in office.
>
> The RGA could be an important ally for Palin—who is now busy fund-raising—because it's willing to spend money. On Friday, for example, the Association announced it would funnel

$750,000 into ads in Michigan, where Republican Dick DeVos is challenging Democrat incumbent Jennifer Granholm.

While working for Frank Murkowski in 2004, Kris Knauss, the man identified by Stoltze as our RGA go-between, attended an RGA conference to lobby for opening the Arctic National Wildlife Refuge to oil drilling. Apparently he maintained enough contact to become the RGA intermediary with Sarah Palin. As far as I was concerned, as a former confidant of the ethically challenged Frank Murkowski, Knauss was radioactive for our campaign due to his lobbying efforts for VECO. No way did I want this sort of association to tarnish our spotless candidate.

Unfortunately, it seemed, I was alone in that conviction.

As if the August RGA meeting, of which Sarah never disclosed specifics, was not damaging enough, Knauss volunteered additional unhealthy suggestions:

Subject: Fwd: Alaska Oppo Research
From: Kristopher Knauss
Date: Wed, 06 Sep 2006 12:08

To: frank bailey
We need to chat in the near future. The RGA will be in Anchorage next week and a poll is going to the field in the next 48 hours. The RNC put this together and it should be useful in your endeavors. I'm in L.A. today, but I would like to give you and Sarah a heads-up on next week (scheduling/TV/etc.)
Thanks.

Gentry Collins, then political director for the RGA (and current political director for the Republican National Committee, described the oppo research referenced by Knauss as follows:

Good morning all,
The Senatorial Committee came through for us this morning. Please find the Knowles oppo-research book attached. It should be current through the 2004 cycle—there may be more recent mate-

rial, but given our time constraints we should operate under the assumption this is the only oppo we'll have . . . I'll have more for you on the survey instrument in the next few hours.

Sharing this opposition research with our campaign made me nervous. I didn't know if such an action represented a violation, but we'd sworn it was always better to be safe than sorry, and I was already feeling very sorry about the whole affair. I didn't need a law degree to understand that the word *scheduling* in the context of coordination with the RGA was pushing the boundaries of legality. Even if it was within the letter of the law—which seemed unlikely—in politics, the appearance of impropriety can be as damaging as reality. And the specifics of Knauss's mentioning "(scheduling/TV/etc.)"? This was blatantly suggestive of working together. Knauss's email to me went unanswered. Unfortunately, ignoring the problem didn't make it go away. A few hours later, campaign coordinator Kris Perry wrote:

Sarah,
Had a nice conversation w/ Governor Romney. He'd like to speak with you directly and we'll try to make that happen in the next day or so. He's traveling in the morning but will give me a call once he reaches his destination.
Bottom line: they are very interested in the Governor's race and are supportive of your candidacy.

While it wasn't particularly convenient to be scraping in a dollar here, a dollar there, we did *not* break laws. Again I heard her words in my head: "It's better to lose than to win unethically."

No matter our previous faults, I knew that Sarah's ethical limbo bar would never drop that low. So I rationalized the sudden turn of events this way: obviously, in agreeing to meet, Sarah was merely extending a courtesy to the RGA bigwigs; the meeting was no big deal. If Romney, Blunt, Knauss, and Stoltze underestimated Sarah Palin, they did so at their own peril.

Against these RGA concerns, the campaign—money woes notwithstanding—was proceeding nonstop. The final weeks before the election were a blur of signs and fund-raisers and debates. Adding to our stimulus overload of constantly ringing phones, last-second schedule changes, and sleep deprivation, our candidate lacked focus and required constant attention. Being tugged in a million directions, Sarah had difficulty delegating assignments and ordering priorities. She wanted to be everywhere, for everyone. As she'd done before the primary, she consumed gallons of Skinny White Chocolate Mochas, lost weight, and shrunk before our eyes. Any little ripple, and she could slip into a depression or grow irritable. We feared that her lack of impulse control might result in an outburst within earshot of the media. It wouldn't take many public tirades to tarnish her reputation. We did our best to shorten the leash, but with Sarah, there was always the risk that any tether might break unexpectedly.

Growing more diligent in those final weeks, we controlled information and shared regular alerts—often beginning with the morning call from Todd as she left for the office—regarding her state of mind on a given day. We were her shield, and our mission was to keep her happy, shaking hands, kissing babies, and smiling for cameras. At every opportunity, we solicited donations and held benefits, doing our best to get her from one money-raising opportunity to the next. As far as I knew, we had turned our back on the RGA serpent's offer of a financial apple.

One of those eleventh-hour fund-raisers on our calendar featured Dino Rossi, the Republican candidate for governor of the state of Washington. The benefit was to be held at former governor Wally Hickel's Hotel Captain Cook. I was running behind, as usual, and I hustled the half mile to the hotel.

I showed up slightly out of breath and saw the first guests arriving. Gripping the oversized carved oak handle and opening the glass outer door, I entered the hallway and immediately noticed Kris Perry heading across the lobby toward me. Sarah walked briskly a few steps behind. Kris grabbed my arm and said under her breath, "Walk with me and act normal."

Act normal? Those words struck me as humorous, since nothing in this now-crazy life was ever normal. I did as asked, assuming that someone important was about to arrive. Kris pulled me along, all the while glancing around nervously as if she were a Secret Service agent protecting a dignitary. We coasted to a stop at the front door. Kris peered through the glass window, searching outside for something or someone, while Sarah stood behind, waiting for us to make a move.

"Okay, come with me, and don't look at the camera," Kris instructed. I could see that there was indeed a camera set up across the street. On a silent count of three, she said, "Let's go." We headed out, turned left, and made our way up the street. I wondered why we were doing this while guests and their checkbooks were trickling in. Our PR firm of Walsh & Sheppard frequently filmed campaign stops, but surely somebody could have picked a more opportune time and place.

As I had little to do with public relations, I put my reservations on hold. A half block later, we came to a prearranged stopping point, turned around, then retraced our steps and reentered the hotel through the same door we'd exited only moments earlier. "Wait here," Kris ordered, again staring intently out the window. She spotted some kind of signal from across the street and whispered, "Again, Frank. This time, walk slower . . ." Out we went like before, with Kris and me in front and Sarah behind us.

"Am I dressed okay for this?" I asked, still trying to "act normal" and wondering if my jeans and sweater were appropriate.

"You're fine," Kris said, not caring that her tone was dismissive. We reached the same spot on the sidewalk, stopped, spun, and back we went. I thought of asking Kris what exactly we were doing, but she and Sarah each wore that "I don't have time for chitchat" look I'd come to respect. As if in a revolving door with no exit, we went around and around, over and over. In and out, back and forth, five, maybe six times.

"Okay, just you this time," Kris said to Sarah. Out went Sarah, down and back, down and back, down and back. Dressed more formally than usual in a woman's suit, she'd screwed on her practiced, determined expression. All business, she marched ahead, looking as if she were deep in thought about vital issues in advance of a crucial meeting. Each trip the same. For whatever the intended purpose, she did a fine job of looking, as she once said, "governor-ish."

By now the weak showing of barely a hundred guests were funneling into the ballroom just off the lobby. After completing the filming outdoors, we assembled to hear the speakers. This time, the mysterious cameraman who'd documented those nutty round-trip marches up and down Fifth Avenue, had set up in the ballroom to capture more footage.

While striking me as silly, this slice of campaign life would have passed as just one more curiosity, except for an unexpected revelation a couple of weeks later. Having arrived home late at night yet again, I was slumped on the couch in sweats and socks, munching on a slice of reheated pizza and watching the news, when a new Palin commercial came on. It was sponsored by the Republican Governors Association, despite my noncooperation, had decided that Alaska was a worthy battleground state.

This particular spot opened with upbeat music and an inspiring shot of Sarah against a background of saw-toothed mountains blanketed in snow.

"Sarah Palin. As mayor she moved her city forward. She cut property taxes, eliminated personal property taxes, and repealed the business inventory tax. That will move Alaska forward."

Suddenly the music turned dark and dramatic, and the film cut to Tony Knowles walking through interior offices, but with the film in reverse so that he appeared to be walking backward.

"Tony Knowles? We've been there before. The highest unemployment in the nation, and even a push for an income tax. Why would we ever go back?"

Upbeat music again. There was Sarah, marching forward, looking seriously confident and determined. "Tell Sarah Palin to support ideas to move Alaska forward."

My chin dropped. Now Sarah was striding out the glass door of the Hotel Captain Cook and turning left, up the street toward the spot where I'd watched her stop and go back for another take, over and over and over. Same clothes, same day, same event. Was the cameraman from the RGA? I sat frozen. Something was terribly wrong, and the pizza I'd just eaten rose up my throat. Sarah had written in no uncertain terms, *"Our campaign can have NO participation in any 3rd party campaign efforts."*

So what happened from the time of that statement just two months before to this commercial?

Our pledge had been to abandon the so-called entitlement culture personified by the Murkowski father-daughter team. Sarah had complained about Ruedrich withholding GOP funds; did she feel because of that she was now entitled to RGA dollars? There seemed to be no other explanation. She had, I believed, broken the law. No question she endured multiple takes of that nutty march at the behest of a cameraman. Not only that, but she did so in the pursuit of a negative ad ripping our opponent. We'd promised a hundred, hundred times to run a positive campaign, regardless of the political consequences. How could this be? We were the *good guys*, remember? If this wasn't dirty politics as usual, what was?

The realization that Sarah Palin and our campaign were not all that we had set out to be made my head ache. In that moment, black and white yielded to a sad shade of gray; there was no absolute good or bad left, at least not in politics. Paraphrasing the poet Robert Frost, I once believed that we'd chosen the road less traveled, but suddenly this seemed like a superhighway heading toward the same old selfish interests.

In our offices the next day, nobody so much as mentioned the RGA commercial and its obvious coordination with the Palin campaign. Finally, Ivy Frye asked if I'd seen it, and I mentioned the backward footage of Tony Knowles. "I guess I'm a little disappointed," I said. Ivy cocked her head. Stumbling over the explanation, I added, "Just seems it's kind of a negative ad. We said we weren't ever going to go negative."

Ivy scoffed at that notion of negativity, suggesting that this kind of truth telling was always fair game. "Besides," she added, "this wasn't our ad."

Even though I hoped that our collective silence would help the winds of intrigue die down, I was sorely disappointed. But almost immediately, the political foul weather escalated into a campaign hurricane. Knowles's handlers immediately issued a press release accusing Sarah Palin of hypocrisy:

September 22, 2006

Knowles' Communications Director Patty Ginsburg pointed out that just two days ago in Ketchikan, Palin again claimed that hers is a down-home, grassroots, low-budget campaign. Speaking to the Southeast Conference, addressing regional leaders, Palin said:

"Well, my campaign, as it's progressing you've probably noticed it's been a real positive campaign, real grassroots. Not, um, highly financed but literally grassroots with folks all over the state of Alaska understanding that it is time for positive change not more politics as usual."

"Sarah Palin has wrapped herself in a flag of grassroots independence, claiming over and over that she doesn't need lots of money or political players," Ginsburg said. "Well, she must have changed her tune since she's now benefiting from a very expensive, very big TV buy courtesy of the Republican Governors Association, or RGA. . . .

One of the leading contributors to RGA has been Capitol Campaign Strategies, Jack Abramoff's group.

Mentioning Jack Abramoff in the same breath as Sarah Palin became a declaration of war. A federal investigation into former GOP lobbyist Abramoff and his partner, Michael Scanlon, had already scandalized Washington and brought down a host of those close to them. Abramoff's name, along with an association with big industry money, gave Sarah an emotional aneurism. As often happened when Team Palin's weaknesses had been spotlighted, the official response was denial followed by even more spectacular accusations against the other side. Sarah wasted no time punching back, delivering a blistering statement through spokesman Curtis Smith to Kyle Hopkins at the *Anchorage Daily News*:

> That's rich coming from Tony's camp. Not only has Tony benefited from outside ads in the past, we're quite sure the Democratic Governors Association is about to do the same thing.
>
> Plus, if they had done their homework, they would know that ads like these are not at all coordinated through the campaign—that would be illegal.
>
> Maybe Tony can continue to run an illegally high number of ads on local TV in hopes of drowning out Sarah's message. (Check out KTUU records Kyle; I was just told Tony ran too many spots in Prime Time).
>
> If Tony is so worried about affiliations, why did he appoint Bill Allen of VECO to head up his transition team in 1994? Not only is his company under investigation by the FBI, But isn't he the leader of the "good old boy" network Tony's camp is chirping about?
>
> As for the Frugally Paid For ads—those are Sarah's. We created those with funds given to her by hard working Alaskans.
>
> Did Tony waste everyone's time with his dog and pony show about ethics? This latest accusation is not only beyond ridiculous, it flies in the face of the ethics plan Tony read from his notes only a couple of weeks ago.

Bill Allen, the man that Curtis Smith claimed in his press release headed Knowles's 1994 transition team, was currently at the center of a dollars-for-votes scandal that eventually landed a number of Alaskan lawmakers behind bars. In bringing up Allen's name—which in Alaska carried even more of a stigma than the name Jack Abramoff (Allen eventually went to federal prison for bribery and tax evasion)—we'd adopted the Sarah Palin tactic of taking both eyes for an eye. But there were a few problems. Most of our accusations were not entirely accurate. For one thing, Bill Allen had *not* headed up the Knowles transition team. Kyle Hopkins shot off a quick post on his paper's political blog the next day, bringing attention to the inaccuracy.

Posted: September 23, 2006—3:15 pm

What role did Veco executive Bill Allen play on Knowles' transition team in 1994?

The reference to it, via a Curtis Smith quote, in today's story could leave you with the impression that Allen was in charge of the transition team.

Not so, the Knowles campaign said today, providing a list of all the transition team leaders.

Dave Rose and Fran Ulmer were running the team, while Allen is listed as "economic & development team leader"—one of more than 24 team leaders and chairpersons. Janie Leask is also listed as a leader of the economic and development team.

I should have precisely *described Allen's role in the story*.

But, as the saying goes, "The toothpaste was already out of the tube," and there was no getting it back in. Most readers, to our great benefit, would never see the *Daily News* correction and hold the false association in their minds.

While this bout of mudslinging raged on, Curtis Smith received another directive from Sarah:

From: sarah
Date: Sunday, September 24, 2006 6:44 pm

Curtis—there needs to be a strong explanation that the outside GOP Governor's ads are NOT our ads. That we're as frugal and hard core grassroots as ever . . . that outside group doesn't give us money or time or people to work on the campaign . . . they want their GOP Gov's group to grow by one so they're running their ads up here. Those are NOT our ads.

Sarah wanted to frame the controversy solely about who paid for the ads. Over the next several days, the accusation war escalated as the Democratic Party filed an official complaint. According to the September 26, 2006, edition of the *Anchorage Daily News*:

The Alaska Democratic Party says it plans to file an APOC (Alaska Public Offices Commission) complaint against the Republican Governors Association and against Palin. The Democrats say the RGA ads about Palin are not "issues" ads at all but can only be seen as a call for people to vote for her. They also say it appears the Palin campaign and the RGA coordinated on the ad, which isn't allowed. The RGA says the complaint is a political stunt, that the Democrats know the ad is legal, and that there was no coordination involved.

The Dems correctly emphasized what we most wanted to bury: namely, our illegal coordination with the RGA. While my palpitating heart and twitching face said, "Guilty," Sarah convincingly conveyed a "How dare you question my honesty?!?" counterattack. She pled innocent on the charges in a widely distributed email that also dealt the ever-popular victim card:

Sent: Tuesday, September 26, 2006 9:53pm
From: sarah

someone needs to tell me if there is any illegality here that I am missing . . . are they spending more than they are allowed? did anyone coordinate the message with RGA?

surely there is someone who knows APOC rules well enough to tell us if RGA did something wrong here. and I don't mind telling anyone that the local RGA leadership machine is NOT supporting us.

More than anything, I wanted to discover if I was somehow wrong in my belief that we'd broken campaign law and then lied. Was this an irregularity that Sarah simply missed or misunderstood? Unfortunately, the answer to that question was, *not a chance*. Had Sarah, as her husband once shockingly said, "become no better" than those she was trying to replace? Was everything we had worked and sacrificed for in danger of coming to an abrupt end? *Technically*, perhaps we didn't coordinate with the Republican Governors Association to be at the locations shown in the TV commercial, but once there, we absolutely and positively coordinated with the RGA in filming it. No matter how our side spun the words, in this instance we proved ourselves to be penniless morally.

The campaign's official denial to APOC came from attorney Wayne Anthony Ross on October 12:

> Your letter (of 5 October) summarizes the allegations made in the complaint on page 1 of your letter under the heading "Allegations." There are five allegations. Four of them appear to require a response from the RGA and only one appears to be an allegation against the Palin Campaign itself. The one allegation directed against the Palin Campaign appears to be the third allegation, to wit, "that Palin for Governor solicited and accepted a prohibited contribution by coordinating with the RGA," an allegation which the Palin Campaign denies.

The RGA went into spin mode as well, brazenly and unabashedly turning the attack around and accusing our competition of duplicity. As the *Daily News* reported: "The RGA's lawyer, Charlie Spies, called the Democrats' complaint dishonest because he says they know the ad is legal. I think it's a political stunt to divert attention from the fact that Knowles campaign is flailing and hasn't gotten any national support."

While keenly aware of the truth, like everyone else I would not volunteer word one; I would bite my tongue until it bled if need be. At the very moment I needed to stiffen my spine and call out my boss for this ethical lapse, as she had done against her own party, I remained cowardly silent. The media, with its short attention span, would soon look for fresh political red meat. While Sarah is not wired to let sleeping dogs lie, we'd do our best to suppress her desire to counterattack.

Unfortunately, just as it seemed we might succeed in fading to black on the RGA scandal, we faced a second crisis when an unknown came out of nowhere, guaranteeing that our cover-up would not go smoothly.

15

Truth Optional

Politics have no relation to morals.
—NICCOLÒ MACHIAVELLI, AUTHOR OF *THE PRINCE*,
PUBLISHED IN THE SIXTEENTH CENTURY

It was impossible for me to deny: I had witnessed the Palin campaign coordinate the filming of an RGA television commercial with the Republican Governors Association. When confronted by critics, Sarah convincingly decried the allegations as malicious attacks on her good name. Employing a familiar strategy, we counterattacked the Tony Knowles machine for spreading lies and accused his campaign of conducting a host of illegal actions.

As far as dealing with a guilty conscience, I'd suffer in silence, not daring to even discuss this with my wife. However, this was the one instance where I did not feel required, beyond keeping my mouth shut, to protect Sarah from herself. If there were an investigation, I would not lie to protect her or the campaign. Of course, that didn't keep me from begging God to forgive me and let this one slide.

Curtis Smith, our bold and blunt spokesman, was again sent out to "refudiate" (a Sarah word) the accusations. Speaking with the *Anchorage Daily News*, he responded to allegations once again without wavering: "It's unfortunate they feel that this is the best shot they've got," Smith said. "They want to nibble around the edges and do a 'gotcha' on Sarah, when I can tell you there is no 'gotcha' to get."

Curtis was not alone in his unabashed support of Sarah. Once the Democrats started publicizing their outrage at the ad campaign, conservatives—having no reason to doubt Sarah's honesty—sprang to her defense, repeating the assertion that Tony Knowles should be ashamed of himself for crossing the line and suggesting that Sarah might lie. What a bully.

Independent candidate Andrew Halcro made the mistake of agreeing to an interview with Palin nemesis Dan Fagan to discuss the RGA controversy. Halcro, believing himself on sympathetic ground, suggested that he *knew* the Palin campaign had coordinated with the RGA. For one, he claimed, the entire film clip *looked* staged. No matter the truth, Halcro's statement sounded ridiculously subjective. He further noted that in the commercial, Sarah didn't have her large red handbag with her when she exited the building and strolled down the street. To our amazement, Fagan ridiculed Halcro and stated forcefully, "Sarah Palin may be many things, but she is not a liar." The handbag argument even elicited cries of sexism from callers because only women carry handbags. Halcro's voice grew unsteady by the end of the show.

In 2009 Halcro wrote in his blog about these events:

A few days after the commercial started to run, former KTUU reporter Bill McAllister ran a story about the ad, which included speculation from me that the ad looked entirely staged. Both Palin and her campaign responded in anger, denying anything was staged and that they had no idea the RGA was even there shooting an ad. There are always cameras around when we speak they told the press.

Meanwhile, my friend and talk show host Dan Fagan also took up the cause, even to go so far as to call me sexist for saying that the commercial looked staged.

An incredulous Fagan went so far as to say, "*This* is why Andrew Halcro will *never* become governor." Fagan, for the only time in several months, directed his verbal spittle at someone besides Sarah. But the talk show host got it wrong yet again. While I disliked Andrew Halcro, the guy nailed the truth in this case, and no one—including the perennially Palin-bashing, persistently misguided Dan Fagan—believed him.

To drive home the point, campaign spokesman Curtis Smith issued a public statement: "There's no coordination. To imply that, is disingenuous." I don't believe Curtis knew what had actually taken place. Sarah encouraged these kinds of denials. In vain, I hoped this was a one-time affair.

———

I can only guess what went on in Sarah Palin's mind, but I am confident that she convinced herself that Knowles had conducted far worse campaign sins. On top of that, through no fault of her own, our campaign lagged far behind in both money and establishment support. To date, Knowles had spent $640,000, while we'd spent about $226,000. Even Halcro, though bringing up the rear in the race, had sunk more than $200,000 of his own money into his campaign. This hardly felt like a level playing field. We needed the extra help, and while not perfect, we remained—at least relatively speaking—the good guys. (Or, more accurately, I suppose, the *better* guys.) Eventually Sarah would convince herself nothing untoward was ever done, at least by her.

Within days, as the rhetoric died and the crisis faded, we breathed a bit easier. Thanks largely to Sarah's reputation for honesty, we Rag Tags survived the DNC and Halcro attacks.

However, survival did not include forgetting. It wasn't only the dishonesty that bothered me. The negativity in the RGA ads seemed to be the antithesis of what we'd preached so hard against for so long. Even Sarah's daughters weighed in—confirming that nobody in their right mind thought these were anything but attack ads. As Sarah wrote to us, *"Bristol and Willow are arguing it now—W says [the RGA commercial is] totally negative and to 'delete it now, Mom!,' and B says, 'Hey, it's free publicity.'"*

———

When Bristol said, "Hey, it's free publicity," she had no idea of the emotional and ethical price we paid to run those ads in the way we did. How could the campaign have been so blind? For hours on end, I continued to seek ways to rationalize away the reality. Part of me kept saying—even as I wrote this book—"Frank, you're wrong. Something is missing here, a mistake on your part." Could this be a simple public relations film that somehow got into the hands of the RGA and they used it in the same way a reporter might use a clip from a speech to set up a news story? Of course the answer was no, but that didn't keep the thought from festering.

When McGinniss released the unauthorized early text of *Blind Allegiance,* Palin supporters claimed that the evidence presented in the book was circumstantial and that "Sarah Palin would never do such things"—a comment I'd heard a hundred times before. While I knew my story was real and accurate, there would be no way, I thought, to convince critics; Sarah would likely treat the story as the ranting of a former employee, then play the victim and deny. That was, I suspected, one of the things I'd have to live with.

However, a strange thing happened on the way from leaked manuscript to final draft.

"You nailed it one hundred percent." So began an unsolicited response to my accounting of the RGA incident from a participant in the September fund-raiser for Sarah Palin at the Hotel Captain Cook in September 2006. As a result of the publicity from Joe McGinniss's actions, we were contacted by an individual—whose credentials we verified—working on behalf of the Republican Governors Association that day and the next.

"I wasn't paying attention to Frank Bailey," this individual said. "The person who seemed to be buzzing around Sarah Palin for the most part was Kris Perry. Kris and Sarah spent nearly an hour with the people from the RGA, coordinating the shoot along the east entrance. Sarah came in and out, in and out, in and out, just as Frank Bailey reported."

The team of RGA operatives, this person confirmed, communicated directly with Kris and Sarah, letting them know if and when a particular shot was in the can or in need of another take. They also filmed Sarah climbing from a car as if she were just arriving—scenes that I did not witness, likely because I was running late that day. According to this eyewitness, "Sarah very much cooperated with the film crew—wholeheartedly!"

Our source then said, "There was no question that Sarah knew full well who was filming her and why. She spoke to the crew, asking questions about what part of California we had traveled from to participate in the filming." Not only that, but Sarah and Kris were not alone in that knowledge.

As Sarah walked away, someone else on the film crew mockingly commented that with her enthusiasm for their efforts, "If this was a high school, she'd make a great cheerleading advisor."

Our source spoke of a second coordinated filming that was to take place the next day at a Republican Ladies fund-raiser at the prestigious and private Petroleum Club. Sarah, as I'd come to expect, in typical form arrived thirty minutes late, squandering the opportunity to stage additional footage. Had they used that footage instead of the Captain Cook take, it's likely I never would have discovered the ruse as I was not a participant in that event.

With nothing to gain personally from stepping forward, our eyewitness admitted, "I'm not a fan of Mr. Bailey," but felt it was important to set the record straight, especially in light of criticism from conservative commentators after the McGinniss leak.

For that honesty, all I can say is, "Thank you!"

The Republican Governors Association went on to spend hundreds of thousands of dollars on our behalf, blasting Tony Knowles while idolizing Sarah Palin. The whole time, lingering in my mind was how close we came to disaster. And for what? A camera angle to make Sarah Palin look more perfect, more intelligent, more serious, more ready to be governor? This stupid commercial frightened me; we might have derailed the entire campaign over such an inconsequential matter.

Later, even some supporters objected to the tone of the RGA ads. When a longtime Wasilla friend of Sarah's called her and suggested that many people were put off by the tenor of the commercials, Sarah—oblivious to how deeply deceptive she was becoming— whipped out her talking points and wrote to her friend:

> These aren't our ads. Our's are all local and they're very positive. . . .
> This ad Knowles is whining about is from the Republican Gover-
> nor's Association and it's illegal for us to coordinate with them . . .
> these groups run with whatever they want to run with. Kinda' like

the Democratic National Committee spending thousands of dollars in the negative push polls in Tony's race, and the DNC's thousands of dollars they're spending having two paid operatives camped out at the City of Wasilla for days on end trying to dig up dirt.

If this were my ad, it would have been a much better and clever ad.

As she'd done to Scott Heyworth when falsely suggesting that we had no influence on the content of letters to the editor, Sarah demonstrated a willingness to misrepresent the truth, this time to a dear friend. Sadly, I played along. To our little group, I wrote:

> While I hate to use TK's campaign as our measurement, it certainly isn't any more negative than his own commercial saying "This isn't a time for a Governor who needs on-the-job training" and "who isn't an experience negotiator." I really don't think its that bad . . . and I REALLY question if it COULD be construed as some kind of coordination if we told them to stop running them. Couldn't they capitalize on that?

At one point, we did ask the Alaska Public Offices Commission for a ruling on whether we could legally request the RGA to pull its ads. APOC director Brooke Miles responded that while coordination between an agency like the RGA and a campaign is not allowed, her staff would never blast a campaign for calling such a group and telling it to stop airing ads. "A person has the right to ask someone to stop something," she said. We pretended to not hear or comprehend that message and stuck with Bristol's advice that, hey, it's free publicity!

However, knowing what we'd done, covered up, and allowed to continue, the word that best sums up my emotions today is *disappointment*. And not just in Sarah. More so, I am disappointed in myself for having gotten it so wrong and later convincing myself that somehow this wasn't a big deal—that the end result justified any path we chose to get there. I'd bitten into that forbidden political apple and embraced a new, unstated slogan:

Truth optional. Win at all costs.

16

Hello, Governor

By the grace of God, I will not let Alaska down.
—SARAH PALIN, EMAIL TO RADIO HOST
DAN FAGAN ON ELECTION EVE

Frank," Scott Heyworth had said, "in the final ten days of a campaign, there's nothing more you can do. The airwaves are bought up, the flyers are out, the signs are up, and the money is all spent. All you can do is wave signs."

I thought about those words as I got out of bed before dawn on Election Day, Tuesday, November 7, 2006. There truly *was* almost nothing left to do except pray to Almighty God that Sarah would win. We'd done many regrettable things to get to this point, but all of us still believed in her mission to build a brighter future for our children. God willing, volunteers and voters were about to hand over the glass slipper that would complete this Cinderella story.

Around four thirty in the morning, with the temperature hovering around zero, I drove past The Intersection. Anyone who's ever worked on a campaign in Anchorage knows what I mean by The Intersection. This is where the New Seward Highway and Northern Lights Boulevard meet in a blizzard of frantic commuters. Seventy or eighty thousand cars drive by every day, passing our patch of sidewalk near the massive Sears Mall parking lot. During the campaign season, this innocent city block becomes a battleground of banner waving, horn-blowing, slogan-chanting partisans. A core of dedicated Palin volunteers had literally spent the night and camped out on the corner so we'd have the proverbial Boardwalk of campaign real estate, forcing Knowles to lay claim to a lesser space. The sea of red triumphed again.

Parking along Northern Lights Boulevard, I marveled at the dozen or so hardy souls already standing under the cold blue of the street-lights. They surged toward me as I delivered donuts and bagels. Once others arrived, some with young children, we poured coffee and hot chocolate from a thermos. Bundled in layers of bulky winter gear and breath turning to steam, they bounced on toes to keep warm while waving signs overhead. If a truck driver pulled the cord on his horn in short bursts of Sarah-support, a unified voice would respond, "Go, Sarah!" A driver delivering a thumbs-up received dozens in return, along with a "Whoo! Whoo! Whoo!" chorus.

With this corner hyperkinetically alive and well, by half past five I moved on to the corner of Benson Boulevard and Minnesota Drive. With its own tens of thousands of daily travelers, this scene was play-ing equally well for us. Approaching the small crowd, I recognized my brother Stevie handing out signs. Jogging in place and looking splendidly puffy in his padded North Slope arctic gear, only a postage stamp's worth of his face showed through the drawn hood. The sea of smiles suggested that even a wind chill of minus-ten degrees could not ice the excitement of this day for any of the congregated supporters. If these efforts were indicative, Palinmania was sweeping the state. On this day, a once-unknown former mayor from Wasilla was challeng-ing a former two-term governor who had every advantage imaginable except our enthusiasm and Sarah's charisma.

With ice crunching underfoot, I circled around the back of my pickup and retrieved several bulky four-by-eight signs from the truck bed. Working slowly through stiff joints, Steve and I mounted the larger posters as background billboards while volunteers held a hot beverage in one hand and a Palin placard in the other. Throughout the state, by six o'clock the morning commute had begun in earnest; street corners from Fairbanks, to the Mat-Su Valley, to Anchorage, Soldotna, Homer, and beyond were Palin red and vibrating with an-ticipation, mirroring our recent slogan for Sarah: "New Energy for Alaska." Our hope was that we'd motivate drivers who might be procrastinating to detour to their voting place and fill in the oval next to the name Palin.

With enthusiasm high, it became obvious there was no need for my cheerleading, so I left for the main campaign headquarters, noting on my smartphone a series of bullish, anecdotal reports from the valley. By all indications, we had the momentum. At our office, I entered to uncharacteristic silence. The piles of signs were gone and, except for strategists John Bitney and Mike Tibbles, who had their heads buried in folders, the rooms were empty. The two men stopped what was a whispered conversation once they saw me.

"What's going on?" I asked.

"Good things, my man, good things," said Bitney. As if choreographed, they flipped their folders bottom side up, but not before I saw the heading, "Transition," at the top of a cover page. Tibbles studied my face as if trying to read a reaction. The two men, referred somewhat pejoratively by long-term volunteers as "Tibbles 'n' Bits," simultaneously bobbed their heads in a silent signal while folding their hands. Tibbles flashed a quivering half smile I'd come to associate with nerves. Bitney forced a grin that looked as if it hurt his face.

"Aren't you going to help with the sign waving?" I asked. "We can use all the bodies we can get."

"Yeah, I guess I should probably do that, shouldn't I?" said Bitney. He didn't seem enthusiastic, and Tibbles remained silent. Both men, politically savvy and known for their ambition, clearly hadn't expected or welcomed my intrusion. With the polls showing us ahead, I understood that my two colleagues were already moving on. A win today meant that tomorrow would began what is known as transition, that two-month period during which the newly elected governor chose key personnel for jobs and cabinet positions in the upcoming administration.

I suddenly realized that these relative newcomers to our group—and political operatives to boot—were already plotting their own futures in the Palin administration. It dampened my spirits. What was to become of Sarah's Rag Tags after today? We weren't experienced in running government, but we'd been like family and through hard work and learning on the job, we'd done something remarkable in overwhelming the state's political machinery. I understood that Sarah needed experienced help, but she needed close confidants more. John Bitney? Mike Tibbles? Men like these were competent enough, but when push came to shove, would they hold their own ambition and welfare above all others? Bitney had once said to me, "Frank, do you realize how much money Sarah will be in control of if she's elected governor? It's in the neighborhood of thirteen billion dollars. That's billion, with a *b*!" I thought about that comment and understood that for some, this election was as much about dollars as message. Would these two men fall on their swords to protect our governor or her husband? My gut said no.

As for my own motivations, I hadn't volunteered exactly one year before to land a plum assignment if or when Sarah Palin won. Now I was suddenly feeling forced to look to the future through anxious eyes. Did I want this road to end, here, today, after the election results were finalized? With a million thoughts buzzing around in those brief moments, I realized that I desperately needed to continue on in close contact with my future governor and her administration. There was no desire to become a bureaucrat, but if that's what it took to help Sarah make a difference, then I'd do whatever was necessary. The missteps we'd taken these last months were merely growing pains. My desire was to take new insights and use them to protect Sarah and be that commonsense voice to counteract individuals like these two sitting tight lipped across from me.

Sarah had promised that she would find jobs for most of us, but it seemed a generalized proposal that I took on faith. In my imagination, I'd be assigned tasks similar to those I'd assumed during the campaigns, including troubleshooting, locating and cutting waste, and being a supportive sounding board for Sarah in times of stress. What did I need to know about running government to take on these important duties?

"Listen," I said, doing my best to pretend that I had no negative thoughts about interloping professionals, "I'm gonna take off, check on the other offices, and make sure we've got rides for everyone, coffee, hot chocolate—"

"Yeah, you do that, Frank. Mike and I have some numbers to crunch. You know."

Yeah, I thought, *I know, all right*. After grabbing a pile of phone messages from an in-box, I about-faced, hastened for the exit, and breathed in the refreshingly frigid air. It felt good to be away from that disheartening scene and back to what really mattered most: working with *real* Alaskans.

A quick stop at our other Anchorage campaign headquarters, was more positive. Our office manager, and semiretired engineer Mary Havens, had the place humming. Her small stature did not diminish the confidence she instilled in others. "This day has finally come, Frank," she said in that hard to believe voice of a child on Christmas morning. "Just look at all those people, so happy. Twenty hour days, all for this moment."

We shared upbeat reports that we'd heard filtering from word of mouth and discussed the need to paste our newly printed Thank You stickers across our larger signs. As for retrieving the other thirteen thousand signs of all shapes and sizes decorating the state? That would be a massive undertaking for another day. Suffice it to say, with the help of extraordinary talents like Mary Havens, we had an overwhelming victory in the statewide sign war, with advantages of two to one in Anchorage, five to one on the Kenai Peninsula, three to one in Kodiak, three to one in Fairbanks, and twenty to one in the Mat-Su Valley.

My number-one job on Election Day became the same as my number-one job for most of the past year. I'd convey to those volunteers how valuable their sacrifice was to both me and Sarah. And after all these months, it still amazed me how motivating these simple words became. This made my more than one hundred and fifty hours a month on the phone worthwhile.

Sean Parnell's people were down at the next corner, waving signs. Because Sarah had been less than impressed with Parnell's effort, this came as a pleasant surprise. Since Sarah was stuck with him these next four years, I hoped this marked a positive new beginning.

After lunchtime, Sarah arrived at the corner of New Seward and Northern Lights to greet the crowd and wave signs. As she pulled up in her black VW Jetta, she was being interviewing over the phone by Dan Fagan. With the victory appearing close at hand, the talk show host had gone from totally negative to a position of passive-aggressive support. He was saying something like, "I hate Sarah's stance on the oil companies, but we should vote for her because of her stance on social issues. Also, she'll select judges we can live with. Do we want Tony Knowles doing that?" Unbelievably, only days earlier he had suggested that listeners vote for Knowles, saying, "At least we know what we'll get. With Sarah, she'll lock out the oil companies, and business in Alaska will dry up." From my truck, as I listened on the radio to the interview, I thought that Sarah sounded energized and handled herself well. I gave her a thumbs-up when she got off the call. Without missing a beat, we grabbed a couple of Palin signs and headed toward the excited crowd.

What I saw back at campaign headquarters was still gnawing at my gut, so I took the opportunity to nervously ask her thoughts on transition. I let her know that Mike Tibbles and John Bitney were going through the folder when I'd stopped in at headquarters. She placed her hand next to her mouth and leaned in, whispering, "I think transition needs to be you, me, and Tibbles, but only because he's done this before." She was wary to discuss transition, she said, because she didn't want to jinx anything. Her brief explanation relaxed me completely. The job I most wanted, as confidant to Sarah, was secure. What a day this was turning out to be.

The events over the next hours felt like Mardi Gras, a whirl of partying, giddiness, anticipation, and hope. All my up-and-down concerns over the last eleven months vanished. We had only the present and the future, and those couldn't be looking better.

———

For election night, we went back to the good-luck Hotel Captain Cook. Neen was in the room I'd booked for us, putting a few things away and ordering dinner, when I received a call. It was Mitt Romney's assistant. He said that things looked close but recent polling showed that Sarah would likely be governor by the end of the night. "Thank Governor Romney. We're praying he's right."

Around seven thirty, just before the polls closed, we gathered in the ballroom. While Alaskans tend toward informality on nearly all occasions, there was a joyful red formality in tonight's outfits, with men largely sporting coats and ties, and women adorned in dresses and sparkling jewels. We positioned buttons, bumperstickers, and those New Energy for Alaska signs behind the podium, where television cameras would pick them up once Sarah gave her victory speech.

Throughout the evening and into the night, I maneuvered through the crowd, shaking hands and listening gratefully to people's compliments and congratulations. "You did an amazing thing." "This must feel good, Frank." When anyone said, "She's gonna win this thing, Frank," I put a finger to my mouth and say, "Shhh. Don't wanna jinx this."

At one point, Anita Halterman, a dedicated campaign worker who later worked closely with John Bitney came up and hugged me. "So do you know what you'll be doing if she wins?" she asked.

"No, not really. Let's just get through tonight."

"Well," she said, matter-of-factly, "Bitney is telling people that Sarah promised he'd be deputy chief of staff ."

"Oh, really? Okay." My words tumbled from my mouth.

Bitney was saying one thing, telling people he was slated for the significant role as Deputy COS once Sarah was sworn in, while only earlier in the day she had downplayed to me his significance. I believed Sarah but did not doubt that a political vulture like Bitney would be spreading such a rumor, hoping it would generate support. Both he and Tibbles were professionals and had learned the art of manipulation from some of the best in the business. But, then again, Sarah often changed her mind about important issues, sometimes in midsentence. I wondered if in the end she might change course and select her political operatives. Was I headed for the Christmas card list?

"Sa-*rah*! Sa-*rah*! Sa-*rah*!"

The chants brought me back into the moment. Trust—all I could do was trust in Sarah's loyalty. No non-family member had been on the inside longer, so there was no rational reason for me to suddenly feel insecure. I grabbed my laptop and headed off to the left of the stage to set up and check the numbers as they rolled in. Resuming the same drill I'd carried out during the primary, I clicked the Refresh button like an obsessive-compulsive and waited. It was a foregone conclusion that we'd sweep Mat-Su, the Kenai Peninsula, and my hometown of Kodiak. With the exception of the Dillingham area, where Todd grew up, I knew that rural Alaska would embrace Knowles. While the votes in each village were relatively small, the towns numbered in the hundreds. Southeast Alaska, with approximately 17 percent of the state's population, would likely tilt to Knowles.

Everything pointed toward Anchorage as the make-or-break region; if we held close, we'd win. If Knowles carried the city by a large margin, it might be a long night. I felt the knot in my throat tighten with each fresh computer screen shot.

Finally, KTUU announced the results. I'd labored for this day for over a year. As I readied to celebrate, I sought to control my trembling hands and wipe dry my moist eyes. I turned to Sarah and, my voice cracking, said the words "Hello, *Governor* Palin." It sounded odd, like the first time someone introduced my wife as "Mrs. Bailey." Confetti filled the air and voices sang our new governor's name. As Sarah rose, I was magnetically swept along.

Once assembled on stage and looking down at the cheering throng, Kris Perry stepped in as master of ceremonies. It bothered me that my tongue immediately tied itself into a thick knot whenever addressing a crowd. I would have loved to thank our supporters. Eventually Sarah took the podium and unsuccessfully gestured for the "Sa-*rah!*" chants to subside.

Someone with a booming voice yelled, "Are you ready for new energy, Alaska?" The room shook with enthusiasm.

Off to the side, I had barely enough time to catch my breath before people were pressing up to me. Many already had an agenda. We'd been declared victors less than an hour earlier, and special interests were already leaning into my ear with laundry lists of requests. One after the other, including people whose names I couldn't even attach to their faces. If this was what it was like for little ol' Frank Bailey, I wondered if Sarah had any idea of the pressure she'd face beginning tomorrow morning. I now knew that she needed her Rag Tag filter more than ever.

On the march to Egan Center's Election Central, the masses pushed forward in the hopes of brushing close to a jubilant governor-elect. Our red parade arrived to thunderous cheers and sharp whistles. Funneled to the tiny channel 13 platform, Sarah gave her first TV interview as Alaska's next chief executive. The larger stations, channels 2 and 11 in a perpetual battle for ratings and political access, looked on enviously.

We were told that a bitter Tony Knowles had already left the building, not interested in conceding. Our winning margin of 7.5 percent was an embarrassment and an unhappy end to an overly long career.

An hour or two later, once I'd returned to my room at the hotel, I found myself unable to stay awake and watch continuing election interviews. I fell into bed next to my wife, who, because of the massive yearlong commitment, had become too much of a stranger. Sadly, I could say the same of my children. I promised myself that things would change for the better for all of us, personally and politically. Sacrifices and shortcuts would come to an end. Making it all worthwhile, Alaskans would finally have an advocate and fighter running the state. I remembered what Sarah had emailed to Dan Fagan when he came over to our side just days ago: *"Dan, Thank you. By the grace of God I will not let Alaska down."*

With a heavy arm draped across my already sleeping spouse, I closed my eyes and dreamed of those better days.

17

Job to Nowhere

[T]hese guys piss me off with this last round of
rumormongering . . . forgive me for cussing . . .
dang it. Politics suck because you can't trust
anyone . . . I need . . . Godly people close to me.
—SARAH PALIN, EMAILS SENT TO
FRANK BAILEY, DECEMBER 31, 2006

The Wednesday morning after the election, November 8, Sarah
called a meeting in her midtown Anchorage headquarters. Included were Todd Palin, John Bitney, Mike Tibbles, Spokesman
Curtis Smith, me, and a few of Lieutenant Governor Sean Parnell's people. The agenda called for forming a transition team that
would address eventual appointments to the administration cabinet, key commissioners, departmental deputies, and their staffs ahead
of Sarah's December 4, 2006, swearing in. Because many of us had
been promised only vague future roles—and we understood that Sarah's plans might shift from inhale to exhale—stomachs were churn-
ing. Kris Perry, one of Sarah's closest confidants during the campaign,
wasn't invited. What's more, both Sarah and Todd had suddenly
been avoiding her, suggesting she was being subjected to a passive-
aggressive, cold-shouldered good-bye. Full of my own anxieties, I reas-
sured Kris that her fears were unfounded. Eventually Kris was given a
role in planning the inauguration ceremony and later became director
of the Anchorage office, but only after Todd told me during this meeting that she could return only if "she left her drama behind."

From the moment that Sarah and I intersected in the parking lot
ahead of the meeting, it was obvious her "Don't-cross-me" quills were

raised. During the campaign, Todd would have phoned ahead and warned, "Sarah's in a shit mood. Don't let her hear or see anything that might set her off." I was sitting in my pickup when she drove up in her Jetta, parked nearby, and climbed out. Ahead of her, I crossed the snow-dusted asphalt with plowed, dirty snow piled high like winter haystacks.

Beneath a gray sky, I passed the martial arts studio next to our single-story office in a strip mall on the corner of East Thirty-fourth Avenue and Fairbanks Street. Despite the hour, ten o'clock, behind our offices the Moose's Tooth Pub and Pizzeria was already baking the best pizza in the state. Normally the aroma started my stomach growling, but listening to Sarah yell at one of her kids set my stomach growling in another, less pleasant way. Her angry voice contrasted sharply with the sound of children playing in the snow at a day care center a few doors down. As she snapped off her phone and approached the sidewalk where I waited, she greeted me by complaining about her children being a pain before going on to gripe about incessant calls.

"The phone won't stop ringing! These people think because they supported me, they can just call anytime they want!" I thought to myself, *What did you expect, Sarah? You were just elected governor of Alaska in a landslide, and people love you. Is that so bad?* But I wisely said nothing, nodding in faux sympathy. "I can't believe how everyone is asking for something from me already," she continued sharply.

Dressed in jeans with her hair pulled up, she stomped her boots to remove slush and stepped broadly through the front door. Several volunteers who were working on post-campaign cleanup rose from their wobbling chairs at folding tables and began applauding in admiration and respect, as if this were an official coronation. But Sarah brushed right by them, her eyes fixed straight ahead. I kept my distance while acknowledging, shaking hands, hugging, and thanking those who had spent so many hours helping us win the election. As Sarah whisked past, her indifference to loyal followers reminded me of the earlier refusal to visit eighty-year-old Eagle River volunteer extraordinaire Marvin Morrisett. We were but one day removed from the thunderous victory applause by these same tireless workers, and it appeared as if there was a new motto: in with the new and out with the old.

Not long after the meeting attendees arrived, we assembled in an open area with folding chairs arranged in a circle. Sarah dropped her large red bag, which doubled as a purse and briefcase, at her feet and waited impatiently for us to pour coffee and grab Costco cookies left over from the previous night's festivities.

Everyone looked heavy lidded from a late night of watching the returns, while Sarah's scowl and pinched brow left no doubt about her disposition. If we'd hoped to ride a day or two of euphoria after a hard-fought victory, we were immediately disabused.

Pale with Albino white hair, a youthful Mike Tibbles jumped in and began asserting himself, rifling through a list of bureaucrats who should be kept (because they "aren't political") and those who shouldn't (because they "are political"). For a man as political as Tibbles, what this probably meant were those he could control versus those he could not. In short order, Sarah named him director of transition (and soon thereafter designated him future chief of staff). My heart sank. This former Binkley advisor attacked our campaign viciously one day then joined up for position and money the next. Wasn't he the type of professional we had promised to replace once in office? Additionally, Tibbles showed no concern for the grassroots volunteers, an early administration red flag. Yet Sarah embraced him wholeheartedly. After he'd orchestrated the attack ads against Sarah in the primary, I'd confronted him and told him that he was "going down." How wrong I was.

Without missing a beat, Tibbles—who would have to wait a few weeks for his own appointment to COS—immediately recommended that another bureaucrat, fifty-four-year-old Mike Nizich, be named deputy chief of staff. Tibbles suggested that because Nizich had worked in the administrations of five different governors—including the two we'd just defeated, Murkowski and Knowles—his "bureaucratic fortitude" would be a valuable asset. On its face, the man's entrenched career made him seem like he should be Sarah's least likely appointee; throughout the campaign she wore out our ears with "We will bring in new faces, new ideas."

When she endorsed the always-been-there-in-government Nizich nomination, I stuffed a cookie into my mouth to keep from yelling, "What about all our promises? No, no, no, no!" We were twelve hours into the formation of the Palin administration, and our assurances of no more career politicians and lobbyists were being vaporized. In moving from campaign to governing, down was now the new up. If the likes of Kris Perry (and me) survived until inauguration, we'd be reporting not to Sarah but to Tibbles, someone she'd once cursed as an unethical evildoer for his painful and deceiving campaign ads. This new inner circle would become the "Juneau-ites" that Todd, who remained silent throughout this meeting, would later grumble were "just humping her leg."

During the forty-minute meeting, I was given the title of deputy director for the transition team, for which I was to recruit, conduct background research, and pour over resumes from potential members of the incoming administration. No mention was made of a role for me once the Palin team officially took office in less than a month.

For the next three weeks, I waited and watched as Tibbles engineered future positions for those he favored. When my name was not one of them, with pounding head and heart I approached Sarah and her chief of staff in our Anchorage offices. Knowing that Sarah was typically in a "mood" these days as inauguration pressures mounted, I tiptoed as if through broken glass to plead my case. Failing to convey the casual tone I desired, I asked, "Sarah, have you thought about where I might fit into the administration?"

With that too-busy-to-be-bothered shrug, she replied bluntly, "I don't know."

"With my background, I thought *efficiency auditor* of some sort." In a briskly worded run-on sentence, I explained that while it would take some time, I had a passion for streamlining operations and saving money, like I had for the campaign—when we had few resources. I'd done this previously at Alaska Airlines, managing a million-dollar budget. Whatever Sarah might have thought, Tibbles dismissed the notion, saying only, "That's not going to work."

A few days later, I expressed interest in becoming deputy commissioner of administration. This position, I contended, would take advantage of my information technology and human resources experience in the airline industry and called for skills that I'd demonstrated throughout the campaign. Tibbles belittled the suggestion. His ticket to influencing what confederate Bitney once claimed was $13 billion under the governor's control seemed reason enough to deny me any significant role.

Over the next weeks, jobs in the administration filled up quickly. Bitney was named to the cabinet as director of legislative affairs. Another name that would figure prominently in Sarah's future was her new communications director, Meg Stapleton, a former KTUU television reporter. Ivy Frye was named director of boards and commissions, a cabinet-level position responsible for recruiting and screening applicants for a cross section of government jobs and commission appointments.

———

With the inauguration imminent, Sarah's moods swung wildly but tilted toward feeling overwhelmed. She acted put upon, often angry, and stressed to the point of chipping. Sean Parnell sent Sarah an innocent heads-up about the scheduled open house at the twenty-six-room governor's mansion in Juneau in December, suggesting that she have staff attend to the details. Sarah responded: *"I am swamped Sean, and there's been lots of assumptions that I have all the info. on upcoming events. I don't. and I need to plan for many things (even around Todd having to go back to the slope this week), including organizing four kids and their futures in the next four years."*

Curiously, she copied me on her reply, as well as Tibbles, Bitney, Ivy, and Kris Perry, as if to make certain that we all knew what a terrible life she was now leading. Sarah made it sound as if she'd just unhappily learned she was going to be governor of Alaska, when, of course, she'd been planning for this for more than a year. A little later, when names of commissioners and deputy commissioners leaked to the media ahead of formal announcements, finding out who was responsible once again took priority over all else. She wrote Tibbles—but, interestingly, not Bitney—of her findings, while blind-cc-ing several others, including me, about one potential hire in particular: Karen Rehfeld for director of the Office of Management and Budget (OMB).

> at hockey game last night a guy approached to ask if I was hiring Rehfeld for OMB. I asked how he had heard such a thing because I hadn't announced it. He said he heard it from Bitney. there again, it's not a good thing to have folks talking before I'm ready to make any announcements. wonder why Bitney would have spoken to people about it . . . and I perhaps Bitney should not have been told of the intention to hire Rehfeld? Who did he hear it from?

In demanding to know who had told Bitney about the OMB hiring, Sarah was sending a warning that she'd find the culprit and deal with him or her in due course. Since I was still without an assignment after the first of the year, my insecurities led me to conclude that Sarah, by blind-copying me, suspected my involvement in the information leak. Ivy Frye, also one of the email's recipients, likewise grew concerned. When I wrote Sarah directly, letting her know I hadn't even been aware of Rehfeld's status, she came back with one of her simultaneously hard and soft replies (emphasis is mine):

> No Frank . . . no one is "giving me the impression that you are not trustworthy here" . . . that is why *I blind cc'd you on this latest episode—because I trust you.* Quit being paranoid. I cc'd you because Bitney was obvioulsy the leak and I was dinging him on it and I blind copied you so that you'd be in the loop with me on this. . . .
> Either I cc you guys on these things or I keep them to myself and I try to work through these by myself. Maybe it will be easier and less "sensitive" if I do just keep information to myself and I attempt to wade through who's doing what and who's saying what by myself.

In response, I did my best to put this to rest—while expressing my current distrust of Ivy in maintaining confidentialities: *"I got a little 'confuzzled' when you fyi'd me and Ivy together about leaking info. . . .*

Sorry . . . she's not company i'm 100% comfortable in keeping. I'll take off my tin-foil hat and say three times 'I'm not paranoid.' "

Sarah claimed that her cc's were all part of a calculated strategy when she wrote: *"ccing Ivy is our way of reminding her she'd better not screw up with 'leaks' of her own."* In other words, Sarah copied me because I held her trust, but she copied Ivy because she did *not* trust her. If I'd had enough guts, I would have requested the Sarah Palin secret-email cc decoder ring.

On November 11, week two of her pending administration, the *Anchorage Daily News* reported a scheduling change for the inauguration before it was official. Sarah, in a now-patterned response, let us know how incensed she was over the leak: *"[The leak] was a quick lesson for me that NOTHING is confidential . . . between that and the comments i'm receiving about my 'chief of staff' and other positions supposedly already filled, I will remain as tight-lipped as possible through this transition."*

As these distractions assumed disproportionate importance, someone should have asked, *Who cares?* We had a four-year commitment ahead of us, and here we were trying to track down leaks on appointments and swearing-in dates and times. As if this wasn't eating up enough time, we never did cease scrutinizing radio critics Dan Fagan and Rick Rydell, ex-opponent and blogger Andrew Halcro, and the biased reporting of the *Daily News*. Sarah eventually wanted others closely monitored, including state senate president Lyda Green and Linda Kellen Biegel, a blogger who calls herself Celtic Diva. When radio host and critic Shannyn Moore disagreed with the governor on nearly every issue, Sarah believed she understood why: *"The only time I met her, I think she told me she was Miss Homer(?) and we were in a pageant together (Miss Alaska), which don't remember—I think she was insulted that I couldn't remember her."* There was, it turned out, a good reason for Sarah not to remember Shannyn: Shannyn Moore never was in the Miss Alaska pageant. Within months, the list would grow exponentially.

———

By Inauguration Day, Sarah was as crazed as in the final days of the election. Todd stepped back in and repeated earlier instructions for us to back off and cease bothering her. *"[Sarah] has alot of pressure on HER,"* he emailed. *"Getting prepared for her [inaugural speech] tomorrow is no easy task, please allow her to concentrate on that task with out any distractions. End of story."*

———

At one point in late December, Sarah said to me, "Frank, I want you to be wherever I'll be. I just don't know whether that's in Juneau or Anchorage yet." Yet by January 2007, Chief of Staff Tibbles had yet to find me a job in the new administration. Where I once received up to two thousand emails a month from Sarah and the staff, I was down to fifty or so a week. With every passing day, I felt that a return to being a simple man, living a modest life, was inevitable.

By this time, the positions of responsibility were mostly filled. With my feeling that at least one foot was already out the door, Sarah finally and suddenly took initiative on my behalf.

On January 7, she let me know that she had told Tibbles not to put me off any longer. She also told him in no uncertain terms to get it done today.

With his back to the wall, the next day Tibbles assigned me a position he likely hoped I'd reject: assistant to the commissioner of the Department of Administration (DOA). Not director or deputy director, but assistant—way down in the administration food chain. For all intents, I'd been pushed aside—out of sight, out of mind—but not quite pushed out. On the positive side, however, in the DOA I'd be largely shielded from Sarah's chaotic management style, the frantic phone calls, and the knee-jerk reactionary stuff that filled our days and nights. Helping to ease my mind, given Sarah's dizzying mood shifts, I suspected that my hiatus would be temporary.

I told myself there were worse things than learning a new job in a plush office. I'd bide my time, do my best, and trust in God that this was part of His plan.

———

I moved into the Robert B. Atwood Building in downtown Anchorage—home to many of the state's governmental offices, and, at twenty stories, the second-tallest building in the entire state. The distance between Anchorage and Juneau was roughly six hundred miles, but I might as well have been a million miles from the Capitol Building where, on the third floor, Sarah, Todd, and Mike Tibbles wielded their powerful hands in running the state. By February, contact with Sarah, Ivy, Kris, and others started trickling in, never surpassing a handful of emails in a given week. Other grassroots folks who had once been instrumental in Sarah's election expressed concern that they could not get a return call or email for months on end. Prudently, I put my nose down and worked hard while enjoying the nineteenth floor view of Cook Inlet and Sleeping Lady Mountain.

Despite the breathtaking scenery, the work was not good for my ADD self. There were many fine and wonderful people who loved their lives working in administration, but for me, having been at the center of the drive to put a modern-day Queen Esther on her gubernatorial throne, I felt like my usefulness had ended. At our best during the campaign, we felt like family, even when dealing with multiple (and often unnecessary) daily crises. Here the dim lights and insulation from the political frenzy felt sterile. Where were all the phone calls and emails calling for immediate action?

In March, sheer boredom eroded my intentions to wait this out. Never comfortable with inaction, I decided I'd rather end the ride than work in a job that did not seem to directly effect real change for Alaska. For days I reworked a respectfully blunt message, and on March 7, 2007, I finally held my breath, typed in Sarah's email address, attached the letter, and with a hesitant index finger hit Send.

Sarah,
I've wrestled with this for quite a while now, sought Godly counsel, prayed about it, and now it is time for me to clear the slate. I do want you to know that what I'm about to say comes from the backdrop that I have and will always have huge admiration for you and support what you are doing.

Sarah, I was patient. A few weeks of unreturned phone calls from Mike went by before I brought it to you. I know how busy you were then. I've always known that. It is always my LAST resort to ever take up your time. I know how busy you are now and that makes this tougher to send even at this late date. But I need to say this. . . . I need you to know how this went down and see this from my eyes.

So Mike called me back and said that he was offering me the Special Assistant. I said "Mike, I'm feeling a little awkward here because I didn't do this for a job. I did it to make a difference. So I am grateful, yes, but what I can tell about that job (Special Assistant) is that I don't really have the responsibility to make the difference that I want to. Can you check on the Dep. Commish job and get back with me?"

He said he would call me back Monday. He did not.

Instead, Todd called Monday night and asked why I had turned down a job. He made it clear that I was being ungrateful, and that many others didn't get the opportunity to work immediately in the transition position. I reminded Todd that a year ago, when no one else followed through on their word to help out, it was me, Kris, Clark, and Kerm. Period. That's not ungrateful. That is a fact. I didn't have to work for free. I CHOSE to work for free, and later just to cover expenses. I worked my BUTT off. . . . Sarah, we had 80+ hour weeks over and over and over again this summer. That was a blow to be considered ungrateful by a Palin. A big one.

One of Todd's points was "Do you think you can handle testifying in front of [Senate Democratic Leader] Hollis French?" My response was, "I'd do it just like every other new thing I've done this year. Did I think I could pick up the phone and call Wally Hickel and ask for his endorsement?" I was rarely afraid of a new challenge. What I lacked in experience I always compensated for in effort. Always. . . .

So my question is this, Sarah. I fought for you. Why didn't you fight for me? I'm left with the impression that you didn't. Why believe the nay sayers on my abilities? I know I didn't have Juneau experience or State experience, but I thought I proved my value throughout the campaign that I could learn anything and do it well. You constantly preached how you couldn't read folks minds,

and I was clear with what I wanted to you and Tibbles, and none of
the options were afforded me (Boards & Commissions, DOA Dep
Commish, DOT Dep Commish). Why were the grass roots efforts
good enough to win you the Primary and General, but not good
enough to excel in bringing new energy to Juneau and set the standard for state government?

This is not about a position. It is not about money. I fought hard
to make a difference. Instead I have been insulated away into a
comfortable non-policy making position. It was clear that Tibbles
and Bits didn't want me remotely near you. . . . This was their political decision to veer away from the homegrown uphill path of your
campaign.

I'm wired to make a difference Sarah, yet you put those who had
been my adversaries (Bitney and Tibbles) in charge of placing me
into a "thanks very much" job. Remember that I was constantly
on Bitney's case for what I called "setting you up to fail" by spending his time talking with lobbyist when he should've been preparing debate points? Or remember the weekend before the primary?
Who called Tibbles, got in his face on the phone, and asked how he
could, with a straight face, put out a mailer so slanderous that was
misleading and obviously not current? His comment to me was "I'm
not going to share my strategy with you. . . ."

When we at your kitchen table in March were telling you "You
can do this," they were saying that you couldn't, and that you didn't
have enough experience. . . . I just wanted to make a difference.
I will, of course, continue to work hard and do my best as Special Assistant, but my wiring won't keep me here. I absolutely want
to see you THRIVE and SUCCEED as our governor and I can't
do that from my beautiful 19th floor office with a view. Maybe it
sounds ungrateful, but really what it is, is me being real with you.
I am totally grateful, but I didn't want a "thank you job." I wanted
to be a part of "Take a Stand" and "New Energy for Alaska" Again,
I appreciate you taking me along for the ride and the appreciation
you shared with many regarding my role with your campaign. I just
really struggle with how I was handled in the end.

This letter while blunt is sent with respect Sarah. I look forward to your response.

In the subject, line, I asked Sarah to please treat this email as confidential, wanting especially to keep it from Todd, whose passions tended to run from overheated to scalding. Sarah, however, decided not to honor that request and sent my email and her response to Todd and Tibbles. Her blunt apology left me sensing that I had few Rag Tag days left:

From: Sarah Palin
Created: 3/8/2007 7:08:39 AM
Frank—I apologize for whatever I've done to make you feel you weren't "handled right" at the end. You know that's not my intention.

I will ask Todd about making you feel uncomfortable, for that "big blow." I know Todd. He probably wanted to just get to the bottom of the issue and deal with it and skip all the peripheral parts—he no doubt just wanted to ask the question and then state his case that there ARE SO MANY people everyday asking for something. . . . Many [requests] were reasonable, some make no sense if everyone truly has the same goal: to do God's will, to serve the people of this state in whatever capacity is available.

You accuse me of not "fighting for you" . . . believe me, I did.

I will go back to the drawing board and start asking around again about other positions. Frank, the job description you wrote for yourself wasn't going to work through in a newly-created position. The duties you described could work beautifully, though, in the special assistant assignment you were offered and accepted. I am reading a book right now called "You Don't Need a Title to be a Leader" and it can explain much better than I the principal that I'm trying to get across re: a person's ability to make a difference where you are today.

Additionally: I trust Tibbles . . . [and] Bitney. I will defend them against any accusatory tone—specifically anything Tibbles did in the campaign for the candidate who had hired him to get him elected. And I am thankful for Tibbles, and for Bitney, who have worked non-stop to un-do so many Murkowski blunders and help usher in needed changes so we can start to move forward. I thank God for them and everyone else God has brought together to build a team to serve. Including you and 'Neen.

And so, glad that I'd found the courage to express my heart, I returned to the Department of Administration, waiting for that call signaling either another job or a pink slip. But by late May, I realized rightly so that she had other priorities. At peace with that, I sought out options outside of state government. The Grace Alaska Foundation, a charity associated with my church, ChangePoint, approached me about becoming its executive director, and we entered into preliminary discussions that continued into July. In addition, Neen and I began a two-month process of purchasing two small coffee stands. All the while, my closest confidante from the past remained Kris Perry. Aware of my intention to return to the private sector, in mid-July she phoned, explaining that she'd told Sarah I was planning to leave.

"Frank, Sarah's upset. She doesn't want you to go."

"Kris, I'm doing nothing for her—"

"Sarah wants you to fly to Juneau with her. You two can talk this out."

Kris explained that we'd all go and meet Michael W. Smith, a popular evangelical musician who'd been an inspiration of mine since the age of fifteen. I immediately agreed.

A few days later, Kris, Sarah, and I flew on the state's King Air to Juneau. Sarah spoke of old times, loyalties, friendships, and the need to keep her team together. When we arrived in the capital, we spent an hour or so with Michael W. Smith. Then, unexpectedly, Sarah had me attend a high-level meeting with her, Mike Tibbles, Kris Perry, Fisheries Policy Advisor Cora Crome, and Ivy Frye, the director of boards and commissions.

We discussed one judge appointment and a wide-ranging list of board appointees. After a short while, Ivy was asked to leave the room. The moment she was out the door, Sarah said, "Frank,

Ivy's done a half-assed job getting us input for this judge appointment, and she does not take criticism from me."

She went on to explain her frustration with Ivy's process of vetting the most important appointments a governor gets to make: Alaska's judges. The way Alaska's judicial appointments are made is absolutely fascinating, and I quickly learned that the problem revolved around Ivy's workload more than her willingness to vet the candidates. Between 250 to 300 appointments that needed to be made per year and an office at the time of one (just her), her workload was insurmountable. Nevertheless, it was Ivy's turn to get frozen out.

Within a week of our Juneau trip, Mike Tibbles phoned. "Frank, Sarah wants to know if you'd consider joining the governor's office."

I now owned two coffee stands and was sitting on a potentially exciting offer from the Grace Alaska Foundation. "Mike, I'm not sure I can—"

"She wants to replace Ivy. Sarah wants you to take over as director of boards and commissions. Immediately."

"I'll need a few days to discuss this with Neen."

My wife and I were torn, especially knowing that this would put renewed burdens on her with family *and* a new business. Sarah, who had left me dangling for months, suddenly needed me "immediately." At the annual Governor's Family Picnic only days later, she had Sean Parnell's deputy chief of staff, Kris Showalter, track me down. By the time Sarah caught up with me, she was all warmth and charm.

"So, Frank, does this mean you'll stay? You'll come, help us? We need you."

She was practically begging me to take on a major responsibility.

Unable to resist, I said, "Yes, I'll stay."

All my prior reservations vanished. Agreeing to return felt good. No, it felt *great*. Back in the game, my heart beat with the same anticipation I had the first day I met Sarah when she invited me to the paint-a-thon where I'd met her family and then went home in splattered jeans. In my eternal optimism, the disappointing past—which was full of contradictions and compromise, false hope, and promises—all vanished. All I saw was, once again, the brilliance of our future.

As I analyze those days of reconciliation, there is no question that plans to leave her played a part in Sarah's sudden need to bring me home. Maybe she feared letting go of someone so well versed in her darker secrets? It's possible.

However, I believe that there was another equally important reason.

A couple of months before offering me Ivy's old job, an unlikely burgeoning friendship began. Todd Palin had a project of vital importance. He'd gone to Mike Tibbles and Attorney General Talis Colberg, but found their effectiveness lacking. As I'd become the Palins' "old reliable," he recruited me for a crusade that became an obsession for him and, in short order, for me.

Our shared insanity, I believe, was at least partly responsible for my political rebirth. When our actions blew up in my face more than a year later, the fallout would lead to personal heartache, making me long for a chance to go back in time to the Governor's Picnic and say to Sarah, "Thanks, but no thanks," on that job to nowhere. Instead I was about to become exhibit A in a miserable saga known universally as Troopergate.

PART THREE

Troopergate and Other "Crap Clusters"

18

How Does Firing Trooper Wooten Make Us Safer?

As you can imagine, we're pretty incensensed by this
whole episode. Sarah obviously didn't drop Monegan
over a personal vendetta against Wooten.
—CHUCK HEATH JR., SARAH PALIN'S BROTHER,
EMAIL IN RESPONSE TO CRITICISM BY BLOGGER
AND FORMER CANDIDATE FOR GOVERNOR,
ANDREW HALCRO, WEDNESDAY, JULY 19, 2008

On October 11, 2008, Sarah Palin was less than six weeks into serving as Republican presidential nominee Senator John McCain's running mate. Standing in front of dozens of cameras and microphones, she declared in her isn't-this-great-news? voice, "Well, I'm very pleased to be cleared of any legal wrongdoing . . . any hint of any kind of unethical activity there."

The infamous *Stephen Branchflower Report to the Legislative Council* had just been released, and the governor was conducting a news conference via phone to explain her jubilant reaction to the findings. In summing up matters, she reiterated, "very pleased to be cleared of any of that."

The Branchflower investigation that Sarah so blithely suggested cleared her name began in August when the Alaska Legislative Council hired independent counsel Stephen Branchflower to investigate whether the Palin administration and staff, including me, exercised inappropriate influence on Department of Public Safety (DPS) Commissioner Walt Monegan by pressuring him to fire Alaskan State

Trooper Mike Wooten; when Monegan refused, he was eventually removed from office. Wooten, formerly married to Sarah's younger sister Molly McCann, had a history of run-ins with Sarah's family, including a bitter divorce and custody dispute with Molly dating back to 2005.

What Sarah neglected to mention in that conference call was that while, yes, investigator Branchflower found that the firing of Monegan "was a proper and lawful exercise of her constitutional and statutory authority," Governor Palin also "knowingly permitted a situation to continue where impermissible pressure was placed on several subordinates to advance a personal agenda, to wit: to get Trooper Michael Wooten fired." And "although Walt Monegan's refusal to fire Trooper Wooten was not the sole reason he was fired by Governor Sarah Palin, it was likely a contributing factor to his termination as Commissioner of Public Safety." The findings further concluded that Sarah "permitted Todd Palin to use the Governor's office . . . to continue to contact subordinate state employees in an effort to find some way to get Trooper Wooten fired." Hence, Troopergate.

For Sarah, once she said, "cleared of *any* wrongdoing," the words assumed written-in-stone status inside her head, and devoted followers joined her in wholeheartedly embracing her innocence and near martyrdom at the hands of abusive critics. This time, however—since I was at the epicenter of much of this controversy and knew better— there were no mental gymnastics that permitted me to blindly march alongside the ever-growing allegiant army. To answer her critics who actually read the Branchflower findings and disagreed with Sarah's conclusion that it gave her a glowing recommendation, Sarah, through her attorney Thomas Van Flein, condemned the report as a means to "smear the governor by innuendo." Sarah's legal counsel wanted everyone to understand that Mr. Branchflower and those who hired him were evildoers, doing their evildoing best to victimize the soon-to-be vice president of the United States of America.

Along Sarah's road from scandal to self-proclaimed innocence, much of the residual blame fell at my feet—not that I didn't deserve a sizable dose. By allowing myself to be sucked into a family vendetta,

I did something monumentally stupid and wrong that took this from rumor to unprecedented PR disaster:

In February 2008, I phoned one of Walt Monegan's deputies and made known the Palin family's frustration with Trooper Wooten.

This ill-advised call was one of dozens—several directly to Walt Monegan—made by individuals connected to the Palin administration. The difference was that the man I phoned, Trooper Lieutenant Rodney Dial, recorded our twenty-four-minute conversation. (In a classic example of our tiny big state, Dial had been the Palin for Governor sign coordinator in Ketchikan.) Worse, the release of that tape in mid-August 2008, six months after being recorded, came in the midst of howling denials by Governor Palin that anyone had ever pressured Monegan regarding "his rogue and dangerous trooper." She removed Monegan, she swore, because he was a failure and the department needed a new direction. Due in no small part to the timing and hard evidence from the recording, I became known as the "the Troopergate guy."

My family suffered alongside me, largely in silence, while Sarah and Todd Palin resorted to doing what they had done so often in the past: deny, deny, deny. "His comments were unauthorized as well as just wrong," she said about my February phone call during a hastily called press conference on August 13.

By this time we all understood that truth was something to be dragged out only when convenient. The deception we'd constructed had consistently worked miracles in keeping Sarah's ambitions on course, and if nothing else Sarah Palin continued to believe in miracles. For her to survive this latest mess, all I had to do was die a thousand deaths for the proverbial greater good. I did just that, including offering my resignation on three separate occasions, but not without wondering, *What is the greater good?* Did it extend beyond Sarah's personal ambition?

At the time of the *Branchflower Report*'s release, Sarah was on the presidential campaign trail, wowing crowds by informing them that Barack Obama was "pallin' around with terrorists" and that she had said "Thanks but no thanks" to the so-called Bridge to Nowhere—

a proposed $233 million federally funded bridge connecting the Alaska mainland to Gravina Island's fifty residents; the project was eventually cut, but not before becoming a symbol of wasteful pork-barrel spending. The renewed furor from the independent investigator's report was unwelcome but did not appear to have the derailing effect that McCain-Palin critics had expected. For reasons best left to political analysts, Sarah remained Teflon. The stench of Troopergate hung over her, but it was like secondhand smoke, lingering and unpleasant, but dissipating. For those of us remaining behind, especially me, the stink was everywhere. If you Google "Frank Bailey," the name will be forever linked with "Troopergate," "Wooten," and "Monegan." But it's my fault. I made the call (and did so much more). It was wrongheaded, even if I believed what I said was true: Wooten is not a sympathetic person and, arguably, has no place in law enforcement.

Despite that, there were many questions I should have been asking. How was destroying Mike Wooten relevant to our job of governing Alaska? How was it remotely worth the hundreds and hundreds of man-hours spent trying to do so? How, for the love of God, would destroying him personally and professionally make the first family safer, as Sarah and Todd swore repeatedly was their main concern? And if safety was a real concern, Sarah forgot all about that when she complained about the inconvenience of having troopers accompany her on trips in and out of state. In an email to Todd on March 4, 2008, copied to those of us who would follow up, she ordered, *"No more security. It's a flippin waste of money."*

This saga, unfortunately, epitomized the worst of Sarah's dysfunctional psyche and administration, including the compulsion to attack enemies, deny truth, play victim, and employ outright deception.

And while the seeds of the scandal were planted back in 2005 and continued unabated into 2008, the pathos was exponentially elevated when John McCain reached out to Sarah Palin as a savior for his floundering presidential ticket. As such, these events directly related to McCain's own incompetent vetting process. As political perfect storms go, this resembled two Category 5s meeting head-on.

19

Loose Cannon,
Ticking Time Bomb

When all else fails, there's always delusion.
—CONAN O'BRIEN, SPEECH TO HARVARD UNIVERSITY'S
GRADUATING CLASS OF 2000

Way back, in October 2006, Sarah briefly introduced me to the problems with her ex-brother-in-law when explaining why the troopers' union, the Public Safety Employees Association (PSEA), did not endorse her for governor. She believed that the organization's then business agent, John Cyr *"persuaded the PSEA . . . folks to back [Tony Knowles]."*

> Hmmmm—John Cyr is the union dude who defended my ex-brother in law, Trooper Mike Wooten, last year while Mike was under investigation for shooting my nephew with a tasar gun, for getting busted for drinking & driving, for drinking in his patrol car, for illegally shooting a cow moose out of season without a tag, etc. Cyr wrote us a letter telling us to knock off our questioning of Mike, basically.

By the time we'd won the election, however, I had no recollection of this specific communication, only that there was a personal reason for PSEA endorsing the wrong candidate. For all practical purposes, the Trooper Mike Wooten saga began for me in earnest less than a week after the general election. During those early postelection days,

I remained a central figure in organizing Sarah's agenda and fielding calls from those in government who needed to schedule meetings. One of the earliest of these was Gary Wheeler, head of what was to be the governor's security detail.

A day or two after the election, I arranged a sit-down in our midtown Anchorage office. When Wheeler politely requested that this be a private meeting between him and the Palins, I gathered up my laptop and papers to leave, but Sarah said, "Frank, you can be here for this." Only a couple of days removed from chasing down votes one at a time, I already felt that I was being distanced from the day-to-day decision making that had been part of my prior menu of duties. I could see that the power structure was changing, with political operatives taking over for us longtime Rag Tags. This small token—pulling me into a private meeting—was welcoming.

The session began rather curiously, I thought, as Wheeler chose to devote the initial moments of face time with the governor to discussing the importance of the previous governor's private jet that Sarah eventually made into a symbol of her frugality by selling—listing it, for a time, on eBay. He claimed that the Department of Public Safety needed such a resource to respond rapidly to threats across the state; if she didn't need the thing, they did. This discussion became a window into our new world, one where everybody seemed to have an agenda and a request, legitimate or not. Unfortunately for DPS, Sarah's sweet smile and "I'll hafta think on that, Gary," was nothing more than polite lip service. With the massive popular support she'd receive for disposing of Murkowski's folly, there was no way she would sacrifice that to a department she believed was already eating up substantial budgetary resources.

Having stated his case on the jet, Wheeler proceeded to the topic of security. Todd said little, sitting back and staring through those cold blue eyes, stroking his chin from time to time as if he had something on his mind but had decided to withhold. Acting as if I were in a class lecture, I sat off to the side and took notes while Sarah sat behind the desk, legs crossed and hands folded. Wheeler gave an overview of how security operations had worked in the past, then asked if DPS needed to be aware of any threats to the Palin family. Sarah began a lengthy detail of how her ex-brother-in-law, State Trooper Mike Wooten, had tasered his stepson, driven drunk in a patrol car, shot a moose illegally, called her daughter Bristol an "effing bitch," and threatened to put an "effing bullet" in her "effing" father if he paid for an attorney to represent Sarah's sister Molly in their divorce battle. Clearly upset and having no interest in disguising her disgust, she went on to blast the department for allowing this "animal" to continue to wear a badge and carry a gun.

"DPS has done nothing. He's a loose cannon and a ticking time bomb. He told Molly that he'd 'take your sister'—me—'down.' Then they put Mike in Wasilla, let him be a trooper in our own city. Gary, what are you people thinking? He's in a patrol car, with a gun, saying he'll take me down, and you put him in my backyard." Todd's mouth turned down while he pressed his hands together hard enough to make gravel from stone. The only thing that likely kept him from exploding was Sarah's thorough job of disemboweling Wooten. "I'm afraid," Sarah continued, "and I mean it. I'm sure he'd do it; he'll pull over my son Track one day and plant a bag of drugs under a seat during a search and bust him just to embarrass the family."

The meeting left me shaken, and the ugly possible outcomes of a rogue trooper swam furiously in my mind.

So real was the threat Sarah described that I asked myself: If this lunatic came at her with a gun, would I throw myself in harm's way to save her? With hands trembling too hard to continue note taking, I told myself I would. Same way I'd sacrifice myself for my wife and children, I'd give my life for hers. Later, when I spoke to Kris Perry about all I'd heard from Sarah, I said, "This guy Wooten is nuts. I could see him going postal and could walk in one day and blow Sarah or Todd away." In short, I believed Sarah's every word.

While I never forgot the drama of that meeting, the name Wooten faded as Sarah ascended from governor-elect to governor. As I was shuffled off to the Department of Administration for the next few months, a world apart from the mainstream I'd been accustomed to, I heard nothing more until, out of the blue, Todd contacted me for the first time in months. Sometime around April 1, 2007, he said, Trooper Wooten, the guy whom I'd learned months ago was a threat to the Palin family, was riding on a snowmobile (Alaskans call them "snow machines" or "sleds") while supposedly collecting workmen's compensation insurance. Todd had a photograph, a sure indictment, he claimed, of fraud. He convinced me that Wooten was gaming the system and his outrage became my outrage. As a lifelong conservative, I believe that government welfare is a policy reserved for extreme hardship and the abuse of that benefit is unforgivable.

"Frank, this dirtbag is supposed to be flat on his friggin' back. Claims he hurt his back pulling some dead guy out of a ditch. Riding that huge sled, does he look too hurt to work?" Todd pointed to the photo of a giant, muscle-bound man atop a machine that weighed the better part of a half ton. "Dirtbag's collecting a big chunk of his pay snow-machining in the back country. Look at him. The guy takes steroids and is as big as a tree. Hurt? That's bullshit, Frank. He threatens my family, and DPS does nothin'. You know people that deal with comp, right? Is there a fraud unit? He needs to go."

In my days as a lower-level airline industry manager, I handled over a hundred employee relations cases and had some familiarity with the administration of workmen's comp. For the first time in many months, I felt needed. My enthusiasm for Todd's mission acted like fast-drying glue to a sudden friendship.

"I'll pass a copy of this along to Brad Thompson," I promised. As state director of risk management, Brad had responsibility for investigating incidents that might result in an asset loss to the state, and I told Todd, "If he's not the guy to do something, he'll know where to go with this stuff." Though Sarah and Todd had spun the truth repeatedly over the past year, I did not doubt anything Todd said; I was bordering on that class of person you can fool all of the time. As I'd done for Sarah a hundred times, I was prepared to fight for her family.

———

From that first moment Todd reached out to me and feigned outrage, I became an active participant in the dump-Wooten game. I was a fully committed believer that Trooper Mike Wooten was all of the adjectives Todd had hurled at him: "cheat," "fraud," "loose cannon," "ticking time bomb," "scumbag," "sleazeball," and (ironically, because

Sarah used the term as a positive in her own book, *Going Rogue*), a *"rogue* cop." Once again, how getting Trooper Wooten fired would make the family safer never did enter my mind.

Later that day, via email, Todd sent me a packet of information on Wooten. At the time, I scrolled the first couple of screens on my BlackBerry of what were a dozen or more letters and emails and forwarded the information to Thompson, my intention being to give him enough ammunition to get Trooper Wooten fired, which was, unequivocally, what Todd wanted to see happen. Because I was preoccupied and felt that I already had all the important details, I did not then plow through Todd's Wooten file—which included copies of multiple verbal and written attacks on the trooper by the Palin family. As a result, I had no inkling of the three-year family vendetta. Nor did I realize that the judge presiding over the Molly McCann–Mike Wooten divorce, Judge John Suddock, had issued multiple warnings against the constant belittling of the trooper. Suddock said, "Disparaging will not be tolerated—it is a form of child abuse." Later he threatened to curtail Molly's custody rights if she and her extended family did not back off. He concluded by suggesting that if the relentless attack continued, the court "will not hesitate to order custody to the father."

Likely because there hadn't been a public record of any Palin-Heath letters of complaint, after she removed Walt Monegan from his commissionership at DPS, Sarah started perpetuating the sound bite to anyone who would listen—inside the office and out—that "neither the Palin nor the Heath family had ever filed a single complaint against Wooten." To this day, I wonder how her conscience allowed her to say something that was so blatantly false. Unfortunately, supporting documentation regarding her lie had to be removed from this book at the insistence of the Alaska attorney general's office.

All of the damning information I had on Wooten and Monegan was filtered and editorialized by the Palins. Therefore, what I did not know was that while Sarah was claiming that neither she nor her family ever filed a single complaint against Trooper Wooten, an email that she'd written to Colonel Julia Grimes on August 10, 2005, was already being circulated. (Like many of the emails cited, it was a part of the packet Todd sent me that I passed along to Brad Thompson.) At the time, Colonel Grimes was director of the Alaska State Troopers and Mike Wooten's supervisor.

In a four-page email, Sarah wrote,

> Let me share again with you just a few of the many episodes in Wooten's recent past that have been discussed with Wooten's supervisors after the episodes were publicly discussed by Wooten with many in our community who are left scratching their heads regarding Wooten's poor reflection of the Trooper mission to prevent loss of life and property as a result of illegal or unsafe acts.

She then, in similarly rambling fashion, detailed a series of allegations collected with the assistance of a private investigator, Leonard Hackett, hired by Sarah and Todd to interview witnesses to Trooper Wooten's troubling behavior. In that incriminating laundry list were allegations of off-duty drinking that included intimidation of another bar patron; being pulled over right after that incident for suspected drunk driving; avoiding a second DUI while driving with his new, married girlfriend by intimidating the officer who'd pulled him over; driving home drunk after a Super Bowl party with his stepson in the car; drinking three beers while driving his family home from a snow-machine trip; being abusive to his former wives (three of them); harboring a disrespect and dislike for Alaska Natives; illegal hunting acts (specifically, killing a cow moose in 2003 while illegally using Molly's hunting permit when she refused to fire at the animal); employing illegal wolf-hunting techniques; tasering his eleven-year-old stepson; physical abuse of Sarah's sister Molly; threatening Sarah's father, Chuck Heath, after he said he'd hire an attorney for his daughter's divorce action against Wooten; refusing to pay a $5 fine at the Mat-Su Borough Landfill; threatening to "bring down" anyone whom he dislikes; claiming that he bugged Molly's phone; not showing up for work to avoid being served with a domestic-violence restraining order; and generally not telling the truth.

Sarah added a PS to the email, explaining that she had *"objectively separated the divorce and Wooten's threats against me and my family with the fact that the Troopers have a loose cannon on their hands."*

Not only did Sarah file that complaint, but her father penned a follow-up letter on October 9, 2005, also to Colonel Grimes. In this message was a fresh allegation. Heath claimed that on September 30, 2005, Wooten "confronted 14-yr-old Bristol Palin, my granddaughter, at a Wasilla High football game. In the presence of others he called her a 'f----- asshole.' This was while he was a member of the Wasilla High coaching staff."

Because they were interviewed as part of the process, Sarah, Todd, and Chuck Heath were all aware that Colonel Grimes was already researching the allegations against Wooten. Grimes had appointed Sergeant Ron Wahl to conduct a thorough investigation. In referencing that, Heath then wrote, "My family and friends who gave statements to Sgt. Ron Wahl are, understandably, uneasy about the fact that Wooten is still a trooper." Heath then repeated many of the complaints outlined in Sarah's August email.

Sarah, upon reviewing her father's letter prior to having it mailed, wrote to Todd:

> this is excellent. . . . Dad should send this, and add that there are many Alaskans who now look at the Troopers in a whole different light . . . because this trooper has never been held accountable. . . . His superiors have been aware of Mike's incidents for more than seven months now, but Mike is still a law enforcement official . . . and as has been reported by many Mike is a ticking timebomb, a loose cannon.

While Chuck Heath's phrase "uneasy about the fact Wooten is still a trooper" and Sarah's throwing in *"but Mike is still a law enforcement official"* do not specifically call for Wooten to be fired, these and several other future comments more than suggested that this was their intended goal, despite the dozens of eventual denials.

Not done yet with their pressure on Colonel Julia Grimes, Todd, again with Sarah's assistance and approval, sent a third message to her on December 2, 2005, weeks after Sarah had filed to run for governor. Todd began his letter by saying, "It has come to my attention that Trooper Michael Wooten will not be charged in his illegal shooting of a cow moose, due to 'lack of evidence.' " Todd attached a picture of the dead moose with the caption "illegal moose." Todd went on to say that he could "only conclude that, this Trooper is above the law," and that because of this, "some Alaskans' outlook towards DPS is evolving into one of distrust and disappointment." It couldn't be lost on Grimes that Todd was including himself and the potential next governor of Alaska in that "disappointed" group. The next paragraphs repeated Sarah's original complaints and added a few others, including Wooten's intimidation of a Wasilla High School cross-country coach. Why, Todd wanted to know, was this "ticking timebomb" allowed to wear the uniform and carry a gun?

A packet of information containing some of the same material that Todd had emailed to me was forwarded by Sarah and Todd to various members of the media as part of a multipronged attack to have Wooten dismissed. In September Todd sent a letter to both Lisa Demer at the *Anchorage Daily News* and Meghan Baldino at KTUU television, suggesting that they investigate Trooper Wooten. When they appeared interested, they were sent specifics, including Sarah's letter. Months later, the Palins continued to follow up and pass along additional information. That same month, another copy of her letter was sent to Curtis Smith, who at the time was part owner of a PR firm. (This was before he became Sarah's spokesperson.) Smith passed along the information to his former employer KTUU News Director John Tracy, with expectations that Tracy *"would light a fire under someone,"* maybe even reporter Meghan Baldino. In December Sarah typed another letter intended for Mark Kelsey, managing editor of the *Mat-Su Frontiersman* newspaper. She began by writing, "Yes, the trooper issue. It's confidential, but: Todd and I will have to sit down with you and let you know what's going on with one of our illustrious law enforcement agents." She explained about having hired a private investigator "to get the facts and only the facts. Then we presented our findings to some top brass." She concluded by suggesting, "An employee with obvious problems may not be most qualified to carry a badge or a gun."

Frank's story begins in Kodiak, Alaska, where the terrain is as unforgiving as it is beautiful (December 2010). *Photograph courtesy of Malcolm Bennett*

Rare tranquility on the waters of Kodiak's St. Paul Boat Harbor (December 2010). *Photograph courtesy of Malcolm Bennett*

LEFT: Humble beginnings from the 2006 gubernatorial campaign, when we sold red Frisbees for five dollars apiece to raise money. *Photograph by Jeanne Devon*

RIGHT: Hundreds of dedicated volunteers operated the Sea of Red sign campaign that blanketed roadsides and yards across Alaska. Here are hundreds of signs carefully stored for a 2010 campaign that never took place. *Photograph courtesy of Eric Siebels*

Our Einstein, Kerm Ketchum, in the Colony Days Parade (August 2006).
Photograph courtesy of Lawrence Wood

Candidate Palin at the Colony Days Parade (August 2006). *Photograph courtesy of
Lawrence Wood*

Candidate Palin addressing her campaign supporters on election night. Also pictured: Janeen Bailey, Frank Bailey, Kris Perry, and Sandy Parnell (November 2006). *Photograph courtesy of Amanda Henry*

Candidate Palin watching election returns. Also pictured: Todd Palin and Chuck Kopp (November 2006). *Photograph courtesy of Amanda Henry*

Janeen Bailey, Governor Palin, and Frank Bailey at the Wasilla governor's inaugural ball (January 2007). *Photograph courtesy of Frank Bailey*

Bristol Palin with Trig Palin in the Anchorage governor's office (May 2008). *Photograph by Frank Bailey*

Frank's son Devin Bailey holding baby Trig Palin in Fairbanks (June 2008). *Photograph by Frank Bailey*

Trig helping Governor Palin review the 2008 capital budget requests (May 2008). *Photograph by Frank Bailey*

LEFT: A protester at the Alaskans for Truth rally (September 2008). *Photograph by Jeanne Devon*

RIGHT: Conservative commentator Eddie Burke counterprotests at the Alaska Women Reject Sarah Palin rally (September 2008). *Photograph by Jeanne Devon*

Governor Palin delivering speech to supporters at the Welcome Home rally in Anchorage. Lieutenant Governor Sean Parnell looks on from the big screen in background. Parnell inherited Palin's position when she resigned in July of 2009 (September 2008). *Photograph by Jeanne Devon*

Governor Palin signing autographs for supporters at the Welcome Home rally in Anchorage (September 2008). *Photograph by Jeanne Devon*

LEFT: Sign-waving supporters on the tarmac at Anchorage International Airport await the return of Governor Palin from the presidential campaign (November 2008). *Photograph by Jeanne Devon*

RIGHT: Governor Palin returning to Alaska after 2008 presidential election. *Photograph by Jeanne Devon*

Governor Palin emails Frank about her concerns related to a reporter at a youth sporting event. Pictured here with Piper and Trig (February 2009). *Photograph by Jeanne Devon*

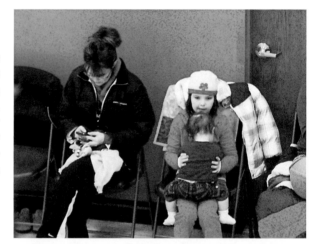

Lieutenant Governor Sean Parnell and Governor Palin serving burgers at the Anchorage governor's picnic. Also pictured: commissioner Bill Hogan, governor's office director Kris Perry, and state trooper Rex Leath, Jr. (July 2009). *Photograph by Jeanne Devon*

Houses ripped from their foundations by large blocks of ice during the Yukon River flooding disaster in Eagle, Alaska (May 2009). *Photograph courtesy of Carol Ford*

Vehicles, trees, power lines, and debris mixed with massive chunks of ice littering the landscape after the Yukon River ice flood disaster in Eagle, Alaska (May 2009). *Photograph courtesy of Carol Ford*

LEFT: Car crushed by giant ice block during the flooding in Eagle, Alaska (August 2009). *Photograph by Frank Bailey*

RIGHT: Rabbit Creek Community Church flood relief volunteers Keith Mallard, Allen Booher, and Frank Bailey in Eagle, Alaska (August 2009). *Photograph courtesy of Frank Bailey*

The legislative council announces the findings of the Branchflower report to the press. Pictured here (left to right): Senator John Coghill (R), Senator Lyman Hoffman (D), Senate President Lyda Green (R), Representative Nancy Dahlstrom (R), Senator Kim Elton, legislative affairs director Pam Varney, Representative Bill Stoltze (R), and Senator Gary Stevens (R) (September 2009). *Photograph by Jeanne Devon*

Beautiful Portage Lake, picturesque Alaska at its finest (November 2010). *Photograph by Cory Pepiton*

As she did with Randy Ruedrich during the 2006 campaign by suggesting that he was behind a series of plots to bring her down, Sarah seemed to believe, with little evidence, that Wooten was responsible for disseminating a host of embarrassing facts and rumors. When poor grades forced one of her kids from participating in sports and when a false story circulated that her son Track was involved in vandalizing school property, she similarly seemed to believe that Wooten was the likely source. In the case of this December 2005 vandalism incident, Sarah also emailed a long list of contacts in radio, television, and print media to discredit the story. She alerted them that *"if false accusations of this sort are coming from a State Trooper who has vowed to destroy our family, then the AST [Alaska State Troopers] organization has a bigger problem on its hands than it did before. (I'm speaking of an estranged brother-in-law who has been under investigation by AST for illegal activity and threats against a family member.)"* Lost on Sarah was the irony of debunking one potentially false accusation (that son, Track, destroyed school property) with another (that Wooten sourced the rumor). Two weeks later, when another story about Track surfaced, Sarah again pointed the finger by alerting her list of media contacts and staff: *"it could be Wooten planting seeds."*

At one point, when older players on Track Palin's hockey team put Ex-Lax in a younger player's cookie as a prank and were disciplined, Sarah reacted by suggesting in an email to Todd and a small list of friends that *"students can't say 'boo' nowadays without getting in big trouble."* More significantly, however, Todd, with her knowledge, sent an email to school officials and tied Wooten back into the discussion. As they'd done repeatedly, they were not satisfied with trying to terminate his employment as a state trooper. They also lobbied long and hard to have him removed as coach of the Wasilla High football team. Todd, in focusing his anger on the school's administration, wrote, *"I am having a hard time understanding the difference between a prank involving a cookie laced with ex-lax and a WHS coach using disgustingly abusive and intimidating tactics while calling WHS student a 'f***ing a**hole.'"* That Wooten remained, at this time, a coach, Todd went on, was reprehensible.

Additionally, the couple solicited letters of complaint from friends who knew Wooten and had a tale to tell. In one instance, a former Wooten friend described him grabbing a beer while at their home, opening it, and driving away while drinking. Many of these reports were sent to Colonel Grimes, to Wasilla High School administrators, and/or as recently as 2008 to me, media outlets, and eventually people like Brad Thompson as fuel to stoke new investigations of Wooten.

Even past and future radio critic Dan Fagan, in his 2005 love-Sarah days, jumped into the game. He spoke directly to Grimes secretly on Todd's behalf, seeking information about the Wooten investigation. On December 17, 2005, he wrote a follow-up, coming close to demanding information or he would be *"going public with all of this if something is not resolved shortly."*

Grimes had already responded to Chuck Heath's letter of complaint, writing, *"I will assure you, as I have assured Sarah (during our telephone conversation) and Todd (during his exchange with Trp. Cokrell), that we take these allegations extremely seriously. . . . I wanted to explain that since these are personnel issues, they are confidential and I cannot discuss them in detail as they are ongoing or when they are concluded."* Despite Grimes's having personally contacted Sarah, Todd, and Chuck Heath, unbeknownst to her, she was being asked to send that message yet another time through surrogate Dan Fagan. She dutifully did so by reiterating in an email, *"Simply stated, the law does not allow for the complainant, the media or the public to obtain the results of any personnel investigation. . . . I am unable to provide any additional clarification as you have requested."* Naturally Fagan forwarded her entire response to Todd within minutes of receiving it.

In an attempt to take some of the sting away from the three-year-long Palin attack on him, Wooten publicly released his personnel file at a Public Safety Employees Association press conference. The 482-page report, along with recorded investigative interviews, were made public on September 17, 2008—the exact day that Sarah claimed that she and her family never filed any complaints against Trooper Wooten. (Her letter to Julia Grimes was inside the file, verifying that misstatement.)

The PSEA documents revealed that Wooten had been investigated exhaustively. That investigation sustained three complaints filed by the Palins and the Heaths and found unsustained approximately twenty-seven others. And despite Todd and Sarah's having described the list of complaints as "coming from the public," every complaint investigated originated from them or from friends of theirs with Palin encouragement and assistance. The most spectacular of those, Wooten's tasering his stepson with a training cartridge, was sustained but merely as the unauthorized use of government equipment, a misdemeanor. The investigation took into account several factors that I had no knowledge of at this time and that the Palins did not ever disclose: the child requested he be tased to prove to his cousin Bristol that he was not a mama's boy, the setting was at low level "test," the boy did not himself complain and told his mother he was "fine," and the event was not reported for nearly two years (and only when Molly filed for divorce). The other two instances cited by Grimes were illegally hunting (he used Molly's permit to shoot a moose when she was reluctant to fire) and having an open beer in his patrol car. Taking all this into account, the violation resulted in a ten-day suspension that was later reduced to five days on appeal by the troopers' union.

When Wooten released his file, the news of his suspension stunned me. Despite later accusations to the contrary, I had never seen or read a single word of Wooten's personnel file. The sad truth is that had I known in February of the disciplinary hearing and Wooten's suspension, no call on my part would ever have taken place to Lieutenant Rodney Dial. Through my extensive experience with employment issues while in the airline industry, I fully understood that Walt Monegan could never—even if he'd wanted to—legally dismiss Wooten under union rules; once an investigation and findings are finalized, there is no recourse to initiate additional punitive action at a later date.

How Sarah could maintain in 2008 that she and her family never filed any complaints against Wooten is a question I'll never be able to answer. Given how many times she and Todd copied that letter she'd written to Colonel Grimes and the numerous occasions they sent those complaints to multiple media outlets and school and government officials—in addition to the hours Sarah and Todd spent helping craft complaints by friends, Sarah's father, and even daughter Bristol, who wrote up her own account of her school run-in with Wooten—it is simply not credible that she forgot.

Despite my own dislike for Wooten and a lack of historical context for the compulsive attacks against him, my becoming Todd's go-to guy in an attempt to destroy another man's life remains inexcusable, representing a lack of common sense or due diligence. I should have known better. By the time Todd approached me to be his ally, I was fully aware that I worked for a couple who felt revenge a sweet drink. I joined in with too much enthusiasm and too few facts.

The combination became, sadly, a recipe for disaster.

20

Attack

Friends may come and go, but enemies accumulate.
—THOMAS HUDSON JONES, AMERICAN SCULPTOR (1892–1969)

Todd's trusting me to be his front man on the Wooten workmen's compensation outrage brought us closer together than ever. Despite that, I still felt outside the inner circle when it came to Sarah, and the person most responsible for that remained Chief of Staff Mike Tibbles. In April 2007 I asked Todd, "Where's Tibbles in all of this?"

"Tibbles?" Todd said, not bothering to hide his disdain. "Mike has zero backbone to follow up on this stuff. It's time to get shit done, and it's us, Frank. You and me. Sarah can't have a loose-cannon trooper running around. What if he drives over someone drunk? What a shit storm that'd be. Yeah, it'll be one-term Sarah."

The message was clear. Todd needed my robotic loyalty to carry out this mission. Before Todd left my Juneau office, I said something like, "I'll do everything I can. This guy's a loose cannon."

A short time after that latest meeting, Todd phoned, breathless and excited. "Frank, the dirtbag lied on his trooper application. He says he got the injury from trooper duty. More Mike bullshit. Guy was already hurt when he applied for the job. I know from a source that knows for sure he left the air force with some kind of disability rating. Can you get this to Brad in risk management?"

"Will do. Absolutely."

"It's important that you keep Sarah out of this, okay? They think she hates the guy, and she can't be involved."

Even though Todd regularly withheld information, depending on the audience, it was nevertheless *my* choice to participate and avoid asking questions, such as how did he receive confidential information from Wooten's military records. Nor did I seek to verify any of the Palin claims firsthand. These allegations declared war on my sense of justice, and I rushed to battle immediately. "You're telling me Wooten's taking state money for something that happened before he took his trooper job?" *This guy disgusts me,* I thought. *He's dangerous and stealing money from the government.* "On top of that," I asked, "he's still able to ride a snow machine? What? Couldn't get the air force to pay him for backcountry recreation?" I jotted on a slip of paper, "prior injury. lied on application. stealing from state. Air Force disab rating. don't forget snwmchn."

"Shouldn't lying on the application be grounds for dismissal?" Todd asked rhetorically. "Your friend Brad? He'll want to know, right?"

"I'm on it, guy."

Minutes after hanging up with Todd, I hustled next door to Brad Thompson's office, where I detailed Wooten's prior injury and lying on his application, and shared my hand-scribbled notes. I explained that this was a dishonorable man who loved the badge and gun and status of being an armed officer, but was willing to milk the system. The anger became a cancer that spread from Sarah and Todd to me, and the only cure was to excise Trooper Wooten. My behavior in all of this *is* the definition of a Palin-bot—and at the time I wore the label proudly.

What I did not know until much later was in that same month, April 2007, Wooten's workmen's comp claim was contravened. He received a letter explaining that his injury was deemed the result of a preexisting condition. In response, the trooper hired an attorney to pursue the matter against the state.

When, a few weeks later, we discovered that Wooten had been put back to work on light duty, Todd did not receive the news well. His fury at the apparent blasé attitude had me feeling vulnerable. Todd wanted inside information that his ex-brother-in-law was going to be punished and, hopefully, fired, and I had nothing of substance to report. In the back of my mind, I feared that Todd was reporting back to Sarah that "Frank isn't any more capable on getting Mike out of there than Tibbles."

Thompson, who was now occasionally receiving calls directly from Todd, patiently explained, "Confidentiality rules prevent me from going into a lot of stuff here, Frank. The situation is being monitored, that much I can say."

None of this kept Todd from pressing. As best as I could without sounding like I was soliciting inappropriate information, I suggested to Thompson, "I understand that it's cheaper to put Wooten back to work in light duty, but with everything else this guy's done, why does the state want to keep him at all? That seems crazy."

Todd agreed this was the appropriate message. "And don't forget this is just between you and me. It's the job of others to get their hands dirty, not Sarah," he reminded me. Each time I recounted a conversation regarding Wooten with anyone in government, Todd's profuse thanks helped ease my anxiety. At least he knew I was trying.

For much of the balance of the 2007 summer, I heard only sporadically from Todd on Wooten and the stagnating workmen's compensation issue. Part of the reason for this hiatus was that we had other crises.

Always with background chaos, we suddenly found ourselves operating on multiple fronts when dealing with enemies and largely self-inflicted chaos. Radio thorn Dan Fagan was stepping up attacks on Sarah's competence and seemed to have eyes and ears inside our administration. We needed to record, dissect, and counteract each criticism with friendly calls, self-penned letters to the editor, and op-eds. We'd phone in and blast Fagan (sometimes directly, other times using willing surrogates), send emails even while he was on air, and complain bitterly at what a bald-faced liar he was.

At one point, Sarah tried to reengage Todd in the battle by directing him to phone Fagan's show unannounced and "call him on his lies." When the radio show host made an off-color remark about those in state leadership being "crack whores," Todd suggested to the inner circle that we combine our mailing lists and coordinate people to call in to his show and then go to his boss—an activity I am sure ratings-magnet Dan would have relished.

Sarah latched onto the "crack whores" comment and took it to the bank. We had meetings, made phone calls, created strategies, and sent emails (that were also removed from this book at the request of the Alaska attorney general's office); and we all invested considerable resources to remove the thorn known as the Dan Fagan radio show from her side. She even tried unsuccessfully to drag other commissioners into the skirmish. Wielding her influence to make a mark in what was scheduled as a meeting about supporting local little league, she encouraged a local businessman to rethink his sponsorship of Fagan's radio show.

While Sarah resolved to never listen, she failed miserably to do so. With her approval, we went after Fagan's sponsors, including computer, furniture, and mattress stores, as well as an Italian restaurant that ran commercials during his broadcasts. In addition to letter writing, we sent them CDs of the offending shows. Sarah reacted by yelling, "Yayy!" In many instances, if she missed the live broadcast, we continued—as we'd done on and off for the past year—to access a podcast or, even more time consuming, a transcript. She also pushed commissioners and government experts to phone in to defend her. Needless to say, we conducted little government business during these hours of listening and plotting.

More troubling than Dan Fagan was the sudden black eye Sarah had suffered because of her handling of the state-owned Matanuska Maid (Mat Maid) Dairy. Mat Maid had lost $600,000 in 2005 and 2006, and the state Creamery Board decided to shut down the business in the spring of 2007. Sarah felt so strongly that Mat Maid should continue operating that she fired the entire state Board of Agriculture and Conservation—which appointed the Creamery Board—and installed her own appointees, who promptly reversed the closure decision. Critics, led by Andrew Halcro, slammed the measure. Three months later, with the dairy having lost another $300,000, the governor was forced to admit that she'd fired the original board in error and that it had made the correct decision. Nevertheless, she continued to drag her feet in deciding how to proceed. Stubbornly costing the state more money, she delayed closure, believing that Alaska would find a buyer to take over the money pit. Todd, recognizing the obvious before his wife did, panicked and sent an urgent email on September 10 to Kris Perry and me that included the following plea:

> MM has to stop the bleeding now. . . . At the end of the day in this blood bath it is Sarah taking all the heat, not . . . the board. With the current direction I fore see Sarah having to go before the Legislature and ask for more money.
>
> Is Sarah getting the correct information or is she being lead to believe there's a buyer out there that's going to stop the bleeding.

Todd was not alone in begging the governor to face reality. A concerned Bruce Anders wrote, *"Keeping alive the myth of a solvent mat maid will cause more pain down the road . . . we may not like halcro, but on this issue he is correct. Shut it down, stop the hemorrhaging."*

Finally, in December, Sarah relented and auctioned off the equipment after finding nobody willing to take on a business that had no prospects for making money. Months earlier, Todd, seeking to deflect criticism of his wife, had asked me to do opposition research on Mat Maid director Terry Clark, a vocal Sarah critic. I discovered nothing damaging, however, and we had little ammunition for attacking him.

Unlike most issues in which Sarah held a personal grudge, the Mat Maid furor died relatively quickly. For the handful of hardcore critics like Halcro and Fagan, this incident remained a stain on her record as a fiscal conservative, but, frankly, the vast majority of Alaskans either did not understand the issues involved or simply forgot about it. As for remaining critics such as Andrew Halcro, Sarah hyperbolically expressed herself by suggesting in one email, *"halcro is a lying $+*#_."* Moments later, she added that he *"is a sinful liar."* A staffer then raised the ante with her own embellishment: Halcro *"is an insulting, arrogant, piece of crap, flippin' liar."*

At least as unwelcome as the Mat Maid affair was Legislative Director John Bitney's reckless fling with the wife of Todd's best friend.

Bitney, championed by his buddy Mike Tibbles, had been hired in part because of his Wasilla connection: he and Sarah had played in the high school band together. But now Bitney was little more than administration dirty laundry. Once found guilty of a breach of loyalty, nothing he did was going to be good enough, and in Sarah and Todd's eyes, he needed to be jettisoned. In July 2007 Sarah ordered Tibbles to fire his friend.

Two weeks later, Bitney, still employed, turned up at a reunion picnic held for former campaign workers. When he began playing guitar for the crowd, it was as if Bitney were attempting to win affection by entertaining those he hoped were still friends. The pastoral setting in Palmer, at the hand-crafted home of the Bensons, on acres of farmland with horses, a warming sun, succulent barbecue, and views of Pioneer Peak, had no effect on cooling Sarah's temper. She cared nothing for Bitney's apparently contrite appeal for forgiveness. Afterward, the moment Sarah climbed into the Suburban for the drive home to Wasilla, she punched the speed dial to her chief of staff.

"Mike, I want John Bitney gone! And next time I tell you to fire someone, I don't want to wait two flippin' weeks! Period."

Yet later that day, Tibbles, even under direct threat from a rabid governor, beat around the bush. He indicated to Bitney that he was being placed on unpaid leave. The final reckoning reportedly didn't come until Bitney, while traveling, discovered his government-issued BlackBerry turned off and his name removed from the state's employment directory. He received official notice only after he phoned Tibbles and asked about his status. Sarah never did provide Bitney an explanation, but she did issue a public statement claiming that the parties had "mutually agreed he would leave his post for personal reasons." No question, from Sarah's point of view, the reason was personal; but there was no mutual agreement. For a short time after this, Bitney became the newest enemy, relegating Mike Wooten temporarily to the back burner.

Almost immediately, Sarah faced questions about Bitney's firing, especially from blogger Andrew Halcro. To members of her team, she explained only a week after Bitney's firing that he should have been let go two weeks earlier for what she called "distractions" that made the quality of his work suffer. That he was allowed an administrative leave now annoyed her, and she threatened to "set the record straight" and let the world know exactly why he was let go. "I won't protect his reputation," she said as if he were there to hear her threats.

While not engrossed in the marathon madness of the Mike Wooten attacks, we mobilized to go after Bitney. A few weeks after his dismissal, Sarah wrote of him in an office email:

Bitney—and perhaps his own right hand man, Fuhs [that being strategist and op-ed writer Paul Fuhs, now out of favor himself]— is hell bent on messing with the Gov's office now that he's not there. He told his new girlfriend that the only reason I got elected was bc of him.

Eventually Sarah wrote, *"Damnit. He's a liar and a slimy lying prick."* Sarah and Kris Perry immediately took to monitoring the reviled *Anchorage Daily News* website for clues that Bitney and his allies were on the attack, as you can see from the following email (emphasis mine):

From: sarah
Date: Sun, 15 Jul 2007 10:48:37
Subject: Bitney

Don't waste your time reading the ADN blog, but know that entries there provide fodder for the media to write stories . . . —Kris and I looked at it recently and have been fascinated by one blogger's turn-around from his support of administration to his slamming of us the past few weeks, *all because of Bitney's departure.* The blogger is Paul Fuhs (he told us his pen name months ago) and he's done a one-eighty.

In another email, she employed the same logic as when blaming Ruedrich for campaign hiccups and Wooten for falsifying family rumors. Despite the lack of hard evidence, she anointed Bitney the person behind a new wave of attacks on the administration and her family. When Todd's employment as an oil field worker became a minor conflict-of-interest controversy, Sarah blamed Bitney. If Fagan had a negative allegation, it came from bitter-liar Bitney.

> Tib—pls be careful with any and all communications with Bitney. He's on a rampage, he's going through a divorce, he's looking to blame someone for his problems and his former boss is a convenient target. He obviously has way too much time on his hands and no supervision.

Sarah, in warning Chief of Staff Tibbles to be careful, was taking no chance with damaging leaks. In this same message, she confirmed that she was still on top of her cyber critics, some of whom were undoubtedly John Bitney: *"From the vindictive blog entries to the last few days of media blow-ups, to the timing of all this—it all points to Bitney. Huge distraction."*

In suggesting this was a *huge distraction*, Sarah was most definitely correct.

Understanding the stakes to him personally, ex-Bitney pal Mike Tibbles joined in waging battle:

> **From: Michael A Tibbles**
> **To: Governor Sarah Palin**
> **Sent: Aug 26, 2007 2:12 PM**
>
> Just a quick update regarding your Bitney concerns . . . I have talked to [others] about being very cautious in their conversations with Bitney. He is obviously trying to use any connection he has to obtain information. From what I hear he . . . [has] been spending a lot of time on the gossip circuit.

Sarah must have nodded her head as she typed a sarcastic reply to Tibbles: *"What a loyal 'long-time' friend that bitney has turned out to be."*

Just as she'd done time after time in overreacting to events and rumors that might have withered under their own inconsequentiality,

Sarah elevated tensions unnecessarily. And we went along. As always, her inner circle understood that our failure to pick up arms and fight alongside her might result in our own BlackBerrys being disconnected and our names deleted from employee records.

The manner in which Bitney was handled became a dry run—albeit on a smaller and less noteworthy scale—for Department of Public Safety Commissioner Walt Monegan's eventual dismissal in July 2008. As she'd done to the Mat Maid board and later with Monegan, Sarah disposed of people, then obscured her reasons through deceit and counterattack.

And while Bitney was front and center for a few weeks, if I'd hoped that there was any chance Todd would not return to *our favorite trooper*, I was to be disappointed. When Wooten reemerged, he would never go away again.

21

Wooten-mania

The Governor has stated, under oath, that the Wooten
matter played no role in her decision to terminate
Mr. Monegan as Commissioner of DPS.
—TIMOTHY J. PETUMENOS, INDEPENDENT COUNSEL
FOR THE STATE OF ALASKA PERSONNEL BOARD,
MONDAY, NOVEMBER 3, 2008, IN HIS REPORT
REBUTTING THE *BRANCHFLOWER* CONCLUSIONS

In a September 1, 2008, Ethics Disclosure form, Sarah, through her attorney Thomas Van Flein, stated: "The Palin family did not learn the results of this investigation [into Wooten] and did not learn the results of the Grimes' discipline until after she replaced Commissioner Monegan." Over the summer, Sarah had raised the stakes even higher when she said, "To allege that I, or any member of my family, requested, received or released confidential personnel information on an Alaska State Trooper . . . is, quite simply, outrageous." Todd, in response to a subpoena dated September 12, 2008, added to their collective denial by stating, "Not until Wooten released, and the ADN posted, his personnel records . . . did I learn that there was a completed internal review by Colonel Grimes and what was done. I learned that there was a ten-day suspension ordered." Not only did they know about the Grimes findings, but Todd, using Sarah's email account (thus it's hard to argue that she was ignorant of the truth), shared these "confidential" understandings with Lisa Demer at the *Anchorage Daily News* as far back as April 11, 2006 (emphasis mine):

From: sarah
To: ldemer
Sent: Tuesday, April 11, 2006 8:59 AM
Subject: Fw: Trooper Wooten

I wanted to update you on the status of Trooper Michael Wooten (dob 8/28/72) on his above-the-law actions. Rumor has it that *Wooten was suspended for two weeks without pay for drinking/ driving in his patrol car, illegally shooting a cow moose, and for shooting his 11-yr-old stepson with a DPS Taser gun.* All the other citizen complaints against this trooper were swept under the rug. Drinking in his patrol car is against the law "AS28.35.029 The Open Container Law," but I guess it's ok for this trooper. It's also illegal for hunters (and troopers) to shoot a cow moose illegally, and how many Alaskans were cited and fined last year for the same crime and were punished for their actions? Shooting his 11-yr-old with his trooper taser gun was reckless and no doubt illegal, and I've read that more than 110 people have died from being shot by a taser gun. What would have happened if the boy had died, would the punishment still be two weeks without pay?

. . . Not knowing what the judge will do in Wooten's custody battle makes it difficult to publicly speak up.

Thanks Lisa,

Todd

It is interesting to note that Todd seemed to know which three offenses against Wooten had been sustained as well as terms of the trooper's original ten-day suspension. No matter the source of his information, to have Sarah and Todd swear in 2008 that they knew *nothing* of this matter is one of those situations where I find myself saying, "I wish I'd known then what I know now."

Over those many months, and while ignorant of this aspect of the Wooten case, I continued to do Todd's bidding. Not content to have Brad Thompson in risk management concern himself with workmen's comp claims only, Todd had me forward additional unflattering information to Brad, just in case he wasn't fully aware of the magnitude of the beast.

From: Todd Palin
To: frank bailey
Created: 7/26/2007 5:35:23 AM
Subject: Trooper above the law

Hey Frank,
Go ahead and forward to Brad if he needs some history of a trooper who is above the law. Make sure when you forward the message doesn't get truncated.
   Frank,
   This will be doctor number 4.
   1 His personal chiropractor,
   2 chose by state
   3 dps dropped the ball and allowed him to choose the doctor. 4?
   When I took picture's of him riding a snow machine one hundred miles from town, April 2, Wooten was very pissed off. When Wooten returned to town a couple days later, he went to his chiropractor than all of a sudden he had a statement saying he can ride snow machines and motorcycles but can't go to work. Is that not black and white, . . . Wooten has said all along that "that f****** bitch is going to run this department into to the ground.". . . The January 15 parks hwy auto wreck that Wooten responded too is where he said he injured himself. . . . The bottom line is that he used workman's comp . . . (to attend basketball games and the thought of being fired for lack of performance) for an injury that he had prior to becoming a trooper.
   . . . And now he wants a settlement, he needs to be punished for fraud.

Is any of this information true? I don't know. Where did Todd get all his information? No clue. Did I send this to Brad? Yes, because at the time, I believed every word.
   On August 17, 2007, Todd emailed me a standard complaint: *"It's very frustrating to hear wooten is still a trooper."* He then spoke of Trooper Wooten's attorney, Chancy Croft. Todd suggested that *"croft*

has no idea about the ticking time bomb he's representing. If he new that thiis animal thretened to kill sarahs dad and threatened to bring donw sarah, would he continue to represent him, he needs to know."

In his normal but quixotic way, Todd was encouraging me to pass along information to Chancy Croft about his client in the hopes that the veteran workmen's compensation lawyer would terminate his representation. If I'd asked Todd about the advisability of including the letter he had me send Brad Thompson, I believe he'd have said "absolutely" and then reiterated, "But don't truncate any of it." On that same day and likely motivated by our conversation, Todd let Kris Perry know, *"It's beyond Sarah and I that wooten is still a trooper . . . what is walt thinking."*

There are a couple of significant things about these summer 2007 emails. Wooten was like a cold sore, liable to pop up at any time. Additionally, Todd acknowledged that it was equally perplexing to Sarah that Wooten was still a trooper. Todd was beginning to question Commissioner Walt Monegan when he asked, *"what is walt thinking,"* which also marked a change in focus. From that moment, Todd believed that Monegan was committed to a law-enforcement blue line that protected rogue cops like Wooten.

In October Todd phoned with yet another joyous revelation. With Wooten still on light duty, he was bragging about drawing a moose tag in the state run lottery, permitting him to hunt in a prescribed wilderness area. "Frank, are you sitting down? Word is that supposedly handicapped Wooten's got a moose hunt planned. What? He thinks he'll have this miraculous recovery by then? My ass he is."

My reaction was to say, "No kidding, Todd?"

"If this isn't clear enough fraud for Monegan and his leg humpin' blue line, I dunno what is."

"We can find out about his getting the tag," I said, immediately willing to renew the fight. "This is blatant fraud if it can be proven."

With Todd's endorsement, I phoned the Department of Public Safety and talked to a DPS spokesperson. In this instance, I made it clear that I spoke only for myself and did not mention Todd or Sarah by name. In that conversation, I supplied the details as given to me by Todd. A bit later, Colonel Audie Holloway, Grimes's recent successor as director of the Alaska State Troopers, phoned back. I immediately put my foot squarely in my mouth when I recited many of the Wooten abuses as I knew them and said, "If this guy's truly done all the things I've heard of and he's still a trooper, than someone in DPS doesn't know how to do an employee investigation." My speech surely sounded like fighting words from an uninformed blowhard. Despite that, Holloway asked when the hunt was to occur. The man, showing great restraint, was respectful and suggested that if I uncovered any additional information, I should feel free to call back.

When I contacted Todd and gave him the blow-by-blow account of this conversation, he appreciated my aggressiveness. Just before he left to collect additional details for me to turn over to DPS, he said, "They're a brotherhood, Frank. They protect their own at DPS, every damn one of 'em. Let me tell you, if you aren't one of 'em, you don't cross that blue line." His accumulated frustration now went well beyond Wooten. The Alaska State Troopers brotherhood—and anyone who defended it—all deserved a gubernatorial spanking.

On September 24, 2007, Todd entered my office, shut the door, and plopped down on the sofa. From under his jacket, he produced a video. "Check this out, man."

On the tape, we watched an overweight man whom Todd claimed to be Wooten being filmed from behind at a high school basketball game. He held popcorn and a drink while wildly cheering and jumping up and down. "Does he look disabled to you?" Todd asked. Since we never saw the guy's face, I am not even sure it was Wooten.

The next day, Todd emailed me a series of new talking points to deliver to Brad Thompson if and when Wooten was finally deposed:

> **Would the tape of him at the ball game help for questions if he's deposed.**
> **What where you doing while you where off on workmans comp. Did you attend basketball games, did you travel hundreds of miles to watch games, sitting for hours on end in a car when you were hurt. The January 15 accident on the parks hwy where you were injuried the ch 2 interview you did, didn't show you in pain.**

Todd concluded by offering an effective summation of his feelings: *"My blood is boiling just thinking about what this dirt bag is doing and the thought of him getting a hudge settlement."*

Sarah and I had no direct communication on these matters, but she was still a player. Spokesperson Meg Stapleton, who eventually became the governor's superconfidante, had her own introduction directly from Sarah on May 6, 2007. Sarah, as she did in nearly every instance when discussing other trooper scandals, felt compelled to include a Wooten tirade. After remarking on a sentence handed down to an officer who assaulted a fifteen-year-old in Fairbanks, she let Stapleton know, *"also confidentially—between this trooper's horrible actions and the message my sister received from her ex (an active state trooper) again this week that he'll continue to 'mess with the governor's sister' and our family by alleging falsehoods (he's done this before)—well some of the state's 'finest' in uniform continue to disappoint."* Sexual misconduct merited fewer than ten words; a man who remained a constant thorn in the Palins' side, five times that much ink.

A bit later, on September 27, 2007, Sarah wrote Walt Monegan an email in which she again mentioned Wooten in a discussion of a Trooper Spitzer, who *"had a bad reputation along with his fellow trooper whom we've talked about before."* For Sarah, while perhaps an accidental admission, she verified prior discussions with Monegan regarding Wooten, something that she would later downplay throughout the eventual dismissal of the controversy in 2008.

Yet Sarah, in the second half of 2008, testified ignorance of *any* action by subordinates regarding Wooten and denied putting pressure on Monegan to fire the man. Making a mockery of these assertions under oath were additional emails released by Walt Monegan to counter Sarah's representations. The first of these was sent by Sarah to Monegan only five weeks into her administration, on February 7, 2007. With the exception of a single sentence concerning a bill designed to handle police officers found guilty of murder, this lengthy email detailed multiple grievances she had with her ex-brother-in-law. The list was bitterly exhaustive, and Sarah suggested that the investigation by Colonel Julia Grimes was "a joke." She maintained to Monegan. *"This trooper is still out on the street, in fact he's been promoted."*

While technically correct that she never said "fire Wooten," Sarah's complaint that he was still a trooper would lead most people to speculate that she did not approve of his employment status. For Sarah, another example of parsing words (eventually under oath).

Not yet finished, on May 7, 2008, Sarah wrote Monegan again: *"I received the other night where an Ak State Trooper recently told a friend of family that he could further 'mess with the governor's sister' by claiming falsehoods about us—well—none of our 'finest' in uniform continue to disappoint."* Not only did this linguistically challenged message point to Sarah's distrust of Wooten, but it highlighted personal animosity toward troopers in general. As Sarah's complaints indicated, she was no less passionate than Todd about Wooten, and the longer the trooper's employment continued, the larger the conspiracy grew and the more the couple blamed the troopers organization.

For someone who swore under oath that she never pressured Commissioner Monegan to fire Wooten, Todd's email unequivocally suggested that her influence had not been powerful enough to have Wooten dismissed. Even if Sarah's assertion that Todd never discussed Wooten with her was true, Sarah's own emails provided clear examples of pressure. And since Alaska's first couple had no off-button to their shared inner rage, they likely shared a lot more than they claimed.

As I believed Walt Monegan to be far from stupid, he undoubtedly read the dump-Wooten messages loud and clear. What none of us understood—with our limited information—was why the commissioner didn't just fire the rogue trooper. I came to share Todd's belief that Monegan was guilty of sacrificing justice for trooper brotherhood. In Sarah's you're-with-me-or-agin-me world, Monegan had, by the end of 2007, chosen *agin*. Going into 2008, our noncompliant commissioner found himself squarely in the Palin crosshairs.

It was, barring a Monegan come-to-Jesus moment, merely a matter of time and a final straw before he felt Sarah's wrath.

22

Accusation Spaghetti

Then Peter came to Jesus and asked, "Lord, how many
times shall I forgive my brother when he sins against
me? Up to seven times?" Jesus answered, "I tell
you, not seven times, but seventy-seven times."
—BOOK OF MATTHEW 18: 21–22 OF
THE NEW TESTAMENT (NIV)

Into the winter of 2007–08, the First Dude ranted ever more frequently over his disgust with the lack of action. "Why the hell
doesn't Walt get rid of Wooten?" This was a question Todd asked
dozens of times in escalating frustration. For me, Todd Palin's indifference to my real job—placing over two hundred board applica-
tions a year and identifying, reviewing, and initializing placements
of dozens of judgeships for Governor Palin's ultimate approval—grew
wearisome. While I agreed with Todd's assessment of Wooten—bad
cop, being protected—after more than nine months of regular and
lengthy calls, visits, and demands to do something, they became a
cruel thief of my already minimal time with job and family. Todd's
was an ongoing assignment I couldn't just tackle and get off my desk.
As Kris Perry was my closest confidante in the administration, I discovered that she too was hearing from Todd incessantly. "Todd just
called again about Wooten" became the second most frequent topic
behind "What kind of mood is Sarah in today?"

In November 2007 Todd launched me into another project. Only
days earlier, I'd learned from Todd that Wooten and the state of
Alaska settled his countersuit after the April contravention of his prior
claim. As part of the settlement, he underwent back surgery at the

state's expense. Todd, who had eyes and ears across the state reporting on Wooten's whereabouts, sent me an email in which he said, *"Must have been a serious back operation, he's already driving around town. I wonder what kind of back operation he had if he's already up and running."* Minutes later, he sent a second email. *"If he had back surgery, the question should be what kind of medication are you on and are you driving under the influence of strong medication. He was spotted driving today."*

There is no way to overestimate Todd's obsession with punishing Wooten. His hope became that if we hurled enough accusation spaghetti against the wall, no matter how frivolous, something might stick. As thin as many of these secondhand reports appeared, I dutifully passed along each one to Brad Thompson and anyone else in law enforcement willing to lend an ear.

Secretly, I prayed that Wooten would just quit his job and put an end to the madness.

In the background, there were two high-profile trooper scandals Todd also focused on as evidence of a blue-line conspiracy. One had to do with Alaska State Trooper Jesse Osborn, who shot and killed an unarmed disabled man at a Kenai highway pullout in 2003. That case was under review and litigation, eventually being settled in 2010 when an arbitrator awarded $150,000 to the deceased man's family.

A second case received even more attention. Trooper Eric Spitzer was charged with using excessive force in 2002 when he arrested Kevin Patrick for driving a snowmobile drunk in Emmonak. Spitzer, at six foot four and 230 pounds, dwarfed the five-foot-four, 140-pound Patrick, yet used a Taser on Patrick while handcuffing him. Examined by a nurse two days after the arrest, Patrick was found to have eight separate burns on his back, shoulder, and chest. When he sued the state in 2005, a jury awarded him $1,800,000. After the state appealed, the parties eventually settled for $575,000 in September 2007.

Because the Spitzer case occurred in rural Alaska, where law enforcement had a history of troubling run-ins with the Native community, and this was the third time that the Department of Public

Safety had to settle excessive force charges against Trooper Spitzer, it was a particularly sensitive matter. Sarah was sufficiently nervous about being implicated in the settlement that she wrote Monegan, *"What I need is just the factual info that proves this was a DPS issue and I was not a part of any settlement. I was not advised, nor requested to participate in this . . . as is the appropriate way of handling such a case. I ask because I've already heard the accusation that 'I' settled with a bad cop."* In other words, because her image was on the line, Monegan's task was to make certain people realize that this was *his* responsibility, not the governor's. In reviewing trooper misconduct cases in general, Sarah let Monegan know in a February 2008 email exactly what she thought should happen to rogue troopers: *"we weed out bad apples in ranks that lead some Alaskans to have this distrust of public safety efforts."* From prior pushbacks, Sarah had learned to couch Wooten criticism in broader brushstrokes. Without a doubt, Walt Monegan and others copied on her bad-apple message (me, Kris Perry, Mike Tibbles, Attorney General Talis Colberg, and several others) understood with arctic-air clarity that Sarah's ex-brother-in-law was exhibit one in the need-to-weed-out imperative.

Todd frequently sent articles on both cases. He would suggest, "Walt would rather cost taxpayers money over and over for these dirtbags instead of pissing off the union and firing their asses." Todd's rage blossomed, and the guilty parties expanded to include Colberg and Tibbles. "They're all worthless," he would say. "Doin' nothin'." Hearing his anger, I became increasingly committed to staying off that villainous list of do-nothings. But that wasn't the whole story with me. I genuinely fretted about the reputation of law enforcement and the abuses, not to mention that I feared Wooten did pose a physical danger to the governor's family.

But Todd never let go of any aspect of this case, no matter how far removed from the present. At one point, he had asked both Chief of Staff Tibbles and Attorney General Colberg for copies of the interviews that Sergeant Ron Wall had conducted on behalf of Colonel Julia Grimes in the original 2005 investigation. In particular, Todd believed that Wall had deliberately turned off the tape recorder when interviewing his daughter Bristol during her account of Wooten's tasering episode. If only Todd could get hold of that document, he felt he'd have the smoking gun needed to expose the blue-line cover-up; in essence, he'd prove that Wall had doctored evidence. When Tibbles and Colberg failed to secure these documents, Todd asked me to try. I made inquiries, had no luck, and realized fully that with every incident, his emotional pressure gauge was trending further into the red zone. I imagined that in thirty years he'd be in a rocking chair with a salt-and-pepper goatee, a great-grandson bouncing on one knee, and Wooten's open file balanced on the other.

As always, I promised to do whatever I could and speak with anyone who would listen and might have some input. Later that February, I phoned Lieutenant Rodney Dial in what became the infamous recorded conversation that hibernated for six months and reappeared shortly after Sarah dismissed Monegan. The call began with a discussion of the Public Safety Employees Association contract negotiations. As director of boards and commissions, my interest was natural, and I thought that Dial might have some insight into the thought processes of those with whom we'd be negotiating.

As with most conversations, I felt I shouldn't let opportunity pass, so I launched into a well-rehearsed critique of Wooten and included the bit about the trooper's driving his children to school while on duty. As the tapes revealed as well, I additionally strayed into Wooten's past offenses, paraphrasing language I'd heard from Todd often enough to dream about it. "Todd and Sarah are scratching their heads," I told him. "You know, why on earth hasn't—why is this guy still representing the department? He's a horrible recruiting tool, you know." I also added a sentence to reflect Todd's conspiracy theory: "I mean, from their perspective, everybody's protecting him."

When I immediately repeated back the entire Dial conversation to Todd, he was clearly pleased with my initiative. "Wow, you think these guys will finally do something?" he asked. "Good stuff, Frank. Great." Within a day or two of this exchange, Todd demonstrated his gratitude by asking me if I'd consider becoming chief of staff if Sarah got rid of Mike Tibbles. "Sarah needs someone she can trust," he said. "That's you or Kris, and she is way too emotional."

Todd repeated the request over the next few weeks. Although I was flattered by Todd's confidence in me ("You just get things done, and Sarah likes that"), I was more interested in becoming deputy chief of staff. The governor needed a COS who knew how to speak to the public, a talent I simply didn't possess.

Shortly after Sarah appointed Monegan as DPS commissioner in early 2007, he named former Wasilla chief of police John Glass deputy commissioner. Glass and Todd knew each other and shared an interest in racing snowmobiles. At Todd's instigation, Glass became someone to whom I relayed Wooten developments on at least three occasions. Our first conversation, the day after my recorded call to Lieutenant Dial, began with my asking—at Todd's request—about the Alaska Police Standards Council, the body charged with disciplining law enforcement personnel, and past levels of trooper discipline. Naturally, Wooten's name spilled out.

Glass was aware of my conversation with Dial and therefore knew what was on my mind. He quickly volunteered, "Frank, the Wooten matter has been taken care of." Later, speaking to investigators, Glass stated incorrectly that he told me Wooten had been thoroughly investigated and suspended without pay. At best, Lieutenant Glass's recollection is faulty, because the first I ever heard of Wooten's suspension was after the trooper released his own file in July 2008. To the contrary, when I spoke to Todd about this conversation, I specifically mentioned that I cynically thought Dial's characterization meant DPS had swept the matter under the proverbial rug.

At Todd's insistence and with his prior knowledge, I phoned Glass a second time in early March to specifically address the issue of Wooten's dropping off his children while on duty. Glass said he would look into the allegations but explained that even if it occurred, it was not a firable offense.

"John, on top of all these other problems, how can this not be important?" I went through the lengthy grievance list. "You guys are just protecting him," I continued, begging him to see the light and care enough to get off his rear end and take action. Glass said he'd make inquiries, a response I interpreted as just one more brush-off.

From reading the *Branchflower Report*, I'd learn that I was not alone in my calls to law enforcement personnel. While I never did speak directly to DPS Commissioner Monegan about Wooten (as Monegan claimed to the media), Chief of Staff Mike Tibbles did several times. Kris Perry, Attorney General Colberg, and at least three others in the administration made over two dozen calls inquiring about Wooten. Todd, it turns out, made many of his calls directly from the governor's office.

———

Entering 2008, we juggled other time-wasting balls in addition to the trooper-bashing main event. One of these was our ongoing priority— that began in the early days of the campaign—to rig issue-oriented opinion polls by television stations KTUU and KTVA as well as radio stations KFQD-AM and KENI-AM, among others. When a January KTUU poll asked, Do you agree with Governor Palin's decision to reject a pipeline proposal from ConocoPhillips?, we frantically submitted votes. Scott Heyworth went above and beyond, getting us a two-point swing within just fifteen minutes. We won that vote handily. A few days later, the station ran another poll: Do you support or oppose the Clean Water Initiative if it harms the state's mining industry? We tried, but lost that one. (Our sentiments were with the mining industry.)

While I actively participated, Ivy Frye, now working in the Department of Administration in my former position, became our after-hours polling watchdog, generating hundreds of responses as needed. For a KTUU listener poll about the gas line—our signature issue—she sent an email blast to her exhaustive contact list, exhorting everyone to vote multiple times. She counseled discretion, as our efforts might be "taken out of context," she wrote, and people might think we were rigging the results. Which, of course, we were. Another KTUU poll asked Alaskans if polar bears should be added to the endangered species list. Sarah strongly opposed this designation, as it would negatively impact Arctic drilling and her pipeline plans. She joined Ivy and emailed friends and family, urging them to vote— multiple times—on this vital issue. During the live online polling updates, it was not unusual for us to email back and forth detailing the minute-by-minute changes in the numbers. While attending legislative meetings, there were times when Sarah, using hard to track BlackBerry-to-BlackBerry PIN messaging, would direct us to target a particular poll or supply updates.

Eventually, even national polls, including one by *GQ* magazine asking about GOP vice presidential preferences, came under our manipulative assault. The team, as far back as 2006, during the Alaska governor's race, went so far as to perfect a way to "power vote" using computer software that voted, cleared cookies so that poll administrators couldn't track the email address, then revoted over and over—a process similar to the one allegedly used to help Bristol Palin reach the finals of the TV show *Dancing with the Stars* in 2010. We became invested in manipulating poll results, as if this indicated some kind of reality and shored up our boss's public persona wherever lacking.

———

Poll rigging was fun and games compared to other imagined concerns. With growing conviction, Sarah continued to believe that her administration had leaks and spent hours trying to devise ways to ferret out the culprits. *"Someone leaked my internal email from this morning to an ADN reporter. It's now posted on the blog. This is amazing. These recepients are our team members."* She often copied Lieutenant Governor Sean Parnell on these messages, as if he needed to know that he and staff were not above suspicion. In a Sarah-inspired strategy, we might leak false information to a single person to see if that information ended up in the media. At one point, Sarah planted a rumor through her Yahoo! account that Kris Perry was pregnant. Sarah believed that if the information did pop up in the media, she could assume her emails were being accessed. For all our clandestine efforts, however, I don't recall catching anyone in the act. Over time, John Bitney, Kris Perry, Ivy Frye, Mike Tibbles, and half of Juneau fell under the blanket of suspicion. In all likelihood, I did as well. Sarah also feared that her home and office were bugged. Under her orders, I arranged to have the head of her security detail, Gary Wheeler, sweep both the Anchorage and Juneau offices as well as the governor's mansion for electronic surveillance. She genuinely feared that there were spies watching us, waiting to take some piece of information out of context and destroy her.

Besides Andrew Halcro and Dan Fagan's harassment, other critics demanded constant monitoring. An acerbic blogger who went by the name of Syrin from Wasilla was the source of many hours of discussion, analysis, and reaction, dating back two years. In typical fashion, she set Sarah and Todd into a mental flameout when she wrote in her blog:

Syrin
Date: Mar 25, 2008—1:15 PM EST Subject: Are We Proud as Alaskans? NO!

Looks are deceiving and so is Sarah Palin, aka Sarah the Incompetent, Queen P, Chavez in drag. She proposed and pushed through with her Democrate friends the largest socialistic inspired raise in taxes, in the history of the world. She supports the idea that the State can seize the property of private industry aka oil producers in Alaska if they don't do what she wants. She has attacked almost the entire Republican majority in the house and senate. She just recently tried to oust the Republican party chair at the annual convention. . . .

Sarah stood by and giggled when a radio shock jock called the Republican President of the Senate a "b****" and "a cancer." Sarah also threatened to support Democrats running against Republicans, if they did not support her tax and spend policies. She did live up to her threat! There is NOTHING conservative or pro business about this fulfillment of incompetence, Sarah Palin! She would be a disaster in any political position. This woman has no self-control and is full of folly. And, it seems unbenounced to the State of Alaska, she announced she is 7 months pregnant w/#5. That is most of her first year in office. She is now over her head . . . pregnant.

When Syrin was outed midyear and revealed to be Sherry Whitstine, a forty-six year old Wasilla Christian conservative, Ivy Frye (heroically) called her at home on a Saturday afternoon and told her, "You should be ashamed!" According to an email from Ivy, *I saw [Whitstine] at a luncheon about 2 hours before I called her. What prompted the*

*call was she went home and blogged that the governor sent her mother
(Sally Heath) and her babysitter (me) as spys to the luncheon and she
named us by name."*

Syrin/Whitstine was not the only critic whom we felt the need
to address. The list of those worthy of at least a portion of our time
became long, but one person in particular rose to the top of the heap
and eventually led indirectly back to the Troopergate disaster. We
generated at least a hundred emails and strategies to deal with State
Senate President Lyda Green, whom Ivy Frye had once worked for
and now despised. Seventy years old, and both a fellow Wasillan and
a fellow Republican, Green had the audacity to criticize Sarah in the
Mat Maid Dairy debacle in 2007, eventually calling for an audit. That
October, Sarah provided to a long list of her confidants the following
heads-up regarding Lyda calling for an audit of MatMaid due to "im-
proprieties" and "conflicts of interest."

**I told her "no kidding there's been problems, that's why we have
a dedicated team of volunteers trying to get information on what
went wrong and then how to right MatMaid." I also asked her if
she's seeking to get information on problems we inherited, or did
she feel we caused MatMaid's problems? She said, "it's both."**

Sarah decided that Lyda's *"goals are evidently not our goals."* A relationship that was once cordial grew toxic. As a result, Green had to
be dealt with. When she decided to run again for the state senate seat
in late 2007, Sarah actively plotted against her, even suggesting in an
email, *"Hey—Ivy even lives in [her] district come to think of it! Never
hurts to rumormonger."* From her governor's office, Sarah instructed me
to seek out opponents to run against Green (as well as other legislators
she regarded as personal enemies, such as state representative Mike
Hawker). As 2008 rolled in, the feud grew. Sarah suggested that *"the
only way [her staff] can work with Lyda is to just keep remembering she's
'Mean, Mean Lyda Green.'"* Sarah tossed Lyda into the same cesspool
as other longer-term political terrorists: *"Gag. I'm tired of every word
I say being picked apart and misconstrued, when lyda, halcro, fagan, etc
get away with outright lies. Especially untruths coming from lyda—she's*

the sen prez and must quite spinning these things without beibg held accountable."

Adopting the same ad hominem language formally directed at Fagan, Ruedrich, Halcro, and the Murkowskis, Sarah remarked, *"She's full of bull. . . . She needs to be called on her lies."*

Green, in Sarah's mind, seemed to be part of a core of critics who complained about everything she did. When the governor made plans to travel out of state to son Track's army infantry graduation, Lyda joined Dan Fagan in criticizing Sarah because her arrangements conflicted with the scheduled State of the State address. Sarah's response was, *"[T]his is an unfortunate indication that some would rather spend time and resources on things other than working together and progressing this state."*

As if we weren't busy enough chasing down critics, the bombshell of bombshells was about to explode: out of the deepest blue, in an email sent while on a flight delay in Seattle, Sarah announced to her remaining Rag Tags on March 3, 2008, that she was pregnant. *"Did Todd tell you?! He was supposed to as he visited with you three (Ivy Frye, Frank Bailey, Kris Perry) lately . . . If he chickened out, here's the scoop: (and only those very, very close will know, for as long as possible so our critics won't have one more thing to criticize) . . . the secret news is that you'll all be aunties, in May. (Oh, Frank, you'll be an uncle.)"* She ended her message with a *"Whoo-hoo!"*

In addition to being stunned that our governor, leader, and sometimes rumored vice presidential candidate was with child, we all felt firecrackers of joy. Kris wrote back, *"Holy flippin' cow!!! How exciting, I think I'm gonna cry because that's the best darn news I've heard in a long time."* Hoping that she could keep matters hushed a bit longer, Sarah added, *"But shhhhh, because I'm getting as big as a house, can't hold my stomach in anymore, but don't want folks to know for as long as humanly possible."* She hinted at the potential of this being a special-needs child, but did so without a hint of sadness—in my mind exhibiting some of that strength of character that first drew me to her campaign.

As I sat dumbfounded, blinking away misting eyes and staring at these messages, I suddenly recalled a conversation I had with Sarah in early 2006, when she asked, "Frank, do you and Neen plan on having more kids?"

"I don't know," I answered, "but a large family is something I always wanted."

"What do you think it would be like—" Sarah paused, failing to suppress a sly smile "—to have a pregnant governor in the governor's mansion in Juneau?"

My eyes lit up, and I said something like, "That'd be a first—and sweet!"

Now, two years later, I reminded Sarah of that moment: *"OMG Do you remember sitting in the campaign office shortly after it was open before things got busy. . . . I was playing the keyboard getting ready for our open house, and you talking about what it would be like to be the first Governor to have a baby?? Absolutely amazing."*

Could she have calculated the public relations advantages of having a child while governor? At that moment the possibility did not enter my pinging mind.

Kris broke my brief introspection when she addressed Sarah's "big as a house" comment: *"I just saw you and you most certainly are not. I couldn't tell a darn thing."*

―――――

When Sarah arrived in Juneau shortly after her startling announcement, she had a rosy glow, and, knowing now what to look for, I noticed the bump under the scarves she wore in a crisscross. We hugged while I stumbled through an emotional congratulations.

"Shhhh!" she hushed, pointing to the door of Tibbles's office. "Tibbles doesn't know yet. It's still a secret."

My eyes watered from smiling so much as I nodded agreement that her secret was safe with me. If ever there was a moment when I'd have understood her desire to resign and reprioritize her life, this was it. Never had I seen Sarah so happy and each of us became infected with her emotional Mardi Gras.

Her desire to keep the pregnancy under wraps "as long as humanly possible" lasted all of one day. On March 4 spokesperson Sharon

Leighow reported, *"Unfortunately, Dan Fagan called me this morning and asked me if you were expecting."*

Sarah responded, *"What a fat idiot he is."* She also wondered about how he heard, since the circle of trust in this matter was so small. She wrote, *"My conspiracy theory mind wonders if anyone has access to our emails. Nothing would surprise me."* Not long after, she stated more emphatically, *"Something's tapped or bugged. How else would he even know to ask less than 24 hrs after only a few people knew?"* Whatever the source, with Fagan somehow in the know, Sarah had no choice but to go public on March 5.

———

Throughout the excited announcements and frenzied planning, Sarah purposely left Mike Tibbles out of the loop. When he wandered into the hallway from his Juneau office while we were discussing how to coordinate the public announcement, he shrugged at us.

"What's going on?" he asked, his eyes darting between the small group that included me, Sarah, Sharon, and Janice Mason, her long-suffering and ever-present Juneau scheduler. The nervous grin Tibbles normally flashed beneath that mop of white hair was gone, replaced by a bewildered expression. "Is this something I should know about?"

Until that moment, he had not known that Sarah was pregnant. She was willing to make an announcement to the world before informing her chief of staff. I shuffled my feet and looked to Sarah. She gave me the "Oh brother, what a pain" look and left it to Janice to quickly explain the governor was pregnant. Tibbles didn't attempt to say the right things: There was no "Congratulations, this is wonderful, Sarah!" or "When's the baby due?" Mike, intensely political and the author of endless schemes, understood that his not having been invited into this intimate conversation meant he was no longer part of the inner circle. This trend of leaving him in the dark when discussing important announcements had begun weeks ago, but for a chief of staff, nothing topped the *ouch!* scale than not knowing your boss was seven months pregnant. Watching Tibbles's eyebrows nearly slide off his face convinced me he understood then and there that, politically speaking, he was a dead man walking. Sure enough, by the end of

April, he was gone. His sin? Besides his distaste for me, I believe it had much to do with not being reactionary enough or blindly jumping to Sarah and Todd's whims.

Ignoring Tibbles's mental arrhythmia, Sarah moved quickly to summon her favorite reporters from the *Anchorage Daily News*, Associated Press, and KTUU News. "So," she said coyly, "you know how I always said I'm going to deliver for Alaska? Well, I'm going to deliver for Alaska." Once the initially confused journalists figured out what she meant, the media madness began. Sarah handed off her BlackBerry to me as I deflected the barrage of incoming messages, numbering into the hundreds. This was an uncharacteristically pleasant news cycle devoid of Trooper Wooten, Lyda Green, Dan Fagan, Andrew Halcro, and anyone else who lurked in our collective consciousness. Sheer chaotic euphoria best describes that brief window of "Happy Days Are Here Again."

Of course, placid waters did not last long. Two issues immediately became irksome. Because she did not look pregnant, speculation arose that Sarah was not actually carrying a child at all. More annoying was the allegation that she was hiding daughter Bristol's pregnancy. Those of us who saw Sarah daily and were there after the birth of Trig know this to be an idiotic story. We also saw Bristol regularly in jeans tight enough to convince anyone with eyes that she was not with child. At first Sarah made light of the story:

From: sarah
Sent: Tuesday, April 01, 2008 2:30 PM
Subject: Bristol

Todd: Don't tell [Bristol] but rumor around the capitol is that she's pregnant. People are so mean. I'm going to nicely pull [Bill] McAllister [KTUU political reporter and soon to be Palin spokesperson] aside and tell him that's not true.

Funny people maybe speculated I'm not really pg, but she is and I'm taking the heat for her! Funny, but pathetic.

The next day, Sarah alerted us that Bristol had already heard the story from classmates who heard that Sarah was not really pregnant, but would be raising Bristol's baby. Sarah described Bristol's reaction:

> She's ticked, but made light of it with, "They think I'm pregnant just because I have huge boobs?" Told her to just tell those rumormongers that they're invited to peer at my stretch marks, that'll prove who's really pg.

When discussing the possibility of feeding information to Sheila Toomey, who wrote the *Daily News*'s political gossip column The Ear, Sarah suggested that Sharon Leighow *"feel out Shelia on it discreetly, play it by ear and clear it up if she's suspecting anything."* Then, for the second time, Sarah suggested, *"Heck—offer to let her see my new stretch marks to prove which Palin is truly pregnant!"*

While the serendipitous suggestion of viewing stretch marks was clearly not a serious proposal, it was nonetheless strange for both the imagery and a deflection from a more simple solution.

————

As with any attack, Sarah decided on a culprit. The most recent number one foe, Lyda Green, became our villain. Ivy got the ball rolling: *"I was just on the phone w [a friend] and he got a call . . . Reports from Juneau that lyda's office is perpetuating the Bristol being pregnant rumor. No doubt [one of her assistants]. I'm callin them on the flippin carpet!"*

In typical fashion, none of us needed proof positive. When Lyda Green first learned that Sarah was pregnant, she told the *Anchorage Daily News*, "It's wonderful. She's very well disguised. When I was five months pregnant, there was absolutely no question that I was with child." Armed with sarcasm like that, secondhand reports from Juneau and guessing at which Green aides were *no doubt* responsible were as good as having the murder weapon, a photo of the crime being committed, and a stadium full of eyewitnesses. Sarah wrote, *"Flippin unbelievable. Wouldn't you think they'd be afraid of being proved wrong when they rumor around the building like that?"*

Don't-mess-with-me Ivy shot back, *"We'll get it taken care of, don't worry. . . . When confronted lyda won't be able to do anything but apologize for her staff. How unbecoming and embarrassing for her office esp when press start inquiring."*

A few days later, Sarah had additional input in an email to spokesperson Leighow:

I was shocked last week to hear that a former Legislative Aide approached my sister at church in Wasilla about the Bristol rumor . . . that's the one that got traced back to Lyda's staff spreading it.

Without any additional intelligence, we accepted that Lyda was out to destroy Sarah Palin and did not care if an innocent teenager got hurt in the process.

———

We continued to fret about and fritter away time on chasing down critics, especially Green, while awaiting Trig Palin's Friday, April 18, 2008, birth, approximately one month premature.

When the Bristol rumors did not die, only four days after Trig's birth, Sarah once again complained:

Sheeeesh—I just can not get over this. Todd just left messages with a couple of teachers out here to have them call him b/c they publicly repeated the rumor and he wants to clear it up with them, but also ask where in the flippin world they heard this. Does anyone have any ideas how to squelch this . . . for Bristol's sake if no other reason . . . —maybe even an [*Anchorage Daily News*] Ear mention, or a crafty reporter could handle it light-heartidly perhaps and put it to rest.

The new suspicion, evidently, is that it's too suspicious that I "flew to Texas" and supposedly came back in the middle of the night and appeared with this baby the next day—ha! That either Bristol really had it or some other stupid angle is the newer twist . . . or that Bristol's still going to have one? (They can't even get their rumor straight.)

Like an untreated infection, Sarah's preoccupation with the story became greater. Sharon Leighhow was given a second heads-up and plea for help.

From: sarah
Date: Tue, 22 Apr 2008 22:12:12
Subject: Bristol Re: channel 13 tonight

Hate to pick at this one again, but have heard three different times today the rumor again the Bristol is pregnant or had this baby.

Even at Trig's doc appt this morning his doc said that's out there (hopefully NOT in their medical community-world, but it's out there). Bristol called again this afternoon asking if there's anything we can do to stop this, as she received two girlfriend-type calls today asking if it were true.

Fortunately, the Bristol pregnancy story remained an Alaska-only witch hunt—at least until Sarah was pegged as McCain's running mate.

The morning of the birth, when escorted behind the hospital double doors, I caught a glimpse of Sarah and hours-old Trig. Dazed, I later joyously snapped a photo of Todd cradling Trig, his sparkling eyes fixed on the infant's face. Todd, for all his faults, unquestionably loves his children deeply.

With a good-wishes carousel spinning around the governor and newborn, I left moments later. Passing through the waiting room, I saw Bristol lying on the couch. Because of all the rumors that still exist, let me say for the record (and I do not intend to dignify the absurdity further) she had *not* just given birth.

In sharp contrast to her fragile emotional psyche, Sarah exhibited remarkable physical willpower as she went back to work only two days later. This display of fortitude reinforced that pioneering spirit she nurtured back in her Wasilla mayoral days. The thought in all our minds was, *Amazing, what a gal.*

With Trig's arrival, my brief vacation from Trooper Wooten was about to end. Todd, nearly as resilient as Sarah, was back on that project immediately. However, I found his fortitude far less inspiring.

Moving as if skating across ice, Todd Palin wasted no time whisking from the birth of his fifth child back to his obsession. During April 2008, a new allegation was born. Todd delivered fresh details about a second incident of Trooper Wooten driving his kids to school in the patrol car. Naturally, he suggested that I make another call to DPS's John Glass detailing these newest revelations ("bombshells," according to Todd). The deputy commissioner listened and reminded me once again that this was not a firable offense, even if it happened as reported. Like a tape-recorded message, I suggested, "The department has done nothing on Wooten; it's all a whitewash. Why is he being protected?"

"Frank, the unions are strong," Glass explained. "There are procedures that need to be strictly followed."

"He has a history. Doesn't anyone know how to do an employee investigation?"

To his credit, Glass politely said he'd look into the incident. He did as promised and later phoned to say that although the allegations were correct, Wooten had obtained permission. "The department was shorthanded, so his supervisor told him to use the patrol car when he dropped them off so that he'd be on call at all times."

I said defensively, "I can't believe they're letting him do that."

When I recited the conversation back to Todd, we both concluded this was likely an after-the-fact rationalization meant to explain misconduct—or, in Todd's words, "another cover-up."

If all this hysterical activity sounds ridiculous and wasteful, that's because it was. And the volume only increased through the next weeks. By early May, Todd was calling or emailing multiple times a week; if he happened to uncover something new, I'd hear from him several times a day. The mounting agitation was also physically evident. His face reddened, drew tight, and his eyes narrowed so often that crow's-feet radiated full-time across his temples.

Meanwhile, Sarah's behavior toward Walt Monegan also changed. She initiated her well-practiced freezing out—the process that we'd seen most recently with Chief of Staff Tibbles. In Walt's presence, she might sigh heavily, as if he were stupidly wasting time. Or she might dismissively turn her back and focus on something else. For those who witnessed this frequent process of falling out of favor, the overriding thought was, *Thank God it's not me.*

By midyear, the noose was being cinched around Monegan's neck. What appeared as an idiotic nonevent in the first days of July represented the last straw. In an emotional explosion, Todd would soon call for an end to the Monegan-Wooten madness. Lyda Green, now nestled alongside Trooper Wooten on the enemies list, was the catalyst for the dramatic denouement that virtually guaranteed an unpleasant final act. Todd directed those of us who did his bidding from behind his familiar curtain—responsible but mostly invisible.

Timingwise, the debacle couldn't have been worse. Another personal crisis *and* John McCain were about to knock on our door just as the "stuff" hit the fan.

23

Head over Heels for Sa-rah

He obliged Cinderella to sit down, and, putting the
slipper to her little foot, he found it went on very easily,
and fitted her as if it had been made of wax.
—CHARLES PERRAULT, *CINDERELLA, OR
THE LITTLE GLASS SLIPPER*, 1697

Sarah was rumored to be on someone's vice presidential list as far back as March 2007. In an article extolling her first one hundred days in office, the *Anchorage Daily News* wrote, "There's even blog talk about the governor as a possible running mate for former New York City Mayor Rudy Giuliani's presidential bid." In response, Sarah was quoted as saying, "Oh come on. I got enough to worry about here in Alaska for the next four years."

In July she told KTUU's Bill McAllister, "I feel like a commitment was made on my part, a deal was struck with Alaskan voters that I would stay put. I would feel like I was not being genuine in my commitment if I decided to run for another office while I was serving as governor."

In an interview with the British-based international publication *Monocle*, Sarah downplayed her chances of being selected but sang a slightly less definitive tone by suggesting that her nomination would bring a breath of fresh air to the GOP:

MONOCLE: You must have heard the recent gossip that Rudy Giuliani, if he emerges as Republican nominee for President next year, might ask you to be his running mate. Would you consider it?

SARAH PALIN: *I think it is so far in outer space, the possibility that he would ever want a hockey mum from Wasilla to be his running mate, that I haven't considered it. I think the obligation that I have here is to serve my four-year term as a governor of Alaska. That's the deal that I struck with voters. There is much more that Alaska can do to contribute to the US and I think I can help it do that as governor. But it would obviously be an honour for me to serve the country. And for Alaska's sake too, it would be very good for our future for an Alaskan to be serving nationally.*

M: *Back to the running-mate question. Say the Democratic ticket is Clinton-Obama, a woman and a black man, you can see why the party might approach you?*

SP: *That's diversity right there, isn't it? Wow! And who do the Republicans have? Good old rich white boys. I think that's another factor that has to be considered by Republicans, that in some way their candidates are a reflection of more politics as usual. Not to slam good old rich boys, but it sure wouldn't hurt for new energy and new perspective to be enveloped by the Republican Party.*

Despite her approval rating in the state hovering around a remarkable 80 percent, Sarah was still unknown outside of Alaska. And with Alaska's three puny electoral votes, her selection seemed impossible. Flattering, but as likely to happen as seeing snow fall up rather than down.

The notion took on less improbability, however, when the Associated Press's Juneau correspondent Steve Quinn wrote a piece the day after Christmas 2007 that put the notion of national office front and center. The reporter, a close friend of Ivy Frye, was a passionate supporter of nearly every move the governor made. In his worshipful article, "Alaska Governor Shows Fearlessness," Quinn quoted John J. Pitney Jr., a conservative political scientist from California's Claremont McKenna College, as saying, "Palin could be an ideal presidential running mate next year. What separates her from others is that at a time when Republicans have suffered from the taint of corruption, she represents clean politics." Quinn and Ivy worked together diligently over the ensuing months to build Sarah's reputation and position her nationally. In what I felt was somewhat manipulative of those involved, Sarah told me on more than one occasion in her office to feed stories through Ivy for Steve because "he and Ivy are like this," holding up two crossed fingers, "if you know what I mean." Whether this comment was true or not, I never had the heart to share it with Ivy. Nevertheless, it was Steve Quinn whom Sarah had summoned as her favorite *AP* reporter to break the news of her pregnancy in March. Later, in a heart-wrenching article after Trig's birth, entitled, "Alaska Governor Balances Newborn's Needs, Official Duties," he detailed the moments when Sarah and Todd first came to know that they would have a child with Down syndrome.

———

Piggybacking Quinn's widely quoted December 2007 article, a Draft Sarah Palin for Vice President website run by Adam Brickley, a twenty-one-year-old college senior majoring in political science at the University of Colorado, began to attract attention. Eventually Brickley's relentless efforts caught not only media attention, but ours as well. Over the next year, leading into the presidential election, we began feeding him information on friends and enemies and held regular dialogues. In the month before her selection by McCain, Brickley claimed to have in excess of three thousand hits per day on his website—at least a dozen of those, I can attest, coming from inside the Palin camp.

Over time, others began to float Sarah's name. *Wall Street Journal* columnist John Fund said Sarah Palin would be one of the best VP choices for John McCain—fortunately, he and others were as unaware as McCain that in January 2008, Sarah emailed her circle that she preferred former Arkansas governor Mike Huckabee over the senator from Arizona as the Republican White House hopeful.

Rush Limbaugh, also in February, put forward the name Palin as an attractive McCain choice. Around this time she landed an interview with Fox News where, I noted in an email to staff, "*Sarah was on Hannity's America. . . . Although he just pronounced her name wrong.*" Hannity, whom I have followed for years, eventually became enraptured with Sarah and embarrassingly canonized her every word, often appearing giddy, as if he'd swallowed silly pills.

Ivy continued to aggressively roll the Sarah-for-veep snowball. In May, when KTUU ran a poll of what was described as the vice presidential sweepstakes, Ivy email blasted her contacts: *"Please go to the KTUU website. . . . Gov Palin is in the lead . . . 55% to 45%—keeps the votes coming in!!"* This pounding for votes in various online polls went on without interruption throughout early months of 2008. We were being paid to run government in Alaska, but our real job was to catapult Sarah Palin's career as the savior of the GOP, America, and the world. Ivy, with full-time Google alerts, announced every mention of Sarah for vice president. She dutifully sent these mentions to her expanding list of contacts.

With typical Ivy devotion, she sent Sarah the following:

From: Ivy Frye
Created: 2/28/2008 7:31:13 PM
Subject: RE: Re: Rush's Site??

Well, I have to get on the record before SP4G [Sarah-Palin-for-Governor] becomes SP4VP. A McCain-Palin ticket is the only chance republicans have to beat a Obama-Sebelius ticket. I don't sense "new energy" or "positive change" when I think of McCain-Pawlenty. You heard it hear folks, that's my prediction. Alaskans are about to take over DC w/ sp leading the way.

By April, Draft Sarah Palin for Vice President founder Adam Brickley was a full-blown participant in our cyber circle. He was at least as well connected as Ivy and emailed his own frequent updates. This one sent our hopes soaring:

From: Unofficial Palin for VP Campaign
Sent: Monday, April 14, 2008 12:31 PM
Subject: Gingrich Plugs Palin for VP!!! (twice!)

Hello Palin fans,
Speaker Newt Gingrich has recently started dropping Governor Palin's name when discussing the "veepstakes," mentioning her

on both Hannity and Colmes and On the Record with Greta Van Susteren! . . . and be sure to tell all of your friends (and/or blog readers) about this amazing development. Speaker Gingrich is by far the most important figure to have promoted Gov. Palin as a national candidate, and I am absolutely ecstatic to hear that he has done it more than once!

Speaking of Ivy, while we had our ups and downs during my time with Palin, I have to say that if Ivy were an attorney, she'd be exactly the type of attorney I would want in my corner. Devoted and loyal like a family member and, like me, often went to over-the-top lengths to support our boss. Meanwhile, Sarah was not on the radar of the GOP rank and file outside of Alaska, but the list of conservative big-wigs who accepted her as viable was impressive: Limbaugh, Hannity, Gingrich, and a growing number of others. In June Larry Kudlow of CNBC, the business network, fell head over heels for Sarah when she appeared on his *Kudlow & Company* show. In this interview, unlike one she previously gave then CNN's Glenn Beck, she did *not* reject the notion outright.

Of all the fawning mostly middle-aged white men, nobody was more infatuated than Bill Kristol, the founder and editor of *The Weekly Standard* and a frequent guest on *Fox & Friends*, and a man I've agreed with more often than not. More strategically, he was an editorial columnist for the *New York Times*; its token right-wing ideologue alongside David Brooks. He'd gone to Alaska on a cruise in June 2007 and sat across the table from the sexy future of the Republican Party. Much as President George W. Bush claimed to have looked into Vladimar Putin's eyes and seen his soul, Kristol understood that deliverance for his beloved GOP lived inside this stunning, five-foot-five Aphrodite from Wasilla. Due diligence was conducted over moose stew, red wine, and winky charm. He did not need to ask about foreign policy or current event expertise. He saw a winner. Kristol began bongo drumming her out-mavericking-John-McCain virtues in every venue at his disposal. By June 2008, he was stating flatly on Fox News that Sarah Palin was a historic prospect for a vice presidential running mate. In public and to his contacts within the McCain camp, he made it known that she was not only legitimate but also the only intelligent choice if McCain hoped to have any chance in the upcoming election.

While none of us believed Sarah to be a sure thing for veep—or necessarily even the front-runner—by midyear we understood that it was a possibility, a development that raised anxiety *and* excitement. In my case, I hit a mental Reset button and convinced myself that everything I believed in 2005 was still true: she was Ronald Reagan in high heels. All disappointment—the deception, anger, distrust, lies, wasted time, vendettas—was a necessary evil for launching her on the national stage. We Rag Tags still in place endorsed her candidacy with every cell of our weary bodies.

While we waited for the vice presidential process to play out, the Palins' personal demands were taking up an estimated 70 percent of my time. Added to the demands of my state job, the workday became a sixteen-hour, seven-day-a-week affair. As the hours in the office grew, time at home dwindled to almost nothing, and my wife and children were once again becoming strangers. Was this what I'd signed up for? Always protecting Sarah's back, fighting personal wars alongside Todd? Dining on coffee, Mountain Dew, Chinese in a box, oily cheddar Chex Mix? The burden of the official and unofficial jobs continued to impact my family, culminating in this email from my wife: *"You care more about the Governor than you do me . . . even Kris [Perry] . . . You bother to call Kris on a regular basis, but you are always trying to get me off the phone. Actions speak louder than words."*

For more than the hundredth time, I begged for Neen's forgiveness, swore I'd try to be a better husband and father, then found myself sucked right back in. Feeling as if I needed Sarah and Todd's approval, I simply felt unable to shut down or say no and walk away. No task was too big or too small. Todd and family needed a travel agent for a room in Seattle? He'd contact me, and I'd follow up with grade-A service, often using my personal credit card.

And I would give them detailed advice on arriving, staying, and where to send the girls to shop. When, after a vacation to Hawaii, they needed to get back home on the q.t. (because Sarah had decided to vacation during the all-important legislative session, a potential PR disaster), Todd knew I was their go-to guy:

Hey Frank,

Sarah is debating whether or not to return to Juneau today or tomorrow. Not having a computer to look into Ak award travel from Maui or Honolulu to Juneau via Seattle\LA, since you are the master could you look into this. She would like to keep it quiet.

Family vacation plans to Mexico? "I'm all over it, man."

While pressure mounted, and Sarah scrambled in the background with the heady possibility of being a heartbeat away from the Oval Office, Todd continued waging the Wooten campaign with me as his windmill-tilting sidekick. Current and past Wooten rubble was weighing heavily enough to crack the first family's emotionally brittle spine. Something major had to give way soon.

On June 30, 2008, that moment arrived in a most unpredictable fashion when Walt Monegan sent an email that started off asking if Sarah had read a report he'd sent over days earlier. Then he wrote:

From: Walt Monegan
To: Governor Sarah Palin
Sent: Jun 30, 2008 2:19 PM
Subject: two things

Governor—
1st [Note: the specific nature of this item and question was deleted at the request of the Alaska attorney general's office. We refer to this as "the Report."]
2nd—Via a soon-to-be-retiring legislator, we have received a complaint that had you driving with Trig not in an approved infant car seat; if so this would be awkward in many ways.
Please know that I am trying to help . . .

The second issue Walt referenced involved a complaint from an eyewitness. This legislator alluded to by Monegan claimed that Sarah, while taking her children on a tour of the Point Mackenzie Correctional Farm, had not buckled Trig into a car seat. In a briefly reported story that died a short and uneventful death, Monegan's heads-up and entreaty that he was "trying to help" had the opposite effect. Sarah and Todd claimed that this was some kind of cleverly worded threat from a cabinet member who wanted to leverage authority over the governor. Monegan, they felt, had latched on to this accusation because he believed that the DPS needed more financial resources *and* because he was tired of hearing that Mike Wooten should be selling cotton candy at hockey games instead of carrying a gun and badge.

Sarah received Monegan's email around half past nine on that last Monday night of June. She immediately fired back, *"I've never driven Trig anywhere without a new, approved carseat. I want to know who said otherwise—pls provide that info now."* This was a command. She needed to know who to attack and needed to know *now*.

In the meantime, Mike Nizich, the interim chief of staff who'd replaced Tibbles, read Monegan's email, ignored the child seat issue, and addressed the Report.

Despite later publicly utilizing the contents of the Report to rationalize Monegan's dismissal two weeks later, Sarah didn't seem to care; all she could concentrate on was the car seat. Her image as supermom was at risk. Forget that she admitted to disliking the click-it-or-ticket law or that I'd seen Todd and Sarah drive off with little Piper climbing from the back to the front to sit on Todd's lap while he drove. We even had a photo of Piper in the backseat of a car after a drive of several hours, asleep *on top* of her unbuckled seat belt.

Sarah's wrath was so great that she did not even understand what Nizich was referencing the report in his email. She fired back thirty seconds after receiving his e-mail, *"What are the details of the report? Who, what, where, what was I supposedly driving, etc?"* That Sarah copied me and several others on these communications meant that she wanted everyone on this *now*. As for Nizich, he undoubtedly pretended that he had his priorities straight all along and ignored the Report; state business could take an unbuckled backseat to this more pressing crisis of challenged motherhood.

We went into frantic overdrive. Not because this was necessarily a big deal, but because Sarah and Todd believed this to be a big deal. Kris Perry jumped in minutes after Sarah sent out her demands. *"This is so flippin' ridiculus. I'm talking w/Nizich about it tomorrow. No details, just 'here you go' at 9:30 at night."*

Sarah agreed: *"unflippin believable."*

I did what I knew was required. I immediately phoned Monegan. After my data-collecting conversation with him, I reported back to the Palins: *"Just caught him at home. He said the complaint did come from Lyda to John Glass who passed it to him."* The moment I identified Lyda Green as the complainant, this morphed from bad to disastrous. The confluence of Walt Monegan, the tarnishing of Sarah's motherhood, Mike Wooten's being protected by the blue-line conspiracy, and now double-rumor-mongering-liar Lyda Green was unimaginable evil. In my mind, I heard the snapping of Todd's already fragile emotional spine followed by the sounds of Sarah's head exploding. In a classic bout of scathing sarcasm, Todd wrote me:

> who does Walt and john [Glass] work . . . Awkward Walt, it's not awkward that one of your finest has threatened to bring down your boss and continues pollute the rank and file with his lie's top priority stuff Walt oh but a car seat complaint is worthy of e-mailing her at 9:30 at night after a very busy day, that is what you call chickenshit.

Adding a busted gas line to this fire, we had the makings of a conspiracy. Monegan let slip in our phone conversation that Deputy Commissioner Glass "is close to the Greens and goes snow-machining with them and such." In passing this along to Todd, he concluded that they were all in cahoots to destroy Sarah Palin at a time when she was about to be put on a worldwide pedestal and potentially be named a vice presidential candidate. In July, after Monegan was let go, Sarah speculated that a more organized plot was brewing when she wrote,

> Walt was in the valley yestereday (ironically, I assume bc Glass and Lyda are in the valley). . . . Word getting back to me on that makes me wonder- did lyda ever meet w Wlat during his tenure? She didn't support him bc of his concealed carry positions and budget issues. It would be telling if she is meeting w him at this controversial

time, if we have info showing she never wanted to meet w him before to help w DPS missions/issues.

No matter that Lyda Green had never supported Monegan as the governor's choice for DPS Commissioner; in Sarah's mind their mutual desire to destroy her was enough to bring them together. Todd did not mince words when he concluded his email with the directive *"The games these guys play, something needs to change."* When Todd sent this, I had no idea how rapidly and ineptly a determined power couple could act.

24

Rogue's Gallery

The person who's always cooking up some evil
soon gets a reputation as prince[ss] of rogues.
—PROVERBS 24:8 [THE MESSAGE]

O f all the Palin complaints about Trooper Wooten and DPS Commissioner Monegan, none was as definitive as Todd's June 30
"chickenshit" email. In this instance, his whup-ass words were no idle
threat. In that moment, both Sarah and Todd reached their breaking
points. As Sarah said to me in response to the pressure, "How much
torture can we take?" After all, Monegan had done nothing about the
rogue, loose cannon, ticking-time-bomb trooper. Additionally, Sarah
and Todd now suspected Monegan, Lyda Green, and Deputy Director
John Glass (who was "close" to the Lyda Green family) of being in a
plot to bring down the governor. As with every other perceived attack
on her, Sarah needed no proof. Nor did I; none of us did. Conjecture
was more than enough.

While Todd cared almost exclusively about the Wooten issue,
Sarah constructed secondary frictions with the DPS commissioner besides Wooten's "head-scratching" continued employment. Sarah, for
all the lip service she gave to being supportive of the Department of
Public Safety, was reluctant to devote additional state resources to the
department, certainly not to the extent Monegan desired. In early July
2008, Sarah went so far as to suggest that DPS management needed
to do their job with the resources they had, just like everyone else. In
other words, they had enough funding and manpower. Period. Being
seen as not devoting sufficient resources to law enforcement, however,

wasn't a smart PR move, so other failings needed to be documented ahead of Monegan's removal. As a result, the governor cited his travel expenses and junkets, while emphasizing what she termed his failure in addressing issues relating to rural Alaska, such as high suicide and alcoholism rates. These logs, some of them legitimate, were thrown onto the fire that had as its primary source of fuel Trooper Wooten's ongoing employment. While it is fair to say that Wooten was not Sarah's *exclusive* beef with Walter Monegan, it is flat-out untrue to say—as she did under oath in the *Petumenos Report*, dated November 3, 2008—"that the Wooten matter played no role in her decision to terminate Mr. Monegan as Commissioner of DPS."

Shortly after Todd's June 30, 2008, pronouncement of "needed change," and days before she had current Chief of Staff Nizich drop the hammer on Monegan, on July 11, 2008, the compulsive need to attack and destroy grabbed hold of Sarah. Within hours of the Lyda Green car seat accusation, Monegan's fate was sealed. Five days later, Sarah began discussing replacements for Monegan.

———

I'd recently reminded Sarah about Kenai chief of police Chuck Kopp—a man I'd known casually and admired. Forty-three years old, with twenty years of public safety experience, he was presently a member of the Alaska Judicial Council, the body charged with reviewing candidates applying for state judgeships. Other than these credentials, nobody had reviewed his personnel files or interviewed anyone who worked with him. Kopp and I had discussions earlier in the year about Sarah and Todd's ongoing concerns about trooper conduct, including Mike Wooten. From those conversations, I came to believe that Kopp shared our trooper concerns. As luck would have it, almost exactly twelve hours before Monegan's June 30 car seat email, Kopp suggested in an email that he might be a sounding board and provide advice on DPS issues. *"If the administration is unhappy and looking for a change, let's talk in person when you get a chance."* Kopp's timing could not have been better. In addition to his obvious interest in the job, he had been a member of Palin's Department of Public Safety transition team. Interest in the job, loyalty to the governor, and apparent law enforcement credibility were ideal. On July 7 Sarah emailed and asked me to discreetly explore Kopp's interest in taking over at DPS once she removed Monegan. As I already had the answer to that question, I replied, *"He's interested . . . he'd love to serve under this Governor."* Thorough understanding why Sarah and Todd were unhappy with Monegan, I added, *"He's also 110% onboard with dealing [with] some of the embarrassing issues that have blackened the eye of the entire Trooper around the state, namely Spitzer, Osborn, etc. I'm sure he'd take the Wooten thing seriously."*

In short order, as he often did in appointments that interest him, Todd became involved. He wanted to make certain that Kopp was no Monegan when it came to Trooper Wooten. I assured him this was a person who would not buck the governor's agenda on any issue. After much discussion, I wrote, *"I've spent countless hours discussing the Spitzers, Osborns, and Wootens of the world with Chuck. I'm confident he's on board."* There seemed little need to discuss any additional qualifications.

Two days later, we had Chuck Kopp in Anchorage interviewing with Acting Chief of Staff Mike Nizich, a man who was looking to remove the *Acting* from his title. The road to becoming permanent was to avoid Mike Tibbles's tendency to respond slowly to Sarah's demands, no matter how knee-jerk reactionary they might have been. As such, we both met with Kopp. Nizich did most of the talking, laying out concerns with department hiring, concerns with the $92 million "Taj Mahal" crime lab proposal that Walt was pushing, requests for additional funding, and what Nizich characterized as Monegan's disconnect from the public face of the department. Representing what I believed to be the deeper concerns, I reiterated that there were civil servants risking their lives, but some troopers seemed "to get away with murder" and allowed to keep their jobs. "The cloak of confidentiality," I explained, referencing Todd's opinion that there was a conspiracy to protect bad apples, "is not good for the department."

Kopp understood and acknowledged that weeding out troublemakers was a top priority.

In a display of decisiveness foreign to his predecessor, Nizich left the interview room and immediately phoned the governor. "We have our man," he declared.

Sarah wasted no time in double-checking with me. I agreed that the interview had gone well and observed that Nizich need only conduct what I assumed was standard due diligence. What I didn't realize was that the bee in Sarah's bonnet had a timetable that would not permit such time wasting. The next day, Thursday, Nizich informed Kopp that in four days he'd be named DPS Commissioner. On Friday, July 11, Sarah ordered Nizich to drop the bomb on Monegan and inform him that his services were no longer required. Offered a demotion to executive director of the state Alcoholic Beverage Control Board, he declined. The next morning, Monegan emailed all the other cabinet level commissioners, informing them of his removal from office. Sarah, who had wanted to wait until the following Monday to announce both Monegan's removal and Kopp's appointment, was hopping mad. This unilateral announcement just showed "Walt's true colors," she fumed.

————

What was intended as a family outing to the wind-carved, salmonrich Whiskey Gulch on the Kenai Peninsula became squandered "kid and daddy time." Word was leaking about the pending change at the Department of Public Safety. Instead of spending uninterrupted hours with my long-neglected kids as planned, two cell phones and a buzzing BlackBerry stole my attention. Coordinating messages with Nizich, Kopp, and Sharon Leighow made irrelevant the Cook Inlet vistas, which brought to mind a luminous Thomas Kinkade painting, with blooming lupine, bald eagles feasting on salmon, steep beaches, and rolling bluffs of the lower peninsula. Already running a day late due to the craziness at the office, my brother Stevie had secured camp before the kids and I arrived. Friday night he asked me, "Dude, why did you even come if you were going to talk on the phone the whole freakin' time?" It was an excellent question with only bad answers.

————

Saturday morning my six-year-old daughter hid my BlackBerry. When I frantically begged her to tell me where, she reprimanded, "Daddy! This is a BlackBerry-free zone." My son said he'd wanted to throw the thing in the fire. In my gut I knew I wasn't being a good father, but Sarah wanted this done now, and what Sarah wanted, Sarah got.

The press release announcing the changes at DPS was drafted that day, July 12, and sent internally at 4:25 p.m., about the same time that I first received Chuck Kopp's updated resume. No interview of superiors or coworkers, no review of personnel files, and not even an updated resume had been reviewed ahead of his appointment. Sean Parnell received his own heads-up in a nine-word email from Sarah the next day: *"We're replacing Walt with Chuck Kopp. . . . It's all good."* Due diligence did not fit into Sarah's schedule. Walter Monegan, union leader John Cyr, and those at DPS who had not jumped through enough hoops to suit the governor had to be punished instantly for their *unflippin' believable conduct*, and Sarah needed to appear organized and ready for a seamless transition. Barring a political disaster, Trooper Mike Wooten would hopefully suffer just deserts at the hands of a newly appointed DPS Commissioner Kopp. As Sarah told her lieutenant governor, "It's all good."

Except that it wasn't. Monday, the announcements became official, and Kopp spent the day fielding media questions. Traveling home from my disastrous family weekend, I phoned to ask how day one went. Suddenly the conversation took an unfortunate turn. Kopp mentioned casually that he'd been tagged with a sexual harassment complaint in the past. Sarah and Parnell, he insisted, knew the details, having been informed when he worked on the governor-elect's transition team, a revelation that Sarah hadn't mentioned. With a groundswell of support for Monegan, questions were being raised about his dismissal, thus making Kopp a target. Potentially, this seemed like a bull's-eye pinned to his back. Did Sarah, Parnell, or Nizich really know? Kopp explained that the "situation" had been investigated, and he was exonerated. I hoped the "situation" was also long forgotten.

Between a lack of sleep mixed with a new dose of dread, I considered other potential traps waiting to be sprung. Sarah rarely thought through decisions and never listened to dissenting opinion, so there was no use lamenting the lack of planning and speed with which this appointment took place. As always, we'd scramble if/when things became messy. In the meantime, Sarah had not so much as spoken to her new DPS commissioner, and I worried that a reporter might ask Kopp, "When did the governor interview you?" Um, never.

That Monday night, I wrote the governor: *"Wondering if you had a quick minute to call Chuck and congratulate him . . . He could then respond, 'yes we spoke this morning actually' If the question came up."*

The next morning, Sarah responded: *"Called him. Great convo . . . I'm calling kenai to thank them for releasing him! :)"*

In the meantime, Todd continued to wage his bad-cop battle. He suggested to Ivy Frye that she email complaints against Monegan and Cyr directly to troopers as a means of rallying support, not to mention "to piss them off." *"The rank and file,"* he suggested, *"need to hear the rest of the story. The PSEA continues to protect bad cops."* In conclusion, he suggested that Ivy delete a handful of troopers from their mass message, including Mike Wooten.

Sarah didn't enjoy the second-guessing that was going on in the media, but she was at peace with her decision. That lasted until Tuesday afternoon, Kopp's second day on the job, spokesperson Sharon Leighow informed the governor that the media had gotten wind of a sexual harassment complaint filed against Commissioner Kopp in 2005 while he was the Kenai Chief of Police. Kris, in a panic, told Sarah that reporters were asking if she knew of the allegation during the transition.

Sarah naturally denied knowing anything of the sort. Ironically, information surfaced later suggesting that it was Walt Monegan who delivered the news in early 2007 when considering Kopp for an appointment within his own department. Later, when the *Anchorage Daily News* confirmed that Kopp's accuser had emailed Sarah prior to the appointment, we took another PR thrashing. To make matters worse, it was discovered that several additional emails from this complaint were also sent to her attention.

Sarah, characteristically, suggested that others were at fault for not forwarding emails to her. She subsequently ordered Leighow to explain to the paper that she was innocent of ignoring warnings. She never even saw the emails; yet, she lamented, the *Daily News* wrote as if she'd purposefully ignored the *"accuser's offer to provide me information."* People needed to know that Sarah was the victim here.

Commissioner Kopp held a press conference. He sought to explain that the situation was not as it seemed. My personal opinion holds that Chuck Kopp is a decent man, and I believe there were important details supporting Chuck that the media disregarded in the case. But my opinion did not matter. The PR worsened as the anger over Monegan's dismissal grew—especially at DPS, where loyalty to him was strong. When criticism for the pick grew to ridicule, Sarah went from claiming publicly in a press release, "There is no substance to the complaint filed three years ago and Commissioner Kopp continues to have my *full support*," to cut and run. On Friday, July 22, 2008, Chuck Kopp resigned after less than two weeks on the job. Unlike Monegan, he received a severance of $10,000. Naturally, that led to speculation this was hush money. Sarah explained that since he'd been asked to leave a paying job, compensation was the fair thing to do. (I heard from a source close to the situation that Kopp was asked to sign a nondisclosure agreement ahead of the payment.)

While Kopp needed to be more forthright with issues, regardless of whether they'd already been raised, Sarah's abandonment of him and lack of foresight to have her team explore political land-mine questions before his appointment was brutal to watch.

Much later in 2011, Chuck was recognized by the Supreme Court for his years of contributions to the Alaska Judicial Council, where he faithfully served prior to his twelve-day appointment as commissioner.

Throughout all this, beginning back on July 9, we faced another interpersonal avalanche. Sherry Whitstine, aka the blogger Syrin from Wasilla, was jabbing Sarah with her sharp stick by suggesting that the governor had engaged in an extramarital affair with Todd's best friend back in 2005—a story later rehashed by the *National Enquirer.* When Whitstine's message appeared on the *Daily News*'s online message board, Sarah had to react. *"OK dokay—enough is enough. I am calling ADN."* That the governor of any state would personally respond to a rumor, especially by directly phoning the state's largest newspaper, struck many of us as inappropriate, as well as unwise. Staffers begged her to not dignify an online message board, but with Sarah, there is no emotional off button. She sent a second email, suggesting that being governor was almost too much of a burden: *"Guys, I may be pretty wimpy about this family stuff, but I feel like I'm at the breaking point with the hurtful gossip about my family that Sherry and others get away with. Bear with me. I hate this part of the job and many days I feel like it's not worth it.*" Suddenly we had to contend with seemingly too much: there was the car seat charge, the alleged affair, Monegan's unpopular dismissal, and dealing with Kopp's PR disaster, followed by his resignation.

But the pain Andrew Halcro was about to inflict on the administration would bury all these other matters.

25

Truth Be Told

Tough when truth doesn't necessarily win out.
It is the way of politics sometimes.
—FRANK BAILEY, EMAIL TO A FRIEND,
THURSDAY, JULY 24, 2008

From Sarah's point of view, Walt Monegan's dismissal, while the subject of criticism, was, everyone agreed, within her rights—even if he was replaced with someone whose background we hadn't properly vetted. Her acting like a pricked balloon when given a heads up from her DPS commissioner over a child not being strapped into a car seat was totally irrelevant.

As firm as her ground seemed, on Thursday, July 17, the soil suddenly shifted, and her foundation of technical righteousness crumbled.

Monegan did not understand why Sarah dumped him; nor did one of our most prominent enemies. When Andrew Halcro interviewed Mike Wooten for his blog, the trooper made a number of startling claims, leading Halcro to conclude that Governor Palin had canned her DPS "commissioner because he fought too hard. Governor Palin fired Monegan because she understood too little and wanted a puppet as commissioner. But there was another reason that contributed to Monegan's ouster; a more alarming reason." Hitting the nail hard and true, he summed up by writing, "But more alarming than any budget battle, Monegan said no to firing a State Trooper who had divorced Governor Palin's sister."

The morning of Halcro's explosive blog, I drew the short straw and had to escort Sarah to a speaking engagement for congressional candidates who'd flown up to Alaska to visit the 19 million acre Arctic National Wildlife Refuge. When we arrived, Sarah was, per usual, greeted as a celebrity. I had to literally push her through the throng to the podium. While she delivered her speech, KTUU television reporter Jason Moore tapped me on the shoulder. "Hey, Frank, have you read this stuff on Halcro's blog about Mike Wooten?"

I half laughed, suggesting that anything originating from Halcro was not worth the cyber ink used to print it. "No, I don't follow Andy's blog."

"Well, maybe you should. He's alleging Monegan was let go because of the governor's ex-brother-in-law. The trooper. I'd like to talk to her after this event, ask her a few questions."

The smell of media gunpowder sent my nose twitching. "Sorry, not likely," I said, my eyes roaming the room for further signs of ambush. "We have another pressing event to go to right away." While a fabrication, I realized that surprise confrontations did not bring forth Sarah's finer moments.

The minute the governor finished her speech, I intercepted her. While she basked in the wild applause, getting Sarah to focus on my warnings about the reporters and Halcro's comments bore no fruit. Worse, she spotted blogger Sherry-Syrin-Whitstine in the audience and insisted that she publicly confront her, all the while unaware that massively embarrassing allegations were being fed like hungry fleas on a mutt's belly.

But the persistent Jason Moore nabbed Sarah before she could get to Syrin from Wasilla. "Governor, could I have a word with you about Monegan?"

"That's a personnel matter, and I really can't comment," she said, still focused on a confrontation with an enemy.

"Andrew Halcro says it's about your brother-in-law. Monegan wouldn't fire him."

Finally, in her face, I saw the realization that somehow her multi-year vendetta against Trooper Wooten was being exposed in the worst possible manner, and this situation represented yet another confluence of familiar enemies coming together: Wooten, Monegan, and Halcro.

Not to mention Lyda Green, who would shortly call for an investigation.

"Governor," I said, clutching her elbow, "we need to move on. No time for interviews. Uh, our next appointment and we're running late."

Another reporter, with camera lights glaring, shot off a question before I could redirect Sarah toward the exit. "Why did you fire Monegan? Was it because . . ."

Sarah's eyeballs came unhinged. She stammered and said something about Walt not being fired; he'd been reassigned to another agency but declined. Wooten? No connection. Halcro? Hadn't read him.

"Governor, your meeting!" I reiterated, more firmly this time. "We have to go."

We left, but not before the damage was done.

Later that day, Todd came at this from another direction. He assumed that because Halcro's blog contained so much detail, he must have received inside information. Todd emailed: *"From Halcros blog, a bunch of lies, but he must have access to Wooten's investigators final report from Walt or John Cyr. I would check Walt's computer to check if he printed a copy of the report before he left his office and gave it to Halcro."* It escaped my attention at the time, but Todd seemed to be suggesting that he knew what was in Wooten's file. How? Had he seen the file firsthand, despite later swearing under oath that he hadn't?

Fortunately, I ignored Todd's request to visit Monegan's computer.

Over the next six days, we convened around the clock rehearsing what information was seeping out to the public and how to handle things. There were no good answers. On Wednesday, July 23, Sarah met with several of her cabinet members, including me, Kris Perry, Sharon Leighow, and Deputy Chief of Staff Randy Ruaro. The governor sat hunched over, her hair hanging uncharacteristically limp and unbundled. With a pinched, pained expression, she appeared to have aged ten years in two days. On the radio, we listened to Dan Fagan interviewing Halcro: both were claiming that Sarah Palin ruined Walt Monegan's career because he wouldn't do her bidding and unfairly fire a trooper. Unanimously we cursed the evil things being said without admitting that many of them were true. Finally Sarah lifted her head and said, "No one's talked to DPS about Wooten, have they?"

Incredulously, I looked around the room at the others. We all knew there was constant complaining about Wooten. Furthermore, many of us had, at one time or another, articulated Palin grievances when interacting with people in law enforcement. And, given that I'd related to Todd Palin every word I could recall after each DPS conversation, I had little doubt Sarah was aware of at least some of what I'd done and said. Her question defied common sense. Her suggesting that "No one's talked to DPS about Wooten" was her way of saying, "If asked, I want everyone to deny ever mentioning Mike Wooten to anyone, anytime. Okay?"

We were assembled in the governor's seventeenth-floor corner office with its view of downtown Anchorage. Storm clouds blanketing the horizon seemed suddenly to breach the windows and enter our room as I admitted, "I have, on more than one occasion, discussed Wooten. I've spoken to John Glass, others."

"About what?" Sarah asked.

"Wooten on his snow machine, driving his kids to school in his patrol car."

Sarah's attention turned to her BlackBerry as she let the conversation die. She didn't want to hear any of this because it would fly in the face of reality. A day or two later, she had Sharon Leighow issue the following statement: "Outright, the first family unequivocally says there was never any pressure by them, or the governor's staff, for Monegan to fire their former brother-in-law. Governor Palin says, 'All I know is what the facts are and what the truth is. And the truth is never was there any pressure put on Commissioner Monegan to fire anybody.'"

When I read those words, I wished the governor had edited out the part about her staff. Also, I'd have felt a bit more sanguine about the "truthfulness" if she'd managed to find a way to exclude her husband from that blanket denial as well. With calls for an investigation growing, surely the fact that Sarah knew this statement to be disingenuous at best would surface.

If she expected me to lie under oath, she'd be disappointed.

If asked about calls, I'd relay to the best of my knowledge exactly what was said.

And while I had heretofore avoided implicating Todd Palin, continuing to do so was going to be increasingly difficult. For anyone to suggest that his unrelenting goal was *not* to destroy Wooten, including having him dismissed as a state trooper, would seem on face to be ludicrous.

For days, Sarah, Todd, and the administration spokespersons continued to deny any connection with Monegan and Trooper Wooten. It was as if all those meetings between Todd and me had never existed. In their alternate version of reality, Todd hadn't hand delivered photos, articles, or so-called testimonials of Trooper Wooten's misdeeds, nor had he repeatedly instructed me to forward that information to people in government on his behalf. He conveniently forgot about relaying the results of the investigation of Wooten to members of the media.

What I didn't understand was why Sarah simply didn't say, "Yes, one of the reasons I let Walt go was that we had rogue troopers—including Trooper Wooten—who had no business wearing a badge or carrying a gun." All she had to do was release everything that she and her husband had compiled on the guy. Who in their right mind wouldn't agree with her? Sarah's sister Molly seemed to understand the soundness of this strategy best. She phoned me shortly after one of my disastrous press interviews to remind me that Wooten had recently threatened, "Get ready for the show! I'm gonna take down your sister." She believed that if all the dirty laundry were aired, the story would have a satisfactory conclusion.

Just before Chuck Kopp was forced to resign and muddy the waters even further, Assistant Attorney General Mike Barnhill interviewed me. I candidly told him everything I could remember, leaving nothing out about Todd, Sarah, Tibbles, Monegan, and Wooten. Afterward, Sarah and Kris Perry immediately asked about the interview. I shared all. They seemed nervous, and I could almost hear them thinking through their own stories so as to avoid contradicting anything I'd said.

The following day, Acting Chief of Staff Nizich summoned me. My name was being bandied about as the key player in the Get-Wooten-fired saga. Dan Fagan incessantly hammered me on the radio, while the television stations rolled unflattering clips of me stumbling through interviews. Lack of sleep, concern for my governor, feelings of guilt, and grief for the pain I was causing my family translated into a gnawing in my gut as I entered Nizich's office. Without much fanfare, he told me that they had become aware of my conversation with Lieutenant Rodney Dial back in February. As I'd already told them all about it, I wondered what the big deal was. Then he launched his uppercut: "The call was taped."

As he began playing the six-month-old recording, I had to admit the conversation sounded bad. All of the administration's protests about never pressuring Monegan were about to be dashed, and I was to blame. Not because I was alone in doing what the first family wanted me to do but because I'd been *recorded* doing what the first family wanted me to do.

Once we'd listened to the entire conversation, Nizich said in his best prosecutorial voice, "Frank, you say that others shouldn't do anything to embarrass the governor. Well, this will be highly embarrassing to her."

Yeah, this *was* embarrassing, but the reasons went far beyond me. Even while Sarah swore that nobody put pressure on Monegan, she knew of my call because I'd told her about it only a day or two earlier. Sarah made the decision to misrepresent the truth, not me. I said nothing in my defense, though, because inconvenient facts were not on today's menu.

"Did the governor ask you to make this call?" he asked.

"No."

"Did Todd?"

"No."

Nizich asked why I felt compelled to suggest that I was speaking on behalf of the governor. I said it was a stupid mistake. He wanted to know how I had all this information. "Did you ever see Wooten's personnel file?"

With that question, there was no longer any way to protect Todd and, as Nizich was one of our team leaders, I decided to let him fumble around with trying to downplay Todd's role in all this. "Mike, it came from Todd. Every file, letter, photo, and accusation . . . every bit of information on Wooten came from Todd. He was aware of this call to Dial, thanked me, and was pleased.

"Other calls? He sometimes knew ahead of time; always knew before or after. Always encouraged me, gave me information to pass along, let me know he appreciated my efforts. Wooten is a bad cop, Mike. I agreed that he needed to be dealt with for the good of the troopers, but my actions were always on behalf of Todd and Sarah, no matter what they say now or in the future." I didn't say these things in anger at the First Dude; my defensiveness was directed at Nizich for not at least pretending to support my position. Later, when he was to blame for not vetting Kopp, he likely came to understand more fully that abiding by the demands of his bosses often had negative consequences. For now, he seemed intent on blowtorching me in a show of effective loyalty to the governor.

Later that day I spoke with Sarah. She wanted to know about the Dial recording. "Was he leading you on, fishing for information?" Sarah acted supportive, looking for an angle to attack back. She indicated they'd be releasing the tape to the public rather than wait for independent counsel Stephen Branchflower or her legislative enemies to do so. She felt it would ease some of the sting if she addressed the issue directly and gave her side of events first.

"This is on me," I explained. "I'll take the hit. What's worse is I don't know how I'm going to avoid the question about Todd when this tape hits the media. Everything I had came from him. I already explained that to Nizich."

"I'm expecting they'll lump Todd and me together in this. What's the worst they can do, Frank? Impeachment? I guess then I'll go home, and life can be normal again."

Go home and be normal? The way she said the words held no relief. She was miserable, and that made me feel like the single, solitary cause of her problem. In that moment, I foolishly believed nothing could get worse.

When I went home later that night, I couldn't begin to explain this mess to my wife. Sleep? The nightmares were disturbing. I wondered if I'd ever experience a pleasant dream the rest of my life.

I decided to resign, believing this was the bullet I'd eventually eat. No way out. Sarah needed me to somehow save her from further damage. But even in this desire to end my political life, I'd fail. With John McCain on the horizon, other less public solutions were required.

———

Wednesday, August 13, the day after Nizich played the incriminating tape and scolded me, the governor's office was fully staffed with the brain trust—who, in this particularly matter, had no interest in my two cents' worth. For hours they debated how to navigate the public handling of the Bailey-Dial recording.

I was certain of two things that morning: (1) this was the worst day of my life, and (2) at some point I'd throw up. I was to soon become the publicly humiliated wounded mule headed for the glue factory. My job had always been to make Sarah shine, but somehow my actions had mired her in what she referred to as the "biggest crap cluster" of her political life.

Through the windows, high above downtown Anchorage, I could see boaters at the mouth of Ship Creek. I envied their lives of hard outdoor work in the most gorgeous waters on the planet. They enjoyed honest chatter about where to secure the day's catch instead of schemes to limit damage and, barring that, redirect attack. How did such a simple guy like me end up in the lion's den? Loyalty? Stupidity? Or both?

Just past noon, spokesperson Sharon Leighow came to my office. "The governor is ready to see you," she said.

Dragging my feet, I followed. Once inside the governor's office, I looked around the room at the dreary faces of Attorney General Colberg, Acting Chief of Staff Nizich, Assistant Attorney General Barnhill, and recently hired Communications Director Bill McAllister, and Sharon. I felt like a mouse in a room full of cats. At the center of it all was the governor. Sarah's white leather outfit was likely meant to convey purity to those outside this room. For me, however, it merely highlighted a fire-engine red face. She was furious. Yesterday's supportive demeanor—when I patiently answered all her questions about Todd, Dial, and my screw-up—had vanished. Now I'd discover how she really felt.

"So," she began, as if lecturing one of her brood, "you know we're going to have to do this right. Those in the legislature, like Hollis French"—she spit out his name, clearly disgusted that this man would be at the forefront of calling for an investigation—"will come out with this information if we don't." The plan was to volunteer the facts, explain, and place the blame right smack dab on me.

I nodded as a lump of saliva wedged against my Adam's apple. "When?" I asked.

Sarah indicated it would begin shortly after the lunch hour.

"Governor?" I asked. "About what we discussed last night? How do I answer the media without getting into where I got the info?" With blindly loyal eyes I was still trying to figure out a way to protect Todd Palin.

Just then, Barnhill jumped up and scurried around the table and whispered in Colberg's ear. The attorney general cleared his throat and said, "Um, we can't be giving you any advice here."

Everybody nodded agreement; no advice for Frank Bailey. *Great.* As there was no chance of swimming, they were saying I was on my own to sink once the cement dried around my feet.

Sarah made it clear that she did not want me at her press conference, so I wilted away to wait for my turn, afterward, to face the cameras. "I'll make myself available at four o'clock for interviews," I told her.

"Yes, fine," she said. "That's best."

As Sharon and I stumbled back to my office, she patted my hunched shoulders and told me to hang in there. It was a small gesture, but it meant something. Nobody else seemed concerned that I was in way over my head.

While Sarah approached the podium to deliver her statement, I sat at my desk, phoned the call-in line that would relay the press conference, and listened. Understanding that there was only one noble thing left to do, I crafted a resignation letter. "It is apparent that in light of candid comments I made regarding my impressions of Trooper Wooten, I improperly and incorrectly characterized some involvement by the governor in my request for DPS to follow up on some issues. This is 100% incorrect." I went on to exonerate both the governor and Todd as best I could.

As I put the finishing touches on the six short paragraphs, Sarah's press conference began. With every word, my personal dismay grew. The governor was masterful, delivering words like "totally wrong," "shocked," "totally unaware," and "appearance of pressure" with the edge of a razor, slicing away my skin along with the truth, allowing my insides to bleed. Sadly I nodded in agreement: I deserved her blame.

Toward the end of the question-and-answer session, a reporter asked, "So, can we ask questions of Frank Bailey? Is he available?"

Watching the replay later, I witnessed the governor's head swivel around. She asked, "Where is Frank?" She looked right and left, playing for the camera. "I don't know where he is." She made it seem as if I were hiding, when she was the one who told me *not* to be on camera with her. "Does anyone know where he is?" Her entire act made me out to be a guilty coward, slinking away to hide under a rock.

Sharon Leighow came to my rescue when she piped up, "Frank will be available for media at four o'clock."

"Oh," was all Sarah said, as if this were the first she'd heard of it.

As I watched my governor's painful theatrics, I literally spoke to the wall, "What? Where am I? Hey, I'm sitting here trying to figure out how in the hell I'm going to protect your husband, that's where I am!" The bus was rolling forward again, running over that last square inch of me it hadn't already squished.

Despite growing feelings of betrayal, I made the decision to own up and take blame. While waiting for my public beheading, I sent Sarah my resignation letter. Not long after, Nizich, almost excited—maybe because Sarah had done such a great job and the storm now centered on me—entered my office. "That letter you sent the governor?" he said. "She doesn't want it. She told me to tell you, she doesn't want it."

What? In my mind, I was a former employee. A skeptic might suggest that Sarah figured it was better to have a still-loyal minion rather than a formerly loyal minion speaking to the press. When I finally did face the media, I played the part of rogue overzealous state official, inappropriately acting on my own without any outside prompting. When asked how I knew about Wooten's employment records, I said, "I'd rather not say."

While this made me appear guilty of improperly accessing confidential records, I remained committed to not implicating Todd Palin or, potentially worse, Sarah. At the time, I questioned how much she actually knew. After many months, I became convinced that she knew much more than she let on. Did Todd go for long drives or stow away in the garage to spend all those hours on the phone with me, retelling the chronicles of Wooten? He had even used the phone in the governor's office for many of these conversations. Was he left alone all those times, with open access to state resources and classified information?

After my media debacle, Todd phoned—not to say he was going to take some of the heat and admit his role—but to buck me up *and* remind me of an important talking point.

"Holy jeez, Frank. Holy jeez."

"Yeah," I said. "Tough one today."

"We love you, Frank. We love you, man. You gotta know that Sarah didn't know *anything*, though."

I mumbled something that was meant to signify I understood without admitting I didn't believe a word of that last sentence. Todd finished as he began, "We love you. Holy jeez, Frank."

We hung up, and all I could think was, *Sarah didn't know?*

Amazingly, my phone rang off the hook, and my BlackBerry filled with more messages than I could possibly return in a month. I found the support I was receiving to be stunning. Sure, most messages came from acquaintances, but these people had also been passionate supporters of Sarah Palin. Those who knew little more than what they'd heard and seen in the media, believed her representations at the press conference to be self-servingly shallow. "She threw you under the bus" and "It's not right that she and Todd don't take any responsibility" were said or texted numerous times. I took great pains not to agree with anyone's analysis publicly, but I felt a tiny bit of relief that some people saw the reality despite Sarah and Todd's public song and dance.

The owner of internet publication *AlaskaReport*, Dennis Zaki, phoned and said, "It's shit what Palin did to you! You can't tell me she did not know."

"If she did, Dennis, I have no firsthand knowledge."

"I've always liked Palin, but this was bad, Frank. Your face is everywhere. KTUU has a poll out, asking viewers if you should be fired."

When he said "Your face is everywhere," that mirrored a recurring nightmare of mine, not unlike the dream where someone leaves his house without any clothes. For me, I preferred the possibility of being naked in public so long as I was anonymous.

Dennis then said, "Have you ever thought of running for office? Hey, you've sure got the name recognition now. Nobody in the state doesn't know Frank Bailey. Do it, run for governor!"

For the one laugh I'd had in days, I remain grateful to Dennis Zaki.

I fled to my brother's house in Chugiak later that night. My cell rang incessantly, but I didn't answer until I noticed an important number. Sarah was calling. Stevie recalls more of what was said than I do:

> The conversation started out tame with you explaining how uncomfortable you were with being the single confirmed target of the "investigation" of abuse. As you paced a hole in my laminate flooring in the kitchen, your tone changed. I'm not sure what was said, but you ramped up and clearly yelled at the phone. You told Sarah that your name was trashed and that your public integrity was run through the mud. You explained that while her name was tarnished, your name and family's reputation would never recover from what they'd done to you. I remember thinking, *Frank is yelling at the governor in my kitchen!*

Actually, I do recall saying in an angry voice, "You'll be fine, but I'm trashed. There's a poll on the web asking if I should be fired, Sarah!" I felt like a spinning plate, one that Sarah had to keep in orbit and keep close and within her control. If I did quit, she'd lose me, and

I knew many more damaging things than did "disloyal" Walt Monegan. At that moment, I was determined to leave the rat race called government and start from the ground up, rebuilding my life like I'd done as a poor kid in Kodiak, when our family had nothing, not even enough food or heat some days.

I think Sarah was more than shocked by my reaction. When I told her I intended to leave, she became worried. The next morning, Thursday, she phoned again. We spoke for about forty minutes. "Frank," she said, "former governor Jay Hammond once told me he sought out people who were reluctant to serve. He didn't go for the bigwig types. He looked for the good salt of the earth people. That's you, Frank. There are only a few of us left. You, me, Todd, Kris. The state needs you, and Alaska needs me. I refuse to accept your resignation, Frank. In fact, I told Todd I wouldn't even open your letter or read the email you sent."

"But even if I wanted to stay, all it would do is make your agenda more difficult to carry out." I was pleading with her to not make this difficult. In my mind, I already had both feet out the door.

"If you go, Frank, then I go." She repeated that statement three times. "Take the rest of the week off to think."

As I'd witnessed many times before, Sarah could put the genie back in the bottle like no one else. No matter the nature of the breakup, if she wanted, she'd calm matters and suck a person back into the fold. As always in these situations, she sounded genuine, and I believed her. We would weather this storm together.

By Friday, Sarah did what Sarah often does: she flip-flopped and was again furious with me; there was no longer any "together" in any of this. When we spoke, she sounded harsh and stiff, with an accusatory tone. She said the Alaska Department of Law wanted to know what I'd done with regard to Wooten and Monegan. I explained that I'd been interviewed by Assistant Attorney General Barnhill and told him everything I remembered about my contacts with DPS. After this testy conversation with Sarah, I renewed my pledge to resign. I again emailed my resignation letter and asked my wonderful Juneau administrative assistant, Selina Kokotivich, to pack up my desk and send the contents to my house, including the private investigator's file Todd had handed me weeks ago in case someone went through my belongings.

A short while later, Todd phoned. "Frank, I hear you're still trying to quit. Don't. Sarah, she's all over the map on this, but she'll come around. One minute she's on your side, the next minute she's listening to Nizich and she's agreeing with him that you need to go. Jeez, Frank, we need you. Hang in there. You'll see."

As luck would have it, my friend Phil offered up his property in the Mat-Su Valley, and shortly after Todd's latest call, I prepared to escape and take the family camping. While refueling, my wife texted Sarah, asking her to call and discuss an idea for handling the media storm. When the phone rang, Neen put the call on speaker. Sarah was sobbing and trying to catch her breath. She had something confidential to share but was so upset she couldn't get it out. She hung up, telling us she needed a minute or two to recover. Whatever Sarah had to say was important enough to cause the governor of Alaska to break down into an emotional mess. I prepared for the worst. Maybe some of our earlier behaviors during the campaign were being uncovered and wrapped around this latest nightmare. Possibly another phone call— as there'd been nearly two dozen by at least four insiders—had been recorded, maybe even one from Sarah or Todd directly. Clearly this was the old Sarah, needing to reach out to the Frank Bailey who had been the original Palin-bot and Rag Tagger. Someone whose blind allegiance had known no limits and who, even now, was arranging to have incriminating investigator's documents commissioned by her husband hustled from Juneau to his house. Thursday she'd said that if I quit, she'd leave. Friday she'd turned course and seemed ready and willing to see me gone. Now on Saturday, August 16, 2008, she was in need of sharing a piece of shockingly confidential information and wanted my wife to listen in as well.

What could it be? If I'd been forced to guess, there would not be enough days in eternity for me to get it right. Just when it seemed that our fan could not possibly handle any more, we found ourselves dodging tons more flying scat.

26

If You Go, I Go—Maybe

omg. what a crap cluster.
—SARAH PALIN, EMAIL TO FRANK BAILEY,
TUESDAY, JULY 22, 2008

That Saturday morning, desperately in need of getting out of town—away from the media and the images of me being ripped to shreds on the television—I had thoughts of utilizing my fast-food-fueled overweight self to smash my smartphone, which no longer seemed so smart. Next I'd toss my BlackBerry under a tire and see how flat its microchips might get beneath the weight of a fully loaded camper. When Sarah first rang, too distraught to speak, I was gassing up, buying thirty gallons that would take the Bailey family hours and hours away from the scandal and to a place where news didn't roll on an endless cycle and people didn't yet know enough to ask, "Oh, so you're the Troopergate guy, huh?"

It was my failure to destroy my electronic connection to the world that allowed the governor to make a return call. Still distraught, she managed to say, "Bristol—"

What happened? I waited for the governor to catch her breath. Was Sarah's daughter injured? This seemed beyond Lyda Green or Halcro or Syrin spreading some nasty rumor. Those things sent us into a frenzy, but this was more. Although Sarah was an emotional creature, she didn't cry often, and when she did, she had the ability to recover quickly and transform hurt into anger. Now she sounded wounded and completely defeated.

"Bristol," she began again. "She's pregnant . . ."

Immediately, my reflex was to reassign myself the role of protector. I knew that all of those who'd earlier spread rumors of Bristol being pregnant when it was a lie would now crow, and that pissed me off. The Bristol I knew was a kind child, thrown into the cauldron of politics against her will. She likely had the least desire to see her family life exposed. My heart bled for her. I thought back to Todd, months ago, telling me how unimpressed he was with this boy who had been hanging around. In his blunt but prescient manner, he'd remarked, "Bristol doesn't have to fall for the first guy that sniffs up her skirt."

Of the pregnancy, Sarah said that only Neen and I, along with Kris Perry and Sharon Leighow, knew.

"I left the decision to her," Sarah explained, "and Bristol wants to keep the baby."

"Bristol is a strong girl. She'll get through this," I said.

Sarah eventually returned to the topic of Todd, Wooten, and Troopergate. She reiterated that Todd had worked behind her back.

For Sarah, if she said something often enough, she'd come to believe its truth and, in her mind, so would others. Her current pain drove me to temporarily not care about truth.

Completing her round-trip on whether I was in or out of favor, she begged, "Frank, I'm telling you again. If you go, I go, we all go. This is unjust." We spoke for ninety minutes before finally hanging up. She said she and Todd loved me. As for me, despite frustration and disappointment, I'd never stopped loving them.

On the recommendation from my friend and then pastor Karl Clauson, I phoned and "hired" an attorney, Greg Grebe, that same day. More than a mere lawyer, Greg shared my faith and reminded me that God was a God of truth, and I needed to lay everything out there and trust in Him. After the previous two and a half years, resting on the rock of truth was a very hard thing to comprehend. I had drifted so far. I explained the basics of what happened, saying, "Yeah, I spoke out of turn, Greg. I said I was speaking for the governor, but she did not know I was making the call."

Greg listened and afterward gave me the best news I'd heard yet. "Frank, I can't see how you have any criminal exposure here." He then advised, "And do not say anything more to the media." Greg refused to take a dime of payment for his time and expertise. He felt that at this particular time, it was his duty to be there for me and speak truth to me. That gesture is something that will stick with me forever.

The next day, Sunday, August 17, Sarah invited my family to her house for another heart-to-heart talk, choosing to meet face to face because Todd feared the phones were tapped and their attorneys warned there should be no colluding over evidence in the ongoing investigation.

We drove down the gravel drive, past the thick trees shielding the Palin house from the road, wondering whether supportive Sarah or hostile Sarah awaited us. With the sun hanging low in the early evening sky and reflecting off the lake that ran to the back of the red-planked house, we were greeted by Todd. He was mowing the lawn. "Hey, man," I said.

"Hey, Frank." Todd broke away from his mowing, and we shook hands. I knew him well enough to see in his face relief that we'd come. He clearly felt a need to clear the air and lessen the tension we all felt.

Willow and Piper shot hoops off to the side while Bristol watched. Her shirt was too short and her round belly showed, but only if one knew what to look for. (Later I was informed her youngest sister was unaware of the pregnancy.) She came over and gave Neen and me a hug. "Look at you," I said, catching the glint in her eye. I couldn't help but worry that while only seventeen, she had a massive secret that would soon be revealed to the world.

Inside, we removed our shoes while Sarah, tending to Trig and still dressed from church with her hair piled high, greeted us. Our kids broke away to play with the two younger girls. Todd joined us inside.

Sarah and my wife and I sat in the kitchen at their island table while Todd stood across from us, behind the sink. Earlier that afternoon, Sarah had met for four hours with her newly hired personal attorney, Thomas Van Flein. She said, "I told Tom after leaving church today, dedicating Trig, that this whole thing is all bullshit." She then said, "If they," meaning Monegan and DPS, "had just cleaned out their own mess, none of this would have happened." For the first time, Sarah spoke the truth. She was finally admitting that if Monegan had only gotten rid of his bad apple trooper(s), he'd still have his job, and she wouldn't be in the middle of this crap cluster. She continued, "The DPS is always more interested in covering up for their brothers in blue and not crossing that blue line than in dealing with people like Mike and Spitzer." For someone who swore she never discussed any of this with her husband, the two of them spoke in nomenclature lock step. Never spoke to him? How, if true, had all of us, including Sarah, come to parrot one another as if reading from the same script?

Rather than ask these obvious questions, I again volunteered to resign for the greater good. Sarah shook her head no and said, "I'll get rid of you when they get rid of Wooten."

That day, in their kitchen, just the four of us, the truth finally filled the air. No pretense about Wooten not being the central issue. He was front and center, and Sarah was as much on board as Todd. Sarah let us know, without any doubt, that had Monegan taken care of his own lousy troopers (or at least Wooten), none of this would have happened. Todd claimed, yet again, that "Lt. Wall shut off the tape recorder just when he was interviewing Bristol, right at the point when he asked if Wooten really tased his stepson. He didn't want to hear the frigging answer and have it on record. Cover up for what? A loose cannon, a ticking time bomb . . ." Now, in danger of being caught in the act, Sarah needed me to continue playing along. She and Todd fed me the "Sarah didn't know" line again and again and again until the line from Shakepeare's *Hamlet* sprang to mind: "The lady doth protest too much, methinks." Little wonder Todd did not want this conversation conducted over a potentially bugged phone. Even today, they will likely deny the truth of what was said in those unguarded moments. For the record, I say wire each of us to a lie detector, and let's see who has truth on their side.

Sarah soon drifted back to the immediate problem. She dropped the news that the state's Department of Law did not believe that Todd had provided me all the information I'd relayed to Lieutenant Dial about Wooten. Law suspected that I'd illegally accessed Wooten's personnel file. Since both Todd and Sarah knew the truth of the matter, it struck my wife and me as weird that she'd offer this information as if it were a topic of debate. We all knew that what The Department of Law thought was dead wrong.

My wife and I asked why we didn't just have a press conference together and sort this out. Nobody could blame Todd for going after
Wooten. Unfortunately, only Neen and I thought that this joint mea
culpa was a good idea. Todd didn't add much except to say repeatedly that this was all "ass backward." I'd have greatly appreciated it if
he'd said something about admitting to the state's lawyers that he was,
in fact, the source of every tidbit of Wooten intelligence I possessed.
When I asked him why he couldn't be more forthright, he managed
to grunt nonanswers that translated into noncommitments. He did
insist, however, that we were a team and that "we need to stick together. Our enemies want us to fall apart." I read that to mean, "We
need you, Frank Bailey, to cover our backsides."

Sarah nodded sympathetically throughout but continued to insist
she couldn't comment either way, since she was not involved. She did
say several times, "God brought us together." In other words, suggesting that "What God has brought together, let no man put asunder."
My wife and I missed the unstated fine print indicating this was a
one-way commitment.

Sarah eventually turned the conversation to her financial plight.
"Tom," her attorney Thomas Van Flein, "said defending against this
investigation could cost us lots of money." She mentioned something
about a legal defense fund.

"I say we have a huge dinner, five thousand dollars a plate," Todd
said. After a brief pause, he pushed further and, without a hint of
humor, added, "Then we make a list of those who pay up, and we give
'em board position on *good* boards."

Sarah laughed for maybe the only time that day. "No, we don't operate like that, but Bink and Murky would, in a heartbeat."

The governor expressed additional concerns as well. Just a few
weeks earlier, she had called for her loyal attorney general, Talis Colberg, to conduct his own investigation, a clear means of gutting whatever Branchflower would find. She complained to us there were those
in the legislature who said her efforts amounted to "tampering with
witnesses," and that he made her plan to disclose these "findings"
problematic.

Just before exhausting ourselves of new topics after nearly five hours, Sarah said as she walked us to the front door, "Don't tell anyone, but I am not running for governor again. I'm not sure what is going to happen with Trig . . ."

My wife interrupted and asked, "Is everything okay?"

"Yeah, but he won't be like other kids, Neen. He will need us forever, and that is a new concept for me."

With that new nugget, we departed, managing to suddenly feel sorrier for Sarah than for ourselves. Her ability to snatch sympathy from the jaws of blame is nothing short of genius.

———

The very next day, Sarah told me to stay at home while they sorted out the Monegan mess. Midmorning, she instructed me to phone in to her official state line. When I did, she put me on speaker for Chief of Staff Nizich to hear. Her tone of voice made it clear that mean Sarah was back, sharpening her knives for guilty me.

"I need to know everything, Frank. Why does the media think you're guilty?"

"Governor, I've told you everything I can remember." *More than once*, I felt like adding.

She grilled me, going over territory covered at her home on Sunday. I repeated everything truthfully without reminding her that she had acknowledged knowing Todd was my source of all information. In an uncharacteristic outburst, I said, "Why don't you ask Todd where he got all this stuff?"

"No, Frank, I'm asking you! I know you think I'm being wishy-washy, but the Department of Law still thinks you did something wrong here."

She concluded by telling me I'd be put on administrative leave retroactive to the day before, pending the investigation. With an ounce of her former support, she concluded by saying, "At least it's with pay."

27

Imprudently Impulsive

[T]he governor was completely vetted by the campaign.
—McCAIN ADVISOR DOUGLAS HOLTZ-EAKIN, STATEMENT
TO THE PRESS, MONDAY, SEPTEMBER 1, 2008, TWO DAYS
AFTER SARAH PALIN WAS ANNOUNCED AS THE
REPUBLICAN PARTY VICE PRESIDENTIAL NOMINEE

Do you want me to tell the truth?
—PINOCCHIO, TO THE FOX AND THE CAT, DATE UNKNOWN

Beginning with my leave of absence, I started having fractured dreams centered around Trooper Wooten confronting me, gun in hand, ready to put one between my eyes; or, in a second nightmare, seeing a whirl of flashing lights pulling up to our house followed by blue-vested cops busting down the door, arresting me and then sending me to a maximum security prison where I'd never see my family again. During the day, things weren't any better. Sleep deprivation and humiliation entwined like a cord around my neck.

There was a single moment from the previous Sunday at the Palins' lakefront house that did manage to seep through this sieve of panic. At one point, late in the evening, my wife serendipitously said to Sarah, "One day, when you're president, we can spit in all these jerks' faces."—a reference to those who purposefully held my recorded call as ammunition to inflict maximum political damage. As for me, internally, I felt I had handed by boss's opponents those "bullets" and wished for the chance to be the sole owner of my mistake with that call. After Neen's comment, I noticed Todd and Sarah sharing a quick, knowing look, as if they were guarding a secret. Unbeknown to me, that *something*, whatever it was, was the other gigantic reason for Sarah's fickle treatment of me and her refusal to deal honestly with anyone or anything. That reason had a name, too: John McCain.

———

By late August, I was days into what was to become a nearly five-week suspension from my official duties as director of boards and commissions and my unofficial role as Palin gofer, warrior, and loyal pincushion. Much of my information now came indirectly from Ivy Frye and, to a lesser extent, Kris Perry, who was now distancing herself from my radioactivity, and Todd Palin. I was, however, aware that by the time the Republican National Convention was set to begin in Minneapolis–St. Paul, Sarah had multiple messes on her hands that would preclude lesser mortals from being plucked from obscurity into the heady realm of GOP royalty.

There was Syrin spouting about an affair, asking on the *Anchorage Daily News* blog, "What peculiar branch of Christianity does Sarah believe in and teach her family? That it's ok to have an affair with her hubby's best friend when he's at work kind?" Worse, Senate President Mean Lyda Green, among others, had yelped enough that on August 11, Stephen Branchflower began his investigation after the twelve-member bipartisan Alaska Legislative Council voted unanimously to look into the dismissal of Walt Monegan. That investigation promised to drag on for at least a couple of months. From being in the center of Troopergate, I knew there was no way their conclusions were going to be pleasant for us. Next on the list of vice presidential obstacles was the hiring and dismissal of Monegan's replacement and the payment to him of $10,000 after it was discovered he'd been subjected to a sexual harassment complaint while police chief of Kenai. Finally, at the top of these mountainous crap clusters, how would abstinence-advocate Sarah possibly explain that her own seventeen-year-old daughter was pregnant, and the father was a self-professed *redneck* hockey-playing high school dropout?

Were Senator McCain's other choices so distasteful that Sarah's baggage was worth the price? Pawlenty, Romney, Bobby Jindal, Tom Ridge, and Joe Lieberman were worse candidates given what was going on in Sarah's life? Bill Kristol, appearing on *Fox & Friends* in

August, said, "Obama can pick a boring choice like Evan Bayh, and McCain can pick an exciting choice like Sarah Palin."

Media reports suggested that Sarah was a last-minute brainstorm of a selection, a name that rose to the top at a Sedona, Arizona, meeting between McCain advisors headed by senior campaign advisor Steve Schmidt on Sunday, August 24. Whether the case or not, Sarah was first formally notified she was under serious consideration, with initial requests for information, that very day. Then, three days later, on Wednesday, August 27, she was flown to Arizona, arriving in Flagstaff around ten at night. The very next morning, the governor was offered the job as John McCain's running mate.

His vetting team, led by Arthur B. Culvahouse Jr., was under the gun to approve this "high risk, high reward" selection. In a 2009 speech to the Republican National Lawyers Association, Culvahouse said, "Me and two of my most cynical partners interviewed [Palin] and came away impressed." On Monday, September 1, two days after the announcement, McCain advisor Doug Holtz-Eakin maintained that Palin "was completely vetted by the campaign" before being chosen. However, Culvahouse's initial interview with Sarah was after her 10:00 p.m. arrival in Flagstaff on August 27 (which, if they were part of that conversation, apparently made those two "cynical partners" easily impressed). More startlingly, as of ten in the morning on Tuesday the twenty-sixth, nobody in the McCain camp had seen Sarah's financial disclosures, tax records, or the formal lengthy vetting questionnaire delving into her background, because Sarah had not yet finished preparing them. Culvahouse, only a day or two from having Sarah offered the job as running mate, seemed nonplussed and asked in an email for the tax returns only *"if possible."* As late as nine thirty that night, at least some of the financial documents were still being assembled by Todd with the assistance of Kris Perry. Again, not that Culvahouse seemed particularly concerned. He indicated to Sarah that he did not intend to begin sifting through these materials until the next day anyway, which happened to be the Wednesday Sarah arrived for her face-to-face with McCain.

So as far as I could see, the process was (1) review Sarah's file for the first time on Wednesday, (2) interview her late that night, and

(3) based on that, it's *welcome aboard* the Maverick Express by around eleven in the morning on Thursday, August 28. How, as Mr. Holtz-Eakin implies, this qualifies as "completely vetted" will forever remain a mystery.

Was there any other investigation going on that made financial data and questionnaires irrelevant? Likely not much. With Troopergate news stirring things up in Anchorage, the two people most likely to be questioned were me and Walt Monegan. Neither of us ever had a word with McCain's people. Sarah contacted Culvahouse on the matter for the first time on August 25, explaining away the situation in a single emailed sentence: she said that her decision to replace Commissioner Monegan (an at-will political appointment) perturbed the police union, and the *"senate Democrat leader called for an investigation of the issue."* Sarah and Todd had done a thorough job of preparing me to parrot their claims that Sarah had no knowledge of anything Wooten, but thanks to the serendipitous "vetting," that turned out to be unnecessary.

As for the other bombshell, did McCain and handlers know about Bristol's pregnancy? Sarah had yet to publicly announce it, so unless she volunteered the information—not something she'd likely do if it risked some prize she coveted—that seems unlikely. Nowhere in the personal data questionnaire was such a revelation required. Fortunately, this didn't become much of a campaign issue.

Did Culvahouse and his vetting team speak to Sarah's family ahead of her nomination? Her three daughters were told the couple was going on a trip to Ohio to celebrate Todd and Sarah's wedding anniversary and not told of the nomination until Thursday. Sarah's mother had no inkling on August 20 as she asked Sarah on that day if she was even going to the convention while bemoaning the fact she'd heard McCain might choose someone as distasteful as Joe Lieberman. On August 27, Sarah's mother blithely discussed her desire to see victories in their upcoming elections for Sean Parnell (running unsuccessfully for Alaska's lone US House seat) and presidential hopeful McCain, unaware of her daughter's impending nomination.

Nor did McCain's staff contact brother Chuck Heath. On Thursday, August 28—the very day Sarah was offered the position—he bet Sarah that Pawlenty would get the nod, even though, as he said, the numbers favored Romney. He did joke that maybe Sarah was the dark horse. *"Who do you think will be the nominee?"* he wrote her; Sarah responded early the next morning, August 29, *"Me???? Turn on your TV in an hour."* Within two hours, on his seventy-second birthday, McCain made the formal announcement. Brother Chuck owed McCain's new running mate a skinny white chocolate mocha.

As for me, I was as clueless as everyone else. Upon hearing the announcement, I stared at the television hard enough to sting my eyes. As I listened to McCain speak of the gritty, full-of-fightin'-spirit and compassionate Governor Sarah Palin, a recurring question nagged at me: How could Sarah do this to Bristol? Later on, when a reporter asked just that, Sarah laughed and said, "Well, that was going to be revealed pretty soon anyway. I don't know what I can say about that. It is what it is."

"Going to be revealed pretty soon anyway"? "It is what it is"? Instead of having to live with a few thousand Alaskans knowing about her mistake, this sweet, sensitive girl was about to become the most recognized unwed mother in modern history, her life unfolding before at least five hundred million people worldwide.

As for failing to do their homework, that's not to say Culvahouse and senior advisor Schmidt did no due diligence. After the failed presidential campaign, when Sarah was complaining about being charged by the GOP for her own vetting costs, we learned that the vetting process hadn't actually begun in earnest until August 31, 2008—three days *after* the nomination. (And it was "coincidentally" the very next day Sarah and the campaign announced Bristol's pregnancy.) McCain and his campaign—by claiming in public that she was fully vetted—pulled a page from our playbook, apparently issuing misleading half-truths to hide their ineptitude. Vetted? Yes. Vetted in an intelligent and timely manner? No.

In simple terms, the woman who nearly became the second-most-powerful person in our country was chosen on a whim. Sarah didn't like McCain much during the primaries, believing that he was "weird" and "wishy-washy." Regarding her choice as his running mate, she might have added "imprudently impulsive." In their lack of planning and attention to detail, it seemed that Sarah and McCain shared reckless madness and little else.

––––––

Sarah spent the first few days as the vice presidential nominee much as Chuck Kopp had as the commissioner of the Alaska Department of Public Safety: battling controversy. Naturally, Bristol's pregnancy was major. There was a silver lining to that cloud, unbelievably, in that it put to rest once and for all the notion that four-month-old Trig Palin was Bristol's child, and Sarah had faked a pregnancy to hide the fact. I knew the original rumors to be idiotic, as my family had gone for a weekend in the middle of March to the Palins' cabin at Safari Lake, after Sarah made her own announcement. Todd restricted Sarah's physical activity, and in one e-mail reminding her that *"your in no shape to ride a snow-maching."* Later, Neen and I witnessed Todd sweetly describing "Sarah's glow and grow," referencing the joy and girth of her being pregnant. And while the original false-pregnancy suggestion bothered Sarah, she resisted releasing medical records that would have quashed the story, so this new, shocking revelation of Bristol's would have to suffice.

The next first-week tempest was the suggestion that Sarah had been a member of the Alaskan Independence Party (AIP), whose mission was to force a vote on Alaska's secession from the United States. On September 2, four days after McCain's announcement and one day after announcing Bristol's pregnancy, Sarah emailed me: *"Frank! Being accused of having been a member of Indp Party in the 90's. Not true but gotta prve it. Got voter reg lists? Talk to eddie burke* [then proud fellow Palin-bot, whom after years of being used finally admitted he was merely "trash along the road, Frank, just trash along the road"] *who'd know this? Very important!!!"* It turned out that while Sarah hadn't been a member, Todd had been *for seven years* until Sarah made her first bid for statewide office in 2002. To make matters a bit stickier, Sarah, while governor, taped a welcoming address for the AIP's 2008 convention. Eventually Sarah demanded that the McCain campaign address the issue and back up her claim that Todd had simply made a mistake when he checked the AIP box on his voter registration form. But McCain's people refused. Schmidt, in a scathing rebuke, wrote, "The statement you are suggesting be released would be inaccurate. The inaccuracy would bring greater media attention to this matter and be a distraction." To address the issue would, he suggested, take a political pimple and turn it into an infected wound. This was a matter that, left alone, would die under its own inconsequentiality. "Just tell whoever asks that Todd loves his country." Sarah didn't care that Schmidt was correct in his assessment. She was furious then and likely remains furious to this day.

Unfortunately, other matters did not die their own unimportant deaths. As if she were wandering around in a fog as thick as a damp rag, Sarah kept blindly running into the wall that was Troopergate. Her one-sentence explanation to Culvahouse may have been sufficient to land the nomination, but as chow for a hungry press, it wasn't going to satisfy. "I'm cooperating fully" and "there never was a connection to Trooper Wooten" became push-button responses. Not long after, however, through her lawyers, Sarah refused to cooperate with Branchflower. And Todd, along with a number of others, including Ivy Frye and Kris Perry, refused to comply with subpoenas issued by the state legislature after receiving questionable legal advice (that eventually led to formal legislative censure). On the side, she schooled all of us, *"Gotta change the term 'Troopergate' to 'Tasergate.' "*

In that regard, I notified Sarah that radio champion Eddie Burke *"ends his radio show every day by saying, 'hug your kids, don't taze 'em!' "* And I further won favor when I suggested, *"Also need to get Hannity a few more details on Wooten . . . Heard him talking about Wooten today saying, 'well he might have changed his ways but he tazed the Governor's newphew.' "*

Unfortunately, not every news outlet had the "objectivity" of Fox News, and Sarah's denials did little to abate what would dog her throughout the McCain-Palin campaign as others piled on. Almost immediately, comic actress Tina Fey began a brutal parody of Sarah on *Saturday Night Live*. Sarah, in an unusual reaction to critics, actually endorsed the idea of appearing on *SNL* and wrote to us, *"I go on SNL and play Tina Fey, I interview her as she plays me. (The questions we'd ask 'me' could reflect the ridiculousness of media's irrelevance.)"* While the satire was biting, Tina Fey's portrayal seemed not to have any negative effect on Republican voters. What was more searing were the sound bites Sarah supplied by way of her painfully botched interviews with Charles Gibson of ABC and, especially, with Katie Couric of CBS. When Gibson asked her about the Bush doctrine, she blankly stared at the television camera. Now, probably 90 percent of the country wouldn't have known exactly what that meant, but Sarah's lost, fumbling look was at least as harmful as her knowledge gap. Then, when she said of Russia and her foreign affairs expertise, "They're our next door neighbors and you can actually see Russia from land here in Alaska," Tina Fey turned that into the infamous line, "I can see Russia from my house!" At least in the ABC interview, some loyalists found a way to put a happy face on the experience. Conservative commentator Phyllis Schlafly emailed, *"Please tell Sarah that her interview with ABC was a fabulous success."*

Worse than Gibson's grilling, during the Katie Couric interview, the following exchange proved humiliating to all of us:

> COURIC: *And when it comes to establishing your worldview, I was curious, what newspapers and magazines did you regularly read before you were tapped for this—to stay informed and to understand the world?*
>
> PALIN: *I've read most of them again with a great appreciation for the press, for the media—*
>
> COURIC: *But what ones specifically? I'm curious.*
>
> PALIN: *Um, all of them, any of them that have been in front of me over all these years.*
>
> COURIC: *Can you name any of them?*
>
> PALIN: *I have a vast variety of sources where we get our news. Alaska isn't a foreign country, where, it's kind of suggested and it seems like, "Wow, how could you keep in touch with what the rest of Washington, DC, may be thinking and doing when you live up there in Alaska?" Believe me, Alaska is like a microcosm of America.*

Steve Schmidt, McCain's senior campaign strategist, later said of the interview and Sarah's failure to identify a single source of reading material, "I think it was the most consequential interview from a negative perspective that a candidate for national office has gone through." Why did Sarah not name anything, when we knew she spent a fair amount of time reading? The answer boils down to image management. Sarah's media diet came exclusively from local sources, including the *Alaska Journal of Commerce, Alaska Business Monthly,* and the *Anchorage Daily News.* In addition, various administrative assistants put together a compilation of stories from major Alaskan news sites each morning. This document, referred to as "Daily Clips," ran in excess of thirty pages, and Sarah digested those capsulated reports by eight o'clock each morning. To suggest she didn't read is wrong. However, in her mind, admitting to this regional-only emphasis would have made her appear less interested in national and international events—which *was* absolutely the case. Instead of honesty, she panicked and, once again, made matters infinitely worse.

As I sat and watched this salt-in-the-wound interview, I raised my eyes and asked the ceiling, "Why can't she just tell the truth?" It's not as if she had to admit she spent nearly as much time reading negative bloggers as she did substantive news. Her interest in Alaskan affairs was totally appropriate for a governor. Instead she searched vainly for an answer that would cast an intellectual glow and wound up coming across as empty headed.

Naturally, the blame for this debacle fell not on Sarah but on the "Gotcha!" nature of the media, with Katie Couric allegedly being the biggest trap setter. The wound still festered in May, 2009 when Couric made a joke at Sarah's expense while speaking at Princeton University. CNN contacted the governor's spokesperson in an email and asked for a response to Couric saying, "Coming here was a real no-brainer! After all, I can see New Jersey from my house!"

Todd responded on Sarah's behalf by emailing, *"She's [Couric] another dead fish that is going with the flow."*

In June 2009, nearly a year after the dreadful interview, Sarah emailed her staff of Couric, *"She SUCKED in ratings before she stumbled upon her little gig mocking me . . . She did Almost lose her job before that VP interview."* Confirming that Sarah held grudges in perpetuity (despite repeated denials), while on Sean Hannity's show, she was asked if she'd ever do another interview with Katie Couric. Sarah replied, "As for doing an interview, though, with a reporter who already has such a bias against whatever it is that I would come out and say? Why waste my time? No."

Officially, Couric's name was added indelibly to the enemies list.

———

Numerous lesser distractions crept in as well. Spokesman Bill McAllister sent a daily list in mid-September that included *"sundry questions"* such as did she believe dinosaurs and humans coexisted at one time. He was also being asked about her policy regarding forensic rape kits, and did Wasilla, while she was mayor, charge victims for these? The media, in light of Sarah's claim that she had military command experience as head of the Alaska National Guard, wanted to know how she shared decision making with the adjutant general of Alaska, Craig Campbell. Sarah's reaction to all of these queries was a frustrating reply: *"Dinosaurs even?! . . . I . . . continue to be dismayed at the media."*

The governor's tanning bed and who paid for it got play. Silly though it was, Sarah became furious: *"the old, used tanning bed that my girls have used a handful of time in Juneau? Yes, we paid for it ourselves."* In what seemed to happen often, Sarah displayed a tin ear for cause and effect when, only a few months before installing this unusual item, she declared May *as Skin Cancer Awareness Month* in Alaska. In part, the press release read (emphasis mine), "Skin cancer is caused, overwhelmingly, by over-exposure to ultraviolet radiation from the sun and *from tanning beds.*" Sarah's anger only grew as blogs wrote, "What's the difference between a pit bull and a hockey mom? Answer: A tanning bed."

Unfortunately, Sarah's change of venue to the national scene did not lessen our collective paranoia, either. Fear of leaks and sabotage migrated south with Sarah, fueled in part by my own insecurities. I wrote to her that, *"judging by the hard left news slant they take and some interviews I've seen on CNBC and Fox, I have every reason to believe that Yahoo upper management is supporting Obama's candidacy. . . . To be safe, we should assume that anything in a Yahoo account should be considered available for snooping eyes by Yahoo company."* We took measures to guard what we said on our Yahoo accounts from that day forward.

Throughout, Sarah complained about the focus on Bristol and her other children. Why should her daughter be the subject of conversation? We had little reason to believe that the Obama campaign played any part in the frenzy that emanated from blogs and tabloids. Despite that and her own consternation, Sarah was in favor of dragging Obama's and Biden's children into the discussion (and by extension, hers as well). Two weeks into the campaign, she asked in an email, *"Do Obama's kids attend public school? Did Bidens?"* She was angling to juxtapose her own kids' public education against the elitist private schooling of her rivals' children. To his credit, Sarah's chief handler from the McCain camp at the time, Tucker Eskew, replied bluntly, *"We're not going to be talking about anyone's kids."* When I read that note, I applauded. Despite her frequent interpersonal myopia, Sarah should have had enough decency to never ask the question in the first place.

When Alaskan Republican congressman and former critic Don Young sent a message through Sarah's chief of staff that he'd like to speak to the vice presidential nominee, Sarah wrote, *"Pls find out what it's about. I don't want to get chewed out by him yet again, I'm not up for that."* Incredibly, there was also a time when Sarah refused for months to be interviewed by conservative talk show host Laura Ingraham. In mid-2009, Laura sent me an email asking why Sarah had done every show but hers. I answered, *"Honestly? Someone has convinced her that she'll have to study for a week to do your show, which is BS."* Even a Dan Fagan interview, far back in the campaign days, sent a shudder down Sarah's back. After accepting an invitation to appear to discuss her signature gas line plan in August 2006, she wrote, *"I'll be grilled by Fagan. I don't even want to go on that day. I do not trust him AT ALL. I don't know why others are thinking I should be there."*

In these avoidance behaviors, where, I wondered, was that Reaganesque steely spine that Sarah admired so much and, in her own book, eventually claimed she possessed? Was she ready to confront a world full of tough political leaders—individuals who would make Katie Couric, Laura Ingraham, Dan Fagan, and local congressman Don Young look like wet cotton candy?

This new campaign, from the very first day, resembled our two years in office: crisis, reaction, victimization of Sarah, and counterattack. Even from Alaska, those of us supposedly charged with running government were spending enormous amounts of time defending the governor-turned-national figure. Whenever Sarah asked for anything, I'd take care of it, whether that had to do with sorting out Todd's Alaskan Independence Party mess or trying to get Sarah booked on *The O'Reilly Factor* at Fox.

Sarah claimed to be in control of both her campaign and the state, but in hindsight, she seemed not so much in control of either. The best word to describe Sarah and Alaskan governance after September 1, 2008, is *disconnected*. From my perspective as director of boards and commissions, charged with recruiting individuals for dozens of state jobs, including judgeships, getting Sarah to focus and make decisions became impossible. There were forty or fifty board memberships per month that needed to be addressed, and approvals from her were not forthcoming. Sarah's Chief of Staff Nizich, in frustration, often resorted to making these decisions on his own. Government by chief of staff? That's not what Alaskans deserved, but Sarah refused to turn over the reins of power to Lieutenant Governor Parnell. Regardless of the governor's claims that everything was getting done and she was in communication with her team daily, plans for running the state by BlackBerry were not working. Every task became backlogged while decisions were made at the last minute and often without Sarah's input. If we thought her focus while in state was weak, we came to discover how out of focus she could really become.

At best, we muddled through.

From Kris Perry, who was on the campaign trail with Sarah, I got an earful of campaign gossip and, those reports made me wish to be a direct part of that inner circle. Kris spoke highly of Texas Governor Rick Perry, of whom, she said, Sarah had grown quite fond. Sarah also liked Joe Lieberman; he seemed genuine, concerned, caring, and full of integrity. Senator Lindsey Graham of South Carolina was McCain's best friend, and they traveled together nearly everywhere. Kris and Sarah were not fond of Graham. McCain himself was absolutely and completely run by his staff, a robot that did whatever campaign manager Steve Schmidt told him to do.

Hearing these and other tidbits made it all sound like our own little Alaskan political cauldron but on steroids. In addition to missing the action, I felt as if the Palins needed me there. Friends encouraged that perception by asking, "Why aren't you with her?" Others suggested that, "Frank, you wouldn't be letting her parrot the same old responses she gave at the Republican Convention over and over. She needs you!"

The weeks after that August 29 announcement to the days just preceding the November 4 election were at times whirling by and other times a broken clock. Like studying for a big test, the load was excruciating, and I looked forward to having the process grade out. In this case, it was a pass or fail, win or lose, move on or come home. As November 1 arrived, I sensed a mounting level of optimism from Sarah. She seemed more energized, and many of the hounding inquiries had played out; the news cycle was finally focusing on poll numbers, red states versus blue states, mock electoral counts, and how much love Sarah Palin was generating everywhere she went.

All seemed better, if not quite perfect. Then, as if still wandering around in that dense fog of naiveté, Sarah once again slammed into a PR wall.

28

Losing the Presidency: Who's to Blame?

Three Days to go. I shall be fasting and praying for you—
for your intercession—and for victory. I love you!
—SARAH PALIN, EMAIL TO FRANK BAILEY AND
PRAYER WARRIORS, SATURDAY, NOVEMBER 1, 2008

On November 1, 2008, there were only three days left before America would decide whether to make Sarah Palin a fixture in the West Wing or send her shuttling back to Alaska a loser, but forever transformed into a celebrity's celebrity. The numbers seemed to favor an Obama-Biden victory, but we knew that polls often didn't tell the whole story.

Having no impact on the McCain-Palin campaign was frustrating for me. The same sound bites played repeatedly by television ads and talking heads took the unhappy place of the 12,500 yard signs along Alaskan roadsides and banner-waving supporters on freeway overpasses. The days of scrimping pennies to buy a button-stamping machine were replaced by lobbyists' marshalling special interest millions into buying influence on all sides of the political spectrum. Could it be that we were only two years removed from chasing a governorship on a grassroots shoestring? Less than two years earlier, Sarah couldn't cut and paste on Word and drove around with expense and contributor receipts piling up in her backseat. Now she pretended to have expertise on international issues she had not heard of three months earlier. What did she know or care about Iranian nuclear proliferation? Until she had speech coaches train her, she couldn't pronounce *nuclear* any better than President George W. Bush. Given the lack of vetting by McCain, clearly he didn't care about any of this. Stage presence, charisma, looks, charm, youth, and the all-important gender factor mattered. With the larger stage, photogenic Sarah could still rally the troops like nobody before and might yet make a difference for the "weird" old guy who was dragging down their ticket. The new, nation-wide legion of Palin devotees could yet carry the day. As we preached, people underestimated her at their peril.

Incredibly, I mostly still believed in the myth of Sarah and her ultimate mission. When she requested we pray for her, I joined others in imploring God to grant victory. Fighting mental suppression, however, a piece of me could see that she was in over her head, and I looked forward to having her return and recommit to our original more modest ambition of building a better Alaska. Troopergate pain notwithstanding, we Rag Tags had survived the worst, and the road, while bumpy, was no longer filled with land mines.

On that November 1 Saturday when she emailed that she was fasting for victory, I received a second Sarah email. She'd added the word *Help* to the subject line. Surprised, I clicked to open, but this time the tone was anything but positive. She was in emotional freefall.

From: SHP
Date: Sat, 1 Nov 2008 10:58:34
Subject: Help, Re: Three Days

We were just pranked, horribly, by a Canadian radio station . . . a fake, humiliating interview I gave to who I was told was the French president.

Turned out to be an awful prank. This will be international news. Very bad.

Gotta pray that what the enemy just meant for bad will be turned into something good. Somehow.

What? A fake call from French president Nicolas Sarkozy? How could McCain's people have allowed such a thing to happen? Sarah emailed me and others because she needed our help. Prayer, words of encouragement, and, if possible, action. *Do something, someone, please.* Shouldn't McCain's people be there for her? What kind of a numb-skull campaign were they running?

I Googled *Palin+Sarkozy+prank*. Unfortunately, finding informa-tion wasn't difficult, as some heretofore-unknown Montreal radio jokester by the name of Marc-Antoine Audette—part of a duo call-ing themselves the Masked Avengers—just became internationally famous. The prank, news-viral within minutes of being aired, made Tina Fey's *SNL* spoofs look like Pulitzer Prize journalism.

I found an audio recording of the interview and listened. At one point, Audette said he loved "the documentary they made on your life, you know, *Hustler's Who's Nailin' Paylin?*" This was a reference to a ri-diculous porn movie made with an actress dressed up as Sarah, seduc-ing Russians who came to her door in Alaska.

Sarah said in response, "Oh, good, thank you. Yes."

Equally ridiculous topics continued as Sarah responded giddily, oblivious to the setup. As I forced myself to listen with hands cover-ing across my shaking face, I understood she'd somehow managed to let her love of celebrity get in the way of good judgment. Painfully, I began to suspect this wasn't the fault of McCain or his staff. Anyone who knew her well understood that Sarah was impulsive and difficult to rein in.

At one point, Sarah enthusiastically suggested to the faux Sarkozy, "We should go hunting together." And then added, "Well, I think we could have a lot of fun together as we're getting work done. We can kill two birds with one stone that way." The "kill two birds" pun when referencing hunting was unintended. She seemed flattered when told that Sarkozy's wife was jealous of his speaking to her, clearly seduced by whatever this important man had to say. In a particularly wincing moment, when told that Sarkozy's wife was a former model and "hot in bed," Sarah said, "Oh, I didn't know that."

Audette asked if husband Todd was also known as "Joe the Plumber." Sarah said "no." Then fake Sarkozy said, "We have the equivalent of Joe the Plumber in France. It's called 'Marcel, the guy with bread under his armpit, *oui.*'" Sarah acknowledged the plight of the working class, and the interview continued.

For what felt like hours, a dozen or more topics were covered, each more ridiculous than the last. Finally the Canadian interviewer came clean, likely because Sarah never seemed to catch on.

> *AUDETTE: I really loved you and I must say something also, Governor, you've been pranked by the Masked Avengers. We are two comedians from Montreal.*
> *PALIN: Ohhhhhhh, have we been pranked? And what radio station is this?*

In no time, the Canadian press released a story that began, "In an over-the-top accent, one half of a notorious Quebec comedy duo claims to be the president of France as he describes sex with his famous wife, the joy of killing animals, and *Hustler* magazine's latest Sarah Palin porno spoof. At the other end of the line? An oblivious Sarah Palin." In the article, Marc-Antoine Audette, the prankster who played Sarkozy, said of his victim, "You can see that she's, well, not really brilliant." As if this weren't bad enough, the comedian later said they had a hard time setting up the prank because Sarah and her staff didn't know who the president of France was.

Sarah's request for prayer seemed like the only thing that might help. I sent out a quick email trying to reassure her: *"We just prayed that God would use this for his Glory. You've been thrown every other curve by the media and this is one more thing to chalk up. He will use it for His Will."* Sometimes "His Will" is a painful lesson that we need to learn, something I know from experience all too well.

Later that night, the campaign stated that Sarah was "mildly amused" at having been the object of the prank. Suggesting that Sarah was amused struck me as the perfect example of putting lipstick on a pig.

Ivy Frye and I knew that had we been there to protect Sarah, this never would have happened. Ivy wrote, *"They got thru the secret service and all of her many, many experienced staffers? Why aren't we on the rd w them again??"*

I wrote back, *"Yer tellin' me!!!"*

The reason for believing we might have saved Sarah from herself?

Approaching any Election Day, Sarah required tighter reins on her activities and a higher human wall to deflect stress. McCain had assigned as her babysitter Tucker Eskew, a veteran GOP operative with whom Sarah butted heads. Eventually, by mutual consent, they had little contact. Sarah needed blindly loyal bodies to protect her from her own haphazardous impulses. We understood that; McCain apparently did not.

———

Despite a string of embarrassing moments along the presidential campaign trail—lowlights being the Gibson and Couric interviews along with the Sarkozy prank—Sarah's army remained immune to her foot stubbing. That core of passionate, allegiant believers fed off her vague rhetoric and pointed attacks on challenger Barack Obama. Crowds were fervent, resembling an *Elmer Gantry* revival meeting more than a political gathering. And the more harshly Sarah berated the media, the greater her popularity and visibility. The more guffaws, the more real she seemed to both hard-right conservatives and the burgeoning group that would later form the Tea Party. Senator McCain became an afterthought to Sarah's star attraction.

Being taken off my five-week suspension and back on the job as director of boards and commissions in late September, I joined in the excitement of the imminent election, especially energized by knowing that I'd been there from the very beginning. The day before the nation was to vote, November 3, 2008, brought that same gnawing anxiety I'd felt in past elections. The biggest differences were my being thousands of miles away and one additional layer of anxiety about to be unveiled.

Largely ignored until this day, Sarah had earlier taken a second preemptive step to counteract the Branchflower findings. After chasing down witnesses to discover what that investigation was likely to unearth, Sarah realized those efforts on her behalf were blatantly biased. In a follow-up act, on September 15 she filed an ethics complaint against herself with the Alaska Personnel Board, asking it to review her dismissal of DPS Commissioner Monegan. Tim Petumenos, an Anchorage-based trial attorney whose firm once handled the $15 million bond issue to finance the Wasilla hockey complex that was Sarah's signature project as town mayor—a conflict of interest that critics believed should exclude him—was hired to conduct an investigation that tilted in what Sarah believed was the correct direction. He conveniently scheduled a press conference to announce his findings less than twenty-four hours before the polls opened. Anticlimactically, he concluded no probable cause that Governor Palin had violated the state's Executive Branch Ethics Act in her dismissal of Walt Monegan. He relied predominantly on her testimony to arrive at this conclusion. I welcomed what I eventually came to understand was undeserved vindication. Critics weren't placated, but Sarah and Senator McCain used the report to vilify the earlier Branchflower conclusions.

Palin attorney Tom Van Flein issued a press release: "Mr. Petumenos determined that the Branchflower report's findings that Governor Palin abused her power had no legal basis and that Governor Palin did not violate the Ethics Act as Mr. Branchflower incorrectly asserted."

The *Anchorage Daily News* minced no words in a strongly disagreeing "Our View" column four days later: "Petumenos' analysis reads as if it could have been written by the governor's own defense lawyer. His exoneration of Palin was conveniently released just a day before voters nationwide decided on her bid for the vice-presidency." The editorial concluded, "[I]t is definitely not OK for a governor's staff to spend a great deal of their publicly paid time settling a personal score for the governor's family. Petumenos uses some creative legal hairsplitting to argue that state ethics law does not cover that kind of behavior, when the plain language easily supports the opposite conclusion."

With Petumenos providing a welcome breeze to the McCain-Palin ticket's sails (whereas the newspaper editorial appeared after the election), November 4, 2008, represented a conclusion to the wild ride I'd been vicariously watching from afar. On Election Day, Sarah and Todd briefly returned to Alaska and scheduled a freeway caravan on their way to a voting photo-op in Wasilla. Bruce Anders, Neen, and I stood by the roadside, bundled in down coats and waving mittened hands as Sarah's black Suburban, trailed by a fleet of other black SUVs, approached in the predawn darkness. Gusting wind cut to the bone while we inhaled swirling snow mixed with exhaust and watched the lead car slow down and draw the others alongside, stopping at Sarah's favorite mocha stand. I removed mittens and pulled out my BlackBerry. With stiffened fingers and steamed breath escaping through the scarf draped across my mouth, I fumbled with a brief note: *"Just watched you pass by . . . we are praying! Can't wait to give you a hug. We are so proud. Neen, frank and bruce."*

A few hours later, after she'd voted and talked to the media, the SUV motorcade returned, on its way to delivering the Palins to the campaign jet that would shuttle them back to McCain's campaign headquarters at the Arizona Biltmore in Phoenix. As the red taillights of the procession faded, I remembered how Sarah had said during the Alaska Republican primary that she had proudly cast her vote for Mike Huckabee instead of Senator McCain. For Sarah, running with a lesser candidate wasn't an issue; after all, it was widely rumored that McCain greatly preferred his buddy Senator Joe Lieberman over her, but simply couldn't get the far-right wing of the party to sign off on the former Democrat's social agenda.

Election night came, and instead of the familiar red-washed balloon-filled ballroom at the Hotel Captain Cook, Neen and I sat home in the living room, sinking into our overstuffed sofa. While the television commentators blah-blahed, I reverted to my habit of clicking Refresh on the laptop, watching the electoral map turning red or blue as the evening wore on.

Voting for her, I was internally at odds. I was beginning to have doubts Sarah was anywhere close to being a sound choice for second in command. Not only that, she seemed to dislike the job of being a political executive. In one PIN message she sent me about two weeks before the election, she asked me to pray she would win so "we can leave that place"—reminiscent of her oft heard comments that "Juneau is evil," meaning that she was clearly sick of dealing with the mounting nuisances of being Alaska's governor.

At least McCain was a war veteran and had substantial political experience. But what if something happened to him? *Was she truly an effective governor?* At times, Sarah admitted that the office was overwhelming. More than a year before McCain selected her, touting her executive experience and governing skills, she sounded lost. She shared in a long phone conversation that she was buried by the "never-ending to-do lists" and the necessity of having to whine at departments to get what she wanted done. This was clearly not what she expected when she campaigned for governor in 2006.

Sensing I was unable to pick up her spirits, I joked that if I lost my job I'd be "making lattes full-time" instead of fighting bureaucratic battles. Her response was darker, saying she expected she'd get fired before I would.

Experiencing emotional difficulty managing a state with fewer than a million people, what would President Palin do if a rogue nation like North Korea went nuclear? Would she be preoccupied with typing messages on the *Anchorage Daily News* blog? Would she use the FBI to monitor Dan Fagan's radio show or dig up dirt on Katie Couric? The IRS, would it suddenly run audits of former political opponents, bloggers, or editorial critics? Would she fire dissenting voices and find out too late they were right and she was wrong—as she'd done with the entire Board of Agriculture and Conservation over the Matanuska Maid Dairy debacle in 2007? Did we want Sarah and her thin skin anywhere near that red button after that 3:00 a.m. phone call, as Hillary Clinton had warned of Barack Obama during their hotly contested primary races?

It became increasingly obvious as the hours ticked by that Obama would win. Our prodigal governor would be coming home. Part of me felt she'd be relieved, another part expected she'd go into the blame-attack-victim mode of dealing with frustration. More likely, she'd vacillate between the extremes.

Once the final results were announced, I cradled my BlackBerry and thought about what message to send Sarah and Todd. I'm a simple guy, and I sought to be brief while offering positives. I wrote: *"You guys are awesome. Hard fought fight. Palins woke up a sleeping Republican electorate and ignited Mc's campaign."*

With my message being one of what must have been thousands, I didn't expect a response. Todd responded in seconds, *"Did Ted win."*

Todd was asking about Alaska's forty-year senator Ted Stevens, who was running against Anchorage mayor Mark Begich while embroiled in scandal. Just the prior week, Stevens had been convicted of seven bribery-related felony charges. I reported back that, nevertheless, Stevens was in the lead by five thousand votes. Again, a reply in seconds: *"Rooooggggeeerrrrr,"* Todd's equivalent of Sarah's *"Whoo-Hoo."* (Eventually Begich was declared the winner by a margin of a little more than two thousand votes.)

Into the late election night, Neen and I sat quietly on our stuffed leather couch. Glued to the television, we watched McCain's gracious concession speech. Staged outdoors under a starry Arizona sky with a wall of palms waving in the night breeze, McCain and wife Cindy shared the stage with Sarah (dressed in blue—where was her signature red?) and Todd. She looked sad and frail. McCain thanked Sarah, calling her "the best campaigner I've ever seen." The crowd erupted while she looked ready to weep. Once he finished, McCain gave Sarah that short-armed hug of his, just as I turned off the TV.

Next morning, Sarah wrote, *"Thank u frank! And pretty wild about ak races (national), howd local races go?"* That afternoon, another message from Sarah: *"Party at the airport tonight—we want to see and thank the amazing pro-America pro-Alaska folks who really do care!!! Kris has details. Can u put this together on short notice?"* With that directive, I was already back to work on Palin personal requests. My having something to do—even if organizing a thank-you gathering for a losing candidate—beat sitting around waiting and wondering. We went to work sending out email invitations and notified the press of the pending tarmac get-together.

A few hours after sending me her party wishes, Sarah granted her first postdefeat interview to CNN. The reporter, having edited an earlier interview, played a clip asking Sarah about her plans for 2012, since speculation was already rampant about a presidential run. Sarah at first ignored the question and spoke of Alaskan energy issues. Similar to election night, she appeared haggard and sad, her hair resembling spider webs in disarray. She attempted a brave smile, but this time it had none of that neon glow. With resignation in her voice, she said:

I cannot even imagine running for national office in 2012, and I say that though of course coming on the heels of an outcome that I certainly did not anticipate and had not hoped for, but this being a chapter now that is closed and realizing that it is a sign to unite and all Americans need to get together and help with this new administration being ushered in.

Suddenly, looking at the shock in her face, I realized she not only expected the miracle of victory but hadn't prepared herself emotionally for defeat. The reporter then asked about accusations from McCain insiders that she was a "diva," and about "going rogue" and about the internal tension in the campaign.

An indignant Sarah responded by saying, "It is absolutely false that there's been any tension, certainly from my part or my family's part . . . there's absolutely no diva in me." The tone was similar to her saying, "Nobody in my administration ever applied pressure to have Trooper Wooten fired."

Returning to a live camera, the reporter addressed the in-studio anchor and said that Sarah's response did not agree with what she'd heard from campaign insiders, and there was much more to be revealed from the McCain camp. I nodded knowingly.

———

Sarah's plane was due at eight-thirty. We'd managed to gather nearly three hundred well-wishers to brave the ten-degree Arctic cold. Each time a plane approached, the crowd screamed, "Sa-*rah*! Sa-*rah*!" and hoisted signs reading You Go Girlfriend, We Love You Sarah, and We Got Our Gov Back!!! As it became increasing frigid and windy, reports trickled in that Sarah's plane was delayed. Finally, at least a half hour late, a JetBlue E-190 that had been repainted with the McCain-Palin logo on the side landed and pulled to a stop about forty feet from where we had gathered behind a rope.

As passengers disembarked, the chants grew. After the press corps hobbled down the stairs onto the tarmac, Todd, the kids, and Sarah finally emerged out the plane's side door. She made her way carefully, teetering on a very tall pair of black high heels, bundled in a black trench coat, appearing thinner than I'd ever seen her. She straightened her shoulders and lifted her chin, her hair no longer wispy but once again pulled back in that signature clip. On the trip back, she'd applied makeup to highlight and complement her eyes and cheeks. Then, as if she'd been reborn, she flashed that smile and began speaking as if she'd never left, saying that this was not a wasted effort. Everyone in the country now knew the message of Alaska, from energy to seafood, and the nation was waving little Alaskan flags. If she harbored resentment in defeat, it did not show. Everyone marveled at how gracious she was.

At one point, while answering questions from the press, Sarah explained political reality this way: "Politics is rough-and-tumble, and people need to get thick skin, just like I've got." I'll never forget that sentence. Sarah Palin may have many qualities, but thick skin has no place anywhere on that list. One thing I've learned is that Sarah had the capacity to deny her own frail emotions while projecting them onto others, specifically those she regarded as wishing her harm. Her hatred of those opposing her was really all about their hatred of her. Had I thought hard enough, I could have predicted I'd eventually join that list.

When she finally finished with the press and returned to her shivering Palin devotees, the crowd began to chant "Two thousand twelve! Two thousand twelve!" Sarah smiled warmly and did not take off in the SUV with Todd until she'd shaken every hand within reach. The energized campaigner extraordinaire was, at least for a moment, back.

———

For many in the McCain camp, once they underwent their own it's-not-my-fault postmortem, they blamed a distracted, unmanageable, and at times emotionally complicated Sarah Palin for the Republican defeat. Maybe Sarah wasn't what they expected, but whose fault was that? Sarah didn't change; she'd always been distracted, unmanageable, and emotionally complicated. What impact did the Sarkozy stunt have on the election results? Or Tina Fey's lambasting Sarah on *Saturday Night Live*? Did the Gibson and Couric interviews really make a major difference? Whatever the negatives, when the results came in and McCain lost by 7 percent and more than eight million votes, Sarah walked away with a larger and stronger army of Palin Gremlins and Palin-bots. She returned to Alaska with a greater tag than Joan of Arc or Queen Esther. For millions, she now wore the mantle of *savior*.

For those of us left behind during the campaign, we conducted our own November 2008 postmortem. I expected we'd do what Kodiak Island villagers did when hit with volcanic eruptions and tsunamis: regroup, rebuild, move on. Sarah's loss in the 2002 lieutenant governor's race turned into a blessing that helped catapult her to the governorship and nearly the vice presidency of the United States. This setback, too, would be a part of God's plan.

In an old refrain, I convinced myself we'd learn from past mistakes and return to the job of governing the great state of Alaska. We still had plenty of time to get back on course and accomplish much in the remaining two years of Sarah's first term. After that? Maybe grab a Senate seat and go to Washington and accumulate some real national and international experience in preparation for another run for national office in 2012 or 2016.

Part of me felt disappointment, but an even bigger part felt relief that we'd go back to being a team. I'd had enough of insecurity these past months. Time to get over the worst of Troopergate and the fear of losing my governor to an administration run by a man who excited none of us, including Sarah and Todd.

I felt the next two years suddenly had a predictable course, proving once and for all that as a prognosticator, I stink.

PART FOUR

Death Spiral

29

Reentry

As far as I know, Sarah "ditched" most of her original
Rag Tag Team . . . Might say we were all thrown under
the wheels of her car as she drove away . . . Sarah may
very well be the real "phony" in the final analysis?
—FORMER BLINDLY ALLEGIANT PALIN-BOT
AND DEDICATED VOLUNTEER UPON SARAH'S
RETURN TO ALASKA AFTER McCAIN LOSS

Just two years earlier the biggest problem in launching the political career of our Reagan in a dress was making certain the name Sarah Palin was front and center on every Alaskan's mind. Now, the former Wasilla High beauty queen with the nickname Sarah Barracuda had returned as one of the most recognizable names and faces in the world. She was Cinderella with a closet full of glass slippers and would soon have a bank account overflowing with untold millions. As huge as the state of Alaska might be, it suddenly felt too small for the celebrity of Sarah Palin.

Friday, November 7, 2008, the first day Sarah arrived back to work as governor, the ladies working in the Anchorage headquarters decorated her nineteenth-floor office with balloons and signs that read We Love You, Welcome Home, Girl, and We Missed You. The local media swarmed the lobby, pressing forward in competition to ask a question that would later be played back for a public infused with Palinmania. Just outside her door and away from the cameras, I waited, shifting from one foot to the other, fidgeting with keys and change in my trouser pockets, wondering if she'd hug me in welcome or dismiss me as the man who added to her Troopergate crap cluster.

Sarah arrived, dressed in a suit with her new signature color: black. After a grueling campaign, she appeared less perfect, a bit worn, but still able to command attention. Without someone to guide her through the mass of cameras and microphones, she looked less sure of herself than in the past, her eyes and head moving side to side as if trying to find a point of focus, some spatial balance. I detected a hint of vulnerability, a woman unaccustomed to having to explain defeat. In my own insecurity, I felt like a person weathering a troubled political marriage and, no matter the pain, needing desperately to keep the relationship alive. In the past, I'd have shielded her from embarrassing confrontations and, if necessary, guided her through to the sanctuary of her office. Now I watched, not sure on what ground the foundation of our relationship was built but certain it was not the firm rock of past years.

Reporters swarmed Sarah and launched into questions about her plans for 2012. She said, "My participation on a national level, it will all have to do with what it is that Alaska needs and how Alaska can progress and contribute to the US." A few questions and answers later, she added, "Just being very thankful to get to hustle back to my governor's office here and get to work as the governor. I tell ya, this is the . . . this is the best job in the world, being the governor . . . You know, Todd and I both said this morning, it's going to take some getting used to not . . . not being I guess out and about and seeing a different city every few hours . . . We'll miss that."

Reading her voice, a reporter asked, "Are you sad?"

"Not sad at all. In fact energized. I think certainly feeling like it's a little bit of a different level because of the perspective now that I have about what national politics are all about." I recalled her recently writing me, *"pray that we win so we can all get out of that place."*

I'd also heard her say or write, "I hate this damn job." I hoped she meant what she was now saying, that she had a new appreciation for the honor of serving her state as its governor.

Leaks from McCain's staff were being circulated, one of which indicated that in preparation for her vice presidential debate, a confused

Sarah thought Africa was a country rather than a continent. When a reporter asked about those rumors, I thought, *So what?* What did any of that have to do with Sarah's once-again job of running Alaska? In three years together, we'd never once spoken of Africa or Israel or any foreign country other than our neighbor Canada—and Mexico as a warm vacation destination. During the campaign for governor, when Mitt Romney was the Republican Governors Association, Sarah didn't even have a clear idea who he was. As she wrote after the gubernatorial election, *"I argued with Frank and others, as I insisted his name was MILT, not Mitt."*

Sarah needed to make a joke of this line of questioning and move on. Instead she lashed out. "If there are allegations based on questions or comments I made in debate prep about NAFTA, about the continent versus the country when we talk about Africa there, then those were taken out of context. And that's cruel, it's mean spirited, it's immature, it's unprofessional, and those guys are jerks if they came away with it taking things out of context, then tried to spread something on national news. It's not fair, it's not right." It was Sarah's reaction, calling people jerks, that became a future sound bite at least as much as the original Africa gaffe. Long before this Q&A, I'd come to believe she'd never learn that lesson.

It did not get much better when asked about the legislature and her reputation as a polarizing figure. She seamlessly borrowed two year-old talking points and spoke angrily, "My ability to work with Democrats, Independents, and Republicans all together has never changed. So if there's criticism that I've changed and all of a sudden become an obsessive partisan, then it's not accurate criticism."

For Sarah, her run for national office had not been in the least bit partisan. With the hypnotic power of words, she'd say over and over she had run a positive campaign and fully believe it.

When finally the inevitable question about Troopergate was raised, Sarah said, "I don't know. I'm just happy that Troopergate truth was revealed there also and, in fact, I'm going to keep on calling it 'Tasergate,' as a matter of fact."

A follow-up question about Monegan's conflicting recollections was danced around as the press conference ended. To applause, Sarah turned away, the reporters trailing her as if being pulled by invisible strings. Sarah rounded the corner and headed toward me and a handful of staffers. Forcing a half-lipped smile, she spread her arms, shuffling down the line, one embrace after the other. I stood back as loyalists pressed to Sarah. She then said to each, "Bless you, thanks for all your hard work, thank you, thank you, thank you . . ." She approached me last. "Thanks for what you're doin', Frank," she said, patting me on the back as she gave me a hug that felt refrigerator-magnet cold. With that, Sarah headed to her office, once again the everyday governor of seven hundred thousand Alaskans. Only from here on, the once-open door to the governor's office would remain closed, and once-welcomed intrusions were no longer welcome—for the next weeks, the least-welcomed visitor being me, the Troopergate millstone.

———

Sarah hadn't ever really been a full-time governor before being nabbed by McCain. All of us, including Sarah, juggled our paid positions around the need to counter criticism. In my case, I had additional duties as Tonto to Todd Palin in his quest to destroy Trooper Wooten as well as filling in as family travel agent, opposition researcher, and occasional designated Sarah Palin punching bag.

For her return engagement, Bruce Anders, long-time consultant and speech and op-ed writer, sought to address some of the issues Sarah would now face. He decided she needed a well-constructed organizational plan to facilitate reentry. At my encouragement, he wrote a blueprint in mid-October and updated it just prior to Sarah's return. Bruce proposed a sound strategy to work with the legislators in Juneau so Sarah might build a record of success that would further her national aspirations for 2012 and beyond. There was talk about Sarah possibly running for a US Senate seat in 2010 against Lisa Murkowski. Having trounced Lisa's father in the governor's race, this Palin versus Murkowski challenge, if successful, would mean that she had taken down two Murkowskis. The thought of double payback was an attractive inducement. Furthermore, a seat in the Senate seemed a logical launching point for Sarah's future career and would quell the cries of critics who said she lacked the experience necessary for higher office.

The offset—a big one for an ego now a bit more than outsized—was that a Senate run would feel like a step down after believing she was going to be a heartbeat away from the presidency of the entire nation.

Bruce addressed all these issues in his plan. Naturally, he received no indication from Sarah that she understood or even read his work. Bruce then did what I often did: he tried going through Todd, hoping the governor's husband might see the wisdom of planning ahead. In mid-November, Bruce told me about those efforts. Todd's reaction was, "She can't kiss up to those jerks, [Democratic legislators] Les Gara and French. Don't you understand they are trying to kill her?" State Senator Hollis French had, after all, initiated and managed the Branchflower investigation. Other so-called leggies from both sides of the aisle had voted 12 to 0 to proceed with that same witch hunt. Compromise and working together with them were no longer conceptually possible.

Bruce suggested it was important for Sarah to rise above this and play politics at a sophisticated level. He then asked, "How's she going to handle the expert snakes in DC if she can't intelligently handle Juneau lightweight politicos?"

Todd, in classic brush-off, told Bruce, "Write out your thoughts and forward that plan to me."

Bruce did so, listing among other things that Sarah should not seek a Senate seat because "Alaska needs her as their Governor—badly. There is so much she needs to get done here, not as a candidate for higher office. Further, if she intends to be a contender in 2012 (or even 2016), she needs to have a strong record of achievement as an executive, as a leader—not a freshman cog in the US Senate." While Bruce agreed with Todd by saying that "Gara and French want to ruin Sarah," he suggested that "this is what politicking is all about . . . Use it. Play them. Make them help without even realizing it. Look at how Clinton co-opted Gingrich: played him like a fiddle . . . So as painful as it is to write, I honestly believe that she needs to reach out to exactly the people she doesn't want to."

Bruce Anders was only suggesting what Sarah always swore—even as recently as her statements to the press the day she returned to Anchorage—that she was a uniter of all parties. There was no question in our minds that she had the skill set to charm anyone. However, ability and desire did not often meet when it came to embracing those who might be plotting behind her back or speaking ill of her. What Bruce suggested was a political chess game: a difficult and focused battle to win by applying our avowed goals of sound fiscal and social policies wrapped around lofty ethical standards. In this, he was implying we go back to square one and start over. Unfortunately, Sarah was not interested. Her schedule was now overflowing, but not with cabinet meetings or discussions about appointments or strategy conferences with deputies and commissioners. There were literally hundreds of requests for appearances, interviews, and invitations to travel around the country. Political celebrities phoned nonstop. One call Sarah spoke about with pride came from former president Bill Clinton. Sarah described it as a thirty-five-minute discussion in which Clinton had words of encouragement and told her that his home state of Arkansas did not vote Obama. She suspected from this discussion that Clinton did not support the president-elect.

Even Todd was getting requests from the *Wall Street Journal*, the *New York Times*, and the television show *Extra* to be interviewed for a story about his participation in the Iron Dog snow-machine race. With so much important celebrity, when groups and commissions in Alaska needed to meet to discuss business and budget, many were told that wouldn't be possible.

She didn't need local and state allies, not with Newt Gingrich regularly emailing advice like suggesting she not answer difficult questions but instead "reframe it into the question she wishes they asked," or better yet, "When your opponent has posed a question designed to put you on defense, the right strategy is to destroy the very legitimacy of the question and pose a new question of your own." Loyal legal advisor Wayne Anthony Ross, who defended Sarah against numerous attacks both formally and informally, became irritated he was being snubbed. Ivy Frye forwarded me a message from him saying, *"I haven't heard from Sarah at all, so I presume that is bad. I have written her at least 4 times asking for 15–20 minutes of her time and you said you even told her of my request. I am beginning to get concerned. Annoyed even."* WAR had yet to learn that one minute you're in, the next you're out.

If he was still around for minute three, he might find himself landing right back in Sarah's good graces.

Tyndale House Publishers, a Christian book publisher, wanted her to write a book. In normal times, Sarah might have jumped at that, but such a small publisher—Christian message notwithstanding—held no interest. These weren't normal times, and Sarah had plans to have others, including me, assist in writing a book that would paint a glowing picture, settle old scores, and sell millions of copies. "Thanks, but no thanks" to Tyndale, WAR, and state commissioners.

For all the "new best friends," as Sarah referred to those who had recently joined her army of admirers, the number of angry detractors at home grew. Many voters noticed they had a distracted governor. Despite Sarah's strong support nationally, the great majority of letters to the editor in the *Anchorage Daily News* were unfavorable. As a result, the tattered remnants of Sarah's Rag Tags were remarshaled to deal with the fallout. Ivy Frye, always ready for action, was the first to suggest firing up the mothballed letter-writing team. To those on our old list that still remained (a dwindling crowd) and those new best friends:

> Friends, I'm sick of opening the Anchorage Daily rag every day to see 10 negative, anti-Sarah letters. Their coverage has become completely biased, and unfair since she was chosen as the vp pick. Today was the worst I've seen—not one positive letter, and 6 negative ones. I encourage you to write 1 positive, pro-Sarah letter each and send it to the ADN. We, the silent majority, need to rally the troops again. Please pen just a few sentences of praise, congratulations, or thanks for her awesome work. And if you have friends that will do the same, please let 'em know I sent mine this morning.
>
> Thanks guys!! Ivy

Unfortunately, times *had* changed. Ivy's cry for help met with limited success. Her uncle, Mat-Su master campaigner Don Benson, faithfully submitted the only letter.

The lack of enthusiasm indicated the troops now felt weary of constant minicrusades, and rallying them was no longer a simple matter.

And while shortly thereafter—by mid-February 2009—I'd be brought back into the inner circle as tightly as before, I too felt that fatigue. We worked as hard as ever but with dwindling enthusiasm. And as the Palins' prospects for fame and wealth grew, so did the deterioration of our dream for a better Alaska. Blind allegiance was being substituted for Sarah's blind ambition. Our Queen Esther was about to forget about saving her people.

Punishing enemies and wealth accumulation became a full-time job.

30

Sleeping Dogs That Lie

I did them no wrong, but they laid a trap for me.
I did them no wrong, but they dug a pit to catch me.
So let sudden ruin come upon them!
Let them be caught in the trap they set for me!
Let them be destroyed in the pit they dug for me.
—KING DAVID, PSALM 35:7–8 OF THE OLD TESTAMENT (NLT)

During the McCain-Palin campaign, I found myself often in Sarah's penalty box (brought back in the game only during a crisis), subject to that well-executed freezing-out process. Because she needed my knowledge of her darker secrets kept close, I managed to survive this excommunication. Upon her return in late November, my cooperation held less value. Had I resubmitted my resignation, it's likely that security would have had me on the street before the ink dried. But unlike others, such as former campaign manager Kelly Goode and chief of staff Mike Tibbles, I had fewer options. Given the shellacking to my reputation during Troopergate, I had to closely consider how, if I left my position, I would support my family. In the meantime, I would suffer meetings behind closed doors that did not include me and omission on insider emails.

I continued as director of boards and commissions, but progress slowed to an unsteady drip, as Sarah didn't much care about state business, and I wasn't on her need-to-return email list anyway. Governor Sarah was physically back in office, but distractions mounted, and time was increasingly devoted to either chasing fame and riches or battling what Sarah characterized as the forces of ever-mounting evil. Despite the release and passing of reports from the harsh Stephen

Branchflower and the kind (at least to Sarah) Timothy Petumenos, the odor of Troopergate lingered into the new year. McCain campaign lawyers, who swamped Juneau and Anchorage during the election, had vanished, and the residual legal fallout again landed in our laps.

The remaining issue had to do with legislative subpoenas to testify, issued by Branchflower in September. Attorney General Talis Colberg had earlier advised administration officials they had the *option* but not the *obligation* to comply. Taking Colberg at his word, several insiders, including Todd Palin, Chief of Staff Nizich, Deputy Chief of Staff Randy Ruaro, and confidantes Kris Perry and Ivy Frye, chose the no-thanks option. Four months later, the media and critics put pressure on the legislature to investigate the no-shows. Leading Anchorage television station KTUU used its nightly opinion polls to ask viewers, Should the legislature pursue punishment for ignored Troopergate subpoenas? Wayne Anthony Ross, despite his frustration at having recent requests to meet with the governor spurned, sprang into action. As I'd done when making calls on behalf of the governor and her husband, WAR understood the best way to get back in Sarah's good graces (so long as you are not embarrassingly caught doing so) was to be, using one of her favorite words, "proactive." He fired off a letter to KTUU stating his objection to the premise of the poll. As we knew from numerous behind-the-back emails blasting him, WAR did not respect or like Colberg, so there was no surprise when he laid the blame on the current attorney general: *"Unfortunately, the AG did not take a clear position on the validity of the subpoenas. As a result, having been left to their own devices due to the indecisiveness of the AG, the involved State employees were forced to obtain their own legal counsel, at great personal expense, to advise them on the proper procedure."*

Ivy Frye, who originally solicited WAR's assistance, recoiled from this strategy. In an oops-that's-not-what-I-meant response, she wrote:

It's [the letter to KTUU] good. Thank you for doing it. However, my point was not to hang the AG out to dry (even though I disagree with him privately I didn't want to do it publically, afterall he is on our side . . . If you write the ADN or any other media organization I don't want you to say anything about the AG, please just focus on the point that subpoenas weren't ignored and if the tables were turned the legislature would also exercise their rights to challenge subpoenas.

The once tight team was beginning to unravel. Earlier, Ivy couldn't get those effusive letters to the editor out effectively and now she couldn't rein in WAR. He said, "With a friend like Talis, who needs enemies? He makes Pontius Pilate look decisive."

The January 30, 2009, *Anchorage Daily News* took an alternate view in an editorial written in response to WAR's and Colberg's representations. In part they claimed, "Colberg's discredited advice about the subpoenas helped delay the Troopergate investigation, just as the controversy was heating up in Gov. Palin's vice-presidential campaign. In this case, Colberg's unapologetic defiance of the Legislature (which issued the subpoenas) served the interests of his boss, not of justice."

In our never-say-die world of counterattack, Talis Colberg was urged by press secretary Bill McAllister to write an op-ed explaining his position on the subpoenas. Colberg suggested we "let sleeping dogs lie." The attorney general's decision not to respond was strategically sound but politically toxic. He should have known that with sleeping dogs, the Palin way was to tie cans to their tails and jab them with knitting pins. From that moment, I began counting on my fingers Colberg's final days.

A week later, on the morning of February 6, 2009, the Alaska State Senate dealt with the lack of responsiveness during the Branchflower investigation by drafting a Senate Resolution of Censure (SR 5). Hollis French, the chair of the judicial council, made comments on the senate floor that included:

As you know, this last fall the Senate Judiciary Committee issued a series of subpoenas, and a number of the subpoenaed witnesses did not show up in conformity as the subpoenas require. . . . The subpoenas were lawful, and the subpoenas were disobeyed. . . . The resolution [SR #5] memorializes the fact that contempt was committed by a number of witnesses, but it also recognizes that this was a rather unique set of facts. And it recognizes that once the suit [to quash the subpoenas] was tossed out of court, the witnesses quickly complied with the request for sworn written statements made by Special Counsel Stephen Branchflower. The swift cooperation is in the language of law a mitigator. It lessens the wrongdoing, and for that fact and that reason, the resolution calls for the imposition of no penalty. The resolution strikes a balance, and I believe it is a good and proper balance. I urge your support, and I ask for the support of the members.

Senate Resolution #5 passed by a vote of 16 to 1. Todd Palin, Ivy Frye, Kris Perry, and seven others were found in contempt of the senate. Maybe because everyone felt a need to recircle the wagons, around this time my position in the inner circle was magically restored. Suddenly I was back on the war wagon, manning my former position as soldier, confidant, and friend. In response to RS #5, Ivy shot off an email to our attorneys, copying back-in-favor me as well:

Created: 2/6/2009 11:35:40 AM
Subject: Re: Senate Resoltion holding us in contempt

Absolutely flippin ridiculous this grandstanding by French to further his own political career. I think we need to respond via oped in the ADN similar to the emails that were sent to KTUU. They want to hold us in comtempt yet don't want to penalize us? Give me a flippin break. The whole thing is a bunch of bs. And again, good names, reputations, relationships have been affected by some legislators on a political witch hunt. I'm preaching to the choir, I know. You two have been great. Standing up for us, looking out for the governor and defending our honor. Pretty frustrating though.

With Wayne Anthony Ross blasting him and Sarah needing a scapegoat, Colberg found himself in a place nearly every Palin employee eventually fell. Once before, I'd asked myself why Sarah's campaign for governor did not include anyone who had been instrumental in her earlier political efforts. The answer became increasingly clear: surviving her serial dissatisfaction was, ultimately, impossible. Four days after RS #5 passed, Talis Colberg became Alaska's former attorney general. The governor's office issued a press release:

> For Immediate Release No. 09–26
> Attorney General Resigns
>
> February 10, 2009, Juneau, Alaska—Governor Sarah Palin today accepted the resignation of Attorney General Talis Colberg. Deputy Attorney General for the Criminal Division Rick Svobodny has been named acting attorney general.
> "I determined that it was in the best interest of the State of Alaska to move on and pursue other opportunities," Colberg said. "It was an honor to serve for the past two years."
> "Talis is a highly intelligent, thoughtful and reserved scholar who brought considerable legal knowledge and great personal integrity to the position," Governor Palin said. "I appreciate his willingness to serve, and as the search for a new attorney general begins, I will look for someone with the same strong moral character as Talis. I wish him well in his future endeavors."

Republican Jay Ramras, an unfriendly legislator who was only a notch or two below Randy Ruedrich on the Governor's GOP enemy list, saw through the boilerplate PR and suggested of Colberg's resignation, "He took a bullet for the governor." Funny turn of phrase, as that's exactly what I vowed to do way back in those first days as a volunteer: take a bullet for Sarah if necessary. As for my fellow bull's-eye, I regretted what happened to Talis Colberg. In my opinion, he is a good man who never should have allowed his allegiance to a person trump his duty to Alaska. He too was trying to wrap his arms around a scandal where there were no heroes, nearly everyone on all sides of this issue from Monegan to myself carried some guilt. Like many of us, in that he struggled.

———

Colberg's resignation triggered embarrassing fallout. Sarah did not want anyone to suspect she might have pressured the AG to resign.

Within hours, Ivy shot off an email to Fairbanks attorney Joe Miller asking if he'd help deflect potential rumors.

> Joe:
> Are you guys still running your website? If so, can you get some information out today? Or do you have friendlies in the media up there I or you can talk to?
> The AG Talis Colberg resigned today. He truly did resign on his own, but I fear the spin will be the governor asked for his resignation, which she had absolutely nothing to do with! Talis is a great, hard working guy, but the work at the dept has come to a grinding hault because of relentless FOIA [Freedom of Information Act] requests and ethics violation inquiries . . . There is no end in sight to these frivolous requests . . . Not to mention an under current from some legislators who want Talis gone. Thanks.

As events would unfold, Ivy's concerns over Talis Colberg were wasted. Sarah would do what Sarah does best: take a bad situation and manage to have everyone forget it by pushing the pendulum off the grid in the opposite direction. Sarah's office had released the promise "I will look for someone with the same strong moral character as Talis." As far as Sarah was concerned, the replacement was an easy decision. She chose somebody who would fight to the death for her, no matter what. The choice boiled down to only one man, Wayne Anthony Ross. Regarded as equally loyal but smarter and infinitely more aggressive, the person who helped push Talis Colberg out the door was perfect. We'd replace a poodle with a pit bull.

Only one small problem. The slice of support for WAR was small, confined mainly to the religious right. In a world requiring legislative confirmation of the selection, the nickname fit perfectly, and the bloody WAR began.

31

Clowns to the Left,
Jokers to the Right

So what do we do? And who is going to do it?
—SARAH PALIN, TO IVY FRYE AND
FRANK BAILEY, MAY 27, 2009

Sarah and Todd Palin may have disliked Levi Johnston, the eighteen-year-old father of Bristol's unborn child, but during the campaign they needed him. Originally summoned from a sheep hunt in the Alaskan wilderness, Levi was fitted for a suit, received a hundred-dollar haircut, had someone teach him how to speak only when spoken to (keeping his comments to "yes, sir" and "no, sir"), and was then jetted off to the campaign trail as Bristol's fiancé. While not an ideal situation, the lipstick on this pig was thick and expertly applied by a PR machine with, by now, a tremendous amount of porcine makeup experience. The storyline went: while they might've made a mistake, make no mistake that these kids are heading toward a happily-ever-after life together. Amazingly, the vast majority of supporters found this an inspiring fairy tale, and the couple was enthusiastically cheered whenever trotted on stage to stand with Sarah and/or John McCain.

Once the campaign ended, however, Levi Johnston instantly became an ex-fiancé with a penchant for publicity. In early April 2009, he appeared on the nationally syndicated *The Tyra Show* and hung out a load of dirty laundry about his relationship with the Palin family, including the assertion that Sarah was probably aware the young couple were having sexual relations, he was not allowed to take his son out of the house, and he and Bristol did not always get along.

This interview landed Levi on a list of unfavorable persons that was already lengthy and about to become seriously long.

Through spokesperson Meg Stapleton, the governor responded:

> Unlike Levi, we feel that the very private details of any personal relationship should be held within the sanctity of the family. We will not walk word for word through the inaccuracies in the spotlight of the media or tabloids. Suffice it to say, the interview is quite troubling. Again, it is clear to me that Levi does not have the best interest of the child in mind—only his own.

Naturally, we individually and collectively did *walk word for word* through Levi Johnston's statements despite pledging not to do so. Sarah kicked off the process by writing us,

> I did not, and would never, let two teenagers "live together" . . . and either Levi is lying, Tyra Banks is erroneously teasing her show with that claim, or they got Levi to say that, somehow taking it out of context. Todd and I are sick about that claim. Levi stayed at the house those first nights after Tripp was born, with the purpose of helping the baby and Bristol through the night.
>
> That lasted perhaps a week—he did not live with Bristol, we would have never permitted it, and bristol would never have wanted such a thing.

In July Sarah continued to monitor her almost son-in-law. When someone filed an ethics complaint against her, alleging she illegally received payment for granting interviews, we did opposition research on the complainant and managed to tie him back to Levi. Sarah wrote to her ghost biographer Lynn Vincent, copying her inner circle for support:

> Lynn . . .
> Levi-the-puppet had a press conference yest in his attorney's office, then today one of his attorney's clients (a James Brown imperson-

ator, I kid you not) filed a charge that I am getting paid for radio and tv interviews. Levi lied in his comments, too, re: a Palin reality show and other things (btw he's trying to go by the name "Ricky Hollywood" now- it's even on his answering machine his friends say)

Lots of craziness lately- straight out of "The Thumpin" [Chapter Five in *Going Rogue*] and Saul Aulinsky's "Radical" book (that Michelle Obama recently publicly quoted). Your investigator should be put to work connecting these dots to prove this is a scheme that's orchestrated from afar, and they're successful in some respects re: destroying their opposition.

Sarah was developing her own plan to do something she did quite well: she'd seek to destroy her opposition from afar.

When two days later Levi was interviewed by Ann Curry on NBC's *Today* show, Sarah pledged, from that day forward to boycott all major news outlets except Fox. In finalizing this decision, she wrote:

Sickening, sickening. I watched levi this morning. Journalism ethics are non-existent. They sat there and let the coached puppet spew one lie after another, starting with "when I lived there . . ."

Sarah then continued, *"What good does it do to ignore FOX and keep talking to networks?"* She pledged, from that day forward, to boycott all major news outlets except Fox. In finalizing this decision, she wrote:

Every time we participate with the bad guys we are telling viewers/ readers: "go watch them! Tune in to what they have to say to bash us today!" I can't do that anymore. I am through with the idiots who use and abuse us—we can NOT win them over, I hate giving them ratings boosts. . . .

Lesson learned. Final one. Networks are not our friends. Talking to them harms my family, admin, record, reputation, Tripp, etc.

No more.

We came to employ a strategy we referred to as "reaching out to surrogates with our talking points." That surrogate list included *Weekly Standard* editor and Fox News contributor Bill Kristol, GOP advisor Mary Matalin, former special assistant to President Bush Jason Recher, former Bush aide Steve Biegun, GOP executive director Nick Ayers, chairman of the GOP Michael Steele, Rush Limbaugh, and Fox News hosts Glenn Beck, Greta Van Susteren, and Sean Hannity. We could normally expect them to repeat any coordinated message we sent. In a scramble, the mainstream media often picked up on the message in an attempt to catch up on our Fox News scoops.

The strategy of selective media access spread from networks to local media and online reporters. For a time, Anchorage television station KTUU was put in the penalty box for a series of unfavorable comments that began with Chuck Kopp's resignation. Certain reporters at the *Anchorage Daily News* were also excluded from access, while others, who were labeled "friendlies," could count on the occasional exclusive. At one point, Sarah decided to temporarily withhold all comment to the paper when she disliked a story about her opposition to President Obama's pick of Katherine Sebelius to head the Department of Health and Human Services. She wrote, *"More bullshit headline grabbing unethical journalism at work."*

As for Levi Johnston, despite the valuable media insight she gained from dealing with his treachery—speak only to surrogate outlets—he joined Sarah's two-eyes-for-an-eye list. Furthermore, with Sarah's return to Alaska, this was just the beginning. For all of us, the trials and tribulations were about to become Job-like.

––––––

Some enemies faded for a time, never discarded but—with the list as long as it was becoming—placed into a kind of cretinous cold storage. Others remained intact, never quite as oppressive as Trooper Wooten, but near enough. The most persistent new thorn was a formerly fervent supporter, Andree McLeod.

McLeod—who, for the sake of full disclosure, filed a complaint with the Alaska attorney general's office, seeking to derail this book—

had tried and failed to secure a position with the state shortly after Sarah's gubernatorial victory. At the time, we attributed her incessant attacks as sour grapes. Sarah wrote of McLeod's efforts:

Created: 5/6/2009 10:59:10 PM
Subject: Re: labor team

[Andree] verbalized to me, many times, the "you can bend the rules" plea, when I would tell her to go through the system to get a job. Bizarre encounters at the capt Cook and other places, following me around.

And the preoccupation with McLeod wasn't a short-lived thing. Two months later, Sarah was increasingly disturbed:

From: gshp
Date: Tue, 14 Jul 2009 22:22:27
Subject: Andre. Fw: Ethics charges Re: David Horowitz

Kris—pls make Meg take no prisoners on this one . . . Need to publicize Andree . . . begged for job. I know we tried it once, but must prove it this time. What are they going to do, fire me? WAR should give quote, I'll give one too.

Whatever McLeod's gripes, she correctly understood that campaign reformer Sarah Palin had not upheld that promise once in office. McLeod took it upon herself to become a watchdog of an administration run by a woman who said repeatedly, "Hold me accountable." Arguably going overboard—and I believe she did—McLeod took on the hold-accountable challenge with massively more energy than Sarah exhibited in managing government.

McLeod filed requests—technically, an Alaska Public Records Request (PRR)—for documents and emails she felt would show that Ivy Frye and I had illegally campaigned for Sarah on state time. In January 2009 she filed a formal complaint with the state, alleging that persons, including Kris Perry, while working on state time had also participated in Sarah's vice presidential campaign. She even sent informal complaints about the dress code in state offices after being "astounded at the amount and magnitude of cleavage being exhibited by female employees."

In what I can describe only as a growing pattern of petty counterattacks, we latched onto this last item in an attempt to bring disgrace to a persistent critic: leaking this story, via our spokesperson, to the *Anchorage Daily News* political gossip column, The Ear. In Sarah's book *Going Rogue* (page 354), she discusses this incident in the broader scale of ethics charges:

> We tried to keep a sense of humor about the fact that the media took Andree seriously after Mike Nizich, my chief of staff, received a fresh complaint from her, this time alleging that women in state service wore their clothes too tight. Breasts were apparently spilling from blouses all over the 49th state and Andree demanded I do something about it. After the string of nutty complaints she'd already hit us with, this one just cracked us up. I told Nizich and Kris: "yep, that's my job. I'm the state Cleavage Czar. I'll get right on it."

We'd somehow survived Troopergate; now we were being hounded by an insurgent critic who wouldn't quit. As such, we created—over this silly dress item—something that came to be dubbed Cleavage-gate. Radio host and fellow blind allegiant Eddie Burke joyfully took up the cause. In early May, McLeod attended a fund-raiser for a local mayoral candidate. Burke confronted her about her rejection for a state job and the PRRs, while secretly recording her answers. He also suggested he might file a FOIA (he actually meant PRR) of his own, asking for all of McLeod's communications with the state for use on his radio show. As governing the state of Alaska seemed a half-hearted hobby rather than an important job, we were now reduced to initiating bring-down-Andree-McLeod games. Ivy listened to Burke's radio show and described the fun: *"Eddie [on his show] played audio of him confronting andree mcleod at the . . . fundraiser last night. She couldn't*

answer if she ever asked for a state gig and got frustrated and called him
an a hole. He played it twice. Pretty funny."

Joining in, Kris replied, *"Man wish I would have heard that. Did*
she sound unbalanced? Well, when eddie's foia gets fulfilled, there will be
multiple instances to show that she did [request a job]."

Sarah loved the image as much as anyone. She wishfully replied,
"well let that foia get filled soon."

Everyone's newest hero, Eddie Burke, added, *"I busted her ass on*
this. She's soooo nervous about the foia and can't answer anything...
When I'm done with her she will wish she never filed anything against
the gov."

Sarah loved the proactive actions. *"Well it's about time someone gets*
the ball and goes downfield on offense." Funny that Sarah wrote this as
if we hadn't already been an offensive force for over three years running. We were many things, but passive was never one of them. Sarah
even ordered a search for secret financial backers when she wrote, in
May 2009:

> We gotta find out [who is funding McLeod]. Someone's paying
> for these foias. And her expenses. She hasn't worked since right
> after the election. She just filed an apoc [Alaska Public Offices
> Commission] complaint (in addition to foia) demanding to know
> about todd's discount on snowmachines in '08.

In the end, not one of McLeod's seven complaints—filed from
August 8, 2008, through May 8, 2009—was sustained. However,
Sarah agreed to reimburse the state in order to settle one ethics complaint over ten state-paid trips taken by her children. This was glossed
over as if it were a clean bill of ethical health. In other instances, the
lines she crossed were questionable, though not considered illegal.
With each dismissal, we celebrated, high-fived, and whoo-hooed as if
this proved we were still, as Sarah once claimed, "the last of the innocents."

And as always, reality mattered not half as much as appearance.

In order to distribute the message, Spokesperson Meg Stapleton—

with Sarah's full endorsement—offered a recommendation after one of our victories:

> Make sure [we] hype up whatever legally works, but something like: "More public monies proving the Governor's innocence in yet another frivolous complaint filed by Andree McLeod. This complaint was filed following discussions with state Democrats and in coordination with liberal bloggers. This complaint followed another request for a position within the state—this time in the attorney general's office and in anticipation of Wayne Anthony Ross' hiring. (Can we release all the above information without causing problems?)

And while we were about to confront a host of additional foes and turn trivial crises into full-blown disasters, Stapleton's "whatever legally works" email hinted at the next major tumor, one rivaling in intensity other bungled plans: Wayne Anthony Ross as Sarah's selection for attorney general. Unlike other provocative appointments, at least Ross wouldn't have to be fired or forced to resign. He'd never get that far.

32

No New Tricks for This Old Dog

> As somebody in [Governor Palin's] cabinet said the other day,
> "You can't kick every dog that barks at you" . . . I'm trying to
> convince her that she ought not get treed by the Chihuahuas.
> —WAYNE ANTHONY ROSS, COMMENTS TO THE
> HOUSE JUDICIARY COMMITTEE, FEBRUARY 2009

Firing the entire Matanuska Maid Board for making the correct decision to shut down losing operations, annually growing the state budget when she said she would reduce it, and stacking her early administration with professionals she later disposed of might have humbled most politicians. Sarah, with an impressive ability to compartmentalize failure, had, on several occasions after her return to Alaska, the opportunity to prove she had no interest in adopting a more modest management style.

In a little-known (outside of Alaska, that is) appointment fiasco in May 2009, Sarah had participated in the selection of a new state senator when the incumbent, Kim Elton, was tapped by newly elected president Obama to a position in the Department of the Interior. Because Elton was a Democrat, the rules required that the Democratic legislators nominate candidate(s) for the governor's consideration. Although the governor was not bound by the name(s), she must submit a Democratic candidate back to the legislature for ultimate approval.

House minority leader Beth Kerttula was, according to Juneau Democratic Chair Kim Metcalfe, "head and shoulders above everyone else in terms of her length of service, in terms of her readiness to step into the position." As such, hers was the solitary name sent to the governor.

To make a long story short, Sarah didn't like Beth Kerttula because she had gone on national television and said that Sarah was not ready for higher office when nominated by McCain as his running mate. Such a statement became a declaration of war, and Sarah rejected the nomination. The legislators proposed more names. Sarah rejected them all despite continuing to insist she worked well with politicians on both sides of the aisle.

A longtime supporter came up with a clever strategy for dealing with the impasse. She recommended that Sarah submit a *"somewhat goofy Dem, who has never been elected over going with someone who has already proven electability like Kerttula. That gives us a better chance of winning the seat next election."* Sarah loved the idea. Not only punish Kerttula for being a critic, but position the seat for a GOP win by putting in place a *goof.* If we'd ever held to our promise of no politics as usual, Sarah was now about to bludgeon it to death. To make the plot even more delicious, this same supporter recommended Tim Grussendorf, a man Sarah found an ideal choice. Fortuitously, two weeks before placing his name into nomination, Grussendorf changed party affiliation from Republican to Democrat, thus making him suddenly available as a nominee. Mimicking Todd Palin's claims regarding his registration in the Alaska Independence Party, Grussendorf said his prior affiliation was a mistake.

The state senate didn't buy the argument or approve the ill-suited candidate, and so the process began all over again. New names were submitted by the senate for Sarah's consideration, including Dennis Egan, former mayor of Juneau and son of the state's first governor, Bill Egan. She rejected these. Back and forth. Sarah sent over new names, again including the already once-rejected Grussendorf, along with another candidate who had become a Democrat only a month earlier.

Of this process, Senator Hollis French said, "The governor was on the brink of being taken to court in violation of appointment statutes. All because she was trying to rebuke Beth [Kerttula], who during the campaign said one or two things that weren't ingratiating to the governor." Furthermore, "The governor has taken an unusual course which is outside the law and leaves us no choice but to ignore what she's done."

After four weeks of wasted debate and animosity, finally in

April 2009, on the last day of the legislative session, and with the embarrassing threat of being taken to court, Sarah relented. She wasn't thrilled with compromise selection Dennis Egan, but at least she won the battle to punish Beth Kerttula. As for placing a somewhat goofy Dem in the senate, she gave it her all.

––––––

Once Talis Colberg resigned as attorney general, Sarah had another golden opportunity to display her head-scratching decision-making skills.

Sarah, beset with at least thirteen ethics complaints on top of the seven filed by Andree McLeod, needed a friend in the attorney general's office. Wayne Anthony Ross had everything Sarah wanted. A legendary figure in legal circles, he was present at the first Palin fundraiser I attended way back in November 2005 and was always ready to lend sound advice to Sarah whenever she ran into legal and political trouble. In 2006 he announced, "Sir WAR stands ready to support and defend the fair lady wherever and whenever he can." In Sarah's eyes, Ross's loyalty trumped his experience, though his experience was enormous. When he submitted his resume on February 15, 2009, it rivaled a novella in length. Born in 1943, WAR had lived in Alaska for forty years and began practicing law in 1968, when he was appointed as assistant attorney general for two years. He listed over thirty current club and professional memberships as well as ninety-eight former memberships. He had page after page documenting extensive employment history, military service, teaching experience, political experience, public service, awards, publications, hobbies, religious preference, and family information. I also knew him to be a bit of a character, riding around Anchorage in his red Hummer with vanity plates proclaiming WAR. He was brilliant and conservative, with the religious right—including the pro-life Alaska Family Council headed by tenacious religious conservative Jim Minnery—strongly supporting him. On March 26, when Sarah announced Ross's appointment, she felt optimistic about his chances of being approved by the legislature. After all, never before had a nominee for any cabinet position, including attorney general, been rejected.

Unfortunately, critics and the press were not inclined to give WAR a free pass. They dredged up a letter Ross wrote in 1993 and published in the *Alaska Bar Rag* (a sometimes irreverent quarterly legal newspaper) called homosexuality "a lifestyle that was a crime only a few years ago, and whose beliefs are certainly immoral in the eyes of anyone with some semblance of intelligence and moral character."

Further, Ross wrote an article that appeared in the *Anchorage Daily News* on September 17, 1989, only six months after the *Exxon Valdez* disaster entitled, "It Is Time We Quit Crying Over the Oil Spill." Nearly twenty years later, many Alaskans had still not gotten over that so-called oil spill. Other criticisms surfaced and all stops were pulled out to ensure WAR did not win confirmation, including defamatory rumors of sexist comments, strong anti-federal-government positions, and opposition to Alaskan subsistence hunting preference, which allows Natives a preference in hunting and fishing rights. His position on the executive committee of the National Rifle Association was used against him by his opponents. While not necessarily hurting him with his conservative base, WAR was being cast as having a far-right, preconceived agenda that did not attract anyone identified as moderate or left leaning. Women's rights groups, the gay community, and Alaska Natives were up in arms over the nomination. The day after his nomination, a CEO from a prominent Native corporation called and asked, "Frank, how on earth could Sarah nominate Wayne without having you lay the groundwork within the Native community? People trust you, Frank." He lamented that while he liked Wayne personally, his selection was handled so poorly and without respect for the Native community that it was doomed to fail. What he did not know was that the appointment was largely handled by Meg Stapleton, the political spokesperson for the Palins at the time and not a state employee.

When it came time for Ross's confirmation hearing in mid-April, Democratic representative Lindsey Holmes asked Ross how he would view cases involving homosexuality. Ross compared homosexuality to his dislike for lima beans. "Let me give you an analogy. I hate lima beans. But if I was hired to represent the United Vegetable Growers, would you ask me if liked lima beans? No. Because my job is to represent the United Vegetable Growers."

In the midst of all of this, an ethics complaint filed by Linda Kellen Biegel, who blogs under the name Celtic Diva, became an issue that WAR promptly embroiled himself in. Biegel maintained in her petition that Palin used her position and state resources for personal financial interests by being "a walking billboard for Arctic Cat, a private for-profit company and family business sponsor." In this instance, attending the Iron Dog race in her official capacity as governor, Sarah appeared on camera wearing Arctic Cat winter clothing that prominently displayed its logo. Some perceived this as poor judgment because Arctic Cat was a major sponsor of Todd Palin during the Iron Dog snowmobile race. Prior to these hearings, Sarah and WAR had spoken extensively about the complaint. Ross assembled a team with "some common sense . . . to review this whole problem and to resolve it." He then added, "I wonder how state government can work at all when a governor has to pay attention to such Bravo Sierra"—*Bravo Sierra* being military slang for BS.

So, when the topic came up at his confirmation hearing, WAR was ready when Republican representative Jay Ramras asked about the governor's provocatively wearing Arctic Cat gear at the finish line of the race. Ross flippantly replied, "She *was* provocative—she looked very good in them, didn't she?"

Ramras was not amused. "To a lot of Alaskans, she looked like a walking billboard . . . The governor looks good every day, and she doesn't need to adorn herself with merchandise that promotes a company . . . where her husband enjoys an endorsement from." Interesting comment from a sitting lawmaker who annually peppered TV with ads paid for by his hotel chain promoting himself conveniently during election season.

If this were the only distraction, it would be enough to send Sarah into a funk. But Sarah, and by extension all of us in her administration, had other crises to hold hands with WAR's confirmation. When on April 3, KTVA (Anchorage channel 11) ran a tease banner ahead of its news programming—"Palin's Sister Arrested"—it sent us into a typical to-hell-with-anything-else frenzy. Spokesperson Meg Stapleton shot KTVA an email explaining, *"It was the Governor's husband's half-sister and not her sister."* She demanded an immediate correction and warned, *"You could have a lawsuit on your hands if one of the Governor's sisters sees that tease."*

Sarah immediately sent out the disclaimer *"Absolute bullshit grabbing headline."* Meg phoned our media relations person, Sharon Leighow, while Sarah ordered us to figure out a way to correct the mistake. Meg, not satisfied with her email, phoned the station, only to discover that Sharon had beaten her to that punch. We recorded each of the next few news shows in an attempt to document if and when the story about the arrest changed. Eventually the story became clearer. Todd Palin's half sister was arrested after police claimed she broke into a Wasilla home for the second time in a week to steal money.

The station itself gave us no comfort. Sarah wrote, *"they stand by their 'story' and lectured [us] about 'if you'd have LISTENED you'd hear we didn't mention the governor.' Then ktva did a story tonight reporting 'Levi Johnston said he and Bristol practice safe sex, most of the time.' When has a teen's sex life EVER been reported on in the news? Never have I heard a celebrity, a criminal, anyone's sex life reported as a hard news story. This is insane."*

From Todd's sister back to Levi Johnston and his comments to the media, this became a distraction that lingered for days.

———

In the midst of all this, in an effort to fire up her newly blossoming Lower 48 conservative base, Sarah indicated she planned on rejecting 31 percent of Alaska's estimated $930 million portion of the federal stimulus money designed to aid states with economic recovery in March. We hadn't focused on state government hardly a minute since her return as governor, and now our administration was returning nearly $300 million, of which $170 million was earmarked for programs to help economically disadvantaged and special-needs students. The total represented nearly $450 for every man, woman, and child in the state. She explained, "I can't attest to every fund that's being offered the state in the stimulus package will be used to create jobs and stimulate the economy." Not surprisingly, this was not widely popular in a state with economic difficulties, far-flung school districts with no road access, and one of the highest high school dropout rates in the nation. Critics argued she was sacrificing Alaskan interests while positioning for national prestige and a role in the burgeoning Tea Party movement that was flexing its muscles as the anti-government-handout party. Unfortunately, Sarah was still governor of Alaska and this would become another crap-clustering decision.

Sure enough, a month later Sarah ended up accepting $900 million of the monies while vetoing only $28.6 million tied to what she said were the adoption of building codes. The governor, according to Sharon Leighow, changed her mind after the public weighed in during legislative hearings. Mostly she changed her mind after taking a public relations beating. Even so, critics continued to hammer away as she became one of the few governors in the country to reject any federal stimulus funds. Sarah grew both worried and puzzled. *"We have hundreds of millions of $ in [our budget] for 'energy relief' and conservation and weatherization . . . and none of those are tied to obama's universal building codes . . . It's a $10 billion dollar budget to serve 670,000 people, and they're going to freak about $28m (with expensive strings attached?!)."*

During this critical juncture, KTUU ran a poll asking, Do you agree with Governor Palin's decision to reject federal stimulus energy funds? All of us invested time, energy, and emotion into linking our computers and utilizing our software into generating votes in favor. We watched the results on a minute-by-minute basis.

Ivy reported: *"We're up 75% to 25%."*

Sarah responded, *"Oh thank God!"*

Ivy's next update was less positive: *"In 10 minutes it went from 71 to 60 to 47. I think it was hijacked. Still working on it though."*

The poll was hijacked? If so, the thieves must've had better vote-rigging software than us.

I wrote: *"Can't let 'em win."*

Sarah responded: *"Argh!!!"*

Ivy tried to buck us up: *"Ugh. I know. It aint over yet though! Were gaining on 'em."*

We furiously sent in more and more votes. I cautioned, *"When this is done plz everyone delete these mssgs re: poll."* I later forgot my own warning.

When the poll closed, KTUU posted the results:

Channel 2 News Staff
Thursday, May 21, 2009

Anchorage, Alaska—In a poll conducted by Channel 2 News Thursday, May 21, 2009, respondents were asked if they agreed with Gov. Sarah Palin's decision to reject federal stimulus energy funds.

Here is the official question and results of the 3,473 people who voted: Do you agree with Gov. Sarah Palin's decision to reject federal stimulus energy funds?

Yes 53%
No 47%

All polls conducted by Channel 2 News and KTUU.com are unscientific.

We won what was definitely an unscientific poll (with me alone devoting three hours of what should have been family time to affecting the results). While it didn't change reality, Sarah felt massive relief. Irrationally, we all did.

In August—despite the bogus poll indicating public support—the legislature voted 45 to 14 to override Sarah's veto of the $28.6 million.

———

While my friend Wayne Anthony Ross was still broiling as the main course, the side dish distractions mounted. Sarah, with a national platform, felt a need to poke her opinions into any and all controversies with an eye toward winning favor with a national conservative base. When Miss California, Carrie Prejean, suggested that she'd lost the 2009 Miss USA title because she gave an answer during the contest stating she believed marriage was exclusive to a man and woman, Sarah became involved, motivated per usual by criticism. In an email bemoaning the fact that Fox News slammed her for "not defending" Prejean, Sarah said:

From: gshp
Date: Wed, 13 May 2009 20:47:18
Subject: Statement needed re: Miss CA

I got slammed on Fox News today for "not defending" [Carrie Prejean], . . . I think it would be good to have that statement out there that of course I support this young, strong woman who voiced her honest opinion on stage—then got punished and crucified for doing so. . . . I know if I were in her shoes (and I have been) it does mean a lot to have someone with the balls to publicly speak up in support. I've asked for [Donald] Trump's contact info so I can thank him, too.

Minutes later, we learned that the governor and Miss California had a connection that went through Sarah's biographer-to-be (in a book deal announced only the day before): *"I did speak to [Carrie] on the phone and we voiced our support for each other. She goes to lynn Vincent's church, small world, that's how we hooked up last week."*

Sarah and staff debated a strategy to rebut the critique. The initial suggestion was for Sarah to call reporters and document her efforts on Prejean's behalf, but as Sarah wrote, *"If I call those reporters then I'm on the hook to answer all their other questions they want."* Long ago Sarah learned that answering unfriendly reporters' questions was a bad idea. Instead she suggested the story be leaked:

This is an easy one bc it was already sporadically covered—that we spoke on the phone and I told her to ignore the hypocritical idiots who've put themselves in seats of judgment and crucified her for exercising her right to speak. She and her mom are extremely supportive of us, too. She texted bristol to encourage her, too!

Sarah asked Ivy to get on this ASAP and google Carrie's dad's comments to further the leak and add it to more supportive statements showing Carrie's strength for standing up for her beliefs.

Meg Stapleton, pulling over to the side of the freeway, attacked on a second front: *"I am driving from Wasilla and pulling over to write a statement. We will put it on Facebook and let it go viral with its 600k friends."*

In addition, a press release on Sarah's behalf stated in part, "The liberal onslaught of malicious attacks against Carrie Prejean for expressing her opinion is despicable. . . . Carrie and I spoke soon after the attacks started; I can relate as a liberal target myself."

The question we failed to ask was, What does this possibly have to do with being governor of Alaska? While it had nothing to do with Alaska, it had plenty to do with publicity. Fox News made this an ongoing story, giving it wall-to-wall coverage. Sean Hannity in particular latched on with both hands. With Sarah suddenly an outspoken supporter, he had gorgeous Prejean on one arm and sparkling Governor Palin on the other. He appeared a happy man. The *Washington Post* wrote that "with this action, Sarah Palin has re-appeared on the national stage."

If Sarah had been off the national stage, she'd never make that mistake again. Alaska was officially too small a pond for this whale of a celebrity.

As for emotional merry-go-rounds, Sarah still had Wayne Anthony Ross, the mounting problem of the vacant senate seat, Carrie Prejean publicity, her half-sister-in-law controversy, and, in an event she'd turn into yet another manufactured crisis, a mess I'd come to call Touristgate. Without so much as a single layer of thin skin remaining on any of us, the Rag Tags were spinning out of control. All we had to do now was take notice.

33

Them's Fightin' Words

You shall love your neighbor as yourself.
—BOOK OF JAMES 2:8 OF THE NEW TESTAMENT (NKJV)

If Sarah was having a tough time of it with her return to Alaska, Wayne Anthony Ross was about to be roughed up even more. His confirmation hearing for attorney general did not go well, and a history of blunt comments made for painful sound bites. Tim Towarak, chairman of the Alaska Federation of Natives summed up the feelings of many who took offense to WAR's rhetoric when he said, "It almost looked like [Governor Palin] was rubbing our face in Wayne Anthony Ross's appointment . . . Like rubbing our face on the ground, saying, 'Here, take this.' "

To make matters worse, WAR weighed in on the battle to fill Kim Elton's vacated senate seat. When Sarah sent names back to the senate Democrats (including two already rejected) after having refused all previous nominees, her move was declared improper. Ross told *Daily News* reporter Sean Cockerham at the time, "It seems to me the most important thing that can be done by the senate is not argue with legal or illegal but to appoint somebody to represent Juneau." When Ross denied making the statement, Cockerham—a widely respected reporter—produced the tape of their interview. As a private citizen, a person might be forgiven for offering ill-conceived legal advice. As candidate for AG, Ross's lack of concern for "legal or illegal" and subsequent denial were awarded a failing grade.

The wave of negative reaction to past and present statements came as a surprise to Sarah. She emailed me, Meg, Ivy, Kris, and Todd:

> Unbelievable. The excuses being used to not confirm WAR. Even some NRA "friends" trying to think up reasons. If/when this confirmation fails tomorrow, I will know that I am much more "out of touch" with Alaskans than I ever imagined. It's a kangaroo court down here, absolutely sickening. We'll need to be ready with some messaging tomorrow.

On Thursday, April 16, 2009, the legislature voted down, for the first time in Alaskan history, a governor's nomination for attorney general. The tally went 35 to 23 against. House Speaker Mike Chenault, a Nikiski Republican said, "I think he is too controversial for the state of Alaska. We've got in some people's mind a controversial governor, and I think that he just has too many controversies out there."

In a telephone interview with the *Anchorage Daily News*, Sarah said, "I think there was a lot of politics of personal destruction involved in this and that's a shame."

Ross, who I personally believe would have made a fine attorney general, hid his disappointment like a true gentleman by suggesting to the newspaper, "I had a neat office for two and a half weeks, and I was attorney general under the law for two and a half weeks for the state of Alaska. And the big question I have now is whether they will put my picture up with the other [former attorneys general] for only two and a half weeks' service."

For WAR's supporters, Sarah received much of the blame for his failure when on the day of the vote she was in Indiana speaking at a Right to Life event. They claimed she should have remained in state to collect votes for her friend and candidate. Instead, the sense of the legislature was that she simply did not care enough to be present. Formerly rabid supporters were saying that for Sarah, being an involved governor at this stage was so "yesterday" and that she was clearly absent mentally if not physically from her duties. This growing impression that she cared less about affairs of state and more about the national stage did not serve well toward Ross's chances of being confirmed.

———

Sarah never did feel she should be bound by legislative or political rules in pursuing political appointees (or most other ambitions). In addition to having championed a "goofy" candidate for the state senate seat who simply changed party affiliation in order to be eligible (and totally unacceptable), she responded with a resounding "Amen, brother" when it was suggested (by me, I am embarrassed to admit) that *"you shouldn't be bound by [Alaskan Democratic Party] rules . . . on filling legislative vacancies."*

Exhibiting that rogue spirit and being desperate over WAR's rejection, Sarah seriously plotted to circumvent all those pesky procedures that ought not apply to her. In what she considered a serious proposition, she wanted to know if it was legal to hire WAR as an assistant AG, then later designate him permanent AG. She wondered what the public's reaction would be, as well as the legislature.

Sarah never did go that route, as she received a strong reaction from those around regarding the potential PR disaster such a move would become. Eventually, with reluctance, our governor named respected attorney Daniel Sullivan to the post. But her disappointment lingered. She wrote:

> Some say Ross' sound advice on [the senate seat] cost him the AG job. I believe that had much to do with it, as some seemed to dread him calling it like he saw it and desiring all to be held accountable. His job was in their hands as some chose to believe misrepresentations and untruths told about him. . . .
>
> Biggest disappointment; WAR's rejection . . . secondary is lawmakers "above the law."

The war for WAR ended in a miserable defeat, and as she indicated the day before his rejection, Sarah proved herself much more out of touch with Alaskans than she ever imagined.

For those residing next to the governor's mansion in Juneau, Sarah Palin seemed not only out of touch, but also totally out of her mind.

———

In a controversial decision, when Sarah became governor, she decided to avoid Juneau, the state capital, and elected to work out of our Anchorage offices, a relatively short commute from her Wasilla home. There was running commentary about how the lights in the governor's mansion were never on because the place was always empty. Except for during the legislative sessions, from January to April, the criticism was valid. In front of staff, Sarah made no bones about her hatred for that city. She disliked the excessively wet weather and the citizenry's Democratic majority, along with the political atmosphere, where it seemed everyone was nosing into everyone else's business, especially hers. She referred to the atmosphere as "evil" and the city itself as a "hellhole." We often ended email exchanges by asking, *"What's in the juneau drinking water anyway??"*

Her animosity wasn't lost on the city's residents, as gubernatorial absences sparked rumors that she wished to move the capital permanently to Anchorage. Or better yet, to Wasilla. If it weren't such a political bombshell, no question she'd have made the attempt.

Were it not for the fact that Sarah billed taxpayers a per diem for 312 nights spent in Wasilla during her first nineteen months in office, the absences wouldn't have been a major issue. But she did. In other words, the governor submitted her own Wasilla home as "Lodging" and received reimbursement for choosing to live there instead of the governor's mansion; the allowances added up to $17,000. The man she defeated in the governor's race, Tony Knowles, said of this, "I gave a direction to all my commissioners if they were ever in their house, whether it was Juneau or elsewhere, they were not to get per diem because, clearly, it is and it looks like a scam—you pay yourself to live at home."

Sarah's administration also billed the state an additional $45,000 for daughter and husband expenses, most of these travel related. In effect, Sarah was making the claim that on several excursions (one to New York in October 2007 to *Newsweek*'s Women and Leadership Conference), her family was helping to conduct governmental business. The list of what looked to be frivolous, nonstate family junkets was long and expensive.

To counteract the publicity, Sarah ordered us to analyze former governor travel expenses wanting to know why they didn't pay taxes on the "stuff." If she did something wrong—same way we rationalized earlier campaign abuses—she would claim others were even worse, and she was simply a victim of what she called, "double-standard scrutiny."

Despite these efforts to deflect guilt onto others, in February 2009, it was announced that state officials had determined Sarah owed thousands of dollars in back taxes on her housing reimbursements. When it was patiently explained to her that this was never an issue before because other governors lived in Juneau instead of their original homes as she did, Sarah didn't understand or care. She simply told me that it sucked to be made to look like the guilty one. Without admitting guilt, she agreed to pay more than $8,000 to cover assorted costs related to nine trips taken by her children in 2007 and 2008.

Shortly after, she asked me to "talk her off the ledge." She lamented at the way her own Juneau crew would "allow her to make mistakes," then sit comfortably outside the media spotlight while she bore the heat for their lack of support.

The victims were not the Alaskan citizens who believed they'd elected a crusader for fiscal conservatism. Sarah was the aggrieved party because bureaucrats did not adequately explain the issues, and the media clobbered her over others' mistakes—much in the same way it was school administrators and coaches at fault when her children received poor grades. The distractions lasted for weeks.

For someone like Sarah who was not generous with her time or her money, paying back taxes came as a nasty blow, despite the prospects of millions in book advances and speaking fees on the horizon. Worse still, this story of per diem expenses for staying in her own house was first reported by the *Washington Post*, which meant it became a national story. Always hypersensitive to criticism, this became a deep emotional bruise and would take only a trivial event—similar to Walt Monegan's warning of a child seat violation—to set off Sarah. The governor had said of Wayne Anthony Ross's nomination that there were "politics of personal destruction involved in this, and that's a shame." Yet without an ounce of self-realization and led by Sarah, we would shortly embark on our own politics of personal destruction against a new, nearly defenseless foe. As in most cases, it took next to nothing to set the guns a-blazing.

―――――

In the smallest of pushes on the soft tissue of Sarah's Juneau housing embarrassment, a neighbor living near the governor's mansion—Chip Thoma, a man Sarah had never met—on Thursday, April 23, phoned the state leasing and facilities manager complaining that tour busses driving by the governor's mansion were causing congestion on the severely cramped streets and pollution. He suggested that with Sarah's popularity after the vice presidential campaign, everyone wanted to see where she lived. In response, he posted signs along the tour routes that read Stop Local Tours, and requested that the state consider repainting the mansion from white to a darker color so that it might be less conspicuous.

A half hour after this request was forwarded to Sarah, she began the process of overreaction. She wrote us:

> Really? Is this a joke? I don't even know how to take it . . . except we'll hear that somehow this is my fault that I let the neighborhood go to hell in a handbasket. :)
>
> Kinda' funny!
>
> And Piper and I have noticed a heck of a lot more people hanging around the house and ringing the door bell. Thought that wasn't such a bad thing though, because piper is quite the friendly socialite. I'll cc sharon [Leighow] so she can be prepared for . . . AP twisting something with this.
>
> I'll be back at the mansion on sunday—I look forward to Thoma's anti-tourism activities.

Later that night, this went from "kinda funny" to less so. Sarah contacted Ivy and me at half past nine: *Do they want the mansion moved to wasilla?! Happy to do it if they push hard enough!* About an hour later, she had the idea to use Thoma's request as a means to demonstrate how unfair she was being treated: *"u can spread it to help shed light on the can't win/insanity."*

By the next day, Sarah had hatched a brilliant plan to escalate the issue; Piper would sell lemonade to the tourists. *"Yes. And piper's lemonade stand to really drive the neighbors crazy. It'll blend in with the trampoline that they may feel generates too much "noise" (ie kids' laughter!). What a crew we live in the midst of down there."*

Sarah had suddenly upped the ante by suggesting there were complaints about children laughing and playing. When asked by her spokesperson, "You are kidding—someone complained about too much laughter?!?" Sarah hedged. She admitted this was hyperbolic but seemed an obvious conclusion (emphasis mine):

> Seems some of the general consensus (from the Chip Thoma's of the world) is that we've degraded the place with the trampoline, buoy swing and bicycle in the yard—*I can't attribute the gripes to any one person,* it's just a general "there goes the neighborhood" whine lately because more tourists (local and outside) are stopping by. Pretty ironic, because if these neighbors keep pushing hard enough (after they bitch and moan about us spending "too much time" in other parts of AK as I do my job) *we'll be more than happy to set up shop where neighbors aren't so bugged having a First Family living nearby. Like Anchorage—could be nice.*

On the following Tuesday, she felt giddy that she'd been able to use Piper to goad her newest enemy: *"Piper made $43 at her lemonade stand here yesterday and is donating it to the March of Dimes charity walk on Saturday. She says the next time she's not going to advertise it 'For Charity.' I don't blame her."*

Despite mother and daughter lamenting their pledge to donate the money to charity, the PR would prove brilliant. Sarah requested that Sharon Leighow contact media ASAP. Sharon, in a courageous bout of common sense, suggested that a wiser route would be to ignore the neighbor's complaints and not make it a story. Sarah hated the idea:

"I say we do a pre-emptive presser on the Chip thoma/neighbors issue. The 'stop tours' signs are such a strange thing . . . Illustrates we're darned if we do, darned if we don't."

If Sharon wasn't enthusiastic, others were. Sarah moved on: *"Ivy— pls get this out bc it shows what a kangaroo court this is that we're trying to serve in."*

In another brainstorm, we decided to push this story to the broader media focusing on Sarah's made-up speculation that Thoma was pro- testing children at play and lemonade stands. The real reason for all of this time spent on building a case to embarrass and, if possible, de- stroy one man's reputation was made clear a half day later:

> And, I just had to pay out thousands of dollars to the IRS for NOT staying in the mansion during it's renovations—and took a lot of political heat in Juneau for not being there—and now the tables are turned and I'm taking heat for being there.
>
>   It's more a tongue-in-cheek, ironic look at the kangaroo court I try to deal with: damned if I do/damned if I don't. It really doesn't have anything to do with Chip, per se
>
>   . . . it's more a commentary on the insanity.

So, with nothing against Chip per se, Sarah decided *"I know that I know . . . that (this tourist controversy is) a good issue for us . . . so ivy pls get it out there."* With that encouragement, we went into discredit- Chip overdrive. A few minutes later, Ivy let us know, "I got pics and an awesome story getting ready to go out for the news cycle."

Later that night, Meg Stapleton, now the spokesperson for Sarah- PAC (Sarah's Political Action Committee), wrote that she'd gone to Sean Cockerham at the *Anchorage Daily News* with an innocent, funny heads-up; he might just want to investigate and write a human interest story about a cute little lemonade stand and an ogre living next door:

> Sean,
> I didn't know some of the information here, but this is what I was calling about. Did you know Piper has a lemonade stand?! I think

this is a good news story because the news was there listening to the complaints that the Governor wasn't in Juneau every day.

Anyway . . . this isn't from me—I don't want to get involved in state stuff. Just got a laugh . . . and thought you might enjoy.
Thanks,
Meg

Meg didn't want to get involved in "state stuff" but did anyway.

After supplying talking points to the *Conservatives4Palin* blog contributor Joey Russo wrote an article entitled: "Juneau Resident Attempts to Close Down Piper Palin's Lemonade Stand." While a fabrication, we managed to have published a nasty spin on what started out as bus congestion and pollution and turn this into Sarah's Juneau crucifixion. In the article, Russo claimed that "one Chip Thoma is the man behind a movement to close [the lemonade stand] down" and that his reasons for doing so included being "sick and tired" of the Palins . . . It seems that Mr. Thoma doesn't enjoy the Palin children very much." He suggested that any man who opposed little girls and lemonade stands needed "to grow up."

When Sarah read Russo's article, she wrote, *"This is hilarious! And pip's planning the stand again for the next sunny day."* This time, Sarah proudly let us know, *"(Piper) made $44 for March of Dimes at the last one. This time she says she's keeping the $. Very cool."*

Stories spread widely across conservative blogs, where writers referred to Thoma as "sick," "unhinged," "a drunk," "drug-addicted," and "in need of therapy." Sarah feared, however, that because Sharon Leighow originally opposed attacking Thoma, we might have missed an opportunity to maximize this public relations coup:

> Now Chip [Thoma] is lying, claiming he never said this had anything to do with the Palins. Bull. He said earlier it's been since the VP run that the neighborhood's going to hell in a handbasket, and I have the flippin cartoon he hands out to the tourists w a drawing of me saying "I'm never in Juneau, don't ruin the neighborhood trying to glimpse a vacant house on you 'voyeur' tour . . .
>
> See, I wanted to get out ahead of this and provide another reason

why I need to get out of Juneau more often, instead, Chip got to
spin the story his way. I hope we didn't blow an opportunity.

When the online version of the newspaper *Juneau Empire* did publish a story that dealt with the congestion and narrow roads, Sarah
became angry. *"I wish [Sharon Leighhow] would have listened to me
and been proactive . . . I KNEW a reporter was going to cover this and
we'd lose the spin opportunity . . . Our folks pulled back and didn't do
what I asked them to do with getting the story out there first (it's front pg
Empire, but spun wrong)."*
     Three days later, when another conservative writer picked up on
our *spin* for the story, Sarah's mood improved. Warner Todd Huston
from NewsBusters.org wrote a scathing article focusing on Thoma's
mythical attack on Piper: "Palin Haters Livid at Juneau Tourism, Outraged Over Little Piper's Lemonade Stand." In the meantime, Sarah
had instructed us to continue leaking pictures, emails, and encouragement to Sean Cockerham at the *Anchorage Daily News* in the hope
that he'd bite and agree to write about this outrage. In a coup of sorts,
the newsman took the bait with an article on May 8, 2009, "Bus Traffic at Governor's Mansion Irks Activist." Cockerham quoted a written statement from Sarah that elicited whoops of joy when we read it:
"I wanted to offer him to hide Piper's trampoline further in a corner of
the yard . . . if it's a matter of not giving anyone anything to look at so
they'll go away then I'd ask Piper to not giggle so loudly on her buoy
swing or bicycle in the yard." She also managed to get in print a jab
at her critics: "We've been slammed if we're not here enough, but now
the table's turned and the message is we're creating chaos because we're
here too often."
     Thoma was quoted as saying, "She is obviously coming after me,
and I've never met her before." Our reaction to that line—aside
from smiling at the man's misery—was, "You betcha we're coming
after you."
     For the days we wasted on discrediting Thoma, we cared about
little else and nothing about him; critics ceased being human beings
worthy of sympathy once we attacked. By the time we finished with
our politics of destruction, he surely regretted ever mentioning the

governor's name. He learned firsthand why so few people were willing to speak out against Sarah Palin. The costs were enormous. At Sarah's direction, we had managed to construct a story with almost no basis in fact that painted her and daughter Piper as victims. In what I can only now describe as a shameful waste, this is what we did more than anything else in all our years together, go after those we disagreed with or simply didn't like. Alaska deserved better of us. We deserved better of ourselves.

In ending his article, the unwitting Cockerham gave us the biggest laugh we'd had in months when he quoted Sarah as saying that she loved Juneau and liked to see it shown off to visitors. "It's beautiful here," she said. Then, as if believing it possible in a city she believed was hell on earth, she concluded by suggesting, "Enjoy!"

Next up? David Letterman, charges of plagiarism, and one last bigtime dodge-the-bullet crisis.

All this and less than six months back as prodigal governor.

34

A Twenty-Ring Circus

Without promotion something terrible happens . . . Nothing!
—P. T. BARNUM, AMERICAN SHOWMAN
AND HUCKSTER (1810–91)

Late in Sarah's run for governor against Tony Knowles, Dino Rossi—the Republican candidate for Washington State governor—participated in one of our much-needed fund-raisers at the Hotel Captain Cook in Anchorage. If Rossi expected any long-running loyalty in return for his efforts, however, he would join a long line of former allies who found Sarah's passion a shifting wind. When he sought the Washington GOP Senate nomination in 2010, Sarah endorsed his rival. This was a pattern that was about to repeat itself with a much more notable political personality.

On the back of her successful attack on her neighbor Chip Thoma, Sarah suddenly found herself being accused by Huffington Post contributor Geoffrey Dunn of plagiarizing phrases from a 2005 Newt Gingrich article in a speech she gave in Anchorage. Naturally, panic ensued, and we spent the next two days attacking those who made the allegations and went about "correcting the record" by bombarding our Fox News and blog surrogates with denials. In defending herself, Sarah reached deep to elicit sympathy by reminding everyone she had a son in harm's way:

It is my firm belief that this latest attack centered on false allegations to attempt to destroy my reputation crosses the legal line.

My son, serving in Iraq, and those with him and those who have gone before him, protect us all to make sure our freedom to speak is protected; this lie harms everyone.

Sarah's attorney, Thomas Van Flein, wrote a legal letter of defense that Ivy and I distributed to everyone on our extensive email lists. Then Newt Gingrich rode in on a proverbial white horse, calling the allegations "just silly." His defense and staunch support during her vice presidential campaign should have earned him a lifetime debt of gratitude. However, just as Rossi learned, Sarah was a what-have-you-done-for-me-today friend. Four days after her speech, Newt—perhaps unbeknownst to him—landed on Sarah's enemy list.

This transformation had to do with a speaking engagement on June 8 at the Washington DC Convention Center. Sarah was invited to be the keynote speaker at an annual congressional fund-raising dinner. As was her custom, she hesitated before accepting, and, we were told, Gingrich was invited as a fallback. A suddenly dis-invited and miffed Sarah threatened not to attend before begrudgingly relenting.

There was nothing unrelenting about her anger, however. The subsequent vitriol over being denied a speaker slot made more un-derstandable Sarah's prior rabid reactions to other enemies, includ-ing Ruedrich, Stambaugh, Wooten, Monegan, Green, Syrin, Biegel, Obama, Murkowski, Bitney, Knowles, Halcro, Thoma, French, Cyr, Branchflower, Fagan, Binkley, Couric, Gibson, McLeod, and even Senator McCain and staff.

On June 7, the day before Gingrich's speech, Sarah wrote:

From: gshp
Subject: Fw: Newt

I don't know why we have to protect the elites who do things like this so we don't "ruffle feathers" by keeping it to ourselves. Newt "uninvited" me yesterday to speak at tomorrow's NSRC [NRSC, the National Republican Senatorial Committee]. I was the surprise guest . . . I know Meg [Stapleton] leaked it to Politico, then would get up to do a surprise speech and introduction of Newt. So . . .

I went from being the invited keynote speaker back in February, to just the surprise introducer of the speaker this month, to the back-of-the-bus'er ("sit down and shut up") the day before the event. One of the organizers told Meg last night that Newt pulled the plug, said he didn't want me to "steal the show".

. . . maybe there's something others see in Newt. . . . Keep this confidential until we figure out how I'm supposed to explain flying all the flippin' way across the country—leaving my baby at home—to be at this dinner, then we get accused of dodging the substantive events like the NSRC, when in reality they kicked us to the curb. I hate politics.

That same day, Sarah added more insight:

Yes, (Newt/GOP) are egotistical, narrow minded machine goons . . . but all the more reason God protected me from getting up on stage in front of 5000 political and media "elites" to praise him, then it be shown across the nation. At some point Newt would have shown his true colors anyway and we would have been devastated having known we'd earlier prostituted ourselves up in front of the country introducing him and acting like that good ol' rich white guy is the savior of the party.

Ivy gave Sarah much-needed love while—as if necessary—whipping up the governor's passion. (In all fairness, I was equally on board.)

I don't know the politically correct thing to do here, nor do I think I care to know, but my gut says no way in hell you're taking the heat for newt on this. . . .

Screw all of them that are scared or jealous or have their egos bruised because YOU inspire the people that truly matter. I absolutely hate the way you are treated and it's a toss up if it's easier to stomach it from the other party or our own.

All I know is, YOU have a gift from God. Keep using it. Screw Newt and let him take the heat himself.

Of Gingrich's speech, Sarah wrote, *"Zzz. Wayyy long."* By comparison, actor Jon Voight's speech was *"bold"* and *"kicked butt."* Newt had inflicted one of those slights from which Sarah would never recover. Newt Gingrich, beware, she's not wired to forgive or forget.

Fortunately for Sarah's peace of mind, David Letterman was about to put us in a much stronger offensive position with an off-color joke at Sarah's expense on his late night television show. With his actions, we'd now have the luxury of ignoring the DC slight and could devote full attention to attacking the comedian and putting Sarah front and center on the national scene.

We'd take the strategic game plan we used against Juneau neighbors and apply that to a much bigger target, proving we were definitely ready for prime time.

———

From the beginning of 2009, Sarah's chief of staff, Mike Nizich, along with Lieutenant Governor Sean Parnell, assumed most of Sarah's administrative duties, as the rest of us, most especially Sarah, wove our way through and around one distraction after another, whipping up a frenzy that became all-encompassing.

On Monday night, June 8—literally on the heels of Sarah's humiliating demotion at the congressional fund-raising dinner—CBS *Late Show* host David Letterman pressed our react button hard. He took note that Sarah had attended a New York Yankees game with her daughter. He made a joke about the governor looking like a "slutty flight attendant." Even less funny and more offensive, he said, "One awkward moment for Sarah Palin at the Yankee game, during the seventh inning, her daughter was knocked up by Alex Rodriguez." The daughter who attended the game happened to be fourteen-year-old Willow.

Sarah had us mobilized within hours. She crafted a statement of disgust and instructed us to ensure its extensive distribution:

Subject: Letterman
Sent: Jun 10, 2009 5:46 AM

Concerning Letterman's comments about my young daughter (and I doubt he'd ever dare make such comments about anyone else's daughter): Laughter incited by sexually perverted comments made by a (60-yr-old?) male celebrity aimed at a 14-year-old girl are not only disgusting, but they remind us Hollywood has a long way to go in understanding what the rest of America understands: acceptance of inappropriate sexual comments about an underage girl, who could be anyone's daughter, contribute to the atrociously high rate of sexual exploitation of minors by older men who use and abuse others." **Governor Sarah Palin**

Within forty-five minutes, we had a media target list, and spokesperson Meg Stapleton wrote, *"I will forward to: Rush, Greta, Glenn, Sean, O'Reilly, Norah O'Donnell, Matt Glick, Kate Snow, Wolf Blitzer."*

Meg also took responsibility for putting everything on Facebook after having crafted a statement for Todd's attribution: "Any 'jokes' about raping my 14-year old are despicable. Alaskans know it and I believe the rest of the world knows it, too."—Todd Palin.

When Letterman claimed his joke was not aimed at fourteen-year-old Willow but unwed mother Bristol, Ivy would have none of that:

From: ivyfrye

Pretty unbelieveable. It was little, 14 year old Willow he was talking about. That's why ppl are outraged. Levin and O'Reilly, and right wing blogs jumped on it. The elite media would never think of saying something like that about obama's kids . . . although Levin said it to make a good point. Hopefully he's not canned over the comparison.

Meanwhile, Sarah's fervor escalated by the minute: *"What a freak Letterman is becoming—taking on Bristol again? I wish people would be outraged at his hypocrisy and sexism—and that they'd do something about it—tho smarter people than I will have to think of what to do."*

By day's end, we felt we'd won the day. From Ivy: *"Good covg all the way around today, I think. Great comments on Hannity w guest Ann Coulter. Rush, Ziegler and Eddie had great shows today, too, talking the gov's record up and defending her family."*

In case we were underestimating her passion, Sarah later added, *"Watched the Letterman clips Old man pervert creep."* Even Sarah's biographer, Lynn Vincent, joined in by writing, *"What an asshole."*

Two days later, armed with a robust supply of adjectives to describe David Letterman, we were still full steam ahead. Sarah had her Google alerts capturing every headline and especially liked this one: "New York Lawmaker Calls on CBS to Fire Letterman for Palin Comments." With an "Amen!," she wondered why Alaskan lawmakers weren't as responsive: *"when one of their hometown native girls* [Willow] *gets hit nationally they say nothing."* With that, she decided that we should *"lead the charge for ak legislators. Good issue . . . to jump on."*

With persistence, Sarah ultimately landed on the *Today* show with Matt Lauer. By now, Sarah had managed to tie Letterman into a national crisis when she said, "No wonder young girls especially have such low self-esteem in America . . . and that does contribute to some acceptance of abuse of young women." Sarah's Juneau neighbor complained about bus congestion, and that became an attack on children laughing, trampolines, and lemonade stands. David Letterman, at eleven thirty on a weeknight, made a horrible and demeaning joke that few would have heard had Sarah not turned it into a four-day battle cry that escalated into accusations of child sex abuse. And in both instances, the media ran with it.

Lauer pointed out that Meg Stapleton had issued her own off-color comment when she wrote, *"It would be wise to keep Willow away from David Letterman."* When Lauer asked Sarah if she thought this also in bad taste, she answered, "Hey, maybe [Letterman] couldn't be trusted, because Willow's had enough of this type of comments and maybe Willow would want to react to him in a way that maybe would catch him off guard. That's one way to interpret such a comment."

What bothered me—as well as two of her commissioners and a syndicated national radio host—was that she could have been talking about moving Alaska's energy policies forward and striking a new deal struck with Exxon to partner with her gasline project, AGIA. Instead, she used what should have been *Alaska's time* and turned it into *Sarah's time* to continue noisily kicking the Letterman can down the road.

Newt Gingrich once counseled the governor to reframe any question she didn't like into the question she wished the interviewer had asked. In her *Today* show response, she implemented a frequent and superior strategy: answer a question you don't like with a string of words that make absolutely no sense to anyone listening. As if just hearing her voice were enough, Sarah's word salad responses worked like a charm. Matt Lauer nodded and moved on.

Just after the Republican primary for governor in 2006, when *Anchorage Daily News* reporter Tom Kizzia suggested that smoothing over missing facts would no longer work for Sarah, that voters and critics would demand more, he was mistaken.

For Sarah and supporters, facts were as irrelevant as comprehensible English.

———

The attack formula worked on even trivial matters of emotional distress; with Sarah, no slight was ever small. Briefly, when Sarah was snubbed as speaker at Bristol's Wasilla High School graduation in May 2009, we chose at Sarah's behest to make that another story of unfair suffering. The campaign began with Rebecca Mansour's blog *Conservatives4Palin*. She reported that Sarah was "the first female governor of their state and the first female vice presidential candidate nominated by the GOP. She was a Wasilla Warrior—the co-captain of the 1982 championship girl's basketball team. She was the former two-term mayor of Wasilla. And now she is not invited to speak before an audience in her own hometown."

Mansour then asked herself why. In seeking an answer, she effectively escalated the issue by suggesting a massive conspiracy that went all the way to the Oval Office: "I don't know the answer, but my suspicion is that everything changed for her the moment she dared to challenge Barack Obama."

Step two was to feed this story to the *Anchorage Daily News*'s Sean Cockerham. He dissected the outrage in his *Alaska Politics Blog* by repeating the *Conservatives4Palin* dis-invitation claim while including an embarrassing account of the high school principal's nonexplanation.

Meg Stapleton issued a statement on Sarah's behalf, reprinted by Cockerham, that made it clear the governor was being a mature adult about all this, despite the unfair treatment: "At the end of the day, the Governor is excited to sit back and enjoy this graduation with no pressure on the stage and in the spotlight. She will relish the moment with the family."

As was frequently the case, the public face masked reality. Sarah let us know she was far from "excited to sit back."

From: GSP
Sent: May 14, 2009 9:10 AM

Argh! . . . The students asked that I speak, months ago, and the class advisor was setting it up until a few weeks ago we hear—then the principals said no.

So, not only do I not speak, but they won't have me up on stage shaking the kids' hands, as every other governor who's ever attended graduations does. I'll be in the audience, which is fine. I'm trying to keep a sense of humor about it—at least I don't have to stress about thinking up another WHS grad speech, I've given quite a few of 'em. :)

The moral of this story is that no matter how insignificant, there is always an opportunity to escalate an offense via unsubstantiated innuendo, play victim, generate sympathy, and attack an enemy.

———

The media, we believed, held us to a higher standard, something we once swore we'd welcome. Now this seemed unfair. In an April example of this burden, Ivy wrote:

It seems that big liberal Biden is once again getting a free pass. No media outlet has played the recent video of Ashley Biden snorting cocaine even though her father fought to create a drug czar cabinet post. Isn't that news worthy?

Moreover, the media has routinely avoided talking about Ashley's other indiscretions such as being arrested and marijuana usage.

Sarah couldn't have unhappily agreed more:

Wow. That's amazing. I did not know any such thing (the coke video) existed. I saw another publicized slam of Todd's old 1980—something DUI again and wondered why does Obama get a pass for his drug use at the same time Todd got busted for drinking beer/driving in the ol' metropolis of Dillingham. Double standards, amazing. When I heard CBS/ktva report on Bristol's "safe sex or not" issue, as a totally serious hard news story, I knew this "new normal" is so perverted as to seem hopeless.

By now, we were far too busy pointing fingers to be concerned about our own standards, higher or otherwise.

———

Even after Sarah resigned, self-inflicted agony continued. Helping to fill the twenty rings of distraction, even old foes joined our circus. When KTUU reporter Rhonda McBride conducted a television interview with ex–Palin high school friend and fired cabinet member John Bitney, we needed to spend time correcting the record. As was her blunt style in addressing problems, Sarah wrote: *"Why'd Rhonda say Bitney was my campaign manager? And bitney sits there in the interview w/her lying about his role even in the debate when I interrupted murkowski and binkley and chided them—bitney says he told me to do that. He's such a flippin lying jerk."*

I added my two cents: *"Cattle-prod Bitney wasn't even IN the campaign until after the primary is my recollection. He wasn't there for that debate, I was the only person there."*

Sarah responded: *"He's a freak . . . Damnit. He's a liar. How can we call him on this. He's doing this to position himself/Harris for gov's run . . . Rhonda needs to be told she was buffaloed."*

Five of us went to work, devising an expose of Bitney. We decided to contact multiple KTUU reporters, not just Rhonda McBride. Meg called. I called. Ivy went out and cyber-blasted the story. Others phoned their contacts. We mobilized, an army of righteous workers acting like seven-year-olds.

Sarah reminded us: *"He was lobbying for nurses assn in Juneau, ivy reminds me (she was w lyda at the time) . . . Bitney wasn't even around."*

For five or six hours, we scrambled. That night, at half past eight, Sarah had another thought: *"I hope bitney claimed that title [of campaign manager] with Rhonda so she can open her bias eyes to the truth— that he's a liar. I'm happy to email her to tell her Kris [Perry] was manager, as ktuu reported how many times?"*

Kris added: *"Bottom line, he came on late. Did a crappy ass job. Didn't even attend debates . . . And wasn't campaign mgr. And as I said before—slimy, lying, prick."*

Sarah confirmed that assessment: "Or in the words of the wise sage Kris: slimy lying prick."

––––––

In retrospect, all of these issues seemed trivial and unworthy of our efforts. Sadly, in the trenches with people who believed otherwise, I failed to see it that way. We felt bombarded from all sides by missiles, without realizing they were no more than spit wads. Eventually the accumulation of overlapping tail-chases began to wear us all down.

The end was near.

35

You're Never Rich Enough

One can never be too rich or too thin.
—THE DUCHESS OF WINDSOR

B y early May 2009 Sarah's poll numbers in Alaska mirrored the amount of time she was now spending on state business: both were down dramatically. When Sarah saw results from a Hays Research poll that would be reported the next day, she alerted us, *"Ugly headlines coming tomorrow re: my astounding drop in poll #s. To go from 80+ percent to 50 percent is dramatic. Things aren't going well."*

We responded as expected, with Ivy suggesting we should commission a more friendly pollster to do a second poll—much as Sarah had commissioned a second Troopergate report to defuse the *Branchflower Report.* Meg Stapleton recommended in an email we explain that the numbers weren't bad *"when you literally have the Obama administration and the . . . [Democratic National Committee] targeting her!"* I wrote Sarah, *"You are the best thing to ever hit our state, but I realize this doesn't help us tomorrow."*

Strangely, Sarah was disappointed, but not half as angry as I might have expected. She wrote back, beginning with a note of humility.

> Well, I'm sure [I am] NOT the best thing . . . but I hate going down without a fight and I hate drowning in the crap we've been going through ever since the D's reared their head in opposition, and brought too many R's along with them.

We have no smoking gun that proves we're being targeted by the bad guys, so it probably sounds to many like I'm a whining b#*(h who stubbornly refuses to govern in the public's best interest. We've tried a lot of different things to get Alaskans to see truth, nothing seems to have worked.

Uncharacteristically, Sarah suddenly had more interest in being above the fray, wishing to downplay the horrible numbers. She made sure we understood that *"the defense/explanation of poor poll#s shouldn't be attributed to me unless the comments are very humble, almost apologetic for letting down Alaskans. Don't . . . attribute "it's not my fault" whiny—sounds to me."*

Where was this suddenly rational reaction coming from, and why did we adopt a policy of not fanning the flames? Normally, this would be a weeklong battle to set the record straight. For some reason, this died with an hour's discussion and a handful of emails.

The explanation for ignoring disastrous polling news undoubtedly had something to do with an event we couldn't have foreseen.

Opportunity had guided Sarah's handling of Troopergate ahead of her selection as vice presidential nominee.

Opportunity now guided Sarah's subdued handling of declining popularity: when negotiating a multimillion-dollar book deal, even Sarah realized that drawing attention to dissatisfied Alaskans wasn't a great move. Besides, outside of her home state, people and conservative commentators still loved her. And they had way more purchasing and marketing power anyway.

———

Sarah Palin announced her HarperCollins book deal on May 12, 2009, while rumors of the multimillion-dollar deal began months earlier, and negotiations for *Going Rogue* surely commenced no later than early April.

At Sarah's insistence, people in her circle devoted hours to constructing a book that would memorialize the myths Sarah wished to build around her life. Our introduction to Sarah's collaborator on this project, Lynn Vincent—a senior writer for the conservative Christian publication *World*—came by way of an email from Meg Stapleton, which deliberately misrepresented the nature of the project.

Subject: Interview assistance private
Created: 5/7/2009 6:09:51 PM

Hello everyone!
Frank and Ivy meet Lynn. Lynn meet Frank and Ivy.

Lynn is a reporter for World. She is trustworthy and is doing a huge in-depth piece on everything Palin. We would love for you guys to interview with her—candid—good and bad and Lynn is going to work with us on final product.

Everything from growing up Alaskan to the campaigns, time in office, accomplishments (Ivy—like you sent me earlier), family life, friends and allies.

Suggestions for other interviews. She has spent time with the Governor and Heaths already, too.

Lynn would like to conduct the interviews with you both tomorrow. Could you all please coordinate with Lynn as to best time?

Thanks, guys!

This "in-depth piece on everything Palin," we assumed, was going to be a favorable piece for *World*.

Vincent wasted no time and contacted me the next morning, Saturday. With that, she began a process that took up hours and days, with especially Ivy Frye (not then a government employee) supplying information, anecdotes, chasing down information, and constructing a sanitized version of all relevant memories. When, on May 11 in a phone conversation, Vincent accidently revealed that this was a book rather than an article, Meg Stapleton immediately emailed, *"I heard you talked to Lynn today and something was mentioned that shouldn't have been. Please keep it a secret until it is announced. I know you recognize the importance!"* After three and a half years, Meg really needn't have bothered; all of us were accustomed to keeping secrets, and one more would simply be lost; a snowflake in a blizzard.

For the next two months, as the manuscript progressed, Lynn Vincent became an insider, bolstering Sarah in times of stress and criticizing foes that continued to materialize throughout the collaboration. In an effort mirroring our op-ed production, Sarah's skills were best confined to offering directives on what needed to be included:

From: gshp
Date: Wed, 3 Jun 2009 14:37:46
To: LynnEmail
Subject: Re: Today's Political News From The Editors of US News & World Report and

This is the topic Ivy was writing about the other day. Lynn—we need you to watch that Media Malpractice dvd we sent w you. I finally watched it—it is very, very good at explaining some of the things that must be incl in book. Thanks

From: gshp
Date: Sat, 11 Jul 2009 06:29:34 +0000
To: LynnEmail
Subject: Important dot-connecting.

Lynn—it's very important we capture all the craziness due to adversaries' last minute attacks in the last weeks of my tenure . . . there were two more frivolous charges filed this week, plus many more foias, plus hordes of natl press up here trying to dig for dirt. Ivy, et al can help you get all this info, there's a lot.

For Sarah, she had other great ideas for material, suggesting *"Lynn—once in awhile check my twitter accnt, I post my principles there as they apply to what I'm doing w policy as governor."*
Second only to Lynn Vincent, Ivy worked harder than anyone on the text, sequestering herself for a while in Hawaii in the late spring, devoting herself full-time to production. Always a researcher, at one point she prompted: *"Lynn—I'll send you my draft. It shows how a Natl*

sales tax will further hurt our economy, and what the governor has done on a local and state level to invite business, provide basic services and infrastructure, and eliminate or reduce the tax burden on Akns."

I always felt that Sarah, in suggesting topics for op-eds that others wrote and she signed, truly believed she was the author or at least had the right to claim authorship. She also found it unpleasant to share credit publicly, making it difficult to elevate anyone to the status of coauthor. Lynn Vincent wasn't mentioned in the book's acknowledgments until after five others who'd helped construct *Going Rogue*, and was cited only for "her indispensable help in getting the words on paper." Maybe she'd been discarded by then? Knowing Sarah, that was possible, if not likely.

———

Despite the millions of dollars rolling in from the book and an agent fielding requests for $100,000 speaking engagements, Sarah wasn't financially satisfied. In the midst of this and before the windfall was made public, she initiated a legal defense fund to pay for defending herself against ethics charges while governor. Most of her contributors—including my wife and I—made far less than 1 percent of her new income. We gave to Sarah because she asked, and this was a way to confirm our loyalty. From people far less wealthy, our hero gladly solicited money she didn't need. Nearly $400,000 was raised from April 24, 2009, until the fund was declared illegal in the last week of June, 2010, because the fund inappropriately used the term "official" on its website, implying Palin's endorsement as governor. Sarah blamed bad advice from out-of-state attorneys for the error. The money was returned to contributors. Within hours of the old fund being deemed improper, she launched a new fund and continued to raise money—this time legally—despite having earned an estimated $12 million in the first nine months after resigning. We received several letters begging for money to pay for bills she believed were caused by evildoers.

———

For Sarah, these were exciting times filled with amazing and great expectations. By announcing her resignation on July 3 (effective July 26), the multimillion-dollar check would arrive, and she'd be treated like a queen and flown around the world in luxury and paid several hundred thousand dollars to deliver the same speech over and over again. When questioned about her motives, as Ralph Hallow of the *Washington Times* did a week after her good-bye speech, she'd react petulantly and demand a retraction. Regarding the *Times* article, she emailed, *"Ralph is an idiot . . . Dang him—we need to get him to correct this . . . And I didn't resign bc of the 'tough political hits' as he reports! I did it bc Alaska is getting screwed."*

While "idiots" like Hallow still "bloviated"—using a word popular with Fox News's Bill O'Reilly, one of Sarah's favorite personalities—dealing with them from the outside would become easier and easier. Especially as she was now rich and, once again, had access to the national stage.

For me, however, a final event—seemingly small in scope but symbolic of everything wrong with what we'd done these past years—finally broke me down. Certainly Sarah's quitting hurt. She was turning her back on all she'd promised our state. And no question her motives were material gain, no matter what convoluted reasoning she blurted out in her resignation speech.

More important than Sarah being a quitter, the beginning of the end started with a controversial appointment in March 2009 and led to a feud that left me dumbfounded. With all our mean-spirited ways, never did I believe Sarah Palin would embarrass a man of God and refuse a cherished cause. And for what end? Nothing more than one last attack on a perceived enemy and a few extra dollars. It's as simple and as complex as that.

This painful chapter would complete my journey from true believer, to misguided allegiant, to back home to the simple life I'd been meant to live. With that final break, more than any time in my life, I gave thanks that mine is a loving and forgiving God.

PART FIVE

End Times

36

Troopergate: The Sequel?

Insanity: doing the same thing over and over
again and expecting different results.
—ALBERT EINSTEIN, PHYSICIST (1879–1955)

Sue their ass. I kid you not. Why do we let the haters
keep doing what they're doing without fighting
back? Isn't that the definition of insanity?
—SARAH PALIN, EMAIL TO HER INNER CIRCLE, MAY 27, 2009

When resignation day arrived on a Friday, July 3, 2009, Sarah correctly cited the various ethics complaints as distractions to governing, and no question many of them were pointless. But more time sucking than these were the self-inflicted distractions (battles over the state senate seat, Wayne Anthony Ross's attorney general nomination, declining then accepting the federal stimulus money), personal attacks on enemies (Juneau neighbors, Letterman, Gingrich, too many others to list), and trips out of state meant to showcase her national aspirations (annual Alfalfa Club dinner in Washington, DC, *Newsweek*'s Women and Leadership Conference in New York, Right to Life speech in Indiana). Not to mention that she had a book deal under way. If attacking a neighbor's reputation was more important than governing, certainly a million-dollar payday was even more so. These were the real reasons government in Alaska was grinding to a halt.

During and after the speech, my phone rang nonstop. A Fox News producer called: "You're the Troopergate guy, right? Can we talk?"

After an "Ugh," I said no.

Throughout the weekend, I spewed the company line. "This is the right move for her. The right move for Alaska." "She's being hounded, can't get anything done for the people . . ."

I filibustered past the truth: since her return after having been on a national ticket, Sarah had come to care less and less about the state of Alaska. Amazingly, despite knowing all this in my head—if not yet in my heart—the process of unraveling my most important non-family relationship had little to do with Sarah's lack of interest in her job or resignation but began behind the scenes in mid-November 2007. At that time, the governor had her first opportunity to nominate an Alaska Supreme Court judge when Associate Justice Alexander O. Bryner retired on October 31. The court, made up of a chief justice and four associates, serves as the ultimate court of appeals for the state's district and superior courts and administers the state's judicial system.

Of all the duties I had as director of boards and commissions, handling judicial appointments was priority number one, with appointments to the state supreme court the most crucial of these. The process was similar to selecting Kim Elton's vacant state senate seat: the governor is sent names of qualified applicants for final selection. In this case, the nominees are submitted by the Alaska Judicial Council (three public members appointed by governors, three members appointed by the Alaska Bar Association, and the supreme court chief justice).

The importance and timing of this initial selection became evident when we learned on Friday, November 2, 2007, that the current court decided by a 3-to-2 vote to hold unconstitutional Alaska's 1997 Parental Consent Act—which requires teenage girls to notify their parents before seeking an abortion. With our right-to-life convictions, the decision shocked and disappointed all of us, nobody more so than Sarah.

She was fired up when she called during her commute to Anchorage and said, "Frank, do you realize that when Track dislocated his shoulder, they wouldn't even give him a glass of water until I arrived at the hospital and gave permission? Yet they'll allow a young girl to receive a major operation like abortion on grounds of privacy? This is outrageous." We worked with Sharon to draft a strong press announcement that was met by cheers across Alaska's pro-life community.

Not long after this decision, the Judicial Council sent Sarah four names for her consideration; she selected a solid Catholic in Fairbanks attorney Daniel E. Winfree. This process of nomination and selection was without controversy and would have been a pleasantly smooth footnote to our normally tumultuous administration if not for a confluence of events over the next two years.

The intrigue blossomed with a legal conference in Sarah-sister Molly McCann's child custody battle (*McCann v. Wooten*). These proceedings represented to Todd the endgame in the drama to destroy Palin ex-brother-in-law Trooper Mike Wooten. At the end of the case, Molly McCann ended up with custody of the children. The presiding judge for the Third Judicial District Superior Court, Morgan Christen, although not the assigned judge in the case, conducted a conference between the parties that resulted in a settlement.

Todd phoned me from the courthouse. "The judge," he said, "raked Mike over the coals, said his financials were bullshit."

"Wow," I said. "How'd it happen?"

Todd was joyously breathless, living a moment he'd been praying to see happen for over two years. "Wooten just threw his shit together half-assed and got his ass called on the carpet by the judge." This was and still is the most excited I've ever heard Todd Palin.

Interestingly, Judge Morgan Christen was one of the three candidates recently nominated by the Judicial Council that Sarah passed over in favor of Winfree. When I told Todd this, he reiterated his great pleasure with Christen. "She's amazing, Frank. She kicked his teeth in. It was beautiful." Todd seemed to believe that Christen had won the day for Molly McCann.

Contrary to Todd's impression, a spokesperson for the Alaska Court System said that Christen was never the assigned judge in the Wooten custody case, didn't make any rulings in favor of either party, and played a "very limited role." Furthermore, when the parties had a dispute following the settlement and asked Christen to resolve it, Christen assigned the case to another judge as she had applied for the supreme court position and had a conflict. As she'd done before with the prior opening, Morgan Christen applied for the position. This time, the Judicial Council sent over only two names: Judge

Christen and Judge Eric Smith of the Palmer Superior Court. As director of boards and commissions, I looked into the backgrounds of the candidates and worked with Sarah on evaluating their strengths and weaknesses. Even with glowing credentials, Christen was potentially toxic politically since the Palins believed she was responsible for Molly's victory and seemed inclined to reward her. More than anyone in the world, I knew the compulsive extremes to which Wooten had intruded on the Palin psyche and how tasty was their revenge. Not the most objective to begin with, what rationality the couple did possess would now be like a drop of water in a hot skillet.

From my perspective, there was another major obstacle to Judge Christen's nomination. With Sarah's outrage over the supreme court's earlier ruling against the Parental Notification Act, Christen's former board position on Planned Parenthood in the mid-1990s (a group currently opposed to the Parental Notification Legislation) made her appear antithetical to the administration's avowed position on this all-important issue.

With respect to this legislation in particular, Sarah had only just begun the fight in 2007 with the Supreme Court's ruling and was calling on the legislature to take up the issue in the spring and summer of 2009. When arch foe Senator Hollis French was being obstructionist, she wrote, "[We] *need to rally [the] troops and demand that Hollis French gets thumped on this and the vote is allowed to take place. This is the 3rd year we've tried to get this passed! Ridiculous."* She admonished the churches to take up the fight: *"The churches need to hustle on support of this, the days are ticking by! Where's their grassroots support?"*

Greg Schmidt of the Alaska Family Council Board, a Christian profamily, antiabortion group, sent out a notice to its members in March, applauding Sarah's dedication: "Every Alaskan who values constitutional rights owes a debt of gratitude to Governor Palin for her call to allow a vote on parental rights, specifically consent for an adolescent girl to obtain an abortion. Governor Palin recently made a public call for a parental involvement initiative should the Legislature once again fail to act on this critical issue."

While the Alaska Family Council Board was praising the governor for her stance on parental rights, they simultaneously lobbied against appointing Judge Christen to the supreme court and pushed for Sarah "to select the more conservative Eric Smith for the Alaska Supreme Court. Judge Smith will be more inclined to adhere to our Constitutions' original intent and to turn back the tide of activism that has run rampant on our Court in the past."

Once the two names became public, Todd visited me in my Anchorage office. "So, Morgan Christen's up for Supreme Court . . ."

"Yeah," I answered.

"She's pretty good, eh?" Todd did not attempt to hide his enthusiasm.

"She's qualified, but Jim Minnery and the Family Council crowd will have a fit if she's selected. A lot of them support Sarah—"

"F*** Minnery! Guy needs to have his balls handed to him." Todd's message was clear: he wanted to see Morgan Christen on the court, and if I thought there was any way the Minnery crowd was going to change his opinion, I could forget about it. The pain in my head instantly spread to my gut. Todd was in that "The game these guys play, something needs to change" mode that signaled Walt Monegan's imminent dismissal in July 2008.

A few days later, while in Juneau, I spoke by phone to the governor. I pleaded my case.

"Governor, you finally have clear grounds to send the list back to the Judicial Council and ask for more suitable candidates. They sent you only two nominees, one of which had a role in Mike and Molly's case."

Sarah paused, and I could almost hear the whirring of her thoughts. After several seconds, she said, "Wow! And how did you find out about Christen and Molly and Mike? Is it publicly available?"

In a typically confounding answer, there was no "You might be right, Frank." Or, "This could be an ethical mess." Instead, it was right back to *Will I be caught?*

I confessed, "Todd told me about Wooten's financial mess, the whole story." *Good Lord*, I thought, *I'm right back in Troopergate, about to get my butt kicked because of Todd Palin.* "Sarah, honestly,

I don't know if this stuff is available online, but I've gotta believe someone's gonna dig it up. This is potentially a reverse Troopergate."

A week before the appointment, Sarah called me to her office to once again discuss the situation. She seemed unconcerned about the potential for scandal or the potential uproar from her religious base. "Frank, keep this between us, but I personally think it'd be really cool if we could appoint Morgan. Wouldn't it?"

The word *no* went through my head as I repeated my concerns about Todd's preference. Sarah frowned and didn't want to hear negatives. Our conversation was brief.

Alaska Family Council president Jim Minnery continued to voice his grave concerns about this appointment. He asked, "Is there a chance Governor Palin would actually choose Christen?" He seemed as shocked by the possibility as he was dismayed.

"Jim," I said, unable to hide the truth, "yeah, there is a chance. And it could come soon. Don't know what you can do, but whatever it is, I'd advise you don't waste any time."

Minnery wrote a piece and sent it out to the thousands of people on his group's mailing list, asking them to respectfully contact the governor's office and plead for her to not select Judge Christen. He instructed those who did so to additionally thank the governor for all her other great works.

———

When I advised Jim Minnery to act quickly, I didn't have the heart to tell him his efforts had virtually no chance. Being on Todd Palin's needs-to-have-his-balls-handed-to-him list meant his voice was like a tree in a deserted forest, not qualifying as sound. On March 4, 2009, Governor Palin chose forty-seven-year-old Judge Morgan Christen to fill the vacancy on the Alaska Supreme Court. Sarah wrote, "I have every confidence that Judge Christen has the experience, intellect, wisdom, and character to be an outstanding Supreme Court Justice."

Before she could relish how "cool" this nomination was, Sarah received large amounts of critical mail over the selection, much of it from members of Minnery's Family Council. While Minnery wasn't pleased, he took the time to explain to the media he was not upset with Palin, and blamed the Judicial Council for sending only two candidates, neither of which was particularly attractive to his group.

The day after the appointment, Sarah cared nothing for the after-the-fact support. She was angry and wrote about the harm Minnery was causing her with the pro-life base:

> **I just got off phone with a famous pastor Outside who only knew what AFC reported, and he said he and pro-life community in America were heartbroken over what I did.**

She continued, venting that he did not have all the facts and we needed to get our version out. Twenty-seven minutes later, she added, *"Dear God, we gotta do something. I don't know. I am clobbered left and right!!! Help!!!"*

The next day, Sarah, for what seemed the millionth time, managed to paint herself as the victim with familiar *evildoers in the media* unfairly attacking:

> **[I told a concerned pastor] . . . the media was reporting Jim Minnery's AK Family Council's report of this episode—and the pro-life community was reeling. I told him this is more of the deception in the media and from some of our own "conservatives" up here that do not support me . . . and those things are out of my control because the media has unfairly portrayed me and my record and my faith and my family for many months now. I also told him that for pro-life people to have "lost hope" . . . that's tragic because I'm the most pro-life Governor in the country . . . We both agreed it will take a supernatural intervention to turn things around for me—that God's favor is the only thing that can vindicate me.**

Ironically, Sarah latched onto Minnery's comment that the Judicial Board tied her hands with their nominations: *"the AK Judicial Council sent up two names, I'm bound by law to pick from what they send me (until our lawmakers change that law and require more choices to be considered!)."*

From Sarah's *new* point of view, she and Todd never wanted Judge

Christen. Todd's effusive praise and Sarah saying it would be "really cool" never happened. I wondered if I was living a scene in the movie *Groundhog Day*, where I wake up and Troopergate-like denials began all over again.

While Morgan Christen was a highly qualified candidate, I wondered whether she, as a recent candidate for the supreme court and someone who likely knew she'd put her name back in the running in a year, should have considered recusing herself from any part of the McCann-Wooten case. There is no question in my mind that Todd Palin became her champion because of his misperception of her role in that case. In my mind, this is the complete inverse of Troopergate, with Sarah and Todd trying to hand out a plum job rather than taking one away, as they did to Walt Monegan. In my mind, this was an action worthy of being included in Einstein's definition of *insane*.

One last thing is equally clear: the governor and her husband now officially hated Jim Minnery, despite sharing the same God. Nor did it matter that Minnery was leading the fight for parental notification, to which Sarah claimed to be so passionately committed.

When Sarah turned on Jim Minnery and his/their cause—for the sole purposes of making money and causing him embarrassment—I saw how blind I'd become. Finally, Sarah Louise Palin's petty ways and butchered priorities would set me free.

37

No Excuse

"AAUGH!"
—CHARLIE BROWN, EXCLAMATION AFTER LUCY
PULLS BACK THE FOOTBALL FOR THE 539TH TIME

The headline across thousands of flyers sent out by the sponsoring group Alaska Family Council and its president Jim Minnery read:

Please join Governor SARAH PALIN & nationally known conservative STAR PARKER Thursday, August 27th 7:30 p.m. at Changepoint Church Anchorage

The plan was to have Sarah attend the ceremonial signing of the Parental Consent Act citizens' initiative that would hopefully lead to a vote for passage into law—over the supreme court ruling—the requirement that minors notify their parents prior to having an abortion. Slot number one on the petition was left open for Sarah's signature, while the guest speaker, conservative Star Parker, an ex-drug addict and prostitute whose faith in God turned her life around, was to be flown in to share the podium.

The arrangements began on June 27, two months ahead of the event, when I emailed Sarah, *"This week we expect the parental consent initiative to be certified. The sponsors would like to bring up Star Parker to do a kickoff event . . . where you ceremonially become the first signature."*

Sarah wrote back, *"Yes! Awesome! Sooner the better. Great work on this! THIS is the stuff that really matters—thank you!"*

Even with Sarah's penchant for changing her mind, this was such an important issue for her that I had few concerns. There were two things Sarah never wavered from through all our tumultuous years together. She held Ronald Reagan sacrosanct, and she believed in a child's right to life, above all other causes.

Jim Minnery, perhaps because of the strife involving Morgan Christen a few months earlier, was less sanguine. On July 13 he asked me to make sure our commitment was rock solid.

As I'd just received reconfirmation on July 8 from the governor, I assured Jim that we were 100 percent committed. On that day, Sarah even suggested I pass along some advice: *"Tell them if I were in charge they'd do sooner rather than later."* In her mind, no issue had more urgency than this.

On July 16 the only wrinkle needing pressing came from, naturally, Todd. He wanted to know, *"Who is star parker, what have they done for [Sarah]?"* Todd's hint at some kind of quid pro quo made me nervous enough to ratchet up my contacts with Sarah and her scheduler and PR mouthpiece Meg Stapleton. Meg said, "Sarah says she's coordinating this with you directly. Please call her." Sarah reconfirmed on August 1 that she was totally committed and wrote, *"I'm sending to Meg for Aug calendar, thanks."* Meg took the time to also thank me personally for *"taking so much time to put this together."* As if that motivated Sarah, she again wrote, *"Thanks, and thanks for working on this."*

Throughout the process, I indicated to the governor that should she wish to speak, she'd have the opportunity to do so at each of the two back-to-back events. Though not a requirement—Sarah's ceremonial first signature on the petition was the main event—knowing how important this cause was made me suspect she'd want to say something. She was also aware that Minnery's charity would receive a much-needed $500 per ticket, and they expected a large turnout. There was a lot at stake, all of it—by our way of thinking—good.

In one of those be-careful-what-you-wish-for moments, Jim Minnery became fearful that he might get his wish that *Palin has given a commitment to Republican Women Federated down in California. Would be great to get a similar commitment.* On July 30, 2009, only ten days before that scheduled event sponsored by the nonprofit Simi

Valley Republican Women Federated, and after large doses of publicity and contributions of up to $150 a head from an estimated nine hundred people, Sarah demonstrated how strong that "commitment" was when she canceled. The announcement was made public by Meg Stapleton on Sarah's Facebook page, writing, *"Neither the governor's state staff or SarahPAC has ever committed to attending this event."*

Skipping a function honoring Ronald Reagan? Especially as I too believed that she had fully committed, this came as a shock. Since Sarah regularly canceled appointments and appearances, maybe I was being naive. In 2008 she accepted a speaking engagement at the Conservative Political Action Conference (CPAC), but backed out at the last minute. At the time, I thought her reasons seemed legitimate, as it was during the busy legislative session. I should have wondered why she accepted in the first place, though, since the legislative session always takes place the same time each year. On March 14th of that same year, she agreed to introduce future Republican Party chairman Michael Steele at the Alaska State Republican Convention. In this instance, Sarah confirmed definitively on March 1 for her 8:45 p.m. kickoff. On March 5 she had Kris Perry send a note to the organizers: *"Good news! The Governor will be doing the opening Friday in addition to the dinner w/Mr. Steel."* On the very day of the event, March 14, Sarah reconfirmed her attendance as late as five forty-five in the afternoon, but she seemed nervous about what she would say, asking in an email, *"Does anyone know what I'm supposed to say?"* At six fifteen, after finding that she was not officially on the printed schedule, a loophole to her commitment, despite everyone in attendance expecting her, she wrote, *"Hate to bug out but if I'm not listed on program and not expected, maybe I bail without folks minding?"* Around that same time, she phoned me and said, "I just don't feel like coming into town tonight, Frank."

Michael Steele, with his always affable smile, told the crowd Sarah couldn't come because she had very important business to attend to. He paused for a moment, then added, "Family business. The most important kind of business there is." As the anatomy of a cancellation, this was typical, if not classic, Sarah Palin: not in the mood, get others to cover for her.

This disappearing act was followed closely by others. In anticipation of the 2009 CPAC, Joseph Logue of the American Conservative Union announced that despite the prior year's mix-up, Sarah Palin was the first confirmed speaker for the 2009 event. On February 9, a week before the convention, it was then announced Sarah would not attend after all. By this time, few people bothered to listen to the reasons why.

That same February, House Republicans invited Sarah to their annual winter retreat, hoping for a morale-building speech. She claimed she had "pressing state business," but actually went to the elite Alfalfa dinner, a joke-filled political event, at a Washington, DC, venue just across town from the House winter retreat. One House Republican said, "She lied to us."

Getting Sarah to meetings and events was like nailing Jell-O to a tree. On the campaign trail and as governor, Sarah went through at least ten schedulers, with few lasting more than months. Nobody wanted the job because Sarah might fail to honor, at the last minute, the smallest commitments, and making excuses for her became a painful burden. In at least one instance, a scheduler quit after breaking down in tears; another left after being accidently copied on an email from Sarah trashing her.

Even without my extensive knowledge of Sarah's commitment infidelities, the Reagan Library cancellation unnerved Minnery. A few weeks before the event, he wrote, *"With the announcement . . . about the Gov now not speaking at . . . the Reagan Library . . . I've had a few people want me to assure them that she will be at our function."*

I now shared his concerns about a flake-out, so I reconfirmed with the governor. She responded affirmatively.

On Sunday, August 23, four days from Parental Consent D-day, I was preparing to depart on a charity mission sponsored by my Rabbit Creek Community Church to travel north to the town of Eagle along the Yukon River. The region had suffered some of the most severe and destructive floods in modern history, and relief workers were desperately needed. At the same time, after the state supreme court debacle on top of a cascading number of distracting and often ridiculous crises and vendettas, I felt the need to heed a clear calling from God to do something worthy in His name. Being Sarah's lapdog struck me as no longer qualifying on that count.

As I stuffed Cheetos and heavy clothes into a duffle, my cell phone rang. I recognized the number: Todd Palin. He began with chitchat. "How's the family, Frank?" Then, he said, "By the way, Sarah's not coming." Todd didn't care that this was a firestorm in the making. The disappointment, the PR hit, the lack of credibility on the back of just recently canceling the Reagan Library function—none of that sunk in. "She's out of town and won't be back."

Over the next day, I sent Todd wasted text messages begging for Sarah to reconsider. Eventually I had to phone Minnery on Monday afternoon. Jim was home in bed, ill, so I spoke to his wife and dropped the bomb. She said, "People told me she'd do this! This is sickening."

Jim Minnery picked up, so ill he could hardly speak. "Where is she? We'll fly her back. Tell her we have people coming from their hospital beds just to hear her speak."

And what was Sarah doing that was so much more important than helping save unborn children? Todd wouldn't say. Sarah would never say. Shortly afterward, her publisher, HarperCollins, announced that it had decided to accelerate the publication date of *Going Rogue* from spring 2010 to November 2009. Chief collaborator Lynn Vincent lived in San Diego, and when I received a Twitter friend's message about seeing Sarah in a shopping mall there, the evidence was enough to convince me she and Todd now cared most about the millions of additional dollars available to them if the book were to come out before the Christmas holidays.

She could've flown in on the Family Council's dime, flown back down to San Diego the next morning, and missed only a half day of work on her book.

Everything had a price, including being governor of the greatest state in the nation.

Sarah sold us out, every last one of us.

And that she did so and embarrassed Jim Minnery—who had caused her so much misery during the Judge Christen appointment— was undoubtedly a bonus for both Sarah and Todd.

Meg Stapleton claimed that Sarah never committed to Minnery

and never heard anything about the possibility of speaking. It's not Sarah Palin's fault, she said.

There were things in Sarah's life that weren't good and weren't her fault. There were far more things in Sarah's life that weren't good and were her fault, despite a denial after each and every one. This cancellation and outright lie fell squarely in that latter category.

"I welcome being held to a higher standard," she swore a dozen times without once meaning a word she said.

As I spoke with Jim Minnery and his wife that Monday afternoon ahead of the Parental Consent gathering, I had to agree, "Yeah, you're right, it stinks." All I could add was, "I am truly sorry."

Jim Minnery had no way of knowing how sorry I truly was, for *every stinking thing.*

38

Good-bye, Rag Tags

We cannot do great things on this Earth,
only small things with great love.
—MOTHER TERESA (1910–1997)

When the May ice jam gave way along the Yukon River, Eagle—
a town eight miles west of the border between Alaska and
the Yukon Territory of Canada—experienced devastation that even
shocked a community hardened to harsh winters. Ice boulders the size
of freight trains smashed cars, turned homes into matchsticks, and up-
rooted trees, denuding the earth in the process. This was nature's version of shock and awe. Eagle residents found their lives littered with
little more than kindling. For many, surviving the initial catastrophe
was miraculous. Overcoming the aftermath and gathering resources
to rebuild was another matter altogether. When the waters finally re-
ceded, relief workers—many sponsored by churches—sent missions of
aid in the form of funds, supplies, and workers.

Those contributing time or money included conservatives, lib-
erals, whites, blacks, Native Alaskans, Republicans, Democrats,
Christians, Jews, and Atheists. When my church, Rabbit Creek Community, took up the cause, I listened. On August 10, 2009, I took advantage of my diminishing role (and popularity) in the governor's life
to sign on. If ever a man was ready to cut and run, it was me. Long
before the August 27th Parental Concent debacle, I began to feel the
sting of betrayal and abandonment, but Sarah's reprehensible behavior became the final straw that broke the back of this formally blind
camel.

My own mounting estrangement meant that those I once believed friends forever, those who Sarah said God had brought together, began disappearing, putting me smack in the middle of Sarah's efficiently effective freezing-out process. Much of what I'd done for the governor, to protect her from the public and from herself, and do her bidding, I questioned and discovered I now had no ability to justify. We hadn't been good Christians. Far from it. We were dishonest and behaved in a vindictive and hateful manner.

But when I saw the pictures coming from Eagle and realized the suffering these people faced, a page in my book of self-pity turned. Life doesn't end with setbacks. We seek help, reach out to others, and, if we are people of faith, we listen to God. Joining those touched by the tragedy along the Yukon River, I quietly planned my trip to Eagle.

I decided to use my skills not at political backstabbing and counterattack but as a nail-pounding, heavy-lifting laborer. I would focus on what our governor liked to call "Real Americans." Only difference was, I would finally back up words with deeds.

My enthusiasm for the Eagle mission didn't go without a fair share of anxiety, however. With Sarah being roasted in the press for the hypocrisy of skipping out on yet another event—and this time for a cause she wore like a diamond pendant on her political frock—I understood what type of strategy might be implemented behind the scenes. As nothing is ever Sarah's fault, there was only one obvious target: Frank Bailey, how's it feel to be thrown under the Palin bus once again?

And while subtle, I felt the impending crush of those wheels. Despite now being outside the inner circle, I had little trouble imagining the insane outrage at both Jim Minnery and me that Sarah harbored. Still plenty enraged for his comments over supreme court appointee Morgan Christen, plan B eventually kicked in: inflict public humiliation on him and his organization.

Sarah knew the disappointment her absence from the charity event would generate. One constituent, anticipating her presence and a chance to meet her, wrote: "Praise our wonderful Lord Jesus Christ that I will finally get my wish to see our Sarah speak at tonight's event. I have been laid up in the hospital for eight months following a horrible snowblower accident and convinced my doctor to let me out three weeks early to attend tonight's event. I will be there. God bless you, and God bless Sarah."

Rather than honor her commitment and headline the event that took hundreds of man-hours to create, she used the slight as an opportunity to turn and take one "heavy round" shot at the soldier in the trench next to her: Jim Minnery. As for the event cosponsors—including Knights of Columbus, Alaska Right to Life, Eagle Forum, Concerned Women for America, Archdiocese of Anchorage, the LDS Church, and countless individual congregations across the state—they would similarly be disappointed. Sarah, and probably Meg, with their strategic tin ears, likely assumed the outrage would be directed at Minnery's Alaska Family Council—an organization that, whether you agree with its positions or not, has earned a reputation for steadfastly standing by pro-life principles.

When the PR backfired, Sarah did what Sarah always does: point all ten fingers and toes in another direction. She swore she hadn't committed to being there. Others failed to communicate effectively. It was not her fault. None of it. I knew the drill well because I, Ivy, Meg, Todd, Bitney, Van Flein, Kris, and others earned proverbial doctorates in deflecting fault from the governor.

Now it was once again, as it had been during Troopergate, my turn to suffer the blows. As in his earlier disagreement with Sarah, Jim Minnery's biggest sin was voicing displeasure.

At one point, Sarah's anger resulted in her threatening to bring legal action, a not uncommon occurrence in recent years. "If this continues," she said to Minnery by phone, "it'll be my lawyers talking to your lawyers."

Jim Minnery, faced with a powerful former vice presidential candidate threatening to sue him and his nonprofit organization, answered, "What are you talking about? I don't even have a lawyer."

More surprisingly, Sarah once ordered me to do opposition research on Minnery. "Minnery can't be as clean as he puts himself out there to be, Frank. Somewhere there's got to be dirt." She wanted criminal and sex crimes databases searched as well as any blog rumors investigated and court records scrutinized.

Talk about taking a wrecking ball to squish a fly.

When his turn came to defend Sarah after the fact, Todd turned to the recurring topic of money. "It would have cost her five thousand in travel expenses to be there," he explained. This rationale disgusted me, and still does. First of all, what plane trip costs $5,000 dollars? Second, that's the exact amount Todd pledged to contribute to the Alaska Family Council, in an attempt to quiet Minnery. "Five thousand? That should be plenty," he continued, as if this qualified the Palins for philanthropists of the year.

Clearly the money, in light of the untold millions flowing into Sarah's personal coffers, was not an issue. At the time, I didn't have the guts to say, "Todd, not everyone reads dollars and cents into everything they do. Take your five thousand dollar check and shove it."

Through all of these machinations, I guess none of us should have been surprised about her indifference to the Parental Consent Notification commitment. (Oddly enough, Sarah has a perfect track record of attending highly paid appearances.) As much as Sarah Palin hated her job as governor, she was—despite quitting on her constituents—turning it into two things she desired most: wealth and glamour.

Surrounded for years by master schemers, by this time paranoia came easily for me. As the person who secured Sarah's commitment to attend Minnery's rally, I knew I was front and center for the blame bull's-eye. Throughout my preparations to depart for Eagle, the inner circle appeared far too anxious to have me gone. I felt like the parent of teenagers about to be left at home alone for the weekend—they can't get rid of you fast enough.

Meg and Todd asked repeatedly, "So when are you leaving?"

"There's no cell coverage there, right? I hear there's no internet," Todd said.

"So, you're going to be *totally* out of contact?" Meg added.

I took that question to mean: "In other words, Frank, you'll not only be unaware of what I say about you on the governor's behalf, but totally defenseless. Right?"

Once incommunicado, I'd be hit with the same chair as every other foe. Despite working on not caring what they did or said, indifference did not flow easily. My fears rose to such a level that I delayed my departure to allow some of the fallout to run its course; I'd learned to never willingly turn your back on those invisible knives.

Planning for future turmoil, prior to leaving for Eagle, I composed an uncompromising email to Meg, knowing it would immediately find its way to the governor and Todd. Hesitating, I initially didn't send it. Instead, my instinct was to weigh the pros and cons while driving to Eagle. On the one hand, I knew the words would end any ongoing relationship with those remaining Rag Tags. Conversely, with radio commentators like Fagan and ever-supportive Burke, as well as the *Anchorage Daily News*, running wall-to-wall negative commentary on Sarah's hypocrisy, sending an email documenting reality seemed advisable. Adding incentive, putting Meg Stapleton on notice that her incessant spin wouldn't work *this* time held appeal. No matter what I decided, however, the end of being this Rag Tag had dawned. Quite a fall for a guy some referred to as Sarah's right-hand man and others mistook for her chief of staff. From that lofty role to where I found myself in late August 2009, a reverse metamorphosis was complete. I'd gone from political butterfly to what felt like a caterpillar stuck to a bully's shoe.

Originally planning to sleep in my Chevy pickup at the halfway point of my drive, to save money, I instead elected to stop at a typical Alaskan roadside motel just before losing internet connection. Next morning, if I still had the will upon waking, I'd send the blistering message.

Halfway to Eagle, in my threadbare motel with butterflies printed on peeling hunter-green wallpaper, I reread my words to Meg one last time, made my decision, and hit Send, twice. Bang, bang. *Meg*, I thought, *take that!*

From: Bailey
Date: Sat, Aug 29, 2009 at 9:53 AM
To: Meghan Stapleton

Meg,

I'm not getting the point of all of this back and forth, and I'm tired of it.

Bottom line, Gov gave me the green light and I had every indication that she was attending and on board. Why would Todd cancel if she wasn't committed? I noticed Rhonda citing you Thurs night and in another article that the governor never committed. Meg, you know that is false. Not knowing what was said, I hope this was a case of media completely misinterpreting what you told them.

I first discussed with her on June 27 (both events, the fundraiser and the public event at a larger venue), she told me it sounded awesome, yes she'd do it, and that this is the stuff that really matters.

Needing the date locked down, I contacted you on July 17th. Told you I needed a date by COB b/c Star needed to make her plane arrangements. Todd emailed me and asked "who is Star Parker . . ." I let him know and then heard from you to go directly with the Gov on this, which I did.

I mssg'd the Governor with some date options, as Star needed to buy tickets. She told me it was a long way out but August 27th worked. I then pinned her back and said "I am giving them the green light." No word of caution, no change of plans, no "hold off Frank" or anything like that.

I then sent the tentative itinerary July 31st, to which she replied on August 1st saying she planned to be there, and copied in Todd. This is the email you have that stating she was forwarding to you for the calendar. She had questions, some of which I didn't have answers to until just before Todd called to cancel. Again, no word of caution, indication of any change, etc. Star Parker based everything on the governor's date choice and that the event would be with Governor Palin.

Ultimately, the governor made a commitment and she chose not to keep it. That happens, sometimes due to things outside our control. But parsing words at this point doesn't do anyone good. I have never minced words with Minnery when there have been disagreements with him in the past. I have always stood by the Governor when appropriate, but the way this is left hanging in the media says that either Minnery, or myself, ran with something half-baked and not approved.

Press statements that she never committed to be there is simply not true.

Also, I don't like at all that C4P has maligned the organizers for "jumping the gun." Jim and I have obviously had our disagreements in the past, but Joe's final paragraph is condescending at best. It would've been wise for them to leave this alone.

I leave the motel for the Taylor Highway here in a bit, have no idea what sort of connectivity I'll have up there. I hope this gets put to bed immediately. I don't want to come back and find more inaccurate statements in the press.

Frank

A few minutes later and ten miles down the road, I crossed into the Alaskan technological wilderness, where cell phones and internet go to die. No matter what Sarah's reaction, I'd not have to deal with her or Meg for several days.

There is something to be said for simpler days when a person might escape the world by just driving away. When payphones were high tech and cell phones only a ridiculous dream.

With a CD of piano legend George Winston filling the truck, I headed north.

Next stop: Eagle, Alaska.

39

Eagle Mission and Serving God

Work heartily, as unto the Lord.
—APOSTLE PAUL, BOOK OF COLOSSIANS
3:23 OF THE NEW TESTAMENT (ASV)

There was no turning back now. The email had been sent. I found a measure of peace—growing a backbone felt kind of nice. In my considerable experience, nobody had ever sent anyone in the governor's office an email that began with a line like "I'm not getting the point of all of this back and forth, and I'm tired of it."

People didn't tell Sarah Palin they were tired of her behavior. Least of all someone like me, a disciple who'd seldom, if ever, had the temerity to say no to any of her whims. While I reckoned it would take a nanosecond for Meg to shoot the message to Sarah and Todd, I took solace in knowing that no matter what Sarah's reaction, I wouldn't hear about it for over a week. With that assurance, I couldn't wait to arrive in Eagle.

Throughout the drive, I noted the sun arching high and bright. The luminous pink flowers of the fireweed that define the interior of Alaska during the middle of summer had turned to white fluff held upright by dusky purplish stems. Towering blue and black spruce trees stood like sentinels pointing to a sky so rich in blue that I knew this *was* God's country.

Through the clear air, I guessed the visibility at about fifty miles. To pass the time, I sang, prayed, and asked, *What's next?* With a political future unlikely, what would I do? Inspired, I recalled Colossians 3:23: "Whatsoever ye do work heartily, as unto the Lord, and not unto men." What really counts, this verse instructs, is the labor one does when nobody's watching. It isn't work to impress people or to make oneself look busy, it's what you do on behalf of God for no other reason than it is right. My own mom worked harder than anyone I knew and set a high ethical bar for me from day one. Unlike my work for Sarah—albeit stressful with massive hours of personal sacrifice thrown in—I had *not* toiled unto the Lord, not since early in her campaign when Sarah's values and motives felt pure. I had done terrible things to people: for one thing, I had assassinated the character of others. While cowardly hiding behind a cloak of fictitious email addresses and fake blog names, I turned off my conscience and perfected the disturbing art of politically twisting the knife when it was in someone's back by planting savage rumors that were juicy enough to spread like an Interior Alaskan wildfire. Heck, I even helped plot to find a young, attractive woman to embarrass a susceptible sitting lawmaker. The "dirty" list of confessions was audibly spoken in my truck that day.

Now, with my window rolled down a crack, the air across my face felt like the winds of change. Racing at seventy miles per hour toward *working heartily, unto the Lord*, I felt as though my mom's biblical advice was exactly what my life needed.

My route took me to a wide stretch of open flats by the Knik Arm of Cook Inlet, up to the Mat-Su Valley, past Wasilla, through Palmer, and down where the road is blasted from the side of the mountains. Through Sutton and Chickaloon, with peaks on every side, life as usual seemed to fade into the scenery. The Matanuska River peeped through the trees on my right every now and then, tumbling over boulders, shimmering in the sun, and my thoughts turned to the Yukon, the river of my destination.

A drive across Alaska, with its clear air and astounding sights, can be therapeutic. We have caribou, brown bear, Roosevelt elk, pika, chickadee, bald eagle, moose, and lynx. Overhead, hawks ride currents looking for rodents or rabbit to prey on. Add to that mountains so high the snow never melts and rivers full of trout, grayling, and chinook or coho salmon.

A family of porcupine chugged their way across the road; I slowed and veered past. I had neglected my own family for four years, and that was something I intended to repair and make right. Of all my regrets, missing family was tops. I'd even managed to lose my wedding ring during the craziness of the gubernatorial campaign. After nearly losing a finger on a piece of luggage while working for a small commuter airline years ago, I habitually took the wedding band off during physical labor. One day, packing up signs and flyers, it went missing. I spent the better part of an hour searching, but to no avail. The replacement we purchased felt as if the gold were plastic and painted to look real. The loss struck me as symbolic of the Palin years, with unfulfilled dreams and lost opportunity.

In those moments, with cool air drying my eyes, I vowed that when I returned from Eagle, things would change. No more Sarah, no crazy circle of faux crises or outrageous overreaction.

God, family, friends. One, two, and three in priority.

As for this mini-adventure to Eagle? I wasn't sure what to expect. What does one say to those who have lost everything to a merciless wall of water raging down the Yukon toward the Bering Sea? The river they loved, that fed them, that flowed past town every day, had turned on them in an unfathomable rage.

————

As rivers go, the Yukon may be the most underestimated in the Western Hemisphere. Everyone knows the Amazon. Then there's the mighty Mississippi. The Hudson is seen by hundreds of thousands of people every day. And, of course, the Colorado River, whose work of millennia is today's Grand Canyon. But the Yukon (Gwich'in for "Great River") flows in virtual isolation, with only four bridges crossing its length of two thousand miles. Massive by any standard, but largely forgotten by the rest of the nation, we Alaskans are happy to keep it to ourselves.

The village and city of Eagle sit just outside a sweeping bend in that river. Every winter the water freezes. Every spring it thaws, with breaking ice an annual event. But this year, a combination of unusually thick river ice, heavy snowfall, and early record-high spring temperatures created the perfect conditions for disaster. As the warming ice cracked with sounds like war cannons, the river raged, creating colossal ice dams. And the 227,000 cubic feet of water that flows down the Yukon every second cascaded over riverbanks like a massive waterfall gone berserk. A tragedy that put my problems in proper perspective.

For the last hundred miles of my pilgrimage, I listened to a mix CD I'd put together. When a tune from 3 Doors Down began playing, the lyrics captivated me. The song spoke to me in a way I'll never forget. It began: "I guess I just got lost being someone else / I'll never find my heart behind someone else."

"Yes! That's me!" I said like a crazy man, shouting inside a speeding car.

As one is prone to do when driving alone on a long stretch of highway, I further cranked down the windows, turned up the volume, and stepped on the gas. Once the music ended, I said, "Frank, it's time to get back to being who you are, not some political hack." And I played 3 Doors Down again and sang at the top of my lungs.

Second time through, another line from the song about wanting to take back the time that was given away hit home. If only I *could* take back time, I'd send a message to the younger me—the one driving to campaign headquarters back in 2005—this is what I'd tell him:

Turn around and go home.

Go hug your wife and swim with the kids and make a difference in the world without losing your integrity.

Take a harder look and see Sarah Palin not for what you hoped her to be, but for what she is: flawed and unprepared emotionally to be anyone's leader, never mind savior.

But that Frank was gone. The only thing currently under my control was the steering wheel of this truck and the decisions I'd make going forward. I couldn't erase those times when I'd given in to misguided allegiance. All I could do was to pledge, *Never again.*

The remaining hour or two flew by, and Eagle beckoned. "God," I prayed, "provide me the means to help." Adding a more selfish request, I added, "Please let nobody know my past. May I be nothing more than a nameless face, trying to help a troubled community." My desire was to leave behind all the things I had participated in the past four years.

"Lord, let me be simply anonymous."

———

With darkness rolling in, a series of narrow switchbacks lay ahead. I had to hug the steep wall of crumbly shale to avoid the sheer vertical drop on the other—*Welcome*, I thought, *to rural Alaska*. When I had initially asked for directions to Eagle, someone said, "If you end up in the river, you've gone too far." Prior to taking a wet plunge, I spied outlines of buildings and base camp for volunteers.

After parking and stretching legs, I introduced myself to staff.

"Hey. Name's Frank," I said to a man behind the door of the first of several motor homes I came to. "I'm looking for Keith Mallard." Keith and Allen were to be my roommates. Despite all three of us representing Rabbit Creek Community Church, I knew almost nothing about either Keith or Allen. "We're assigned to bunk together. Any idea where I can find him?"

I discovered the check-in man was formally a state trooper from Kentucky. More interestingly, he informed me that one of my roomies, Keith Mallard, was also a trooper. But not from Kentucky. For the next week, I'd be bunking with an Alaskan state trooper.

Did Keith know about Trooper Wooten? Troopergate? Frank Bailey's idiotic call trying to get Wooten canned?

You betcha.

Sometimes God answers prayers, sometimes He doesn't. When I prayed for anonymous status, that was apparently one of His no-candos. Thank God, I believed God knows best.

Meanwhile, the Kentuckian was scribbling onto a rough map. "You're here. I think Mallard's here." He pointed to the location of a camper across the yard.

Unsteady footwork took me toward more than I bargained for when I signed up for this mission work. After I took a deep breath and knocked, the door opened.

"Hey, Frank! I had a feeling it was going to be you." If there was an ounce of doubt about remaining anonymous, his smile laid that to rest. As we shook hands, the man's face displayed no outward animosity. Maybe my taking time to travel up to Eagle and help out was enough. Maybe, unlike me and Team Palin, he understood that "working heartily as unto the Lord" was a good enough recommendation to put preconceived notions on hold.

"Here's the plan," he said. "We're just three guys and we go where needed. We'll check with the volunteer coordinator in the morning for assignment. Simple."

"Sounds good. So, you're a trooper?"

"Captain," he answered.

I nodded. For an hour we spoke of family, the work schedule, and weather. He knew who I was, and I knew he knew, yet we never spoke of it. Once the light went out and I lay in my bunk, I wondered: if the shoe were on the other foot, what would I do?

I had no good answer.

———

After our first breakfast the next morning, the Rabbit Creek trio began working to salvage a dilapidated house about one hundred feet above the river. Descending into the cellar on a rough-hewn spruce ladder, I wondered if the structure above our heads was stable. The receding water had created a large mass of diesel-filled mud that had knocked over the retaining walls and bowed the supporting beams. There was oil-soaked insulation everywhere, surrounded by gravel and wood debris. In a corner, a toppled hot water heater lay like a corpse.

Our initial chore involved shoring up retaining walls when not shoveling and hauling bag after bag of petroleum-soaked earth across a suffocating crawl space, up the wooden ladder, and through the hole in the main floor. The harder we labored, the sweatier and smellier we became, and the better I felt.

After having collectively hauled fifty or more bags out of that hole on day one, my back rewarded me with a purposeful and fulfilling ache. Pain well earned and appreciated.

That night we did not bother turning on the heat in the camper. It felt good having the night breeze flow across my face, taking in cold, Alaskan air scented with cranberry blossoms.

As the days passed, I fell in love. Groups from backgrounds as diverse as Habitat for Humanity, Mennonite Disaster Service (in their red T-shirts), Samaritan's Purse, and Rabbit Creek tirelessly toiled side by side. Workers went about their tasks of cleaning and repairing while members of the community cooked meals in kettles or delivered them in foil containers.

The week passed quickly, each day full of good work, nights promising heavy slumber. I experienced honest teamwork that led to efficient progress toward an important goal. Here the talk was about survival—everyone had a story about watching the water rise and the icebergs crushing cars and homes. We focused on time management, cooperation, and finding parts and tools and pumps.

Meals were a time to refuel, get direction, and take a brief rest before rebuilding a cabin. One evening after playing in Redman Mess Hall I earned the nickname Piano Man, a name so much better than anything I'd been given in recent years. I liked that nickname (especially as we had a man specializing in constructing outhouses whom we referred to as Crapper John). Relearning how simple fun can be came easily as we talked and laughed, listened to the river rumble in the distance, and watched the orange sparks from our nightly open fire rise toward a sky pierced with bullet hole stars.

On the final night, around the fire, the conversation turned to politics.

Part of me dreaded going in that direction, but how, I wondered, was I to get on with life if I hid from the past?

Soon all eyes turned to me. "Politics can change people," I began as I poked the fire with a stick, hoping the flames might contain an explanation that made sense. "It has the power to turn people into something they weren't before—and I'm not just talking about ordinary people, but extraordinary ones as well." I suspected most everyone understood I was referring to Sarah. That the passion and honor I hoped she once had somewhere became lost and corrupted. "The process is seductive, the game addictive, and the feeling of power can end up devastating lives, much like a river of ice, I guess. I've seen it happen to too many people." Keith's eyes read my face, and he nodded.

For a moment, we all watched the sparks from my ash stirring flitter and disappear like excited fireflies. Keith leaned across with elbows resting on both knees, thumbs holding up a squared jaw. "I understand," he said. "Frank, all I know is that you're here—we're both here for the same reason. That's good enough for me."

If ever a man had a right to negative preconceived notions, that man sat across from me; but instead of judging me, he was being a friend. He didn't care about Frank Bailey the Troopergate guy.

———

The morning of our last day, we ate a final home cooked breakfast and readied the vehicles. Single file, we departed, with me taking up the rear. Down that narrow shale and cliff road, slowly but surely. Miles later, my pickup suddenly lurched as a tire hit a piece of razor-sharp shale and blew. As the caboose to the caravan, I was left alone. Eventually to the rescue, a State Department of Transportation employee arrived and raced down the mountain to retrieve Allen—a member of our team—who returned up the mountain to assist.

As we set to remove the blown tire, the lug-wrench spun. And spun and spun. Corroded lug nuts, like a bike wheel with no resistance. We needed a vise grip. I recalled placing the key to the toolbox in the side-door pocket of my pickup, but it wasn't there. I checked under the seat, on the floor, between the seats, in the ashtray, in my pockets, on the dashboard, back to the ground—this time on hands and knees. No key.

Anger, frustration, and a dose of homesickness went into a mighty crunch of my foot into the pickup door. I'll always appreciate the resulting dent, because when my foot landed against the driver's side door, I heard a series of jingles—sounding like a piece or pieces of metal. Surely this was the key—having slipped behind the side-door pocket—rattling down behind the pads.

I flipped open the door and, at the bottom of the door pocket, saw a crack just big enough for a key-sized object to slip inside. I reached in as best I could but felt nothing. Desperate, I tore the door pocket from the upholstery. To get to the key, I needed to do more damage. I began ripping the whole door panel to pieces. Over the years, it turns out, more than just a key had found its way into that crack. As if I'd broken open a four-wheel-drive piñata, spare change flew out and onto the road. Along with maybe a buck ten in nickels, dimes, and quarters was the key. But in that moment, I cared nothing about the toolbox, the flat tire, my desire to get off that rocky road in Nowhere, Alaska, or that key.

I bent down, no longer aware of aching muscles. My eyes riveted on a message I will forever believe came from the God who never abandoned me, who stood alongside me, even while I went off the path of righteousness. In this last week I'd traveled across the most beautiful land His hand bestowed on us, worked side by side with people who humbled me with their moral strength and felt as proud of my labor as I'd ever felt. The result was a pledge to reprioritize my life, to reconnect to family and make up lost time. So, with that in mind, I had to believe the object drawing my attention—delivered with impeccable timing—was something to always remind me of my Eagle mission vows to reprioritize my life.

Among the debris lying on this lonely road was the thing I'd once removed during the early days of the Palin campaign and lost. Reaching down, the metal reflected the day's dwindling light. Etched in tiny letters I read: 11–30–91 JMS to FTB.

November 30, 1991, my wedding day.

JMS, my wife's initials.

FTB, mine.

I took off my replacement ring and slipped on this simple and cherished original.

40

The End

I do think there should be consequences for bad behavior.
—SARAH PALIN, TO REPORTERS, APRIL 29, 2010

By the time I returned from Eagle in late summer, Sarah was physically out of the governor's office. She couldn't wait to get out, get going, and get rich. On July 3 she resigned; on July 26 she was officially an ex-governor. Some predicted that quitting would be the end of her fifteen minutes of fame. Boy, were they wrong. Sarah not only did not fade away, she became an omnipresent fixture on every news show pretty much across the country, the human equivalent of Kodiak Island's tsunamis and earthquake rolled into one tiny package.

But not everyone remained infatuated. Alaskans, whose lives depend on perseverance, could not abide a quitter and saw through Sarah's me-first ideology long before the rest of the nation. Approval ratings, which once surpassed 80 percent, would plunge into the low thirties. Protestors, referring to her tenure, called her "our half governor." Signs read *Quitter* wherever she appeared, even during her book tour in hometown Wasilla. During television filming, a thirty-foot banner proclaiming *Worst Governor Ever* was hoisted over the dock in the Homer Harbor. If she was known to be en route to an event anywhere in state, former supporters who once waved New Energy for Alaska signs now shouted, "You quit on us!" Eventually the Palins found themselves largely holed up in their newly constructed gigantic family compound on Lake Lucille, when not traveling to more supportive red states in the lower forty-eight for $100,000 speaking fees (or, triple that, traveling to Hong Kong). Fox News built her an in-home studio from which she can comment—critically and at times incoherently—on current events. No more ventures into "lamestream media," where unscripted questions might pop up regularly.

———

Unfortunately, my own tiptoe from office drew parting shots from the local media who rehashed all of my misdeeds. Much of it deserved; but all of it stung. Governor Parnell, who I came to believe was an honest man without Sarah's interpersonal loose wires, offered me the airport director's job. For that gesture—actually finding a spot where my fourteen years in the airline industry would prove ideal—I remain grateful. But finally, with lesson learned, I realized that my life was no longer in government, fighting idiotic wars with only Pyrrhic victories. Coffee stands that pulled in just enough to scrape by but left time to spend with my wife and kids would do just fine. While I continued to have an occasional nightmare about Trooper Wooten holding a gun to my head, there were no more hysterical calls from Todd Palin about his ex-brother-in-law riding a snow machine or illegally shooting a cow moose, and no more chasing after phantom enemies or participating in Sarah-orchestrated circular firing squads.

As it turned out, I never did officially resign. No formal letter— as I'd written on three occasions during Troopergate—no exit interviews or gold watch. For the remainder of that August, I continued working while waiting for a replacement to take over boards and commissions. Sarah and Todd, from the moment I returned until I left the offices for the final time on September 7, spoke not a single word to me. Kris Perry, once my closest friend in the administration, gone from my life. Palin attorneys acted friendly and communicated when they needed me in the fall of 2009 to help out with a case involving a college student in Tennessee who'd hacked Sarah's emails. The young man, David Kernell, twenty-two years of age and the son of a Tennessee lawmaker, was accused of obstruction of justice, unauthorized access to a computer, and wire fraud.

As the hacker legal proceedings began heating up later that year, Sarah took a personal interest in one of her favorite pastimes, seeking retribution. Even from a distance, I understood this young man was a target of her disaffection, and she had all her resources lined up to make sure he suffered—I'd witnessed the drill many times and realized this kid was likely doomed.

Having been a participant in nearly every email illegally accessed, I was unfortunately called to prepare a deposition ahead of what became, after much delay, an April 2010 trial. I was reviewing materials while in Palin attorney Thomas Van Flein's office when Todd and Sarah showed up. It had been many weeks since we'd spoken or seen each other face-to-face.

Todd approached and robustly shook my hand. We exchanged small talk while I imagined his thoughts: *With our book about to be released, got to keep Frank close, no matter what Sarah thinks.* I'd like to give the ex–First Dude benefit of the doubt—that maybe in his heart he had some lingering affection for me, for what I'd been through on their behalf. However, I'd been down a long, painful road with him, and I knew I couldn't trust Palin affection, lingering or not.

After my exchange with Todd, and as I copied emails, Sarah entered. I'd seen her withered, thin and drawn, and teetering on emotional breakdown dozens of times. But in that office, as I glanced across the room at her, I found the sight shocking. Her time away from the grind of government seemed not to have been rejuvenating. There were creases scarring her face, and her cheeks sagged. With shoulders pinned back, as if she were ready for a fight, and face focused on the text scrolling across her BlackBerry, she blindly stepped in my direction. I hadn't seen my ex-boss since before I'd left for Eagle, and unexpectedly here we were, only ten feet apart. My eyes locked on her face, and even when she looked up, my gaze held.

With a dry throat that must have hurt, she more growled than spoke, "Hi, Frank." The face I'd once thought belonged to one of God's angels turned hellish.

I bobbed my head and said only, "Sarah," and went back to copying. Crazily, a smile stole across my face; I delighted in realizing her fierce hatred had no effect on me. I felt healed.

When the hacker trial began in 2010, Sarah was the star witness. Once Kernell was found guilty on two counts, a delighted Sarah said to reporters outside the courthouse, "I do think there should be consequences for bad behavior." Having suffered for my own ignorant and bad behavior during Troopergate, I didn't disagree with what Sarah said. But, I thought, shouldn't the half governor be held to the same standard? What of her mountain of bad behaviors? How could a person be so devoid of introspection?

While the hypocrisy still nags at me, being free of the once-cherished inner circle immediately brought a sense of peace I'd found missing for over three years. No longer did I suffer with the freeze-out. Instead, I thanked God for the icy exclusion.

———

Today, when Sarah appears on the television, if I cannot avoid watching, I'll shake my head, knowing that she no longer speaks out of love for state or country but to feed a need for attention. Sometimes I skim an article on her, but never do I finish, as the stories are largely naively written, whether good or bad. And while I came to know Sarah—maybe as well as anyone—there is no understanding her. Not me, not Ivy, Kris, Todd, or anyone else will ever fully explain her many faces or the drama encircling her life. And as bizarre as it sounds, the person who knows Sarah Palin least, is, in my opinion, Sarah herself.

Having achieved most everything she seemed to want—wealth, fame, and glamour—I suspect she—and Todd—are less happy today than when she was pulling kids in a wagon door-to-door in sleepy little Wasilla, Alaska. Many times I simply feel sorry for my former boss. With so much controversy, I know she is in a war with hundreds of simultaneous battles. And while I also know she'd be a disastrous president and is unsuited to be a political leader, I don't hate her, and I never have. More than anything, I mourn her squandered potential and our shattered dreams. I pray that one day I'll see a change in the woman who at one time meant so much to me and to all Alaskans.

Looking back on those four years together, I'll forever miss the dream, but not the reality.

EPILOGUE

I've gone through life never holding grudges because life
is too short and that's why I have a good disposition. God's
blessed me with that—in fact it's not me but Him in me that
has always allowed me to walk in forgiveness and peace.
—SARAH PALIN, EMAIL TO CONSERVATIVE RADIO
SHOW HOST DAN FAGAN, JUNE 18, 2006

Back in May 2009, a buddy on the board of trustees for an educational foundation contacted me about a fund-raiser for college scholarships. His idea was to auction off a bottle of wine signed by Governor Palin. I initially PIN'ed her about the idea, to which she amusingly responded, *"Sure, if we can drink all the wine first. Have Kris sign it."* Several weeks went by and my friend reminded me of the request, so I followed up saying, *"Boss, are you ok with Kris autographing a bottle of wine? My friend thinks this will fetch more than any other bottle for their cause."*

Sarah agreed.

Kris Perry, who signed most of the letters to constituents in Sarah's name, did me the favor of signing the governor's name. After the auction, I wrote Sarah, *"Your signed bottle of wine helped raise $1,000 for scholarships for needy kids."*

Sarah responded, *"Cool! Thanks."*

Without an ounce of guilt—and now, with apologies to whoever paid a $1,000 for a fake signature—we misled the public about this simplest of matters. Why not just send the bottle to Sarah, have her actually sign it, and be honest with everyone? The only explanation is that by 2009, we'd been denying truth so long on large issues that small matters didn't seem worth the effort.

Just as Sarah really believed—beyond comprehension—that she held no grudges and walked in forgiveness and peace, we all became selectively immune to self-reflection. And in wading through this painful memoir, I realize that all of us Rag Tags had similar defects, none more so than me, the person who worked alongside her longer than any other.

The lesson learned, I guess, is that it takes an extraordinary person to deliver more than promises for a better future. We need to not only listen but also dig deeply into the character of our leaders before offering them our allegiance. And, more important, I will never, ever, surrender blind allegiance to anyone again, save God and family.

ACKNOWLEDGMENTS

Frank Bailey:

To my hardworking wife, who labored through this process with me, and to my children who continually make my heart smile. The completion of this book signifies hope for more "BlackBerry-free days." To Rich and Carolynn, the best in-laws a guy could want. To Greg Grebe, God used you as a voice of reason in my life during some very dark days. To my brother, Stevie, who heard me out those nights when I couldn't sort truth from fiction. To the Rag Tags who sacrificed so much: Kerm, Don, Robyn, Clark, "The Marys," Phil, Glen, Mark, Eric, Scott, Curtis, Anita, Bruce, Ramona, Lindsay, Linda, Joey, and Cathy. Two thousand and six would not have turned out the way it did without each of you. Ivy, you were one of the first to call after the press conference; I've never forgotten that. To Jeff Lowenfels, who wisely reminded me to conduct myself in such a way that I could "look myself in the mirror." To my "sister," the road has been long and difficult, but you will always hold a special place. You gave at times when you had nothing more to give. To my best friend Mike, who intently listens to my "wow, what a life" reality show.

To Jeanne Devon—working together? Whoda thunk? To Mister Ken "Show Don't Tell" Morris. Without your brilliantly descriptive writing skills and driving Wall Street personality, this project would never have sustained a seventeen-month trek. The roller coaster has been a wild one, but because of you two, we did it. To Kristin, for your technical talents when I needed them most.

Jonathan, your belief in us and the courage you possessed injected life back into this project when we thought all was lost. You lead a top-notch team. Philis, Jessica, Bruce, and Felice, your professionalism is unparalleled.

To Rabbit Creek Community Church, the "friendliest in Anchorage," you welcomed me with open arms when my cup was empty, then taught me the joy of serving again. You are truly amazing. Finally to my God, who despite my wayward heart and obvious "planks," still loves me. You were with me through those ominous morning drives to Seventh and E in the fall of '08.

Ken Morris:

This book was written inside a cone of silence as an attempt to avoid the kind of furor that Joe McGinniss launched when he released our unauthorized first draft. For over a year, my family maintained our secrets and supported my efforts, despite no assurances that we would ever reach publication. My wife, Amelia, and younger sons, Tim and Colby, kept me sane and offered necessary love and encouragement.

When I sent my two older sons to law school a few years back, little did I realize that investment would one day pay off in the form of helping save this project. Especially second son, Scott, who, in his precious free hours from a full-time job, took a direct interest. His legal council was marveled at by senior attorneys who wondered where I got this brilliant legal mind on such short notice. My daughter-in-law, Sarah (yeah, another brilliant attorney), married to my oldest son, Brett (also a brilliant legal mind), handled contract work and was an amazing advocate of this project from day one. I love you all and am so proud and thankful.

Along the way, I met people who embraced our David versus Goliath challenges. In particular, Professor Tom Field, the brilliant University of New Hampshire authority on copyright law, became my cyber-friend and advisor. On top of everything else, he liked my novels, proving him to be an intellectual titan. No question his guidance and advice were not only comforting but also helped with an understanding of the daunting issues confronting us on multiple fronts. I hope his students appreciate his heart and mind.

In yet another streak of good luck, I managed to find two up-and-coming attorneys on the West Coast who were unbelievably responsive and available twenty-four hours a day when we were issuing cease-and-desist orders, one after the other. To Dean Steinbeck and Peter Bonfante, your amazing hustle and enthusiasm for the fight will never be forgotten.

To my coauthors and best friends forever, Frank Bailey and Jeanne Devon, the mountain seemed to grow faster than we could climb, but climb we did. God bless.

Finally, to Howard Books, never in my wildest dreams did I imagine we'd land on your doorstep. Now that we have, never in my wildest dreams can I imagine not having landed on your doorstep.

Jeanne Devon:

Thanks to my amazing family: my husband, Ron, and my beautiful children who have looked at the back of my head and listened to clacking keys more than they should have. Without your love, patience, and encouragement I don't know where I'd be. Gratitude to all the "Mudpuppies" who show up every day and who have been asking me to write a book since long before this project started. And to my dear friends and editors at The Mudflats: Shannyn Moore, Linda Kellen Biegel, and Jennifer Snoskred—your intelligence, friendship, and willingness to carry water on short notice have kept me going, and sometimes even smiling, through dark times. Thank you to my partners in this unlikely trio—Frank Bailey and Ken Morris—for proving that we don't need to agree politically to be friends, work together, and care about our country. It has been an honor and a privilege working with you both on this project that felt kind of like having a baby, only it took longer. And to you whose good work, love, friendship, and advocacy have helped this effort in so many ways, even if you didn't know it: Debbie Bagdol, Judi Davidson, Zona Devon, Thomas Dewar, Jason Leopold, Debra Potter, Roger Ranch, Zach Roberts, Kara Soluri, Kelly Walters, and those who remain anonymous. To the enthusiastic hardworking people at Howard Books and Simon & Schuster and the Carol Mann Agency, humble thanks for having faith in our team and this project. We didn't know for so long who you would be or even if you would be, but we leapt, and you, our net, appeared, even when it seemed unlikely. Most of all, I am grateful that even though my mother passed away before she could read this book, she got to tell me, "I always knew you'd be a writer." Thanks, Mom. I love you.